Darkness in the Light Series

P[illegible] TOTH

UNDERESTIMATING SATAN

P.O. Box 4102, Elanora, QLD 4221, Australia
Website www.anazao.com.au
Email: phtoth@anazao.com.au

ISBN: 978-0-9806579-0-6

Published by
Anazao Press
P.O. Box 4102, Elanora, QLD 4221, Australia
Website www.anazao.com.au

First Published: June 2009

Printed by
Graphic Print Group
Graphic House, 10-14 Kingston Ave
Richmond, SA 5033, Australia

DEDICATION

This book is dedicated to Heather, my lovely wife.
The most extraordinary person I have met.

ACKNOWLEDGEMENTS

Special thanks to the following people who helped in the editing process:
Fran Platt
Helen White
Leonie Mansfield
Robyn Van Der Zee
Ps Simon & Pat Murray

Particular thanks to Pastors Malcolm and Diana Dow
for their theological expertise and meticulous comments.

Also to
Devorah Carageorges
Deborah Fuhrmeister
for their helpful comments and attention to detail.

Special thanks to Jano and Vlasta Tuchyna

Finally,
to my patient wife Heather who challenged me, like only a wife can, to justify the inclusion of each passage and who, while driving for 2000 km, listened carefully to the draft being read out loud.
Multi tasking women, how do they do it?!

CHAPTER SUMMARY

FOREWORD

In his first book, *The Forgotten Factor in Healing*, Peter Toth of Anazao Counselling gives an understanding of the nature of dissociation and teaches methods of ministry that we have been using to great effect in our counselling through Roaring Mouse Counselling and the Beth Tephillah Ministry Centre, as have numerous other counsellors, clinical psychologists and other ministries to whom it has been introduced. His understanding of the process of dissociation has caused vigorous discussion in counselling circles. It seems to be too radical to some, upsetting too many sacred cows and defying conventional 'professional wisdom'. However, to those who are willing to take the risk of rethinking things too long left unexamined, it is providing remarkably effective tools and a dramatic shortening of the length of ministry to DID, which until now usually took years and often ended inconclusively.

If we could make a comparison that would help to demonstrate the effect Peter's teaching has had on our practice it would be with our first encounter with Dr. Charles Kraft back in the 1990s. We had been warned by those who trained us in prayer counselling against "adopting the methods of Dr. Kraft because he talks to demons!" Some still accept this as a given. However, Charles graciously came to Melbourne and ministered to one of our leaders, allowing us to observe. Once we saw what he actually did, forcing demons to assist in the ministry with no dramatics, while at the same time totally preserving the dignity of the person, it made such sense that we knew we had to learn to handle demons the way he did. And we did so, to great effect. We have enjoyed a long association with him and Meg since then.

In the same way, Peter Toth and his lovely wife Heather have endeared themselves to us. They minister with humbling integrity, and are inspiring in their energetic pursuit of truth and understanding and its application to bringing people into a healthy, effective, and most of all, intimate relationship with Jesus. And as if that wasn't enough, they have helped us to make another great leap in our ability to minister to others.

Once again, in this next book, *Underestimating Satan*, the first in his *The Darkness in the Light* series, Peter takes the bull of conventional thinking by the horns, and turns it over to see what is really underneath it. Peter returns to the scripture passages and "proof texts" commonly used to explain things to do with the kingdom of darkness, but looks at them with a fresh paradigm which seeks to explain the many unusual things he encountered in his ministry to deeply broken and demonized people. The exercise is well worth while, because the result is a worldview-enlarging description of the spiritual realm as it is revealed in the Bible, but often misunderstood by theologians and ministry practitioners, and generally ignored by the average pastor and Christian believer.

Read the book and discover that, contrary to what you may have been told, Satan and his demons are still servants of God, just as they were created to be in the beginning. The only difference now is that they don't like it. Satan and demons operate in the lives of Christians and non-Christians alike, to the degree that we give them legal rights to do so by our individual, corporate or ancestral sin, and within boundaries established at the beginning of creation by God. And even in this they carry out God's ultimate purposes.

Satan is responsible for when and how we die, not just God. Did you know that when Job said, "The Lord gives, and the Lord takes away," he was unintentionally maligning God? How many believing parents have wrongly blamed God for killing their child, and how many boys and girls have been told that God needed their mummy in heaven more than they did? What does that do to a child's willingness to trust such a God?

Have you begun something and then failed, blaming God by saying, "God closed the door?" God didn't close it, if you believe he called you to that task in the first place. So, who did cause the blockage? Our God is not cruel and whimsical.

There is much more - read the book!

Having been given a glimpse ahead by our participation in Anazao's *Cutting Edge Ministry School*, and the discoveries we ourselves are making as we add these principles to our existing ministry, and even more importantly, engage with them in our daily living, we eagerly anticipate the future books that Peter Toth has planned in this series. The coming book, *Satan's Trojan Horse* will probably "blow your mind," as Peter might say.

.

Friends, it is time to take a closer look at what is really happening around us and at our part in it. The time is drawing short and the kingdom of darkness is increasing its activity in response. The ideas in this book are not a sideline, reserved for a few specialists or enthusiasts. Understanding Satan's part in many of the negative experiences of life creates a shift that helps believers grow in trust of the God who loves us. This knowledge is central to a true engagement in the believer's task of working with Jesus and the Holy Spirit in the bringing in of the Kingdom of God, and in preparing ourselves for life in that Kingdom, now and in eternity.

Blessings

Malcolm and Diana Dow

Malcolm has Bachelor Degrees in Mathematics and Theology (Hons) and a Masters in Electrical and Electronic Engineering, and lectured for thirteen years at Victoria University of Technology. Diana has a Diploma in Librarianship and Certificate of Christian Ministry. Her involvement with Christian Women Communicating International, since 1977, includes six years as International Know Your Bible Director, travelling the world to encourage participation in regular Bible study through KYB, particularly in developing countries. Both have extensive prayer counselling training and experience. Passionate about books, they have a personal library larger than many Christian bookshops! They are pastors of Williamstown Baptist Church and Directors of Beth Tephillah Ministry Centre and Roaring Mouse Counselling.

INTRODUCTION

Doesn't it surprise you that as Christians we are not very different from the rest of the world? We don't die any later nor are we any healthier. We visit the doctor as much as the next person. We have the same number of relationship problems. The divorce statistics for Christians are similar to the rest of society. We occupy the same number of beds in psychiatric hospitals as do non-believers. Christians are prescribed medication for depression in the same proportion as is prescribed to others. We aren't any wealthier than non-Christians. In fact, in some Christian microclimates, poverty is exalted!

Something is wrong. Sure, we have salvation to offer the unbeliever and that is no mean gift. Eternal life for free! I don't have to earn it. Now that is incredible. An offer no other religion can match. Yet as for the here and now, the daily grind, well, that is a different story. We can't seem to offer an attractive inducement that has to do with life right now. The secular world looks at our insurance plan for life after death and basically says: 'Sounds great, but what can you show me now to convince me that what you are saying about the future is true?' And for most of us, we are stumped. We don't have an adequate answer. Jesus makes a difference in the hereafter but he doesn't seem to have a tangible impact in our lives right now.

Yes, we hear stories and testimonies of people being miraculously healed, but in comparison to the number of times we cry out to God and nothing happens, these events are few and far between. Yes, Jesus has exchanged, through his death on the Cross, curses for blessing, sickness for health, sorrow and grief for peace and joy. Yes, God is a miracle working God. Yet why do a lot of the people I know, who love Jesus and seek his help for a variety of problems, end up disappointed and disillusioned? They end up with little real progress in their condition. Why did the lovely Christian family across the road have to lose their mother to cancer and leave behind a distraught husband and three bewildered children? Where is the blessing, the health, the peace and joy? Their church prayed and interceded. There were even 'prophesies' and 'words of knowledge' that she would be healed but she died. The church was bewildered and in a state of shock, confusion and disappointment.

Like you, I have asked these questions many times. Uncomfortable questions that we prefer to remain in denial about. Many times I have been exhorted to simply have faith and continue to trust in God because, after all, his ways are not our ways. Like you, I have continued to trust and have faith that God is in overall control. After all, who am I, a mere mortal, to think I could possibly understand the bigger picture that is being outworked. Nonetheless, there has been a lingering dissatisfaction with this answer. There is an internal discord that can't reconcile a God of love and a capricious, unpredictable God who would want to end the life of a much loved young mother when I can give you a hundred good reasons why she should live.

This book is an attempt to make some sense out of these apparent contradictions and to bring a different perspective to this perplexing problem. Over the past few years, the Holy Spirit has given Heather and me some important keys in reconciling these dilemmas. Solutions to problems often happen when we think outside of the box. We take a new and different, perhaps even a radical approach to the problem and find that the 'non-sense' starts making sense. Hopefully we will answer many of the questions raised. It will nonetheless require you to suspend your preconceptions, some of the suppositions you take for granted, and you will need to be flexible enough to consider another alternative. The answers to the questions raised lie largely in developing a more complete and balanced understanding of the satanic kingdom, how it functions and a knowledge of the legal rights system that both the Kingdom of Light and kingdom of darkness use.

Unfortunately, within most Christian denominations today, the devil is written off as a 'has been'. Popular within evangelical and Pentecostal thinking and teaching is the following statement.

> 'We don't need to focus on the devil; we just need to focus on Jesus. Don't give him any more attention than he already gets. Jesus has defeated him on

the Cross and so he is not an issue. He may be a roaring lion but he hasn't got any teeth. If we resist him, he will flee. The IRS doesn't focus on counterfeit dollar notes but they study the real thing so they recognise the counterfeit bill because they know the real bill so well. So too, as we concentrate on Jesus, the devil will be recognized as the counterfeit that he is. Greater is he who is in me than he who is in the world, so I have nothing to fear.'

Consequently, we really don't know our enemy. We dismiss him as a non-event and in so doing play right into his hands. We say we are in a battle. We know it is not against flesh and blood but against principalities and powers, yet we have little idea about who they are and how they operate. We put on the armour of God, employing the shield of faith to deflect the arrows of the enemy. If pressed to explain what those arrows are, the best that most of us can say is 'temptations'. The kingdom of darkness remains in darkness to Christians and Satan and his army are very happy with that situation. They pillage with relative impunity while our patriot missiles remain in their silos.

Based on thousands of hours of dealing with victims of Satanic Ritualistic Abuse and, as a consequence, directly interacting with demons of varying sophistication and responsibility within the kingdom of darkness, we have been forced to re-examine the Scriptures and challenge existing interpretations.

It is important to state that we believe the Bible is God's word; it is his revelation of himself to us and it is the truth. The problem lies in believing that *my interpretation* of what the Bible is saying is the only possible interpretation of the truth. It is the reason we have so many different denominations today! People take a passage of Scripture, place their interpretation on it and dogmatically assert that their interpretation is correct!

For example, we all agree that at the Last Supper, Jesus took the bread and said, *'This is my body'*. He took the cup and said, '*This is my blood'*. Yet Christendom is split in two by the interpretation of these words. Some believe it is to be taken literally; that the bread and wine, when blessed, transform miraculously into the body and blood of Jesus. Others interpret it as only a symbolic representation; no miraculous transformation. One passage of Scripture with two mutually exclusive interpretations! Each camp believes its interpretation is the truth! In fact, adherents to one view have died at the hands of adherents to the opposite view rather than deny their interpretation. While people have lost their lives over which interpretation is correct, it is at least of some comfort to know that the point in question, though important, is not essential to our salvation.

There are, of course, tenets of the Christian faith that are important, on which we all agree and which define being a Christian. These beliefs are not negotiable if you want to call yourself a Christian. Holding them is essential to our salvation. These are most succinctly expressed in the Nicene Creed, the defining statement of what we believe as Christians, compiled by the church fathers in the fourth century. Not negotiable are the following: God is one and at the same time a trinity of Father, Son and Holy Spirit. Jesus, the second member of the Trinity, became man, fully human, dwelt among us, was tempted in every way we are, lived a sinless life, died and rose again. Salvation is only possible by accepting that Jesus, through his death, paid the penalty for our sins; a penalty we could never pay. We appropriate this salvation by repenting for our sins, asking God to remove them, because of what Jesus did, and surrendering our lives to him. At the point of this surrender, the Holy Spirit, the Spirit of Jesus, comes to dwell in us and, consequently, each believer carries the very presence of God within him.

The theology of Satan and our understanding of the kingdom of darkness is not so clear cut. We know that he had a special relationship with God before he rebelled and that he convinced a third of the angels in heaven to rebel with him. He tempted Adam and Eve and they succumbed. As a consequence, man was separated from God. Jesus defeated Satan at the Cross and man was reconciled to God. Satan and his demons tempt us today. Satan will work with the Antichrist and the false prophet to deceive the world. He will be locked up for 1000 years when Jesus returns. At the end of his captivity, he will be released to gather his forces for one last battle with God. He will fail and be thrown into hell forever.

That is all that 99% of Christians know about Satan and his kingdom. It's not very much, really. Just exactly how capable is Satan, as a created being, with his power, knowledge and understanding? Exactly how was Satan defeated at the Cross? Did this defeat affect his intrinsic power? If so, by how much? How does he operate today? Do Satan and his minions believe they have lost the battle against the Kingdom of Light? What does he really look like when he isn't occupying a serpent? Does he have horns, cloven hooves and a forked tail? What role did he play, if any, in the death of the mother of the Christian family that lives across the road? Have *you* actually been tempted by Satan himself or is he too busy to bother with little ol' you? How is his kingdom structured today? How does he infiltrate the church? What are territorial spirits? What difference does it make spiritually, when we go to the top of a high place and claim the area below, a city perhaps, for God? Is putting on the armour of God the best way to deal with the satanic kingdom? What about people who claim they have been abused in satanic rituals and yet have no memory of consciously being involved? When I get sick, what percentage, if any, is the work of the demonic? Which model of deliverance is the best to use? Where should demons be sent when they are cast out? Can Christians have demons? Should Christians be talking to demons? Just exactly how much control does the kingdom of darkness have over my life, as a Christian, on a day-to-day basis?

This book is the first of a series of three that will attempt to answer these questions. It is a study with a comprehensive and meticulous focus on the character and nature of the kingdom of darkness, addressing *why* Satan does what he does and how the complex interactions between God's kingdom and Satan's can be understood. These three books will expose the kingdom of darkness and bring it into the light. Darkness in the light. The reader will also see how the Church has attributed to God what is actually the work of the kingdom of darkness; darkness in the Light.

> *Then watch out that the light in you may not be darkness. If therefore your whole body is full of light, with no dark part in it, it shall be fully illumined, as when the lamp illumines you with its rays.* (Lk 11:35,36)

NOTE

1. Anazao believes that there are six primary ways God reveals himself to us. These are through Scripture, personal revelation, experience, reason, creation itself and knowledge. A detailed explanation of each can be found in Appendix 1.

2. Anazao does not necessarily endorse people, organizations or every aspect of articles quoted in the end-notes.

3. In keeping with the more recent trends in Christian literature, the pronouns used to refer to Jesus, God the Father or the Holy Spirit, such as *he, his, him* will be in lower case.

4. When referring to a non-specific individual, there is interchanging use of he/his/him and she/her. There is no implication that the example used applies exclusively to males or females.

5. The terms "the satanic kingdom" and "the kingdom of darkness" are used interchangeably and refer exclusively to angelic beings.

6. Unless otherwise stated in the text or end-notes, all written material and diagrams are original.

7. Scriptures are always presented in italics. All other quotes are not.

Chapter 1:
INTIMACY

This is a book about the kingdom of darkness, its interactions with God's kingdom, the Kingdom of Light and how Satan directly impacts believers today. Before we can fully understand God's interactions with Satan, we need to briefly refresh our understanding of the different time periods or phases of God's interactions with man.

The first period
God's first interaction with man was the creation of Adam and Eve. They were created sinless. Adam was designed to live forever in a decay free world. There was no sin, so there was no death; not for humans nor for animals.

The second period
The second phase began when Adam and Eve sinned, and as a consequence of their sin, death entered the equation. All creation, including Adam and Eve and their offspring, would decay and die.

> *Therefore, just as through one man sin entered into the world, and death through sin, and so death spread to all men, because all sinned.* (Rom 5:12)

The effects of this second phase, with regard to death and decay, continue to this day.

This phase had some unique characteristics that we currently don't have. Everyone was vegetarian.

> *Then God said, "Behold, I have given you every plant yielding seed that is on the surface of all the earth, and every tree which has fruit yielding seed; it shall be food for you..."* (Gen 1:29)

People lived long lives and existed in harmony with animals. The reason they lived such long lives was because the effect of decay is accumulative. In other words, the extent of decay and death is linked to the time elapsed since the fall and the compounding effect of sin in the world. The change from perfection to imperfection was subtle and gradual. Just because Adam sinned doesn't mean he went from being perfect to an absolute 'bad to the bone' sinner in an instant. Today we live in a world that increasingly reflects the accumulative effect of decay and death. We can objectively observe the accumulation over time of genetic damage within a species and down a family line. The fact that we can intervene and remove cancers, consequently living longer, doesn't mean that decay is any less. On the contrary, there are more cancers and disorders of the body today, both mental and physical, than there have ever been.

Harmony with animals during this period also makes sense because everyone was vegetarian; the animals had nothing to fear! It explains why Noah had no problems getting the animals into the ark. Despite a slow and gradual build up of the layering effect of sin, there was an exponential growth of evil towards the end of this period. Thirteen hundred years after the creation of Adam, God was left with few options. He ended this second phase with a global flood.

The third period

The covenant with Noah on Mount Ararat began the third phase of God's interaction with man. He now gave man permission to eat meat, and as a consequence, there is now disharmony with animals.

> *The fear of you and the terror of you will be on every beast of the earth and on every bird of the sky; with everything that creeps on the ground, and all the fish of the sea, into your hand they are given. Every moving thing that is alive shall be food for you; I give all to you, as I gave the green plant.* (Gen 9:2,3)

There is also a limit on the age of man; one hundred and twenty years.

> *Then the Lord said, 'My Spirit shall not strive with man forever, because he also is flesh; nevertheless his days shall be one hundred and twenty years.'* (Gen 6:3)

The effects of this covenant continue to this day but will diminish during the 1000 year reign of Jesus on earth. This period also marked the separation of people and land. The tower of Babel, in Genesis 11, represents the moving away from a unified language and the beginning of individual languages. At the same time, the land began moving apart. Separate continents were forming. This was very rapid at first but has progressively slowed down over time. The latest theory from creation scientists is that the splitting and movement of continents began during the year of the flood. The flood's impact on the world was huge. The dramatic environmental changes that resulted from the flood led to an ice age which isolated people further, forcing many to survive in caves. This led to the popular myth, prevalent amongst evolutionists, that as man evolved from the ape, he dwelt in caves.

The fourth period

The fourth period was entered into when God chose to reveal his plans and intentions to one man, Abraham. He committed himself to an individual and would build a nation through his seed. This didn't mean he loved other nations less. He simply chose a man, whose heart was in the right place, and committed himself to him and his offspring. His generational line would eventually develop into a separate nation; Israel. Does the nation of Israel hold a special place in God's heart because of Abraham's obedience? Definitely! Scripture tells us that these people are the 'apple of his eye'.

> *For thus says the Lord of hosts, "After glory He has sent me against the nations which plunder you, for he who touches you, touches the apple of His eye."* (Zech 2:8)

Nevertheless, holding a special place in God's heart doesn't mean favouritism. God's increasing revelation of himself is always accompanied by an increasing risk of God's judgment and the nation of Israel exemplifies this principle. Greater revelation always leads to decreased tolerance because ignorance is no longer an excuse. What other nations could get away with, Israel couldn't.

The fifth period

The fifth period began on a mountain and finished on a hill. It began with an earthquake and finished with an earthquake. Sinai to Golgotha was a time when God became much more interactive and directive. Previously, his requirements and directives were generalized. Now they were very specific. God gave Moses 613 commandments, ten of which were engraved on stone. Try as they might, the nation of Israel constantly failed to keep these Mosaic commandments. This was exactly the point that God was trying to make. Relying on our own self-effort and self-righteousness simply ends up with us falling flat on our faces.

During this time, God's purpose was to establish archetypes that would find their completion in the New Testament and in his Son in particular. Some of these archetypes are the animal sacrificial system as atonement for sin, the Passover and other feasts, the layout of the Tabernacle and prophetic discourse regarding the coming Messiah.

The sixth period

The sixth period, or dispensation as these periods are sometimes called, began at 3pm on Good Friday and was ratified in the early hours on the following Sunday morning. One righteous man, who managed to keep all 613 Mosaic commands, rules and regulations and therefore didn't need to be punished, decided to take the punishment we deserved, so that we in turn could appropriate his righteousness.

> *He made Him who knew no sin to be sin on our behalf, so that we might become the righteousness of God in Him.* (2 Cor 5:21)

Important as it was for Jesus to secure our eternal salvation, this amazing weekend in history secured something else that no one had ever had before, not even Adam. It opened up the possibility for Christ to dwell in us; for God to find a home. Not in a temple of bricks and mortar, but in temples of flesh!

On the Sunday evening of that momentous Passover, Jesus appeared in the upper room and the Holy Spirit took up permanent residence in man for the first time.

> *And when He had said this, He breathed on them and said to them, "Receive the Holy Spirit."* (Jn 20:22)

For the first time, God no longer limited himself to being external to man or confined in a particular part of a temple, but he now dwelt in us. The Indiana Jones' of this world can forget about trying to find the Ark of the Covenant. They are surrounded by them; living Arks carrying the very presence of God! Moses could only experience God external to himself. It was a reflected glory that faded with time. Every believer since Easter Sunday has an internal radiance that increases with time. We still enjoy the benefits of this dispensation today, even though this dispensation itself only lasted for 40 days.

This is the first salvation experience recorded in Scripture. Paul states that there are two conditions to be saved.

> *That if you confess with your mouth Jesus as Lord, and believe in your heart that God raised Him from the dead, you will be saved;* (Rom 10:9)

The apostles were the first to fulfil both conditions. They had previously confessed him as Lord and now, standing before them, was the resurrected Lord. They believed, and at that instant, were saved!

With each of the previous dispensations, regarding intimacy with God, as one ended, the next began. Like a relay runner passing the baton to the next runner, each period of God's dealings with us was a distinct period that finished at a certain time. When the fifth phase finished, there was no more obligation for each of us to fulfil the Law to gain acceptance from God. The fifth phase became redundant, finding its completion in Jesus. Now we enter a new phase. This sixth period and the remaining dispensations build vertically instead of linearly. The sixth period is a foundation upon which the seventh is laid and the eighth on top of that and so on. In other words, each remaining period adds an increasing level of intimacy with God without diminishing the previous period.

The Sequential and Layering Effect of God's Intimacy with Mankind

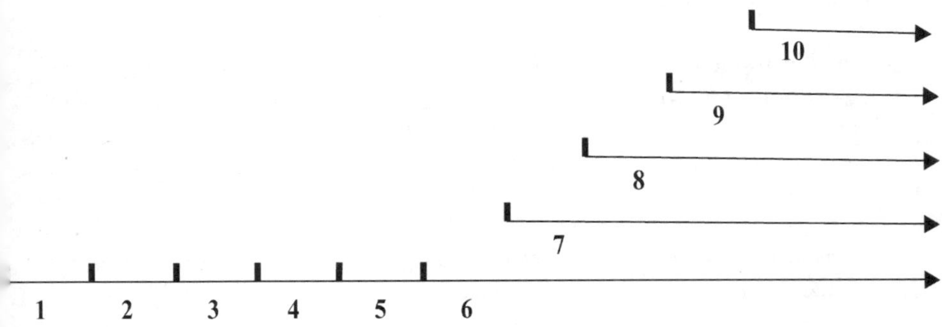

The seventh period

Just when the previous period seemed to have more of God's grace than we could cope with, God extravagantly lavished upon us even more blessing; the fire of his Spirit within us. Pentecost Sunday ushered in the seventh period of God's interaction with man. It wasn't sealed with an earthquake, like the previous two were, but it was sealed with fire; a baptism of fire. On Resurrection Sunday, the apostles received an inbreathed Holy Spirit, part of the package deal every believer receives when we accept Jesus as our Lord and Saviour. Six weeks later, it was an outpoured Holy Spirit that the apostles received. An inbreathed Holy Spirit given by a resurrected Jesus sealed our salvation. An outpoured Holy Spirit given by a glorified[1] Jesus gave us the extra firepower and confidence to live the life God was calling us to. Extra spiritual gifts; new arrows in our spiritual quivers, were now made available to accomplish God's will in our lives more effortlessly. There is a layering effect of the presence of the Holy Spirit in us; a deposit at salvation and a huge endowment when we receive the Baptism in the Holy Spirit.

We are currently in this seventh dispensation and it will continue until the reign of the Antichrist and the calamities mentioned in the book of Revelation are fulfilled. It is likely that the eighth phase will happen in the not too distant future. The continually increasing effects of death and decay that have been building up over the ages will come to a pinnacle in the dreadful events of the tribulation.

After an absence of almost 2000 years, the re-emergence of Israel as a nation in 1948 signified the beginning of the end of this seventh period. The increasing alienation of the nation of Israel and the rise of the Antichrist, the charismatic leader that will galvanize the world under his rule, are the signs that we are waiting for. When everything seems doomed and the Jewish nation has nowhere to turn, they will call upon 'him whom they have pierced' and they will say 'Blessed is he who comes in the name of the Lord'.

> *I will pour out on the house of David and on the inhabitants of Jerusalem, the Spirit of grace and of supplication, so that they will look on Me whom they have pierced; and they will mourn for Him, as one mourns for an only son, and they will weep bitterly over Him like the bitter weeping over a firstborn.* (Zech 12:10)
>
> *For I say to you, from now on you will not see Me until you say, "Blessed is he who comes in the name of the Lord."* (Mat 23:39)

The eighth period

The seventh period began with the return of the Holy Spirit in greater presence and power than previously experienced. So too the eighth period will begin with the return of the Messiah in greater presence and power than previously experienced. The seventh period will end with a global confrontation centered on Israel. So too the eighth period will end with a global confrontation centered on Israel. Just as God intervened, through Jesus, at the end of the seventh period and saved Israel, so too he will intervene at the end of this eighth period.

In response to the nation of Israel finally acknowledging that Jesus is their Messiah, he will return in spectacular fashion as their physical Saviour as well as their spiritual Saviour. Just like General Douglas MacArthur and Arnie Schwarzenegger,

Jesus was the first to say, 'I'll be back!' You can bank on it! There will be a huge earthquake and geological upheaval on his return and Jerusalem will rise to be the highest point in the land with water flowing from Jerusalem down to the Mediterranean and also to the Dead Sea. See Zech 14:2-10[2] (in full in Endnotes).

This geological upheaval with Jerusalem rising above the surrounding countryside is confirmed in Isaiah, as is the increasingly vegetarian nature of all animals and their harmony with man that characterizes this period.

> *In the last days, the mountain of the house of the Lord* ***will be established as the chief of the mountains, and will be raised above the hills;*** *and all the nations will stream to it. And many peoples will come and say, "Come, let us go up to the mountain of the Lord, to the house of the God of Jacob; that He may teach us concerning His ways and that we may walk in His paths."*
> (Isa 2:1-3)

> *And the wolf will dwell with the lamb, and the leopard will lie down with the young goat, and the calf and the young lion and the fatling together; and a little boy will lead them. Also the cow and the bear will graze, their young will lie down together, and the lion will eat straw like the ox. The nursing child will play by the hole of the cobra, and the weaned child will put his hand on the viper's den. They will not hurt or destroy in all My holy mountain, for the earth will be full of the knowledge of the Lord as the waters cover the sea.*
> (Isa 11:6-9)

He once again will come to physically dwell with us, but this time, as ruler of the earth, the king enthroned in Jerusalem. We not only have his presence in us at salvation and his increasing presence via baptism in the Holy Spirit, but now we will be able to physically see him in Jerusalem.

The decay that affected the earth will have reached a maximum at the point of the Lord's return and afterwards it will begin to decline. Then will commence the slow and steady rejuvenation of the earth back to the former glory of the second dispensation. Progressively, people will live longer lives, there will be less and less meat consumed and harmony with the animals will be restored.

> *"For behold, I create new heavens and a new earth; and the former things will not be remembered or come to mind... No longer will there be in it an infant who lives but a few days, or an old man who does not live out his days; for the youth will die at the age of one hundred and the one who does not reach the age of one hundred will be thought accursed... For as the lifetime of a tree, so will be the days of My people... The wolf and the lamb will graze*

together, and the lion will eat straw like the ox; and dust will be the serpent's food. They will do no evil or harm in all My holy mountain," says the Lord. (Is 65:17-25)

Note that the new heavens and new earth don't refer to the New Jerusalem and the New Earth that we will one day inhabit for all eternity. This is because there is still death present. The new heavens and new earth refer to the rejuvenation of the earth and heavens that will occur when Jesus returns and restores the earth from the effects of the tribulation.

We see that people now begin to live longer lives because anyone who dies under 100 years old is considered cursed. The lifetime of a tree indicates that people will be living lives closer to those in the pre-flood (antediluvian) days; hundreds of years. The last verses indicate a return to a vegetarian lifestyle, even for the animals. Implicit is a restoration of harmony with the animals. The world will be returned, progressively over the 1000 year reign, to a state not unlike it was at the time of the Garden of Eden. God will bring everything full circle.

Why? Because God's plans are always completed. What he begins, he intends to finish. He began with man uniquely created in his image with a trinitarian nature, living eternally, living sinlessly, in a decay free world. Sin entered and its consequences, death and decay, immediately followed. God was not perturbed. Despite the devil's intentions to spoil the party, God is going to restore the earth

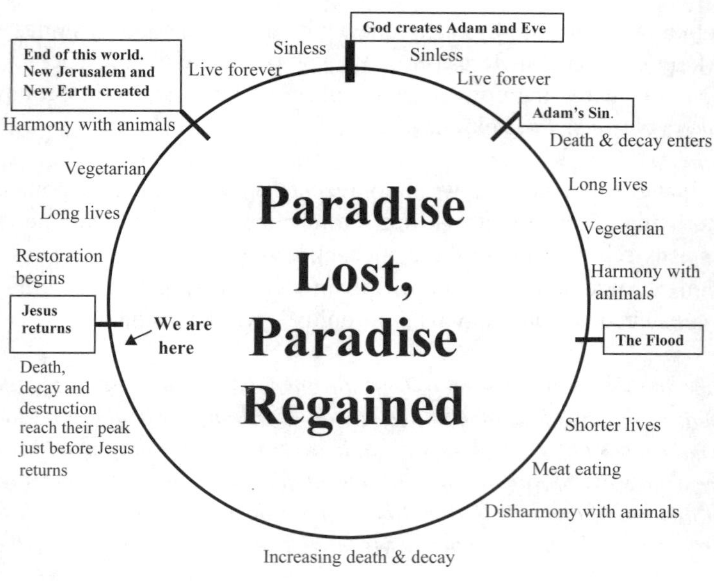

to its former glory. For reasons explained later in the book, man can no longer remain eternally on this earth. This earth must pass away. The circle of salvation will finally be complete when we get our resurrection bodies, living sinlessly and eternally in a decay free New Earth. Hallelujah!

But we are rushing ahead a bit! Before we enjoy the sinless life of the ninth period, Satan, who has been bound during this millineum of restoration, will be released and will tempt many to rebel. This will reach its climax at Jerusalem and Satan's rebels will be destroyed.

> *And they came up on the broad plain of the earth and surrounded the camp of the saints and the beloved city, and fire came down from heaven and devoured them.* (Rev 20:9)

The earth has served its purpose and is finally destroyed.

The ninth period

The eighth dispensation will begin with the establishment of the earthly Jerusalem as the habitation of Jesus and it will last for 1000 years. The ninth dispensation will begin with the establishment of the heavenly New Jerusalem together with the New Earth as the habitation of the Father, Son and Holy Spirit and it will last forever.

Before we can enter this New Jerusalem, there will be the final judgment of mankind. Everyone will receive a resurrection body, whether or not they spend eternity in heaven or in hell. The first judgment will separate the sheep from the goats and determine our eternal destiny.

> *All the nations will be gathered before him, and he will separate them one from another as a shepherd separates the sheep from the goats; and He will put the sheep on his right and the goats on his left.* (Matt 25:32,33)

For believers, there will be extra judgments with regard to the works we have done and the words we have spoken. With regard to works, they will be tested by fire and those that were the result of independent self effort will be burnt up.

> *Each man's work will become evident; for the day will show it because it is to be revealed with fire, and the fire itself will test the quality of each man's work. If any man's work which he has built on it remains, he will receive a reward. If any man's work is burned up, he will suffer loss; but he himself will be saved, yet so as through fire.* (1 Cor 3:13-15)

Those works that were done with the cooperation of the Holy Spirit will endure the fire. We will also have to give an account of every idle word spoken.

> *But I tell you that every careless word that people speak, they shall give an accounting for it in the day of judgment.* (Matt 12:36)

We will now be living in the New Jerusalem, which will be on the New Earth. We will be daily interacting with one another and growing in intimacy with each other and with Jesus. We will be creatively enjoying our new environment and because there is no decay, everything we make will last forever! No more maintenance work and repainting! This dispensation may last thousands or millions of years.

The tenth period

Despite billions of people in heaven, there will eventually come a time when God considers that we have become so connected and intimate in our relationships with each other that we will no longer be considered a group of individuals. Instead we will all be moving, acting and thinking as one unit. When this time arrives, when we are no longer 'brides' but 'a bride', we will marry Jesus[3]. We will be united with Jesus at a level of intimacy that we have not previously experienced. He will now be our bridegroom and we will have entered the tenth and last period that Scripture has revealed.

> *Let us rejoice and be glad and give the glory to Him, for the marriage of the Lamb has come and His bride has made herself ready. It was given to her to clothe herself in fine linen, bright and clean; for the fine linen is the righteous acts of the saints.* (Rev 19:7,8)

The rest of eternity will be spent getting to know our new bridegroom. We will marvel at his creativity and laugh till our sides ache at his sense of humour. We will enjoy creating the most amazing gifts to present to him and become increasingly filled with love and admiration for him. We will adorn our lover with music and all kinds of creative expression. Yet a marriage to Jesus is a marriage with the Father and Holy Spirit are well! We will marvel at the way the three of them make intimacy look so relaxed and easy and they will be our model. We will explore our New Earth with them by our side, and spend the most incredible time enjoying our mansions in the New Jerusalem. Now *that* is something to look forward to!

It's all about intimacy

The link or thread that we can see that runs through these ten periods of God's interactions with man, is his desire for greater intimacy with us. The first period seemed perfect; walking in the cool of the evening with Adam. There was wonderful relationship and intimate fellowship. However, Adam's sin meant

God had to rebuild from the ground up. We can see that each successive period increases God's revelation of himself to man and the level of intimacy increases accordingly. God's more general commitment to Noah, moves to a more specific and personal interaction with Abraham. Subsequently, his reflected glory on the face of Moses becomes an internal radiance beaming forth from his indwelling presence in every believer. At Pentecost, there is now the additional radiance resulting from the outpouring of his Spirit. Growing intimacy is next brought by his physical presence back on earth for 1000 years, which then moves to a resurrected eternal body powerfully imbued with his presence internally and externally. Finally, a marriage with him that will give an intimacy that far exceeds anything that Adam experienced. Intimacy with one another, intimacy with God, intimacy so complete that we will be submerged, encompassed and enveloped by the Trinity.

Graph of Intimacy with God versus Time

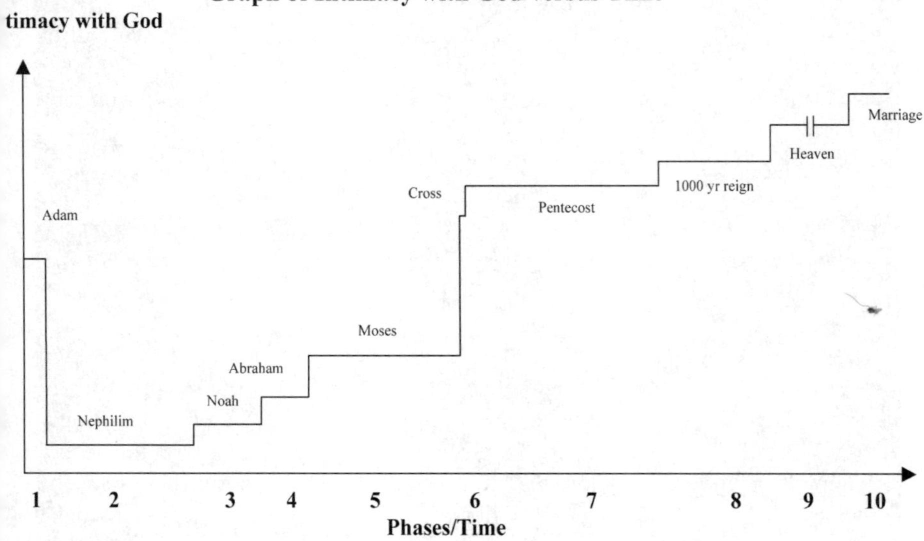

UNDERESTIMATING SA

SUMMARY

- God's dealings with man can be divided into ten periods.

- The first period of time was from the creation of Adam until he sinned. Adam was sinless and there was no death or decay.

- The second period started with the fall of Adam and ended with the global flood. Death and decay entered during this phase but the impact of sin was gradual, so instead of living eternally people still lived long lives. They only ate grains, fruits and vegetables. There was harmony between man and animals.

- The third period started after the flood and ended at the call of Abraham. During this period, immediately after the flood, the earth and people began to physically separate. Man could eat meat and was no longer in harmony with animals. Man's lifespan was set at 120 years. The impact of the events of the first three periods continue to this day.

- The fourth period started with Abraham and ended at Mt Sinai. During this period God, for the first time, committed himself to a man and his offspring, setting them apart as his people to fulfill his purposes.

- The fifth period began with the Sinai covenant and ended at Calvary. During this period, God gave man 613 very clear dos and don'ts. His purpose was to show man how incapable he was of meeting God's exact standards.

- From the sixth period onwards, all the other periods layer upon one another with regard to increasing intimacy with Jesus.

- The sixth period was the shortest period lasting a matter of a few weeks. This period started at the Cross and ended at Pentecost. During this time, Jesus reconciled man to God through his death and, as a consequence, for the first time, God came to dwell in man permanently; each believer became a living 'ark of the covenant' by virtue of the fact that the Holy Spirit now indwelt him.

- The seventh period began at Pentecost and is the period we are currently in. It is characterized by a greater intensity of the life of God in us. The Holy Spirit, given in the sixth period, was present in the Apostles and other believers at the time in a limited manner. At Pentecost, the Holy Spirit was given in a greater measure enabling believers to operate with far greater efficiency in the Kingdom of God, due to nine extra gifts that accompanied this endowment. The seventh period will end when Jesus returns.

- The eighth period will last for 1000 years. It begins with the establishment of Jesus' rule in Jerusalem and will end with the final destruction of the earth. During this time, the earth will be gradually restored to the state of the earth in the second dispensation. People live very long lives, harmony with the animals is restored and everyone becomes progressively vegetarian as animal death declines.

- Paradise was lost at the end of the first period and we are still experiencing the effects of that loss today. Paradise will be regained. God will not be outdone. We will return to the Edenic state that we once had. Everything will come full circle.

- The ninth period will begin with the final judgment and will end with the marriage feast of the Lamb. During this time, we will all be given resurrection bodies. Those going to hell will now endure torment with a physical component to that suffering as well as the spiritual aspects. Those who are righteous through faith in Jesus will now enjoy life in the New Jerusalem which is on the New Earth.

- The tenth and last period that we have knowledge of, begins when Jesus considers that we have developed sufficient intimacy with each other to become one 'Bride'. He will then dwell in us in a deeper and more complete way than we have hitherto experienced. This event will be celebrated with an amazing wedding feast, the likes of which we can't even begin to imagine!

- The ten periods or dispensations tell the story of God's commitment to man despite man's continued rejection of him. It is a story of increasing intimacy until we are as one as we possibly can be with him; submerging into his triune nature.

Chapter 2:
NO EXCUSES

You will have noticed in the previous chapter that Satan barely gets a mention. The focus of that chapter was God's commitment to us and his interaction with us. Satan was an active and important factor in those periods. We turn our attention now to his role. The rest of this book will be spent looking closely at Satan; his character, his actions, the way he thinks, his impact on us. We will examine all direct references in the Bible to Satan and look at the different periods or dispensations that have affected him. It is in understanding Satan; what he can and can't do, what he is allowed to do and not allowed to do, that we will find the answers to many of the perplexing questions that were raised in the introduction. We need to understand with greater clarity, the complex relationship that exists between God and Satan. For too long, our approach to this relationship has been one dimensional.

The first phase of God's relationship with Satan was, of course, his creation and the creation of all the angels and the time before Satan's rebellion. The Bible gives us one passage relating to Satan before his fall. All biblical scholars and commentaries apply this passage from Ezekiel to Satan.

> *You had the seal of perfection, full of wisdom and perfect in beauty. "You were in Eden, the garden of God; every precious stone was your covering: The ruby, the topaz and the diamond; the beryl, the onyx and the jasper; the lapis lazuli, the turquoise and the emerald; and the gold, the workmanship of your*

settings and sockets, was in you. On the day that you were created they were prepared. "You were the anointed cherub who covers, and I placed you there. You were on the holy mountain of God; you walked in the midst of the stones of fire. You were blameless in your ways from the day you were created." (Ezek 28:12-15)

The first reading of this passage is enough to take your breath away! Look at the first part of the first verse. If we didn't know better it could be taken as a description of God. When God created the heavens and the earth and all the creatures, it was 'good' (Gen 1:25). When he created man, it was 'very good' (Gen 1:31). When he created Satan, it was 'perfect'. God's creation of Satan received his seal of perfection, unable to be surpassed. The phrase 'full of wisdom' is not used anywhere else in Scripture. The phrase 'perfect in beauty' is not applied to any other person or creature in Scripture.

That Satan is in a class of his own is stating the obvious. 'Anointed' means set apart. He was a cherub that was set apart from the others. He was 'perfect in beauty'. He was 'full of wisdom'. These two phrases imply highly developed mental and physical faculties. Einstein and Solomon pale in comparison. The phrases: '...in Eden, the garden of God', '...on the holy mountain of God', '... walked in the midst of the stones of fire' all imply a very special relationship with God. A privileged position afforded to no other. A walk of close connected intimacy with God that could only be fully appreciated by one so perfectly created. It doesn't mean that the rest of God's creation wasn't perfect because God cannot create anything that isn't perfect. It means that the level of endowment in terms of capabilities and sophistication that Satan received couldn't be surpassed for a created being.

No Excuses

The second dispensation of Satan relates to his fall. The second part of the Ezekiel passage and Isaiah 14 explain what happened.

You were blameless in your ways from the day you were created until unrighteousness was found in you. By the abundance of your trade you were internally filled with violence, and you sinned; therefore I have cast you as profane from the mountain of God and I have destroyed you, O covering cherub, from the midst of the stones of fire. Your heart was lifted up because of your beauty; you corrupted your wisdom by reason of your splendor. I cast you to the ground; (Ezek 28:15-17)

How you have fallen from heaven, O star of the morning, son of the dawn! You have been cut down to the earth, you who have weakened the nations! But you said in your heart, 'I will ascend to heaven; I will raise my throne above the stars of God, and I will sit on the mount of assembly in the recesses of the north. I will ascend above the heights of the clouds; I will make myself like the Most High.' Nevertheless you will be thrust down to Sheol, to the recesses of the pit. (Isa 14:12-15)

From Ezek 28:17 it appears that pride, the internal focus on self, was the initial part of Satan's undoing. He looked at himself, compared himself to other angels and became proud. Even his amazing wisdom, which he should have used to keep his self-absorption in check, became corrupted as his rampant pride took over. Timothy uses the word 'conceit' to describe the sin.

And not a new convert, so that he will not become ***conceited*** *and fall into the condemnation incurred by the devil.* (1 Tim 3:6)

In other words, he started losing the plot and thought he could take on God (Isaiah 14:14).

Why does such a majestic being who is in close fellowship with God want to rebel against him? Why does the perfect love of God which surrounds you with reassuring joy and comfort make you want to move away and be independent?

We can only guess why this may have happened. If Satan was created first, with a long gap before the creation of the rest of the angels, then the only other being he could relate to was God. This is the case with any first born child who relates entirely to his parents before another sibling comes along. Being a creation, rather than an offspring, Satan nonetheless would have begun his existence in close fellowship with the Father, Son and Holy Spirit. It also means that Satan would have been present and watched with fascination and intrigue as God created the rest of the angels. Perhaps as he observed these comparatively inferior beings, he couldn't help but notice how much closer in beauty, majesty, ability and power he was to God than these latest creations. Since he had no reference point for his own creation, perhaps he thought that he was, or could be, a fourth member of the trinity?! From his perspective, he just 'was' and entered into immediate relationship with the Godhead. Could this scenario be part of the explanation for the phrase, 'I will make myself like the Most High'?[1]

Rebellion

Satan managed to convince a third of the angels to follow him.

His tail swept a third of the stars out of the sky and flung them to the earth. And there was war in heaven. Michael and his angels fought against the

dragon, and the dragon and his angels fought back. But he was not strong enough, and they lost their place in heaven. The great dragon was hurled down—that ancient serpent called the devil, or Satan, who leads the whole world astray. He was hurled to the earth, and his angels with him.
(Rev 12:4,7-9 NIV)

It is intriguing as to why a third of the angels would follow Satan. They were created by God and, we would assume, had the presence of God in a measure, at least around them, if not in them. They were not stupid and possessed moral clarity; they haven't yet sinned. Yet Satan managed to convince as many as a third of them to cast their lot with him. Put yourself in the position of one of those angels. You are not going to follow Satan unless he is a credible alternative to following God. If Satan is like you, just another angel, and God is infinitely more powerful, no angel in his right mind is going to choose Satan over God.

The only logical conclusion is that Satan, at the apex of God's creation, was far more majestic, powerful, intelligent and capable than any of the other angels. Absolutely in a class of his own, as has already been mentioned. Although God is infinitely more powerful than Satan, he masks his majesty and power so that his creatures can tolerate his presence. Because of this, Satan in all his majesty probably didn't look that much different from God. A rank and file angel looking at God and Satan may have seen little difference in the majestic brilliance that both beings presented. They were similar in appearance but the reality is that

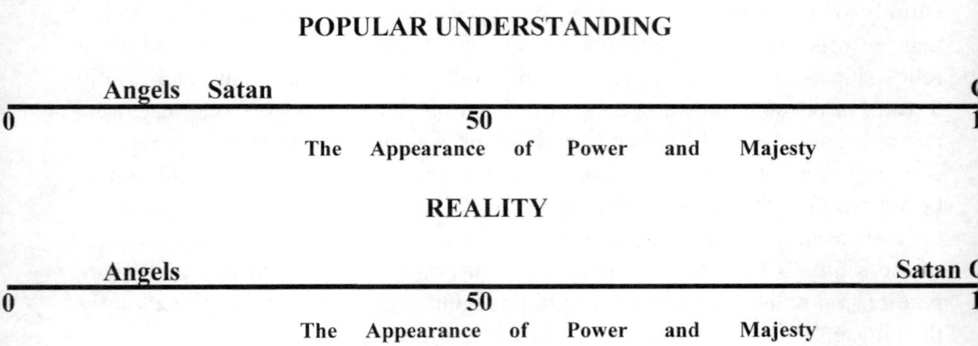

God's brilliance and power is 'way off the scale' in comparison to Satan. Looking at God and then at himself, Satan must have thought that he scrubbed up pretty well in comparison! Then, when he looked at the rest of the created order, the other angels, they appeared somewhat dull and second rate. He saw God getting all this glory and wanted a piece of the action himself.

> *By the abundance of your trade, you were internally filled with violence.* (Ezek 28:16)

Perhaps this verse refers to Satan politically trying to lobby the angels to follow him, not unlike Absalom lobbying the men of Israel by subtly undermining his father David. If he offered credible inducements that were backed by his majestic persona and radiance, it is not hard to imagine angels joining his team. More about this later.

When he does finally show his hand and takes on God and the remaining angels, he becomes the first to make the fatal mistake of all those who lose wars; underestimating the strength of the opposition. It was probably not necessary for God to reveal any more of his majesty than he already had because his angels, with twice as many warriors as Satan's, were able to triumph. Was it a walkover or was it a closer call than we have imagined? I think it was a closer call than we imagined and I think that God observed rather than directly participated.

A puzzle?

Why did Satan reveal his hand when he only had half the number of followers compared to his opponent? Remember Satan is the most capable, intelligent being ever created. He is no fool. Yes, his burgeoning pride is beginning to cloud his judgment, but it is unlikely to have clouded it to the extent that he would make such a fundamental error. No, he would have calculated that his angels plus *himself* should be able to defeat God plus double the amount of angels.

Satan's use of extra dimensions

It raises the question as to what extraordinary powers and abilities Satan possesses that would enable him to calculate himself as equal to God plus one third of the angels? From experience, we are aware that Satan has dimensional capabilities that the other angels don't possess. The third book in this series, *'Darkness in the Light: Satan's Trojan Horse'*, will go into more detail as to what this means. If Satan has the ability to control even one dimension higher than the rest of the angels, it would give him an enormous advantage over the opposition. The phrase, *'The anointed cherub who covers'* (Ezek 28:14) and *'O covering cherub'* (v16) could refer to these extra dimensional capabilities. It would give him an oversight, a covering or God's eye view that none of the others had.

ght of this, the enigmatic verse below takes on a different interpretation from that often given.

> *But Michael the archangel, when he disputed with the devil and argued about the body of Moses, did not dare pronounce against him a railing judgment, but said, 'The Lord rebuke you!'* (Jude 1:9)

Michael, although an arch-angel, is no match for Satan and he dare not insult Satan for fear of the reprisals. Satan's intrinsic power is too much for Michael. In our counselling experience, it takes a significant number of archangels, acting together, to stop Satan from getting to where he wants to be and even then, he can only be contained for a very limited period. One archangel is merely a minor nuisance to Satan, despite the fact that they are on God's team.

Although one would imagine that God is present to some degree in each of his angels, his presence in angels is not sufficient to deter Satan. However, his presence in believers, such as you and me, is sufficient to stop Satan in his tracks. Why is that? I think it is because we are created in the image of God and angels are not. We are created *above* angels. Our trinitarian nature coupled with our positional authority means that God's presence in us is sufficient to take a stand against Satan, and prevail.

Underestimating your enemy

When it came to doing battle with God, Satan doesn't seem to have taken into account God's capabilities when he did his calculations. Yet, as already stated, it is highly unlikely that Satan would have been so stupid as to overlook God as a significant opponent in this battle. Why doesn't he factor in the Creator as a significant obstacle to victory? A possible explanation is that God limited himself to the dimensional realms of his angels and, although he created Satan with extra dimensional capabilities, God only ever related to the angels at their level; within their dimensional existence. This would have meant that when Satan chose to explore the extent of his created abilities, when he moved to a higher dimension, he found that he could 'look down' on God. This would have further inflated his pride. If he thought he was dimensionally one up on God, it is not unreasonable for him to think he could take God on. Pride always leads to a narrowing of focus and this proved to be Satan's undoing. Satan possibly failed to realize that God was not dimensionally limited. God transcends all dimensional boundaries and limitations.

It is important to keep in mind that although Satan lost the battle and his authority in heaven was stripped away, his intrinsic nature is still intact. His intelligence, dimensional capabilities and majestic presence are still as they were.

When God creates a being, whether it is Satan, an angel or a human being, disobedience or sin of any kind doesn't affect the *nature* of the individual. Even after the Cross, Satan still appears as 'an angel of light' (2 Cor 11:14). One of the biggest mistakes Christians make is to think that Satan is an ugly, warted creature with horns, cloven hooves, pointy tail and carrying a pitch fork. This couldn't be further from the truth. When Satan embodies today; takes the temporary form of a human, he is drop dead gorgeous! His physical attributes are second to none. Satan makes any current male heart throb look like the hunchback of Notre Dame in comparison! But Satan is quite happy about us believing that he is powerless and ugly. As he learnt the hard way, underestimating the enemy plays right into his hands!

While sin doesn't affect our makeup, it does affect our standing with God and God can remove anyone from authority. King Nebuchadnezzar's conceit saw him immediately removed by God from his position of authority. Herod's conceit, disguised by his passive acceptance when he was called a god, saw God's immediate judgment fall upon him. Similarly, God's judgment of Satan, for his conceit and rebellion, was that he be 'hurled down to the earth and his angels with him' (Rev 12:9).

The three heavens

Because angels occupy dimensions higher than humans do, it doesn't mean that the satanic kingdom was confined only to our space-time existence of four dimensions when they were hurled down to earth. Rather, it means that they were removed from their place of intimacy with God. This removal is likely to mean a dimensional limitation. The first heaven is the earth, earth's atmosphere and outer space. The second heaven is that dimensional 'in between' region in the heavenly realms that separates the first heaven from the third heaven. The third heaven is the place Paul talks about being taken up to.

> *I know a man in Christ who fourteen years ago—whether in the body I do not know, or out of the body I do not know, God knows—such a man was caught up to the third heaven.* (2 Cor 12:2)

The third heaven is the region that God and his angels occupy and that believers enter when we die. Although God is omnipresent and therefore present in all three heavens, he none the less has a place of dwelling where the heavenly court meets. It is the place where Jesus is seated, in his resurrection body, at the right hand of the Father. It is the place seen and described by Isaiah in chapter 6 and by Micaiah in 1 Kings 22; and also John the Apostle in Revelation 4.

The second heaven is not governed by the laws of physics like the first heaven. It is not necessarily a physical dimension. It is a buffer zone between the first and third heavens, just like the Holy Place was a buffer zone between the outer court and the Holy of Holies. It is the spiritual realm that most directly impinges on our space-time world. Demons and angels monitor our activity, interacting with us by moving from the second heaven into the first heaven and back again. God's angels and Satan's angels interact in this realm. It is the region that believers pass through after death to gain access to the third heaven.

Demons occupy the first and second heavens but now can only enter the third heaven on invitation. Angels, those belonging to the Kingdom of Light, can move freely between all three heavens. It is likely that hell is in the second heaven since the third heaven appears to be the exclusive domain of God and his glory.

The interchanges between the angels of the Kingdom of Light and the fallen angels of the kingdom of darkness takes place primarily in the second heaven. How these

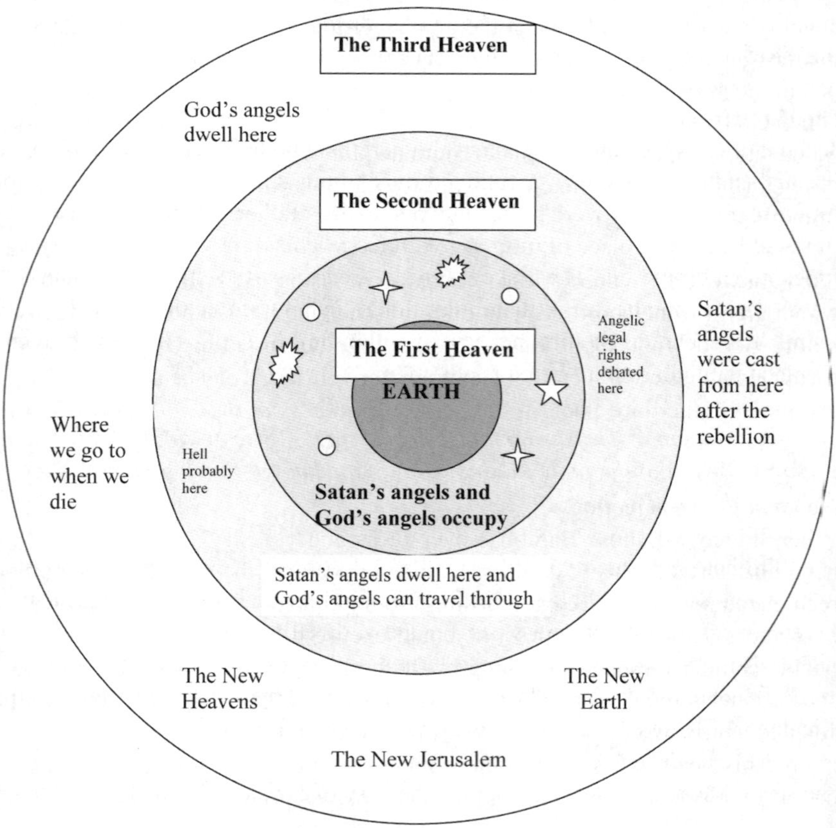

proceed in the second heaven is dependent on the authority each kingdom receives from the territorial and spiritual interplays happening in the first heaven, here on earth. However, it is not a battle, with angels fighting angels, in any physical sense, as some Christian books and intercessors would have us believe. That kind of battle happened once and since the defeat of Satan's army, the courtroom is the new battleground and legal rights are the currency of negotiation. A clear example of this dynamic is described in Daniel chapter 10.

> *Then he said to me, "Do not be afraid, Daniel, for from the first day that you set your heart on understanding this and on humbling yourself before your God, your words were heard, and I have come in response to your words. But the prince of the kingdom of Persia was withstanding me for twenty-one days; then behold, Michael, one of the chief princes, came to help me, for I had been left there with the kings of Persia."* (Dan 10:12-13)

The angel of the Lord was delayed in bringing God's response to Daniel because the demonic Prince of Persia and his assistants had successfully baled up that angel. It wasn't until Michael the archangel intervened, three weeks later, that the message was able to get through. The demonic prince over Persia was able to detain the angel because Daniel was in his territory giving him a legitimate right which God honoured. More about how the Prince of Persia gained those territorial rights later. Nonetheless, Daniel's continued intercession built up enough credits, or legal rights, to legitimize God's intervention via Michael and so 'the mail got through'.

Satan, however, is a special case. Because of his extra-dimensional capabilities, which aren't to be confused with omnipresence, he has the ability to 'accuse us before God day and night' (Rev 12:10) and at the same time be hurled down to earth. How these two seemingly contradictory positions can be reconciled will be examined in the third book in this series, *'Darkness in the Light: Satan's Trojan Horse'*.

No stranger to rejection

When the crowd chose Barabbas over Jesus and yelled: 'Crucify him', it must have hurt Jesus deeply. As his swollen eyes scanned the crowd, he would have recognized many who received healing from him and that meant the betrayal was even more acute. Nonetheless, he could excuse it because he knew how fickle people could be when swept along by the hysteria of the crowd. The betrayal of Judas, Peter's repeated denial and being abandoned by the rest of the apostles, John excepted, would have hurt Jesus far more. After all, for three years he had poured his heart and soul into these men. Yet he knows how quickly fear can distort man's perspective and lead to knee jerk reactions that are later regretted.

However, Satan's betrayal must have been the most cutting of them all. Here there were no easy excuses that could be offered. The most perfectly created individual, who understood better than any other creature the nature of God, betrayed God. The being that was privileged to enjoy an intimacy with God that we can only imagine, turned around and stuck the knife in. He had no flaws. He was full of wisdom. There were no excuses.

SUMMARY

- Satan is the most capable, intelligent being in God's created order.
- Satan sees himself as closer, in appearance, to God than to other angels.
- Satan must have been a credible alternative if one third of the angels chose to follow him.
- Satan wouldn't have taken on God's angels when he was out numbered two to one unless his presence and capabilities made enough difference for him to think he had a chance.
- Loss of authority doesn't affect intrinsic abilities. Satan was still as powerful after his rebellion as before it.
- There are three heavens. The first is our physical space-time world. The second is the spiritual realm that envelopes our world. The third is God's dwelling place.
- Being 'hurled down' to earth means that Satan and his angels no longer have automatic access to the third heaven like the other angels. They can only occupy the first and second heavens and can now only come into the third heaven on invitation by God. God's angels can occupy all three.
- Daniel chapter 10 is a good example of angelic conflict in the second heaven. Not physical conflict but law room debate.
- We don't often stop to consider the enormous amount of rejection God has had to cope with, particularly from those closest to him: Satan, Adam, Judas and the apostles.

Chapter 3:

A PROMISE YOU WON'T FORGET

It wasn't by accident that Satan was sent to earth. God didn't have a bad hair day and later realize he had made a big mistake by sending him and his followers into man's zone. God wanted him here. He hurled him down; down to earth. He wanted Satan to tempt Adam and Eve. Pretty mean of God, isn't it? Not really. God created Adam with one less moral parameter than Satan and the angels. Man wasn't created with the knowledge of good and evil. The angels had it. Man didn't.

The knowledge of good and evil

The angels had the knowledge of good and evil, the ability to make a sinful choice, and a third of them did. God created man without the knowledge of good and evil so that it was *impossible* for Adam and Eve to sin.

It is only when I have an understanding of what good is that I know what is not good and what is evil. Babies and young children have diminished moral responsibility for their actions because they don't know what is good and what is not. Drawing on the wallpaper with a crayon is not a sin if I don't know that I am not supposed to do that. Once I have been told that it is wrong, and I *choose* to do it, it is a sin. Paul sums this up neatly.

> *What shall we say then? Is the Law sin? May it never be! On the contrary, I would not have come to know sin except through the Law; for I would not*

have known about coveting if the Law had not said, "You shall not covet." (Rom 7:7)

Paraphrasing the essence of this verse; if I don't know the law that says, 'Do not draw on wallpaper' then drawing on wallpaper would not be a sin. Since Adam had no 'law' of any kind, he couldn't sin. He had no knowledge of evil. His conscience was absolutely clear. Because his conscience was perfect, just like every other aspect of his makeup, every thought that Adam had was absolutely pure. His thinking and actions never violated any aspect of God's law. It was effortless because he didn't have the dilemma of having to choose between good and evil. When he looked at Eve, there was nothing but love. Lust didn't even enter his thinking. It wasn't an option. All of Adam and Eve's actions toward each other were purely altruistic, purely selfless. Unconditional love was personified in Adam and Eve. They didn't have to make a moral choice because there wasn't a choice to make. They didn't know how to sin because they weren't capable of choosing evil. They didn't know what evil was. They were perfect.

The choice to do evil wasn't an option. Well, almost! There was just one condition. An imaginary dialogue between God and Adam might have sounded like this:

> "See that tree over there, Adam. That's right, that one way over there in the distance. You can't eat its fruit. Don't eat from the tree of the knowledge of good and evil. Don't eat from the tree of the Law. Don't eat from the tree that will unfold for you an immediate understanding of good and the possibility of *not* doing good. Adam, I strongly advise you not to eat from this tree of choices because you will become a slave to it. It will control you. You will become contrasuggestive. The more you know, the more tempting it will be to be disobedient. If it says, 'Don't lust', you will want to lust. If it says 'Don't covet', you will want to covet."

> *...for I would not have known about coveting if the Law had not said, "You shall not covet." But sin, taking opportunity through the commandment, produced in me coveting of every kind;* (Rom 7:7b,8)

Adam responds,

> 'No problem Lord. I've got the picture. No need to worry, I'm your man. I've got enough on my plate with naming the animals and picking fruit! I've got a stunning wife that I'm besotted with so that tree isn't an issue. Just one small tree to leave alone amongst all this blessing that you have given me. You couldn't have made it any easier'.

Adam was right. It wasn't a problem for him at all. Keep in mind that because of Adam's total lack of knowledge about good and evil, it wasn't a *temptation* for him when God told him not to touch this tree. From that point on, Adam never said to himself, 'Will I or won't I?' There was no internal dilemma or tension. Adam was never going to go near that tree.

Provided there was no third party to upset the status quo.

Above all else

God wants everyone to follow him as the result of a free will choice, not under compulsion. God needed to give Adam an opportunity to deliberately *choose* him over other desirable options. God wants us to choose him above everyone and everything else. Hence, he had to present Adam with a choice. A choice that would test him. A choice that would be fair. The same choice that the angels were given; follow God or follow Satan. God was really saying,

> 'Who will you follow Adam? You are my dear and trusted friend, the one with whom I walk in the cool of the evening, the only creature made in my image. Will you choose me or will you also let me down, like one third of my creation did in choosing Satan?'

God sent Satan to earth for two reasons. Firstly, to punish him for his rebellion. Beautiful though the earth was, it was nothing compared to the majestic glory of the third heaven that Satan was now excluded from. Satan was an outcast and his prison sentence was to be bound forever to the first and second heavens. Secondly, to set up a scenario where a High Noon duel would take place for Adam's allegiance. God was saying, 'Your choice, Adam. Who is it to be? Satan or me?'

In Job, chapter 1, God deliberately drew Satan's attention to his righteous servant, Job. Job was happily minding his own business, but in the heavenly realms another transaction was taking place.

> *The Lord said to Satan,* ***"Have you considered My servant Job?*** *For there is no one like him on the earth, a blameless and upright man, fearing God and turning away from evil."* (Job 1:8)

It wasn't the first time this had happened. It wasn't the first time God purposely directed Satan towards man. He had done it once before. He drew Satan's attention to Adam in a very dramatic manner. He hurled him right into the middle of Adam's backyard.

We miss the point if we concentrate on the tree. From God's perspective, the test wasn't, 'Will Adam eat from the tree or won't he?' Eating from the tree was the consequence of failing the test. The real test was:

> "Will Adam listen to Satan or will he listen to me? Will Adam obey Satan or will he obey me? When Satan casts doubt on what I said by using the phrase, *'Did God really say, 'You must not eat...'*, will Adam believe him or me?"

Male passivity[1]
Make no mistake. Adam was there with Eve when it all went pear shaped. Well, fruit shaped! The second half of Genesis 3:6 says so:

> *She also gave some to her husband,* ***who was with her****, and he ate it.*

When tempted, Adam should have stepped up to the plate and said,

> 'Listen serpent, you leave my wife alone. God told us not to eat from this tree and I trust God more than I trust you. Come on Honey, let's go".

But he said nothing. Zip. It was the first sin of omission, the first act of male passivity. It's no wonder males are so passive in matters spiritual today. Adam opted out then and his sons still opt out today. Show me any church and I'll show you more women than men.

We wouldn't have had the twin tower disaster in New York if the sin of Adam's passivity hadn't been replicated in his descendant, Abraham. Sarah had the bright idea that Abraham should sleep with Hagar to get the necessary offspring to fulfil God's promise. Abraham should have said:

> 'No dear, God promised our offspring would be through you and me, not through me and Hagar. Nice idea, and I am tempted, but no. I trust that God will come through.'

But Abraham didn't. He failed to declare what God had promised and the Arab nations were born as a consequence. The rest, as they say, is history.

The hardest word to say
Have you ever wondered what might have been if Adam had said sorry? Would salvation history have been changed with that one simple word? Would God have forgiven and restored him? We will never know. Instead, Adam moved into doing what we all do best; self justification. He blamed it on Eve and, as if that wasn't bad enough, he subtly blamed God as well.

The man said, "The woman ***you put here*** *with me—she gave me some fruit from the tree, and I ate it."* (Gen 3:12)

Authority regained[2]

From Satan's perspective, this temptation opportunity gave him an ideal chance to regain his lost authority. He was once the undisputed pinnacle of God's creation; coverer, overseer of the then created order. Now he is the ruler of an army but with no kingdom. He needs to re-establish territorial authority. Adam has territorial authority. The earth and all it contains belongs to Adam and Eve. It was given to them by God.

God blessed them and said to them, "Be fruitful and increase in number; fill the earth and subdue it. Rule over the fish of the sea and the birds of the air and over every living creature that moves on the ground." (Gen 1:28)

You made human beings the rulers over all that your hands have created. You put everything under their control. They rule over all flocks and herds and over the wild animals. They rule over the birds of the air and over the fish in the ocean. They rule over everything that swims in the oceans. (Ps 8:6-8)

Satan was keenly aware that if he could get Adam to obey him instead of God and do what he asked instead of what God asked, then Adam would come under his authority. The scriptural principle is that we come under the authority of those we choose to obey.

Don't you know that when you offer yourselves to someone to obey him as slaves, ***you are slaves to the one whom you obey****—whether you are slaves to sin, which leads to death, or to obedience, which leads to righteousness?* (Rom 6:16)

When I go to the doctor regarding a health problem and he gives me advice that I act on, I am coming under his authority. I give his words authority because I *act* on his advice. Implicitly, I am giving him authority. If I don't act on his advice, then I won't be giving him or his words any authority in my life. If I choose not to take the drugs he has prescribed for me, I am saying, in effect, 'I don't believe you'. Adam took the drugs. He took a bite. He acted on Satan's advice and therefore gave him authority. Once I act on the first bit of bad or sinful advice, it makes it that much easier to act on the next piece of sinful advice. I lose my clarity and my ability to make the right choice ever so slightly. A fogging, however imperceptible, appears. Just like a frog that remains in water which is being heated, I become a slave to the water I am in. A slave to what is effectively cooking or killing me. Adam's obedience to Satan, and all the rebellion and sinful choices that Satan represented, meant that Adam had chosen death; a slow and progressive killing of himself. He wasn't obedient to the truth he knew. He didn't make a choice for life, a choice to continue living a righteous life. He made a choice for death. The following words of Paul could really be a direct quote from the lips of Adam.

> *I was once alive apart from the Law; but when the commandment came, sin became alive and I died; and this commandment, which was to result in life, proved to result in death for me; for sin, taking an opportunity through the commandment, deceived me and through it killed me.* (Rom 7:9-11)

Satan tempted Adam and got what he wanted; territorial control of the earth. God gave it to Adam; Adam relinquished it to Satan. God was the owner. Adam was the leaseholder. Adam chose to give his lease to Satan. He chose a new landlord. God is still in ultimate control. He is still the owner of all creation but the chain of command has now changed

Before the Fall	**After the Fall**
God	**God**
over	*over*
Man	**Satan**
over	*over*
The World	**Man**
	over
	The World

Adam had his chance

Satan, as a being, is far more powerful than man. Nonetheless, at the temptation, Adam could have resisted him. He could have said, 'No, get out of here' and Satan couldn't have done anything about it. He couldn't posture, turn nasty or threaten. Why? Because he was trespassing on Adam's turf. Just as I have every right to evict a trespasser from my property with the full weight of the law behind me, so too, as the leaseholder of the earth, Adam had every right to tell him to leave and Satan would have had to do so. But as soon as the temptation transaction was over, a whole new ball game began.

Once Adam handed his authority over to Satan, Satan was given the upper hand in both departments; he was more powerful (mentally, spiritually, dimensionally) than Adam and in addition to these natural attributes, he now had authority over man and all of man's possessions. Man became completely powerless against Satan, impotent and in effect, his slave.

When Satan tempted Jesus in the wilderness, he confirmed his ownership of the world and referred back to the Garden of Eden when he said that it had been handed over to him.

> *And the devil said to Him, "I will give You all this domain and its glory; for* ***it has been handed over to me****, and I give it to whomever I wish."* (Lk 4:6)

Was Satan telling the truth? While Satan is a liar and the Father of lies, not everything he says is a lie. He wouldn't be believable if that were the case. Satan knew he had to come up with a really good temptation to sidetrack Jesus. He knew that with Jesus' sinlessness and moral purity, Jesus would spot a lie at 100 paces! He was not going to be so stupid as to tell an outright lie to the Son of God.

The same sin

Adam and Eve committed the same sin as Satan; wanting to be like God. Satan said,

> *"I will make myself like the Most High."* (Isa 14:14).

That was the key factor in his downfall. Satan tried the same temptation on Adam and Eve,

> *"For God knows that when you eat of it your eyes will be opened,* ***and you will be like God****, knowing good and evil."* (Gen 3:5)

Adam and Eve succumbed.

Adam and Eve committed the same sin as the rest of the fallen angels. They chose Satan over God. Satan must have taken some comfort that this new creation of God's was not too dissimilar to himself! Now he had the ideal opportunity to cultivate this new creation to be part of his already extensive army. Wouldn't that be rubbing it back into God's face!

The same sin, the same consequence

Satan's rebellion needed a consequence. Justice demanded it. Containment between the first and second heavens was the first part. Hell began, in a sense, for Satan and his followers, when they were excluded from God's tangible and continual presence in the third heaven.

> *...and they were not strong enough, and there was no longer a place found for them in heaven.* (Rev 12:8).

Hell, at a primary level, is separation from God. Even though the satanic kingdom still had freedom of movement in the first and second heavens, it was not home. It was not what they were used to enjoying. Hell, as a definite place of torment and eternal confinement, was the second phase of God's plan for those who would not repent.

An analogy can be made between England and Australia two hundred years ago. Those who trespassed against the laws of the realm were expelled from England. They were condemned to Australia, a hostile and undeveloped land, without the refinements of home. Early arrivals lamented the absence of the comforts they had taken for granted in the motherland. Although confined to Australia, there were many who could roam freely once in Australia. There were others, however, who once arriving in Australia, were physically confined to four walls of a jail out of which they would never escape.

Like Satan's two phase punishment for his rebellion, man's punishment also had two phases. Just as Satan was excluded from heaven immediately when he rebelled, so too Adam was excluded from Eden immediately after he sinned. Satan and his followers lost access to their heavenly paradise. Adam and his descendants lost access to their earthly paradise.

Since man committed the same sin as Satan, it is logical and just that the second phase of hell, the place of eternal jailing, should be the same for both.

> *Then He will also say to those on His left, 'Depart from Me, accursed ones, into the eternal fire which has been prepared for the devil and his angels.'* (Matt 25:41)

Process, Event, Spirit
As a result of the sin of Adam, death entered the world.

> *Therefore, just as through one man sin entered into the world, and death through sin, and so death spread to all men, because all sinned.* (Rom 5:12)

Instead of everything existing forever, there would now be a slow and gradual winding down of God's creation. Death and decay now affected everything.

> *That the creation itself also will be set free from its slavery to corruption into the freedom of the glory of the children of God. For we know that the whole creation groans and suffers the pains of childbirth together until now.* (Rom 8:21,22)

What transacted between God and Satan that led to death being the consequence of sin? To answer this question, we need to understand what death is. Again it is a multilevel answer. Death is a process, an event and a spirit.

Death is the *process* of the slow and steady decay that afflicts all creatures on earth. All sickness is the process of death. Ageing is the process of death. The process of death means that we are slowly dying from the moment we are created. Aside from biological death, death in relationships and death, decay and fragmentation in society are further aspects of the pervasive tentacles of death. Death is anything that does not lead to life, in the broadest sense.

Death is also the actual *event*, the instant when life ends. For man, it is the point when our soul and spirit leaves our body behind and enters the second heaven, where hell is, or the third heaven, where paradise is. Death is a specific event occurring at a specific instant in time.

Death is also a *spirit*, a fallen angel belonging to the satanic kingdom. The spirit called Death is closely aligned with the spirit called Hades, another member of Satan's ruling elite.

> *I looked, and behold, an ashen horse; and he who sat on it had the name Death; and Hades was following with him. Authority was given to them over a fourth of the earth, to kill with sword and with famine and with pestilence and by the wild beasts of the earth.* (Rev 6:8)

> *Then Death and Hades were thrown into the lake of fire. This is the second death, the lake of fire.* (Rev 20:14)

> *For He must reign until He has put all His enemies under His feet. The last enemy that will be abolished is Death.* (1 Cor 15:20-26)

Death has a personality. Popular caricatures of the Grim Reaper are not as far from the truth as many of us would like to think. For every one of us, the event of death coincides with the spirit of Death calling us into death. The spirit of Death calls us and we die. More about this later.

Separation from God

We have seen that Adam chose to cast his lot with Satan, and because God honours free will choice, there was an automatic separation between man and God. Symbolic of this separation was man being driven from the garden by God. Death of the relationship between God and man, was now formalized. It was set in concrete. Man would now endure decay, which would end in physical death, after which he'd be eternally separated from God.

Why was God so harsh? Surely he could have given Adam another chance. Hey, what's a tiny bit of fruit between friends!

Let's not underestimate the enormity of Adam's sin. God made it very easy for him to stay on the straight and narrow. He could do absolutely *anything* except *one* thing. He was perfect in terms of purity of thinking and human intelligence. He walked with God. Does it sound familiar, like a re-run? He didn't have to struggle with generational iniquity like we do. He wasn't sinned against, as we all are, through imperfect parenting. He wasn't born on the wrong side of the railway tracks. He had no excuses.

Since Adam had chosen to come under Satan's jurisdiction, God left him there. God effectively said, 'You have made your choice, Adam, now reap the consequences'. God's judgment, that the fallout from Adam's sin would be death to all creatures with life, was easy to implement. God simply told Satan to appoint two of his fallen angels and make them responsible for death, and containment after death. Satan appointed Death and Hades.

Whether God's judgment of death, as a consequence for Adam's sin, was determined after he sinned or whether God established all the moral and physical laws of the universe at the instant of creation, is open to debate. The point is that God always binds himself to the laws he creates in order to participate justly in what he has created. It is the foundational premise behind the legal rights system that both kingdoms use. It doesn't in any way diminish God's power and authority. In fact it provides a security for his created order because they are not dealing with an impulsive or reactive God who doesn't play by the rules.

Given the keys

Satan can't believe his luck. It appears to him that God has washed his hands of this latest creation attempt. Satan not only gets the earth and all creation that is on it, but in particular, he gets control of the death of man and maintaining this separation from God after death. Satan has the keys of Hell, the keys of Sheol. He has control of the first and second death; physical death and spirtual death. He gives the keys to his two princes, Death and Hades. The angel called Death is primarily responsible for physical death. The angel called Hades is primarily responsible for spiritual death; the containment of all who die in Sheol. However, their roles overlap. They're a tight team. A dynamic duo. It appears to Satan that God has packed up his toys and gone home, leaving him with the whole kit and caboodle! Satan thinks he's hit the Jackpot!

20/20 vision

It is most important to keep in mind that God has never been out of control. Despite the angels' choice to follow Satan, they are still servants of God. This appears contradictory but it is not. Satan has his own band of followers now and, at one level, is in rebellion against God, subversively trying to undermine God. At the same time, he still has to do what God asks of him. He was defeated. God was the victor. You do as you are told when you are defeated. From Satan's perspective, God's tasks, such as tempting Adam or Job, are further opportunities to wreak havoc in God's kingdom and to establish and solidify his own fledging kingdom. From God's much bigger perspective, it is a chance to test, hone and refine his own kingdom. Satan has a myopic viewpoint and God has 20/20 vision. Satan builds his army without realising that he is inadvertently training God's army.

The last word

Satan enjoyed a certain kind of smugness. He had taken on God and finally won. True, he had lost the battle for heaven, but he had won the battle for earth. Be careful Satan, don't underestimate your opponent. You made that mistake once, don't make it again. Satan's biggest mistake was, and still is, to under estimate the extent of the love God has for all his creation and the lengths to which he will go to win back man's allegiance. Love was no longer a word in Satan's vocabulary. Love was the only word in God's vocabulary. Like David cutting out a piece of Saul's garment when Saul thought he had David on the run, God left Satan a tantalizing morsel concerning his future plans. Like Joseph who put a cup in Benjamin's sack to ensure he would have ongoing dealings with his brothers, God gave Satan a warning that stunned him.

> *And I will put enmity between you and the woman, between your seed and her seed; he will bruise you on the head and you will bruise him on the heel.* (Gen 3:15)

God knew that Satan wouldn't be able to get these words out of his mind. It was a promise Satan couldn't forget.

SUMMARY

- Adam and Eve are created without any knowledge of good and evil. Created in God's image, with a perfect conscience, they didn't know what evil was and hence there was no possibility of sin.

- The knowledge of good and evil brings conviction of sin and a propensity to sin.

- God sends Satan to earth, both to punish him for his rebellion and to provide an antagonist to test Adam.

- Adam fails the same way Satan sinned. He wants to be like God.

- The issue at the temptation in Eden isn't so much about man gaining the knowledge of good and evil as it is about who will win the allegiance of Adam; God or Satan.

- The silence of Adam during the temptation establishes the template that all men still operate under. Male passivity, when it comes to spiritual leadership, is still the scourge of the church today.

- Would salvation history have changed if Adam had said sorry instead of justifying himself?

- We come under the authority of those we choose to obey. Adam came under Satan's authority by choosing to listen to *and act on* what Satan said instead of what God said.

- Adam hands over his God-given control of the earth to Satan. Because Satan is intrinsically a far more capable being, Adam and his descendants are powerless to deal with the new landlord he has installed.

- As a consequence of Adam's sin, the knowledge of good and evil means that man will be a slave to sin. Slavery to sin leads to death.

- Satan's sin leads to exile from the third heaven and final eternal separation in hell. Adam's sin leads to exile from the Garden of Eden and final eternal separation of man from God for those who are unrepentant.

- Death has three aspects to it. It is a process, an event and an angelic being or spirit. It is the angelic spirit called Death that is responsible for calling all men from life into death.

- God assigns to Satan control over the containment of men in Sheol, or Hades, after death. Hades is the spirit in charge of Hades. God gives Satan the keys to Sheol.

- While it appears that God has lost, that God is not in control, there is never a moment when God is not fully in control of everything that is happening. This is true even when events go against his *desired* will. Satan thinks that he is winning, that he has thwarted God's plans, but God uses Satan's attempts to thwart him as a means of building and strengthening his own kingdom. Satan inadvertently plays into God's hands.

Chapter 4:
INFECTED

And I will put enmity between you and the woman, between your seed and her seed; he will bruise you on the head and you will bruise him on the heel. (Gen 3:15)

Reading this verse on face value, free from theological bias and pre-conceptions, it is clear that Satan can produce seed or offspring and the offspring from Eve herself will contend with those of Satan. While 'seed' can be used in a figurative sense, sound exegesis (interpretation of Scripture) suggests that when the same word is used twice in the same verse, the same interpretation should be given to both. Since the seed of Eve is universally interpreted as her biological offspring, the logical implication is that Satan's offspring are also biological. The big question is, 'Who are these physical offspring of Satan?'

Legal rights

The legitimate right to gain spiritual advantage over man, through man's free will choices, began with Adam's sin. This was the beginning of what Anazao, and others, call the legal rights system. The legal rights system originally began with Satan's rebellion. The consequences of Satan's sin were being thrown out of heaven and losing favour with God. The consequences of man's sin were being thrown out of Eden and losing favour with God.

It is understanding and unravelling the legal rights system that both the Kingdom of Light and kingdom of darkness use, that is the focus of this series of books,

'Darkness in the Light'. This approach will answer many of the questions raised in the introduction. Satan has a legal right to do certain things to man, based on Adam's choice to be obedient to him instead of God. God has to honour that. However, there are restraints on how far Satan can go. Satan is still under God's authority. The amount of influence, or legal rights, that each side gets is linked to the free will choices of men. If man chooses selfish actions, the satanic kingdom gains more control. If man chooses more selfless actions, the Kingdom of Light gets more control.

The legal right system, as a negotiable currency between the kingdom of darkness and the Kingdom of Light, began to gather momentum with Adam's first sin. Further legal rights were given to the satanic kingdom when Adam refused to say sorry when confronted by God and instead chose self-justification and blaming. The Kingdom of Light would have gained legal rights with the purity of Abel's heart and his offering. This would have been offset by Cain's jealousy and murder of Abel. You get the picture.

From the transaction in Eden and for the next four thousand years[1], Satan had control over the world. God was still the owner but Satan was the landlord and man the tenant. Satan had authority to do a lot of things to man because of man's initial submission. Nevertheless, since God was in authority over Satan, Satan couldn't act with complete impunity.

The devil's seed

Satan must have gained, over time, significant legal rights to be able to put into effect what has to be the most amazing angelic-human interaction imaginable.

> *Now it came about, when men began to multiply on the face of the land, and daughters were born to them, that the sons of God saw that the daughters of men were beautiful; and they took wives for themselves, whomever they chose. Then the Lord said, "My Spirit shall not strive with man forever, because he also is flesh; nevertheless his days shall be one hundred and twenty years." The Nephilim were on the earth in those days, and also afterward, when the sons of God came into the daughters of men, and they bore children to them. Those were the mighty men who were of old, men of renown. Then the Lord saw that the wickedness of man was great on the earth, and that every intent of the thoughts of his heart was only evil continually. The Lord was sorry that He had made man on the earth, and He was grieved in His heart. The Lord said, "I will blot out man whom I have created from the face of the land, from man to animals to creeping things and to birds of the sky; for I am sorry that I have made them.* (Gen 6:1-7)

The use of the term 'sons of God' in Scripture applies to angelic beings and men. Whenever the term is used in the Old Testament, it refers to angels, both God's and Satan's. Whenever it is used in the New Testament, it refers to people[2]. In the passage above, God would not have allowed his angels to have intercourse with women and so, by elimination, it must apply to fallen angels. Further backing for this viewpoint is that the literal translation of the word 'Nephilim' in Hebrew is 'fallen ones.' *Targum Yonathan* is a well known Jewish translation and commentary on the Hebrew Scriptures. It says that the 'Nephilim' were so named because they were the sons of the fallen angels. Strong's Concordance with Greek and Hebrew Lexicon refers to the word 'Nephilim' translating it 'a feller, i.e. a bully or tyrant: giant'[3]. It states that this is derived from the verb 'naphal' which means 'to fall'[4]. This word is often associated with violence, hence frequently translated 'overthrow, fall upon'. Both translations are correct in that they each provide a different emphasis on the same word that complement each other. The Jewish emphasis on the word as a noun shows us that Nephilim were the offspring of fallen angels. The Gentile emphasis on the word as a verb describes their character. They were bullies who, through their large size, dealt violently with their fellow man.

Secondary Agreement

The book of Enoch is considered to be an Apocryphal book. It is not included in the Jewish Tenakh, the Hebrew name for what Christians call the Old Testament. The Protestant Old Testament is based on the Jewish Tenakh; the books in both are the same, although the order is different. After the Babylonian captivity, in the five hundred years before Jesus was born, Jews were spread all around the world and the Tenakh varied slightly. The Ethiopian Jews included Enoch in their Tenakh and most of the book of Enoch was found intact in the Dead Sea Scrolls. The book of Enoch has a rare distinction among apocryphal books of being quoted in the New Testament:

> *It was also about these men that Enoch, in the seventh generation from Adam, prophesied, saying, "Behold, the Lord came with many thousands of His holy ones, to execute judgment upon all, and to convict all the ungodly of all their ungodly deeds which they have done in an ungodly way, and of all the harsh things which ungodly sinners have spoken against Him."* (Jude 1:14-15)

This is a direct quote from the first chapter of 1st Enoch:

> And behold! He comes with ten thousands of His holy ones, to execute judgement upon all, and to destroy all the ungodly: and to convict all flesh of all the works of their ungodliness which they have ungodly committed, and of all the hard things which ungodly sinners have spoken against Him. (1 Enoch 1:9)

Clearly then, the writers of the New Testament must have been aware of Enoch and its contents and did not consider Enoch too dangerous a book to quote. While new doctrine can't be formed from apocrypha books alone, these books can be used to support and amplify the Tenakh, where they are in agreement with the Tenakh. Such is the case with the Gen 6:1-7 passage. The book of Enoch tells us the names of the spirits[5] that came down and had intercourse with women and the extent of the evil and corruption that resulted. Whether the names mentioned in Enoch are true or not is debatable. Nevertheless the support that Enoch lends to the interpretation that fallen angels had intercourse with women is unequivocal.

The Book of Jubilees is another ancient Jewish apocryphal book, also found among the Dead Sea Scrolls. It is sometimes called Leptogenesis meaning 'Lesser Genesis' in that it retells the book of Genesis. One of the reasons it is considered apocryphal is because of the author's tendency to unrealistically break all events into groups of seven years which he then linked to the year of Jubilee, the year after the 49th year. Interestingly, the translation of Gen 6:1 occurs in Jubilees 5:1 and confirms Enoch's interpretation of these verses.

> And it came to pass when the children of men began to multiply on the face of the earth and daughters were born unto them, that the angels of God saw them on a certain year of this jubilee, that they were beautiful to look upon; and they took themselves wives of all whom they chose, and they bore them sons and they were giants. (Jubilees 5:1)

Some readers may object to the use of other Jewish sources to corroborate or support the Scriptures. It is a serious omission, in my opinion, that the translations Christians most commonly use are translated predominantly by gentiles, rather than Jewish experts. There can be a tendency in our thinking to believe that we gentiles know best when it comes to understanding the Bible, because Jews made the fundamental error of not recognizing Jesus as their Messiah. If they can make such a major error in misinterpreting their own Scriptures, perhaps they have made other errors of misinterpretation and can't be trusted. Therefore, the rationale is that gentile believers in Jesus should go it alone, relying predominantly on their own interpretation.

It is stating the obvious to say that Jews know their language better than non-Jews do. Knowing how to read and speak Hebrew is one thing, but *being* a Hebrew (a Jew) adds an extra dimension and understanding that no gentile can acquire. We are simply the wild olive grafted into the natural olive (Rom 11:17) and we will never have the same innate, intuitive understanding of the Bible that they do. As gentiles, we are apt to see the Bible as principally God's written communication to mankind rather than primarily as a Jewish historical and cultural record that is also God's written communication to mankind. The emphasis is important. We compartmentalize and relegate the Jewish component to merely the vehicle that God used to communicate with humanity rather than seeing the two aspects seamlessly and inextricably interwoven. Reading a commentary on the famous Australian poem and song, 'Waltzing Matilda' by an American or an Englishman is unlikely to be as insightful and accurate as an Australian commentary. In reading translations of the Old Testament, in particular, we would do well to read parallel translations by Jewish translators and commentators and find out what the prevalent Jewish understanding is. I am not saying that they are always right, but a more balanced and accurate interpretation is likely to be achieved when we cast a broader net.

Makeup of Angels

One can imagine Satan's thinking going along the following lines: I have angels under my control; I have men under my control. What about a half breed? To ensure that God doesn't fulfil his promise, if I can gain greater control of men, they will be less likely to give their allegiance to him'.

Perhaps the prospect of having intercourse with the daughters of men was part of the carrot that Satan used to lure a third of the angels to follow him. The fallen angels thought the daughters of men were beautiful and, implicit in that statement is that they were sexually attracted to them.

All angels are male. Despite the world's portrayal of angels being predominantly female in television advertisements, nativity plays etc, every time angels appear in Scripture they are male. The pronouns used in reference to them are always masculine. There are no Scripture references to 'daughters of God', only 'sons of God.'

Fallen angels, or demons, can change their appearance to look like dragons, snakes, gargoyles or any other shape, beautiful or hideous, that will impress or frighten men. From my experience counselling survivors of comprehensive satanic ritualistic abuse, it appears that angels are created, with a default setting to take the shape of a person. In the spiritual realms, angels look like us, whether they are on God's side or Satan's. They have a head, torso, two arms, two legs and, yes, they have a penis. Regarding wings, most angels and demons don't have them. Wings are not necessary for 'flying' since angels exist in dimensions outside of our space-time world where wings for movement through the air are not necessary. A small proportion of angels, such as seraphim and cherubim have wings but the function of these wings is protection rather than movement. The wings of the cherubim that were placed on the top of the Ark of the Covenant had a protective function, not unlike the analogy used in Ps 91.

> *He will cover you with His pinions,*
> *And under His wings you may seek refuge;*
> *His faithfulness is a shield and bulwark* (Ps 91:4)

Again, from our experience, it appears that when demons, in spiritual form, engage in sex with humans today, they are always male. I have counselled a relatively large number of women who have inadvertently had sex with demons. Many of these women are God-fearing believers who have had no direct involvement with the occult at all and are surprised and perplexed at what is happening to them. These demons are given the collective name, 'Incubus'. Women relate varying degrees of sexual involvement from clitoral stimulation to full intercourse. Often clients are understandably embarrassed to share such incidents. Frequently they relate that the sex is the same as sex with a human male in terms of dilation of the vagina, heaviness on the chest and related sensations. It is as though a body is lying on them, but there is nothing there. Sometimes the woman can see the demon and they can appear in every respect just like a man. Less common is interference by 'Succubus' demons which usually involves anal penetration of human males, and females, or oral stimulation of the person's penis. The incidence of Incubus and Succubus interference is much more prevalent in African countries.

Demons can make themselves look like females when they appear as ghosts to deceive people, but when they embody, they always embody as male.

Examples of Angels embodying

The fact that God's angels can embody physically, for limited periods of time, is not in question. Some appeared to warn Lot and he invited them in as guests. Another angel wrestled with Jacob.

> *Do not neglect to show hospitality to strangers, for by this some have entertained angels without knowing it.* (Heb 13:2)

By embodying we mean taking on a covering of flesh, for a limited period of time, and interacting directly with us. Embodying doesn't mean going into the body of an existing person. It means forming a completely new physical entity that looks and acts like a human in every respect. There are numerous stories in many Christian books today of angels embodying to help out the saints. Derek Prince, in his book '*Appointment in Jerusalem*', relates how an angel carried one of his adopted daughters to safety from one side of war torn Jerusalem to another.

Someone I know of personally, who was actively involved in smuggling Bibles into Europe and China, relates an incident of travelling towards Albania by himself in a VW car crammed full of Bibles. Albania, at that time, was the most anti-Christian country in Europe. He was relying on God for a miracle since he had no idea how he would get the car full of Bibles through the border checkpoint. He didn't speak Albanian. Not far from the border, he picked up a hitch hiker who happened to speak English. As they approached the border the hitch hiker said, 'I speak fluent Albanian. Let me take care of the border inspection'. The car stopped at the checkpoint, the hitch hiker rolled down the window, spoke to the guards and they waived the car through with no inspection at all. He relates, 'Leaving the inspection point, I put the car into first gear, changed into second gear, turned to thank the hitch hiker and he was gone! He disappeared. The car door wasn't opened at any stage through the checkpoint and afterwards'. The only possible explanation is that God had sent an angel. It makes the following verse, from Hebrews really come alive!

> *Are they not all ministering spirits, sent out to render service for the sake of those who will inherit salvation?* (Heb 1:14)

Satan's crew can too!

Satan's angels can embody and do. Remember, the angel's ability to embody is intrinsic to their makeup and that didn't change when they lost their authority. There is a popular misconception amongst the general public, including Christians, that demons in their natural state are horrible, wart covered creatures who look like deformed dwarfs or gargoyles. This is simply not true. While they can change their shape and appearance to look like anything they choose, including something grotesque, that is not their natural form or shape. They are angels, just like God's angels. They have simply chosen to follow a different master. Not only did demons embody, but from this passage in Genesis chapter 6 we learn that they had physical intercourse with women and could produce sperm capable of fertilizing a human ovum. They were obviously attractive enough when they embodied to entice women to have intercourse with them.

The uniqueness of man

The angels would have been intrigued watching the creation of Adam because he had a trinity of spirit, soul and body. Man was part of a dimensional existence that was physical. Angels were part of a dimensional existence that was spiritual. They had a spirit and a soul but man was different. He had a spirit and a soul just as they had, but in addition this spirit and soul was inseparably linked to the flesh of this new physical world. It wasn't that man was spirit and soul *clothed* in flesh, it was that the flesh was actually one with the soul and spirit. Angels were a 'bi-unity'; man was a 'tri-unity', made in the image of God. When angels embody they are not a 'trinity' like man. They are spirit and soul clothed in flesh. A bi-unity encased in flesh. A being that looks likes us but in reality is fundamentally different. God had created man as a reflection of himself, just a little lower than himself.

What is man that You take thought of him,
And the son of man that You care for him?
Yet You have made him a little lower than God,
And You crown him with glory and majesty! (Ps 8:4,5)

Unfortunately the King James Version has incorrectly translated the first line of verse five as *"...made him a little lower than the angels"* and this misconception is entrenched in the thinking of many Christians. The NIV continues the error with *"...made him a little lower than the heavenly beings"*. The Hebrew word is 'Elohim' and this word is almost always translated as 'God or gods', rather than 'angels' or 'heavenly beings'. It is translated correctly in the NASB. Incidentally, the writer of Hebrews also mistranslates those same verses (Heb 2:6,7).

Similar soul and spirit

Some may argue that we don't know for sure that angels are a 'bi unity' of the same soul and spirit we have. Because angels had intercourse with women and produced viable offspring, it is unlikely that the union of the sperm of angels with the ova of women was significantly different from normal human reproduction. If it were, we would be dealing with another species but, as will be explained in more detail in chapter 6, Nephilim could reproduce with ordinary humans producing a generational lineage. This indicates that they are the same species, only larger in size. Hence the impartation of soul and spirit at the conception of angel-human offspring is the same as human-human offspring. No one is exactly sure how soul and spirit are imparted to a new being at conception. Does God uniquely impart a completely distinct and different soul and spirit at the moment of conception? Alternatively, does the soul and spirit inherent in the sperm, meet with the soul and spirit inherent in the ovum to produce a new soul and spirit that is still unique and distinct but more closely linked to that of both parents? The latter scenario provides a more seamless vehicle for the transference of inherited generational iniquity.

Conjecture

It is more than coincidental that the fall of Satan happened after the creation of Adam and Eve. In fact, it is very likely that these events were connected. Everything seems to have been okay in heaven up until this point. *All* the angels, sons of God, shouted for joy when the earth was created.

On what were its bases sunk? Or who laid its cornerstone, when the morning stars sang together and all the sons of God shouted for joy? (Job 38:7)

This verse implies that the rebellion of Satan was yet to happen. Rev 12:9 makes it clear that the earth existed when the rebellion took place. The rebellion of the angels in heaven occurred when Adam and Eve were enjoying the Garden.

> *He was hurled to the earth, and his angels with him.* (Rev 12:9)

There was collective joy and jubilation after God had made the heavens and the earth. However, when man entered the scene, and then woman, things started to go awry.

Maybe Satan, who was watching this event, realized that as beautiful, majestic and powerful as he was, this new creation of God's was somehow more intrinsically reflective of God's nature than he was. Maybe that was a factor in his rebellion. His conceit meant that he was not going to play second fiddle to anyone. As he watched Adam and God walking in the cool of the evening, maybe he recognized a quality in their relationship that was absent in his own.

Fascinating females

Imagine the intrigued look on the angels' faces as they watched the creation of Eve. Here was a being quite different from them. Firstly, she was physically different; there were breasts and no male organ. Secondly, her thinking and emotional responses were processed in a manner that appeared to them strange. Their jaws must have dropped when Adam and Eve first had sexual intercourse. Here was a connection between two individuals that they had never seen before. The enjoyment of this act, experienced by Adam and Eve, as well as God's approval of what was happening, would have added to the fascination.

Satan now had a carrot to dangle as an enticement to join his band. If he could promise his followers that they too could enjoy intercourse with this new creature maybe that would convince some to follow him. If Satan could persuade the angels to choose lust over unconditional love, then that might be the thin end of the wedge that would open the door to angels enthroning him as god instead of Elohim. If this was the case, then Genesis chapter 6 is really about Satan making good on his promises. He was letting his boys finally enjoy what was promised before they threw their hats in with him.

Perhaps the 'trade' mentioned in Ezek 28:16 refers to Satan lobbying the angels with his proposition of sexual gratification.

> *By the abundance of your trade You were internally filled with violence, and you sinned;* (Ezek 28:16)

Could the 'violence' refer to Satan's intention to destroy mankind, whether through radically infecting them with half breeds or by direct violence towards men?

The Nephilim

The Nephilim, the offspring of the union between embodied fallen angels and women, possessed some super human qualities. With 50% of the genetic material coming directly from the satanic kingdom, it is not hard to imagine that evil spread at an incredible rate. It was not the angelic genes as such that was the issue but the accompanying demons. The use of the phrase, 'men of renown' in Gen 6:4 doesn't in this case mean 'good renown'. Verse 5 expands on verse 4 saying that the wickedness of man was so great that *every intent* of his heart was inclined to evil. It is likely that the widespread infection of the Nephilim into man's genetic makeup, coupled with the violent behaviour these god-men modelled, meant that soon all of humanity was biologically or morally corrupted by their influence. God was left with little choice but to take the drastic action he did. The only way to remove the Nephilim, to genetically remove their impact, was to eliminate everyone. Everyone, except for someone with a genetically pure human lineage and a heart turned towards him. Noah fitted the bill.

> *These are the records of the generations of Noah. Noah was a righteous man, blameless in his time; Noah walked with God.* (Gen 6:9)

Let's look at the phrase translated *'blameless in his time'* in the NASB and *'blameless among the people of his time'* in the NIV. The Hebrew word translated 'blameless' is *tamim*. Jewish commentators translate the word as 'whole, unblemished, perfect'. Strong's Concordance agrees and translates it as 'without blemish, complete, full, perfect, sincerely (-ity), sound, without spot, undefiled, upright(-ly), whole' [6]. The nuance of the word implies an untainted wholeness or perfection. Its primary application is not moral perfection. The word translated 'time' should be translated 'generations'. It is exactly the same word used in the first part of the same verse; *these are the records of the* ***generations*** *of Noah.* The same word should have a consistent translation within the same verse! The literal translation of this phrase, *'blameless in his time'* should be *'perfect in his generations'*. Several Jewish translations use the phrase, 'perfect in his generations' for Genesis 6:9[7] . The translators of the NIV and NASB didn't translate it literally because it didn't make sense to them[8]. This is because the fundamental assumption of the major commentaries (e.g. Matthew Henry, Zondervan) was that Gen 6:1 doesn't refer to fallen angels having intercourse with women. The translation 'blameless in his time' seemed to tie in better with 'Noah was a righteous man' and so they used this instead. Fortunately, not all Western translations are flawed. The KJV (King James Version) and RAV (Revised Authorized Version) correctly translate this phrase as *'perfect in his generations'*.

If the premise is correct that Nephilim had infected most generational lines and God had to choose a man that was both righteous and untainted in his generational lineage, then the literal translation 'perfect in his generations' meaning 'pure in his generational line' makes more sense. Noah was both righteous *and* he had a pure generational lineage. It is also more consistent with the opening statement of the same verse, *'This is the history of the generations of Noah'*. The author begins the verse by saying he is going to tell us about the history of Noah's generations but the phrase 'blameless in his time' talks about character, not history. The literal translation means the context of the first part of the verse is explained by the second part; *these are the records of the generations of Noah. Noah was a righteous man and his generational line was unblemished.*

Extensive infiltration
Noah was the tenth generation from Adam:

> *...the son of Noah, the son of Lamech, the son of Methuselah, the son of Enoch, the son of Jared, the son of Mahalaleel, the son of Cainan, the son of Enosh, the son of Seth, the son of Adam, the son of God.* (Luke 3:36-38)

In Genesis chapter 5, with the exception of Noah, for each of the ancestors mentioned above is added the phrase, 'and he had other sons and daughters'. We don't know how many additional children each ancestral patriarch had but given the abundance of provision that existed in a near perfect world and the long lives each person lived, it is not unrealistic to assume that each couple had between 10 and 20 children. They were commanded to go out and populate the world and they no doubt took that seriously. Over ten generations, mathematically that means there were billions of people alive on earth at the time of the flood, probably more than are alive on earth today. The extent of the corruption of the human genome must have been absolutely enormous if God can find only *one* who is righteous *and* has a pure generational line. It is highly likely that we are not talking about a handful of angels infecting one generation but a repeated generational assault by a large number of angels producing hundreds of thousands, if not millions or tens of millions of Nephilim and related offspring. It is no wonder that the moral corruption on earth had reached epidemic proportions.

The antibiotic
The flood, as God's solution to man's wickedness, makes more sense when we see it primarily as an antibiotic response to the widespread infection of the Nephilim that had riddled humanity and rendered it moribund. Because of the purity of his blood line and his righteous obedience, Noah becomes the physical saviour of the human race; a forerunner of Christ who through the purity of his bloodline (sin-free conception) and his righteous obedience would become the spiritual saviour of the world.

SUMMARY

- Man's free choices determine the extent to which he will be blessed by the Kingdom of Light or cursed by the kingdom of darkness.
- Every choice man makes gives legitimate access, or legal rights, to either kingdom to influence his life.
- A focus of this book is understanding and unravelling the legal rights system, in a general sense, that both these kingdoms use.
- The phrase 'sons of God' in the Old Testament always refers to angelic beings, whether they are fallen or not.
- The correct interpretation of Genesis 6 is that Satan's angels took on flesh (embodied) and had intercourse with women, producing offspring that were angelic-human hybrids called Nephilim. Genesis 3:15 must refer to biological seed of Satan.
- Angels embody today to help out the saints. Similarly, Satan's angels can embody today to further Satan's plans.
- Angels and demons look like humans. Although they can take on different shapes, their 'default' setting is the shape of a human male.
- Most angels don't have wings. Wings form a protective function.
- Satan's fall soon after the creation of man is no coincidence. A likely incentive Satan offered angels to side with him was the chance to have sex with women. If that is the case, Genesis 6 is really about Satan keeping his promise.
- The angelic interaction with humans is unlikely to have been a small infestation but probably populated the earth with millions, perhaps billions of Nephilim and their offspring.
- The flood is a drastic measure but a viable way to eliminate the Nephilim from the earth.
- A literal interpretation of the first part of Genesis 3:15 regarding Satan's offspring now makes sense in the light of Genesis chapter 5.

Chapter 5:
DARKNESS IN THE LIGHT

After the flood, the next significant interaction that gives us direct insight into the relationship between God, Satan and mankind is the story of Job. It appears that Job lived in the period shortly after the flood, around the time of the Tower of Babel. Behemoth, described in Job 40, can only apply to a dinosaur[1], and we know that the changing climatic conditions after the flood meant that the dinosaurs didn't survive for long. In addition, there is strong scientific support for the belief that the post flood conditions led to the formation of the ice age[2]. It didn't envelope the whole earth, as is commonly believed, and it is likely that the region that Job lived in was relatively unaffected. Nonetheless, the repeated references in Job to ice, frost and frozen sea[3] implies its impact was not lost even on the more temperate regions.

God's interaction with demons

There are not many direct references to demons and God's interaction with them in the Old Testament. Those we do have paint a very different picture from what many Christians believe. A common misconception is that God is either repulsed by demons and doesn't want them in his presence or that demons can't stand to be in the presence of God, because of his holiness.

Separating sin from sinner

God created all the angels. He loves all his created beings, whether they are human or angelic. Just as he loves the human sinner and can separate the sin from the sinner, so too he loves the fallen angels and can separate what they have done, and are still doing, from who they are: wonderfully created beings. God has no problem with fallen angels in his presence. Neither do they have a problem with coming into his presence. They are servants. A servant comes into the presence of the master whenever the master commands it. They do so respectfully. They do so immediately, whether they like it or not.

The interactions between God and the satanic kingdom, recorded in the Old Testament, clearly show God in control as he sends evil spirits to do his bidding.

> *Then God sent an evil spirit between Abimelech and the men of Shechem; and the men of Shechem dealt treacherously with Abimelech.* (Jdg 9:23)

> *Now the Spirit of the Lord departed from Saul, and an evil spirit from the Lord terrorized him.* (1 Sam 16:14)

> *Isaiah said to them, "Thus you shall say to your master, 'Thus says the Lord, "Do not be afraid because of the words that you have heard, with which the servants of the king of Assyria have blasphemed Me. Behold, I will put a spirit in him so that he will hear a rumor and return to his own land. And I will make him fall by the sword in his own land."' "*(2 Kings 19:6,7)

This next passage shows very clearly how comfortable God was in his interactions with demons and, in turn, their respectful attitude toward him.

> *Micaiah said, "Therefore, hear the word of the Lord. I saw the Lord sitting on His throne, and all the host of heaven standing by Him on His right and on His left. "The Lord said, 'Who will entice Ahab to go up and fall at Ramoth-gilead?' And one said this while another said that. "Then a spirit came forward and stood before the Lord and said, 'I will entice him.' "The Lord said to him, 'How?' And he said, 'I will go out and be a deceiving spirit in the mouth of all his prophets.' Then He said, 'You are to entice him and also prevail. Go and do so.' "Now therefore, behold, the Lord has put a deceiving spirit in the mouth of all these your prophets; and the Lord has proclaimed disaster against you."* (1 Kings 22:19-23)

Notice that all the hosts of heaven were there; God's angels were present, along with the fallen angels and they were divided into two distinct groups, one on his right and one on his left. It is likely that the Lord's angels were on the right and Satan's angels on the left, reminiscent of the separation of the sheep from the goats in the final judgment. (Matt 25:32, 33)

If we need any further convincing of God's overall authority and the ease of interaction between the Kingdom of Light and the kingdom of darkness, the first two chapters of Job provide interesting reading.

> *Again there was a day when the sons of God came to present themselves before the Lord, and Satan also came among them to present himself before the Lord. The Lord said to Satan, "Where have you come from?" Then Satan answered the Lord and said, "From roaming about on the earth and walking around on it." The Lord said to Satan, "Have you considered My servant Job?* (Job 2:1-3)

The 'sons of God' in this context refer again to the fallen angels of the kingdom of darkness. It appears that God has called them to attention, like a military parade. Satan himself was also commanded to appear. Notice the relatively relaxed, conversational style of the interaction.

Not equal and opposite

With this misconception that God and demons repel each other, is the underlying assumption that the satanic kingdom and the Kingdom of Light are two opposing camps at war, each trying to gain control of the other. Not unlike the Axis powers versus the Allies in the Second World War or the Russians and Americans in the cold war that followed, with each side plotting and counter plotting. That situation has never happened not even in Satan's initial rebellion.

No contest

God's omnipresence, omniscience and omnipotence mean that he has never for a second, not even a nanosecond, been out of control of the situation. He has been everywhere, right in the midst of Satan and his followers at all times. He has known everything; absolutely every aspect of what Satan is thinking and intending to do. He is all powerful. Satan is no more a threat to God than an atom is to an elephant! There never was a war like we imagine there was, based on our human understanding of relatively even and opposing forces. When your enemy knows absolutely everything about you at all times and is infinitely more powerful, there isn't a 'war'. Yes, in the initial angelic rebellion, God's angels certainly battled and had to trust God and there may possibly have been times when they appeared to be losing, but the outcome was never in doubt. God merely used the battle to train his angels.

Is God responsible for what the devil does?

It is hard to get our heads around the idea that God has control over the satanic kingdom. Our reasoning goes, 'If God is good, pure and holy then he shouldn't have anything to do with the devil and his mob'. If God is in ultimate control of the devil, then isn't he responsible for what the devil does?

The point that we miss with a question like this is that we are not that different from the kingdom of darkness. We are full of pride, just as they are. We sin daily; many, many times a day just as they do. We are selfish and self seeking, just as they are. Equally we could reason, 'If God is so good, pure and holy then he shouldn't have anything to do with humans'. But he does! Why? As has been stated but is worth repeating, because he loves all his creation. That includes the devil and his fallen angels. Our sinfulness doesn't stop God loving us. The devil's sinfulness doesn't stop God loving him. Remember God can separate the sin from the sinner far better than we can! The devil looks at God with eyes of disdain and hatred. God always responds to the devil with eyes of love. God is firm but loving. Satan wants God to respond to him with the same hatred that he has for God. God won't. God *is* love.

We know that God is in ultimate control of the world, yet we don't hold him responsible for what man does. Man exercises free will choice. Each person is responsible for the choices he makes. In the same way, although God is in ultimate control of the satanic kingdom, we can't hold him responsible for the free will choices of the devil and his cohorts. Just as God doesn't agree with the selfish and destructive free will choices we make, yet he allows us to make them, neither does he agree with the selfish and destructive free will choices of the devil and demons, but he allows them to make them. Just as God hopes that we gain wisdom and understanding by reaping the consequences of bad choices, so too he allows the satanic kingdom the ability to reinforce and enhance those consequences in our lives to hopefully accelerate our growth in wisdom and maturity. Just as God is capable of working out his plans for mankind within the free will choices man makes, in like manner he is able to achieve his goals for mankind despite the active efforts of the kingdom of darkness to thwart him. God is in control. Being God means that he is never *not* in control. Sometimes man's wise choices accelerate his plans. Other times man's poor choices slow down his agenda. No matter how fast or how slow the progress, God's will *will* ultimately be done!

Back to Job

Isn't it mean of God to set Satan onto Job? It appears that God draws Satan's attention to Job.

> *The Lord said to Satan, "Have you considered My servant Job?"* (Job 2:3)

It's like letting a Rottweiler loose on a Chihuahua! Why did God do that?

God is always more interested in us developing a closer relationship with him than he is in our comfort. He doesn't mind us being comfortable provided our comfort doesn't lead to self satisfaction and complacency. God wants us to keep a sharp cutting edge. He wants us to mature, to grow in wisdom and understanding. This often involves us continuing to make the right choices in adverse circumstances. God wants us to trust him when the chips are down. He allows trials because refining happens under fire. As the Apostle Peter says, it is the refining fire of trials in our life that tests our faith and trust.

> *In this you greatly rejoice, even though now for a little while, if necessary, you have been distressed by various trials, so that the proof of your faith, being more precious than gold which is perishable, even though tested by fire, may be found to result in praise and glory and honor at the revelation of Jesus Christ;* (1 Pet 1:6,7)

God saw Job's heart. He knew he had in Job a man who loved him. A man who feared him. Although God can see the future, he never allows his foreknowledge to influence Job's free will choices. He knew that despite whatever Satan could throw at him, including at times his four unhelpful friends, Job was likely to continue to place his trust in God. Job would come out a wiser, more mature man. A well honed and sharper instrument in his Master's hands.

A legal rights model

The first two chapters of Job give us tremendous insight into how the legal right system works. Job is often an enigmatic book for Bible commentators to deal with because it appears to be an anachronism. It doesn't fit anywhere. In the context of a legal rights understanding, it is the most valuable book in the Bible.

We know that Satan is the accuser of the brethren, and the first two chapters of this book provide us with a video cam view of how this process works. We see Satan challenging God regarding his protection of Job and the banter that goes on between Satan and God. People are uneasy at the relatively amicable interaction between God and Satan but this interaction is consistent with the rest of the Old Testament references. Despite the banter, God is definitely in control, giving clear parameters for Satan's influence over Job. Initially God gives Satan restricted access regarding what he can do to Job. He cannot harm him physically. We see that Satan has control over the elements and the power over death. He sent down fire and wind which destroyed Job's property and killed his children and he also incited other people to kill Job's servants.

> *Now on the day when his sons and his daughters were eating and drinking wine in their oldest brother's house, a messenger came to Job and said, "The oxen were plowing and the donkeys feeding beside them, and the Sabeans*

attacked and took them. They also slew the servants with the edge of the sword, and I alone have escaped to tell you." While he was still speaking, another also came and said, "The fire of God fell from heaven and burned up the sheep and the servants and consumed them, and I alone have escaped to tell you." While he was still speaking, another also came and said, "The Chaldeans formed three bands and made a raid on the camels and took them and slew the servants with the edge of the sword, and I alone have escaped to tell you." While he was still speaking, another also came and said, "Your sons and your daughters were eating and drinking wine in their oldest brother's house, and behold, a great wind came from across the wilderness and struck the four corners of the house, and it fell on the young people and they died, and I alone have escaped to tell you." Then Job arose and tore his robe and shaved his head, and he fell to the ground and worshiped. He said, "Naked I came from my mother's womb, and naked I shall return there. The Lord gave and the Lord has taken away. Blessed be the name of the Lord." Through all this Job did not sin nor did he blame God. (Job 1:13-22).

God blamed

Notice what Job says at the end of all this calamity.

> *'The Lord gave and the Lord has taken away'.* (Job 1:21)

This next point is very important: Job wrongly attributes to the Lord that which is the work of Satan. God gave permission for Satan to test Job but God cannot be held responsible for what Satan did or the way he did it. What Job should have said is:

> 'The Lord gave and Satan took away'.

From the context of this chapter, this is the only conclusion that can be drawn. Job, of course, was not privy to the heavenly discourse that we, the readers, know about. He didn't have the overview of what was really happening. He just experienced the *effect*; he didn't know anything about the cause. Without a knowledge of the heavenly bargaining that had taken place, it is understandable he would jump to the wrong conclusion. It is highly likely Job did not have much knowledge of who Satan was and what he was capable of doing; hence it wouldn't have entered his mind to blame him. In the forty chapters of conversation between Job and his friends, nowhere is Satan, or the devil, mentioned.

Although unwittingly attributing to God what was actually the work of Satan, Job was not blaming God. His immediate response to all that happened was to fall on the ground and worship God. He blessed God. He doesn't get angry; he doesn't stand up, shake his fist at God and curse or swear. Neither does he move into self-pity, which would be another understandable response in the circumstances. His wife, however, can't handle it. After round two with Satan, when Job is covered with boils, she has had enough. Even then, Job stands firm.

> *Then his wife said to him, "Do you still hold fast your integrity? Curse God and die!" But he said to her, "You speak as one of the foolish women speaks. Shall we indeed accept good from God and not accept adversity?" In all this Job did not sin with his lips.* (Job 2:9,10)

Party Animals

There were obviously sufficient legal rights for Satan to do what he did to Job's servants and family. Satan went all out and used his legal rights for maximum impact. He could have been more subtle but he used the sledge hammer approach. Was it God's intention that all Job's servants and his children would die at that time, all together and in the manner that they did? No. Did God permit it? Yes. Why? Because there were sufficient accumulated legal rights in the lives of Job's servants and children, and even Job himself, for Satan to exercise this right if he chose to. Job's children were sinners like we all are. In fact, the first few verses of this book make it clear that they weren't saints! Like many young adults, they liked a good time. Job was sufficiently concerned with their behaviour that he regularly offered sacrifices in case they had offended God.

> *His sons used to go and hold a feast in the house of each one on his day, and they would send and invite their three sisters to eat and drink with them. When the days of feasting had completed their cycle, Job would send and consecrate them, rising up early in the morning and offering burnt offerings according to the number of them all; for Job said, "Perhaps my sons have sinned and cursed God in their hearts." Thus Job did continually.* (Job 1:4,5)

If Job had to do this continually, his children were obviously making quite a habit of their indulgent behaviour; a cyclical routine of meeting in each other's houses. In fact, they were partying together when the house collapsed on top of them and killed them!

> *While he was still speaking, another also came and said, "Your sons and your daughters were eating and drinking wine in their oldest brother's house, and behold, a great wind came from across the wilderness and struck the four corners of the house, and it fell on the young people and they died, and I alone have escaped to tell you."* (Job 1:18,19)

Wrong application

'The Lord gave and the Lord has taken away' is, in my opinion, the most misquoted phrase in Scripture. Daily, in Christian funeral services around the world, whenever someone dies prematurely, you are likely to hear this phrase quoted. It implies that the person who has died has died because God has chosen to take the deceased away. We make exactly the same mistake as Job made. Except that we have no excuse, we should know better. We have the benefit of hindsight that Job didn't have. We should be saying, *'The Lord gave and Satan took away'*.

The story of Job is not just a one-off event that has no relevance to us today. What's the point of its inclusion in the Bible if that is the case? No, Job is you and Job is me. Job is a man with a simple faith in God. Like many of us, he has children that he worries about and it isn't always smooth sailing in his marriage relationship! He does his best to get on with life, treating others fairly and minding his own business. Sure, you may not have the same dramatic calamities as Job has, but the interaction in the heavenly realms over your life is just the same. Because of the daily layering effect of sin in your life, Satan has considerable legal rights over you and your family. Just as God has a measure of protection over Job, because of his innate righteousness, so too he has a measure of protection over you because of the imputed righteousness of his Son. That's not an excuse to get complacent. Just because you are a believer, doesn't mean that you are immune from Satan. Living on this side of the Cross, as you will see later, doesn't nullify the relevance of Job for us today. Satan petitions God regarding you and your family. If you aren't making regular deposits in God's legal rights account, then as Satan's case against you grows, God's ability to maintain his protection diminishes.

Look around you at the Christian families who suffer calamity, who constantly seem to struggle, who have family members that have died earlier than God ever intended. Do you still think it is fair to blame God or are you starting to see the bigger picture? Are you, like so many others, going to continue to attribute to the Kingdom of Light that which is the work of the kingdom of darkness? Are you going to continue to place darkness in the Light?

> *This is the message we have heard from Him and announce to you, that God is Light, and in Him there is no darkness at all.* (1 Jn 1:5)

SUMMARY

- We mistakenly believe that God is repulsed by demons. God loves all his created beings, including Satan. God has an immense capacity to separate the sin from the sinner.
- All angel were created as servants. Although the kingdom of darkness chose to rebel, their job description didn't change. They are still servants but without privileges.
- There is no dualism between God's kingdom and Satan's kingdom. It is not an 'us' against 'them' scenario. The kingdom of darkness is under the control of the Kingdom of Light.
- God is no more responsible for what the devil does than he is responsible for what we do. He hopes we make the right choices and yes, he still hopes the satanic kingdom will make the right choices, despite their continuous rejection of God. He can still work out his plans within the choices that we and the satanic kingdom make.
- As servants of God, demons are more constrained as to what they can and can't do than humans are. Humans were not created as servants in the same way angels were.
- What Satan intends for evil, God can use to train and hone man, even if on the surface it appears calamitous for man. Job is a good example.
- Job made a mistake when he said, 'The Lord gave and the Lord had taken away'. The context clearly implies, 'The Lord gave and Satan took away'
- This is the most misquoted verse in the Bible.
- The heavenly interactions and their outworking in Job's life are relevant to each person today. Satan's control over death then is still the same today. Job is *you* and Job is *me.*
- We must avoid attributing the work of the enemy to the Kingdom of Light. We dull the purity of the Kingdom of Light by placing darkness in the Light.

Chapter 6:
REINFECTED

Often we ignore the little phrases within verses, that are quite significant.

> *The Nephilim were on the earth in those days,* ***and also afterward****, when the sons of God came in to the daughters of men, and they bore children to them. Those were the mighty men who were of old, men of renown.* (Gen 6:4)

The phrase, 'in those days', refers to the time before the flood, called the antediluvian period. This period lasted approximately 1300 years and is covered by the first six chapters of Genesis. The phrase, 'and also afterward', refers to the time after the flood (postdiluvian). In other words, although these god-men were completely wiped out by the flood, somehow they reappeared after the flood, probably after the time of Job and a few generations before Abraham. That there were Nephilim on earth after the flood, at the time of Moses, is confirmed by the following verse.

> *There also we saw the Nephilim (the sons of Anak are part of the Nephilim); and we became like grasshoppers in our own sight, and so we were in their sight.* (Num 13:33)

This verse is part of the report of the scouts who went to spy out the Promised Land after Israel had escaped from Egypt. The preceding verse says that they were men of *great* size. Moses, the likely author of Genesis, wrote these verses after God established his covenant on Mount Sinai, during the time of the second infestation of Nephilim, about 800 years after the flood. That is why he included the phrase, 'and also afterward'.

After the flood, there were no Nephilim initially. Noah and his sons started a pure human lineage. Following the tower of Babel, the unity of mankind was broken, and man dispersed over the earth, which itself was splitting apart at the time (massive continental drift). It would appear that this re-infection began some time after this because it was an issue at the time of Abraham, 400 years after the flood.

> *Then the Lord said to me, 'Do not harass Moab, nor provoke them to war, for I will not give you any of their land as a possession, because I have given Ar to the sons of Lot as a possession. (The Emim lived there formerly, a people as great, numerous, and tall as the Anakim. Like the Anakim, they are also regarded as Rephaim, but the Moabites call them Emim).* (Deut 2:9-11)

The sons of Anak (Anakim) are called Nephilim in Num 13:33 and Rephaim in Deut 2:11. In this context, it appears that the word 'Nephilim' can be interchanged with the word 'Rephaim'. This makes sense. Rephaim means 'giant'[1]. As we have seen, Strong's Concordance includes the word giant as an alternative word for Nephilim and the Book of Jubilees translates the word Nephilim as giant. A characteristic of the Nephilim is that they were giants. The terms 'fallen ones' or 'feller' and 'giants' are used interchangeably because they were considered one and the same. Aside from the sons of Anak and the Emim, mentioned above, there were another people group called the Zamzummin who were also Nephilim or Rephaim.

> *When you come opposite the sons of Ammon, do not harass them nor provoke them, for I will not give you any of the land of the sons of Ammon as a possession, because I have given it to the sons of Lot as a possession. (It is also regarded as the land of the Rephaim, for Rephaim formerly lived in it, but the Ammonites call them Zamzummin, a people as great, numerous, and tall as the Anakim, but the Lord destroyed them before them. And they dispossessed them and settled in their place,* (Deut 2:19-21)

The background to these passages is found in Genesis 19. Lot was Abraham's nephew. When Lot's wife was turned into a pillar of salt after his escape from Sodom and Gommorah, Lot's daughters, fearing they wouldn't be able to find a husband, slept with their father and produced two offspring. One of these became the father of the Moabites, the other the father of the Ammonites. Thus both the daughters of Lot were with child by their father. The firstborn bore a son, and called his name Moab; he is the father of the Moabites to this day. As for the younger, she also bore a son, and called his name Ben-ammi; he is the father of the sons of Ammon to this day. (Gen 19:36-38)

The Emim and the Zamzummin were displaced to make way for the Moabites and Ammonites so that God could honour Lot's inheritance. How did God destroy the Emim and the Zamzummin? He used a group of kings headed by Chedorlaomer, king of Elam, and Tidal, king of Goiim.

> *In the fourteenth year Chedorlaomer and the kings that were with him, came and defeated the Rephaim in Ashteroth-karnaim and the Zuzim in Ham and the Emim in Shaveh-kiriathaim,* (Gen 14:15)

When Chedorlaomer conquered Sodom, he made the mistake of carrying off Lot and his possessions and Abraham pursued and defeated him.

Setting limits

It makes logical sense that after the flood God placed a prohibition on all reproductive physical intercourse with women by the satanic kingdom. He is unlikely to have gone to all the effort of destroying almost all of mankind to eliminate the Nephilim and then allow the Nephilim to repopulate. There are two possibilities for what happened between God, Satan and his angels in regard to the Nephilim dilemma. After the flood, the satanic kingdom had to obey because they were servants. No discussion. Alternatively, God left it to Satan to deal with this problem, knowing that Satan would be harsher on his followers. Satan wants to be top dog in a manner that continually emphasizes to his fallen angels how much greater he is. Strange as it may appear, Satan's pride means that he cripples his followers to enhance himself. Once again this plays right into God's hands.

God values what he created and although he can diminish the intrinsic abilities of his creation, if he so chooses, he prefers they retain their created abilities so that they can continue to make unhindered free will choices. Satan, however, is not so gracious. Just as man used to castrate his fellow man to look after his harem or to sing in falsetto, so too Satan did something similar to most of his angels. From our counselling experience, although many can still participate in intercourse with humans, it would appear that all the fallen angels no longer have the ability to sexually reproduce today. The only exception is Satan himself. More about that in *'Darkness in the Light: Satan's Trojan Horse'*. It is likely that during this period Satan instituted the heirarchy within the demonic kingdom that exists today. Lower level fallen angels, or demons, simply do not have the same capabilities as those angels closest to Satan. However, Satan did not, at the time immediately following the flood, remove the reproductive potential of *all* the fallen angels. It appears that he did this for almost all but left a few, along with himself, that could still reproduce. Unfortunately, those Princes he did leave rebelled against God and reinfected the earth, producing the Emim, the Zamzummin, the Anakim and perhaps others.

Did Satan allow this rebellion? Satan runs a tight ship. From our experience, Satan is the supreme dictator and no one would rebel against him. Satan allowed a few of his top Princes to go back to earth and strategically re-establish the presence of the Nephilim on earth again. He may well have participated himself. Why did he do this?

Satan listened intently to what Noah had prophesied over his sons, after Ham had exposed his father's immodesty.

> *So he said, "Cursed be Canaan; a servant of servants he shall be to his brothers". He also said, "Blessed be the Lord, the God of Shem; and let Canaan be his servant. May God enlarge Japheth, and let him dwell in the tents of Shem; and let Canaan be his servant."* (Gen 9:25-27)

In this prophesy, God is described as the God of Shem and the descendants of Canaan, Ham's son, are to serve Shem. Satan hasn't forgotten the Genesis 3 prophesy about the offspring of the woman bruising his head. He realizes that 'this offspring' is likely to be through Shem's lineage due to God's blessing of Shem. How can he stop this happening? If Satan can somehow gain control of the land of Canaan, then he has a platform upon which to undermine Shem. Satan thinks he can undermine God, even though Satan is God's servant. In like manner, if he can use Canaan and his descendants to undermine their masters, Shem and his descendents, he might be successful in stopping them.

While the promise given to Shem was enough motivation for Satan to re-establish his giants, Satan would have been even more alert as he watched with interest the commitment of God to one man, Abraham. He would have listened intently to what God said to Abraham or, if that was a private conversation, he would have found out by listening to Abraham and Sarah talking about this Promised Land and its boundaries.

> *The Lord said to Abram, after Lot had separated from him, "Now lift up your eyes and look from the place where you are, northward and southward and eastward and westward; for all the land which you see, I will give it to you and to your descendants forever.* (Gen 13:14,15)

> *On that day the Lord made a covenant with Abram, saying, "To your*

descendants I have given this land, from the river of Egypt as far as the great river, the river Euphrates: the Kenite and the Kenizzite and the Kadmonite and the Hittite and the Perizzite and the Rephaim and the Amorite and the Canaanite and the Girgashite and the Jebusite." (Gen 15:18-21)

Yes! His plan was working, he had guessed right. Notice that the Rephaim are a people group mentioned in the land God was giving to Abraham. Now all he needs to do is increase the presence of his god-men. If he could establish a really strong presence there, then he might be able to thwart God's plans. The world was no longer one people and one territory, as it was before the flood. The land had split apart and people were spreading everywhere. Satan was less interested in the rest of the world; he was more interested in these children of the promise. This time Satan's agenda would be very specific. This time he would control all the lands given to Abraham in the promise and, to be on the safe side, also the land given to his nephew, Lot. When these Israelites returned, which, according to the covenant, they must, he would be ready for them. And ready he was. When the Israelites saw the sons of Anak, men who were giants, they were terrified and because of their lack of trust in God, they wandered a further 40 years in the wilderness.

Where are you, God?

Why did God allow it? It doesn't make sense, after such a dramatic solution to the first infestation. Why would God sit meekly by and allow this to happen? God's omniscience meant he knew this would happen. He could have stopped it. Why didn't he?

When a master has a rebellious servant, the master has a number of options. He can immediately punish the servant and quash the rebellion as soon as it happens. He can allow the servant to rebel hoping that the servant might learn a lesson, just like a parent training his son. He can allow the servant to rebel and use the consequences of the servant's rebellion to further his own ends. God has all these options open to him whenever he deals with Satan. In the last chapter, we established that Satan's viewpoint is often narrow and reactionary whereas God's viewpoint is always much broader and always calculated; never reactive, always responsive. God was comfortable with a localized reappearance of the Nephilim otherwise he wouldn't have tolerated it. He monitored the situation and used this rebellion to his own advantage. He allowed the Nephilim to be there provided they were within his tolerance limits. When these limits were in danger of being exceeded, he acted. He destroyed the Emim and Zamzummim to make way for the sons of Lot, the Moabites and Ammonites, to inherit the land. However, he had his own reasons for leaving the sons of Anak and we will see why later.

Unlike the book of Job, where we are privy to the heavenly dialogue, we can only conjecture as to the extent of God's approval, if any, for what Satan did in genetically re-corrupting humanity. Satan is a defeated servant and yet he hates God. He acts within the legal rights man gives him and he pushes that envelope to the limit. He still has a free will and can also choose to rebel. We know it was never God's intention, at any time, that the kingdom of darkness interact with man sexually in the manner that they did. God would have allowed it because of the enormous amount of legal rights Satan gained from Adam's defection. The first part of Genesis 3:15 confirms this.

> *And I will put enmity between you and the woman, between your seed and her seed; he will bruise you on the head and you will bruise him on the heel.* (Gen 3:15)

God knew that when Adam and Eve fell, Satan would reward his angels by allowing them to have sex with women. It may well have been something that was discussed in heaven between God and Satan before the temptation event, just like the Job dialogue. The verse implies that both God and Satan knew that Satan sowing his seed was inevitable. But did Satan keep to the limits God had set?

Regarding this second infestation, it is possible that Satan simply rebelled and acted entirely of his own volition. It could be a combination of both scenarios: God may have *allowed* limited interaction and Satan abused this limited privilege. Scripture seems to indicate that Satan acted without God's permission.

> *And angels who did not keep their own domain, but abandoned their proper abode, He has kept in eternal bonds under darkness for the judgment of the great day,* (Jude 1:6)

This is the clearest confirmation of Genesis 6 within Scripture pointing to a trespassing by angels beyond God's intended limits and it appears that God punished these errant fallen angels by sentencing them to immediate confinement in hell.

This is corroborated in 2 Peter, chapter 2. In verses 4 to 7, Peter gives a brief summary of God's judgment of the unrighteous and rescuing of the righteous. He relates the examples in chronological order. Because he mentions the angels *before* he mentions the flood, the angels Peter is referring to are almost certainly those of Genesis 6.

> ***For if God did not spare angels when they sinned, but cast them into hell and committed them to pits of darkness, reserved for judgment;*** *and did not*

spare the ancient world, but preserved Noah, a preacher of righteousness, with seven others, when He brought a flood upon the world of the ungodly; and if He condemned the cities of Sodom and Gomorrah to destruction by reducing them to ashes, having made them an example to those who would live ungodly lives thereafter and if He rescued righteous Lot, oppressed by the sensual conduct of unprincipled men... (2 Pet 2:4-7)

The Greek word for hell that Peter uses in this passage is 'tartaroo' or 'tartaros'. It is the only time this word is used in the New Testament to describe hell and it means 'the deepest abyss of hell'[2]. 'Hades' and 'Gehenna' are the other two words used to describe hell in 12 out of the 13 occurrences in the New Testament. The singular usage of this word, 'tartaroo' has led scholars to believe that a separate section or compartment of hell was set aside for these fallen angels. This is confirmed by the Book of Jubilees which says that these angels were

> bound in the depths of the earth and kept separate. (Jub 5:6)

More about Tartaros in a later chapter. The book of Enoch states that rebellious angels

> will be bound for seventy generations under the hill of the earth until the day of Judgment...

but intriguingly it states that this won't happen until

> ...they see all their sons destroyed. (1 Enoch 10:12).

In other words, the errant angels won't be thrown into hell until the last Nephilim is destroyed. Although only secondary support to Jude and 2 Peter, both the Book of Enoch and the Book of Jubilees add further weight to the belief that these fallen angels were confined to hell soon after the rebellion. The condemnation of these angels to hell was premature. It was not what God intended. All fallen angels (demons) have free reign on earth until the final judgment.

The Israelites are ready

After wandering in the desert for 40 years, the Israelites were ready to trust God and take on the inhabitants of the lands that stood in the way of claiming their inheritance. Joshua and the Israelites destroyed the various nations that blocked their path to reclaiming the land promised to Abraham. Of the Nephilim on the earth, the Emim and the Zamzummin had already been wiped out and Moses had destroyed Og, the king of Basham, who was a Nephilim. Og was the last remaining Rephaim related to the area adjacent to the Ammorites.

So the Lord our God also gave into our hands Og king of Bashan and all his army. We struck them down, leaving no survivors. (Deut 3:3)

Only Og, king of Bashan was left of the remnant of the Rephaim... (Deut 3:11)

The last remaining Nephilim that stood as obstacles in Joshua's way were the Anakim. Joshua dealt with these but unfortunately he didn't destroy all the remaining Nephilim.

Then Joshua came at that time and cut off the Anakim from the hill country, from Hebron, from Debir, from Anab and from all the hill country of Judah and from all the hill country of Israel. Joshua utterly destroyed them with their cities. There were no Anakim left in the land of the sons of Israel; ***only in Gaza, in Gath, and in Ashdod some remained.*** *So Joshua took the whole land, according to all that the Lord had spoken to Moses, and Joshua gave it for an inheritance to Israel according to their divisions by their tribes. Thus the land had rest from war.* (Jos 11:21-23)

Satan's plan to use the Nephilim to stop the Israelites settling in the Promised Land had failed. Satan was down, but he wasn't out. There was still hope because Rephaim continued to reside in three cities. Not just any three cities. Gaza, Gath and Ashdod were all Philistine cities. There were still Rephaim in these cities but Joshua let them be. He should have pursued and eliminated them all, while he had the upper hand. He didn't and the consequence of this disobedience was reaped by future generations of Israelites.

For the next few hundred years we don't hear anything about the Rephaim. It isn't until the time of David that they make their presence felt again. Where would we expect them to be found? Among the Philistines, of course, and in particular a certain giant; Goliath of Gath.

Then a champion came out from the armies of the Philistines named Goliath, from Gath, whose height was six cubits and a span. He had a bronze helmet on his head, and he was clothed with scale-armor which weighed five thousand shekels of bronze. He also had bronze greaves on his legs and a bronze javelin slung between his shoulders. The shaft of his spear was like a weaver's beam, and the head of his spear weighed six hundred shekels of iron; his shield-carrier also walked before him. (1 Sam 17:4-7)

That's big!

A cubit was 18 inches or 45cm. A span[3] was 9 or 10 inches, between 22 and 26 cm. Six cubits and a span made Goliath 9 feet 10 inches or exactly 3 metres tall. The tallest man living today is 7 foot 9 inches (2.35 m) and the tallest height reached by a human, that has been verified is 8 ft 11in (2.72m)[4]. This was by an American, Robert Wadlow, in the last century. That makes Goliath two feet taller than the tallest man today and one foot taller than the tallest man of recent history. What is impressive about Goliath was not just his height but his size. He was huge. A shekel was 12 grams. 5000 shekels was 60 kilograms or 132 pounds. Goliath's armour was the weight of an average adult female! When Goliath wore his armour in battle, it was as if a woman had been draped over his shoulders. This would have debilitated an ordinary warrior but wasn't even noticed by Goliath. The head of his spear (excluding the shaft) was 7 kgs (15 pounds). Most spear heads are between 500 grams and 1 kg (1 to 2 pounds). That makes the head of his spear between 7 and 15 times heavier than normal. That is absolutely massive. Goliath wasn't a tall, thin man; he was a man-mountain! He truly was a giant in every sense of the word. Scripture doesn't give us the weight of Goliath or much quantitative information about Nephilim but it does confirm that these dimensions were typical of Nephilim by telling us the bed size of another of the Nephilim: Og, king of Bashan.

> *For only Og king of Bashan was left of the remnant of the Rephaim. Behold, his bedstead was an iron bedstead; it is in Rabbah of the sons of Ammon. Its* ***length was nine cubits and its width four cubits*** *by ordinary cubit.*
> (Deut 3:11)

The bed was 13 foot 6 inches long and 6 feet wide (4m 11cm long and 2m wide). If we allow one foot of extra length in a bed, then Og was probably 12 ft 6 inches. Two features that point to Og's massive size, are the width of the bed and the fact that the writer makes a point of mentioning that it was made of iron. Most people at the time probably had wooden beds but the thickness of the timber required to support Og's bulk, particularly if he threw himself onto the bed, would have made it cumbersome to construct and move around. So he had an iron bed made. If we try and visualize the size of such a man, we can sympathize with the twelve spies when they first saw these giants. The spies were accurate in their description when they said that they appeared like grasshoppers in comparison.

A class of their own

The size of these giants is such that they do not fit within the usual Normal Distribution Curve[5] as it would apply to the current human race regarding size and weight. These giants are not simply tall or large people that are at the extremes of such a curve. These men are several standard deviations beyond these extremes. They can't simply be dismissed as 'big people'; their giganticism puts them in a class all of their own. Outside of the supernatural genetic component that the

Bible indicates is the reason, there is no credible biological or genetic explanation for such size. There has never been anyone recorded in non-Biblical human history as large as Goliath or Og. It cannot be attributed to an excessive supply of growth hormone since that is usually a one-off occurrence, such as happened with Robert Wadlow, and it doesn't account for the large numbers of genetically linked individuals that existed. Neither does a hormonal explanation account for the massiveness of these individuals. Wadlow was tall, but not massive. These giants are an enigma that defies any natural explanation.

Yet just like us

Were they human? Did they have a spirit and soul as we do and therefore could they be saved? The evidence points to Nephilim being human. Aside from their large size, they appeared human in everything they did. They were born of women, ate, breathed, reproduced, died and were limited to the confines of our space-time world for the duration of their time on earth, just like the rest of us. Unlike their spiritual fathers, who could embody only for limited periods of time and disembody, Nephilim were rooted to terra firma and returned to dust when they died. Because of their propensity towards evil, due to their genetic heritage and their own choices, there is likely to be a lot fewer of them in heaven, proportionally, than the rest of humanity. However, those that made wise free will choices and acted in faith will, like the rest of humanity prior to the Cross, be justified and in heaven with Abraham, the patriarchs and millions, perhaps billions of others. The most disconcerting aspect for many Christians to get their heads around is that fallen angels can produce viable sperm that can fertilize a human ovum and produce humans, admittedly large humans, but humans nonetheless.

Think about it. It takes some time for us to mentally digest! Angels can embody, clothe themselves with flesh and produce sperm with the same set of human chromosomes that we have. These are compatible with those of a human ovum and produce a human being. That the human produced is exceptionally large doesn't make it any less human. As we shall see, these giants were capable of reproduction. In other words, they could produce viable offspring themselves. This is even more remarkable because usually if two different species interbreed, the offspring are sterile. For example, if a donkey is mated with a horse, the offspring is a mule which can't reproduce. The fact that viable offspring result indicates that angels are very close to us in many respects.

We are not told whether female giants were produced. It is highly likely that the sperm produced by angels only carried the Y chromosome because angels are a direct creation of God, without female input. This means they wouldn't have been able to produce sperm carrying the X chromosome. This also means that all the first generation Nephilim had to be male. When these Nephilim in turn reproduced, their sperm would have had both X and Y chromosomes like ordinary males. The X chromosome would have been normal, since they inherited it from their fully human mothers. If we assume that the gene for giganticism was linked specifically to the Y chromosome, it means that all boys would have become giants, just like their father. It also means all their daughters would have been of normal size, because they inherited a normal X chromosome from their Nephilim father. In other words, giganticism would have only ever been present in males. However, if giganticism wasn't localized to the Y chromosome, but was spread less specifically through the genome, then females of various sizes would have occurred.

We are more comfortable with relegating the satanic kingdom to horrible, yucky, deformed gargoyle-like beings that are not remotely like us. We find it easier to remain in denial, which is just what Satan wants.

The remnant

It would appear that Goliath must have been one of the last remaining giants of the Nephilim because if the Philistines had many others like Goliath, one would have thought that they would have used them all in their battle against Israel. It is also likely that the writer of the books of Samuel would have mentioned it if there were more than just one giant at the time of David's confrontation. In 2 Sam 21:22, Goliath is referred to as *the* giant in Gath, implying there was only one giant at the time. It appears then that Goliath is the singular exception in the crowd. If that is the case, then we can assume that intercourse between fallen angels and women had ceased a long time before. Perhaps God finally put a stop to all angelic-human interaction at the time when Joshua defeated the Anakim, so that the remnant that escaped to Philistia was the last of the pure Nephilim. From then on, there were no new first generation Nephilim created and the existing Nephilim simply reproduced with women. Over the following centuries, they died off and the gene pool was progressively diluted. This theory has additional support, based on Og's bed; he was three feet taller than Goliath. Goliath, although still tall, was not pure Nephilim like Og. Og would have appeared quite imposing to Goliath just as any person would who is three feet, or one metre, taller than you!

This raises the question of Goliath's children. If Goliath is the last of the Nephilim to have any substantial amount of angelic DNA and he was killed by David, did he leave any young male children behind that in turn grew to be giants like their dad? Fortunately, the Bible tells us the answer and also what happened to his children.

> *Now it came about after this that there was war again with the Philistines at Gob; then Sibbecai the Hushathite struck down Saph, who was among the descendants of the giant. There was war with the Philistines again at*

Gob, and Elhanan the son of Jaare-oregim the Bethlehemite killed Goliath the Gittite, the shaft of whose spear was like a weaver's beam. There was war at Gath again, where there was a man of great stature who had six fingers on each hand and six toes on each foot, twenty-four in number; and he also had been born to the giant. When he defied Israel, Jonathan the son of Shimei, David's brother, struck him down. ***These four were born to the giant in Gath, and they fell by the hand of David and by the hand of his servants.***
(2 Sam 21:18-22)

David killed Goliath and David's mighty men killed Goliath's four sons, who were also giants. This passage only mentions three sons although it says there were four. The three mentioned are Saph, Goliath (named after his dad) and a son with extra digits. This incident is recorded again in 2 Chronicles and provides us with the name of the fourth son, Lahmi.

Now it came about after this, that war broke out at Gezer with the Philistines; then Sibbecai the Hushathite killed Sippai, one of the descendants of the giants, and they were subdued. And there was war with the Philistines again, and Elhanan the son of Jair killed Lahmi the brother of Goliath the Gittite, the shaft of whose spear was like a weaver's beam. Again there was war at Gath, where there was a man of great stature who had twenty-four fingers and toes, six fingers on each hand and six toes on each foot; and he also was descended from the giants. When he taunted Israel, Jonathan the son of Shimea, David's brother, killed him. ***These were descended from the giants in Gath,*** *and they fell by the hand of David and by the hand of his servants.* (1 Ch 20:4-8)

This second version, or retelling, isn't as specific as the first in linking these giants directly to Goliath himself. It doesn't mean that it contradicts the first version; it simply takes a broader perspective. In 2 Samuel, the emphasis is on Goliath as the immediate father. In the 1 Chronicles account, the emphasis is on the generational lineage of Goliath's sons; that they were descended from the giants of Gath. Just as Jesus was the son of Mary and Joseph *and* Jesus was descended from the line of David, so too the giants mentioned in these passages were the sons of Goliath and descended from the giants of Gath. Both statements are true; one takes a narrow view, the other a broader perspective.

The Chronicles account confirms the assumption that Goliath was not a one-off giant but part of the generational line of Nephilim that Joshua failed to completely eradicate.

With the death of Goliath's four sons, it would appear then that the last of the Nephilim have been wiped out. How do we know for sure? Firstly, there is no more mention of giants ever again in Scripture after the sons of Goliath were wiped out. If these men monoliths still existed anywhere else, their presence is unlikely to have gone unnoticed or unmentioned.

Satan incensed

There is another reason that points to the belief that Goliath and his sons were the last of the Nephilim. It occurs in the very next verse.

> *Then Satan stood up against Israel and moved David to number Israel.* (1 Ch 21:1)

Although this verse begins a new chapter, there are no chapter divisions in the original Hebrew. One chapter runs into the next without any breaks or paragraph distinctions. The Jewish scribes only made distinctions at the end of major books. There are no distinctions made between each of the books of the Minor Prophets, such as Joel and Amos; they simply run into each other. Chapter divisions we have today are a relatively recent addition, about 800 years old, to make referencing easy. While the divisions are supposed to be at an appropriate end of a passage, and more frequently are, sometimes they are not. This, in my opinion, is one of those times because the first word of the next verse is 'Then' and this links it to the previous verse. If we take out the chapter division, these last two verses become;

> *These were descended from the giants in Gath, and they fell by the hand of David and by the hand of his servants. Then Satan stood up against Israel and moved David to number Israel.* (1 Ch 20:8 - 21:1)

In other words, as a consequence of David's men removing Goliath's sons, Satan is so angry that he incites David to take a census.

> *Satan rose up against Israel and* ***incited*** *David to take a census of Israel.* (1 Ch 1:21 NIV)

Why would Satan be so angry if he still had Nephilim left? But if these were the very last of his god-men, then he would not be very happy, to say the least! Aside from a brief period after the flood, for almost three thousand years, he'd had some direct influence over man's genetic makeup. Now his final hopes had been removed. He had great plans for these helpers of his. He thought they would thwart God's plans. He thought that the huge size of these 'creations' of his would intimidate and control man's destiny. After all, from Satan's viewpoint, God's idea of how a man should be was rather puny in comparison to the colossus he could engineer. Satan's plans appeared to be working; mankind was infected and thoroughly corrupted but God intervened with the flood. Despite orders from God to the contrary, he would have another go. After all, it worked so well before the flood. The prophecy regarding Shem and the one given to Abraham was a worry and needed to be intercepted. Better stick with what works best. Let's re-infect. First time lucky, second time not so successful. Group by group, one by one, all his Nephilim were progressively eliminated. He must have been fuming when a teenage shepherd boy humiliated him by wiping out his well trained Nephilim warrior. To add insult to injury, the followers of this same shepherd boy proceeded to destroy all of his last remaining hopes. No, Satan was not at all happy with David. David was going to pay and, as we shall see, he paid dearly.

God is always in control

God knew Satan was being disobedient with the second infection but he let him go ahead. He had a twofold purpose; he wanted to teach Satan a lesson and train his own people. Satan thinks size is the key factor. God knows teamwork is an even better weapon. It is not the size of the man that makes a difference but the size of the fight in the man. Satan's champion Goliath, intimidating though he was, wasn't a match for God's champion, David. The god backing Goliath wasn't as big as the God backing David. This was the fourth time God taught Satan this lesson. Satan's god-men, the Emmin and Zamzummin were wiped out by Chedorlaomer, king of Elam and Abraham in turn triumphed over him. Moses defeated and killed the Nephilim king of Basham, Og. The Anakim initially succeeded in intimidating Israel but Joshua eventually triumphed over them. David conquered Goliath. Each of these four men; Abraham, Moses, Joshua and David were, to some degree, archetypes for Christ: First-born of a new people, Lawgiver, Liberator and King. These four indirect confrontations were forerunners for the direct confrontation between Satan and Jesus himself that would take place in 1000 years time. It would begin in Bethlehem and end at Golgotha but the outcome would be the same.

God allowed the Nephilim so he could train Israel not to look at outward appearances. The world looks at outward appearances. God looks at the heart. Satan works on rebellion and independence. God works on intimacy and teamwork. It is not a bunch of isolated giants, acting independently, that will win a war but the teamwork of men galvanized by a common goal. United we stand, divided we fall. A group of shorter basketball players acting as a tight knit team will beat a group of taller players who act as individuals. Israel learnt some valuable lessons in confronting the Nephilim. Satan laughed when he saw the Israelites wandering aimlessly for 40 years. He thought his god-men had won. God saw the bigger picture and was training Israel with such a resolve that these giants would eventually be as grasshoppers to them.

SUMMARY

- The Bible clearly states that there were two infestations of fallen angels producing god-men or Nephilim.
- This second infection occurred sometime after the tower of Babel when the peoples of the earth were scattered over the rapidly drifting continents.
- The second infection appears to be confined to the regions surrounding and including the Promised Land. The reason is that Satan wanted to thwart God's plans to establish a people in that region.
- The people groups mentioned at the time of Abraham that were Nephilim, were the Emim and Zamzummin.
- God used earthly kings to remove these Nephilim to make way for the Moabites and the Ammorites, the descendants of Lot.
- At the time of Moses, the principle group of Nephilim were the Anakim. Moses was responsible for defeating Og, king of Basham. Joshua was responsible for destroying the Anakim who stood in their way of possessing the Promise Land.
- Joshua let some Nephilim escape to Philistia.
- It would appear that the production of fresh Nephilim ceased either at this time or earlier because those in Philistia dwindled over the next few hundred years.
- At the time of David there was only one Nephilim family left in Philistia; Goliath of Gath and his four young children.
- David killed Goliath. Later David's men killed Goliath's grown sons who were also now giants.
- There is no further mention of giants in Scripture. This fact, coupled with Satan's anger against David after Goliath's sons were

killed, indicates that the last of the Nephilim were likely to have been destroyed at this point.

- The distinguishing characteristic of Nephilim was their gigantic size. Based on the dimensions of Og's bed and Goliath, the size of these men was well outside even the most extreme dimensions of human height and weight.

- No satisfactory natural explanation exists that can explain the inordinate size of these people.

- Based on Scripture references, it is likely that some or all of the Nephilim, both before and after the flood, were the result of the kingdom of darkness acting in rebellion against God.

- The enormous amount of legal rights Satan had from Adam's sin may have meant that initially God had little choice in Satan's desire to infect man with his genes. Satan however, abused the limits God had set.

- God allowed the rebellion because it ultimately served his greater purposes; teaching Satan a lesson and training his own people.

Chapter 7:
SATAN AND ISRAEL

Job's children died earlier than God intended. Satan was responsible. Today people around the world, Christian and non-Christian, die earlier than God intends. Satan is responsible. Aside from willful acts of man, based on freewill choices, more calamities and accidents than people probably realize, as well as most sickness that leads to death, are largely controlled by the kingdom of darkness. Even today, even after the Cross, most people who die prematurely die because Satan has sufficient legal rights to end their lives. What do we mean by prematurely? Anytime under the age of 90 to100 years old. God does not want anyone dying prematurely. His desire is that we live to a ripe old age. However, because we build up so many legal rights that the satanic kingdom can use, most of us are at the mercy of Satan and the spirit of Death and Hades as to when our lives will end.

Some readers might be shocked by the last part of chapter 5 and the first paragraph of this chapter. Please bear with me and continue reading the book and you will gain greater clarity on these strong statements. Once we make some changes to our thinking patterns and challenge existing assumptions, a lot more questions will get answered. We will be less likely to be perplexed or presumptuous in the way we judge situations and arrive at conclusions.

Not to be taken lightly

So far we have looked at six very significant events of the Old Testament that involve Satan: his creation, the rebellion in heaven, the Garden of Eden, the

Nephilim, Job and lastly Satan's second attempt at using the Nephilim. Each of these events sheds light on different aspects of Satan's character and abilities. At his creation, we marvel at his beauty. In the rebellion, we are taken aback by the incredible audacity he has to take on God and the extent of his pride. In the garden, we are impressed with his cunning and the subtlety of his temptation. The Nephilim confront us with the uneasy truth that the connection between man and angels may be a lot closer than we are comfortable with. If that's not challenge enough, the book of Job presents a picture of satanic control over our life and death, that many readers will still be in denial about! Satan's infliction of boils on Job shows his control of human physiology, and his swift, almost cavalier manner of dealing out death paints a frightening picture of control over humans.

The remaining two times he appears in the Old Testament are also dramatic in their impact. In both instances Satan is making an attack against Israel. One reference refers to a specific instance in the life of David; the other is symbolic of Satan's continuous attack on Israel, even today. Both have to do with establishing God's presence here on earth. Both situations appear to be calamitous. In both situations Israel is on the back foot. In both situations, God provides hope.

Since the book of Job, God has moved forward in his salvation plan and committed himself to a man, Abraham. From the loins of Abraham have come a people, Israel, and these people are set apart. God invests a lot of time and effort into these people. Satan is no mug. He is watching the situation closely and he is ever mindful of God's warning regarding the offspring of the woman who will bruise his head. The forces of the satanic kingdom are now focused heavily on this fledgling nation. Israel is the meat in the sandwich of a cosmic battle that is far bigger than anything Job had to cope with. Satan intuitively knows that this motley crew, this rebellious group of people that God has committed himself to, will be crucial to his own success or failure in the future.

Satan first named

Satan is first named as 'Satan' in the first book of Chronicles. 'Satan' means 'he who accuses' and he is fulfilling that function in this reference.

> *Satan rose up against Israel and incited David to take a census of Israel.*
> (1 Ch 21:1 NIV)

This is the first verse of a fascinating chapter. This passage doesn't include a heavenly interaction between God and Satan but one can imagine that it was not unlike Satan's request to sift Peter like sand. Why? Because both Peter and David were men after God's heart; pivotal men in God's purposes.

Gold, glory and girls

Satan would have watched with interest David's rise to power, and no doubt was keen to get his hands on him. He would have played a major role in tempting David with Bathsheba and the events that followed. Instead of focusing on his sexual appetite, he knew the sin that would offend God the most would be David's pride. We are all susceptible to the three 'G's; Gold, Glory and Girls (or Guys!). Money, power and sex are three Achilles' heels that most humans are corrupted by. With regard to David, Satan had scored well in the sexual temptation. Now he was about to see if he could do the same with David and his hunger for pride and glory. Whether Satan had enough legal rights to incite David without God's permission is open to debate. The use of the word 'incite' has a very active element to it and to be so aggressive in his temptation of David may have required permission from God. However, as intimated in the previous chapter, Satan's anger at David's elimination of the last of the Nephilim is likely to have been a factor in his attack against David.

What's wrong with taking a census? Didn't God direct Israel to take a census in Numbers 1 and 26? Yes and therein lies the point. It was God directed. There was no need for David to take a census. God told him he would bless him and he had. God wanted David to exercise his faith and trust in him, independent of how many fighting men he had. Even David's right hand man, Joab, recognized it was an ego trip David was on and he was very reluctant to be a part of it.

Why does the writer of Chronicles mention that Satan incited David to take a census? Why couldn't he simply say 'David took a census'? God showed us, in the first two chapters of Job, what was happening behind the scenes. Similarly, God wants us to see the bigger picture; to look behind the scenes. This is another example of God and Satan working hand in hand, without Satan realizing he is fulfilling God purposes. Satan must have been very pleased when David listened to him and took the census. He now could rightly demand that David be punished. God had to agree. God presented David with three options. David indirectly chose a plague. Seventy thousand men died. Oops! 70 000 wiped off your census total, David. Satan was pleased with the irony of it all. Yet God saw David's heart in all this. God used Satan's apparent success in tempting David to train David in the opposite virtue; humility. Just as Peter and Job grew in humility as a result of their experiences, so too David's repentance, humility and sacrificial desire to stand in the gap (v17) were genuine. As a result of David's response, God established the site of his temple and its construction through David and his son Solomon. The place where wheat was threshed by Orman was bought by David and would become God's official residence on earth for 1000 years till the Romans eventually destroyed it. It will be rebuilt again in preparation for another reign of 1000 years. The seed of David will return to the threshing floor of

Orman, the temple mount, and establish God's presence on earth both physically and spiritually.

God always sees the bigger picture. In the midst of failure, there is hope. God used this incident as a means of establishing the precise place where his Son would rule from on his return. Solomon's temple provided for this previously nomadic people an anchor point, a physical reminder of God's presence with them here on earth.

The end of the OT focusing on the end of the NT.
The only other time Satan makes a heavenly appearance in the Old Testament is in his role of accuser against the high priest, Joshua.

> *Then he showed me Joshua the high priest standing before the angel of the Lord, and Satan standing at his right hand to accuse him. The Lord said to Satan, "The Lord rebuke you, Satan! Indeed, the Lord who has chosen Jerusalem, rebuke you! Is this not a brand plucked from the fire?"* (Zec 3:1,2)

Let us look at these verses in a wider context. Biblical commentaries[1] interpret these prophecies in the immediate context of the rebuilding of the temple after the Babylonian captivity. An alternative explanation, one that best fits the detail in the prophecies, is that the primary focus of the book of Zechariah is the second coming of Jesus and the establishment of the millennial reign of Jesus. Zechariah dovetails beautifully with the book of Revelation; one book shedding light on the other. With the exception of small references to Jesus' first coming, all the visions and prophecies are related to events yet to happen.

The focus of Zechariah chapter 2 is the city of Jerusalem when Jesus returns to reign and rule. It is about a huge, expansive city that people of many nations will stream to; a city almost without boundaries. Jesus' light and presence will radiate from its midst. This vision of the man with the measuring line is the third vision detailed in Zechariah. It is concrete, specific and unmistakable in its application to the millennial reign of Jesus.

Chapter 3 is the fourth vision and is more allegorical. It ties in with chapter 2 in that it is about the restoration of Israel.

> *Then he showed me Joshua the high priest standing before the angel of the Lord, **and Satan standing at his right side to accuse him. The Lord said to Satan, "The Lord rebuke you, Satan! The Lord, who has chosen Jerusalem, rebuke you! Is not this man a burning stick snatched from the fire?"** Now Joshua was dressed in filthy clothes as he stood before the angel. The angel*

said to those who were standing before him, "Take off his filthy clothes." Then he said to Joshua, "See, I have taken away your sin, and I will put rich garments on you." Then I said, "Put a clean turban on his head." So they put a clean turban on his head and clothed him, while the angel of the Lord stood by. The angel of the Lord gave this charge to Joshua: "This is what the Lord Almighty says: 'If you will walk in my ways and keep my requirements, then you will govern my house and have charge of my courts, and I will give you a place among these standing here. Listen, O high priest Joshua and your associates seated before you, who are men symbolic of things to come: I am going to bring my servant, the Branch. See, the stone I have set in front of Joshua! There are seven eyes on that one stone, and I will engrave an inscription on it,' says the Lord Almighty, 'and I will remove the sin of this land in a single day. In that day each of you will invite his neighbor to sit under his vine and fig tree,' declares the Lord Almighty." (Zec 3)

Joshua is a symbol of Israel (*who are men symbolic of things to come.* v8) and Satan is yet again accusing Israel. This time, God has had enough. In effect, God says to Satan that the punishment Satan has meted out to Israel has just about crushed her. While he has had the legal rights to do so, and God has allowed it, Israel is just about burnt up and God is plucking her from the fire before it is too late.

Just as he removed his protection over Job, and Satan had free reign, God removed his protection over Israel, and Satan has done his worst. Using the nation of Babylon, Satan gave Israel a body blow that left them reeling for seventy years. Yes, God allowed it and it worked his purposes in disciplining Israel despite Satan's intention to destroy the nation. The kingdom of darkness has used many other nations since then, culminating in the Romans dismantling and dispersing the nation of Israel, not for 70 years but for almost 2000 years. The latest nation Satan has incited to do significant damage is the German nation, with the murder of six million Jews. Out of these ashes a restoration process, in part, has begun with the establishment, once again, of Israel as a nation.

However, in the context of these verses, Israel is still a stick in the fire. Today, Israel is still dressed in filthy clothes. The Lord has yet to rebuke Satan and pluck the burning brand from the fire. Before it gets better, it will get worse. The full wrath of the world has yet to be focused on Israel. When that happens; when Israel is at its most defenceless and she has her back to the wall, then God will pluck Israel out of the fire by sending his Son. Then he will rebuke Satan with the consequence Satan knows about but hopes will never happen. He will be locked up for 1000 years.

The 'Branch'[2] refers to Jesus, just as the stone with the seven eyes refers to the Holy Spirit. Although Jesus did wipe out the eternal effect of sin in a single day on Calvary, this is not the primary application of these last verses in this short chapter. God will wipe out the collective sin, the compounded iniquity, from the nation of Israel on the day of Jesus' return. On that day, as has been explained in the seventh period of God's dealings with man outlined in chapter one of this book, the nation will finally recognise their Messiah and call upon him.

> *...they will look on Me whom they have pierced; and they will mourn for Him, as one mourns for an only son, and they will weep bitterly over Him like the bitter weeping over a firstborn.* (Zech 12:10)

In that collective act of repentance and acknowledgment that he is indeed their Messiah, he will forgive their 2000 year old sin; that of rejecting him. It was that initial rejection and their ongoing rejection since that has stood as such a blockage and barrier to Israel receiving his grace.

Lamps with life-giving oil

The vision outlined in the next chapter, chapter 4, of the gold lampstand and the two olive trees, meshes beautifully with this interpretation of chapter 3. The picture is of two olive trees that supply oil to pipes that fill up a bowl suspended above a seven branched lampstand. From the bowl there are channels, seven in all, to each lamp in the lampstand.

Jews today and in the past acknowledge that the lampstand, or Menorah, is a traditional symbol for Israel. Oil and water are two commonly recognized symbols of the Holy Spirit. The oil flowing into the lampstand represents the Holy Spirit. The complete picture represents the Holy Spirit coming upon the nation of Israel. Zechariah asks the question, 'Who then are the two olive trees?' The angel replies,

> *"These are the two who are anointed to serve the Lord of all the earth."* (Zech 4:14)

Interestingly enough, there is only one other place in Scripture where olive trees are referred to as people. It is not in reference to Zerubbabel and Joshua, as the commentaries assert, but it is in reference to the two witnesses mentioned in Revelation.

> *And I will give power to my two witnesses, and they will prophesy for 1,260 days, clothed in sackcloth. These are the two olive trees and the two lampstands that stand before the Lord of the earth.* (Rev 11:3,4)

The connection couldn't be clearer, even in the use of the phrasing, 'the Lord of the earth'. The phrase 'lampstands' in this context refers to the role of the witnesses as mouthpieces of the Lord in Jerusalem, shedding his light on that dark city through what they say. Linking back to Zechariah, we can now see another important role that these witnesses play that is not mentioned in Revelation.

While Satan will be gloating over the vice like grip his Anti-Christ has over the world, these two witnesses will be the vehicle God uses to convict the people of Israel regarding who his Son is. Over the three years of their preaching, right in the middle of Jerusalem, the Holy Spirit will use the words of these two men to convict the Jews about who their Messiah really is. Day by day, oil will flow from their mouths into each branch of the seven branched candelabra that is Israel. Day by day, the Holy Spirit will do his work and soften hearts that have been so hard towards their Messiah for so long. When the lampstand is full of oil, the breakthrough will come. For the first time, Israel will collectively realize what they have done. Joseph's brothers were stunned as they watched Joseph take off his Egyptian clothing and they finally recognized him as the brother they had rejected. In a similar manner, Israel will stand stunned as they finally realize Jesus as their brother; the one they rejected; the Messiah that they crucified. Then they will mourn for him and call out to him. Just as Joseph was the physical saviour of his brothers, now Jesus will be both the spiritual and physical saviour of his brothers.

Jesus will have waited over 2000 years to hear this invitation. Joseph went to meet his father, Israel, on his chariot and the two wept together. So too after the defeat of those gathered around Jerusalem, Jesus will enter Jerusalem on his white steed through the Gate Beautiful and he and Israel will weep together. As Jesus enters through the gates, he will hear the words that will be music to his ears, *"Baruch ha ba B'Shem Adonai"; "Blessed is he who comes in the name of the Lord"* (Matt 23:39). Then he will begin his reign and rule in Jerusalem.

Satan thought he had victory over David through igniting David's pride, and prevailing. God allowed that to happen because he was more interested in developing David's character. Satan was inadvertently working out God's purpose. David was the archetype or fore-runner of the same scenario being worked out on the same spot but this time not with one individual but a whole nation. This time, while Satan's puppet, his carefully groomed Anti-Christ, will back the nation of Israel into a corner, God will be working out an agenda of his own. This time, Satan will gather the whole world against little Israel and God will be working on Israel's pride just as he had worked on David's pride. This time, when it seems that Israel has nowhere else to turn; when Goliath is about to consume little David, God will provide hope. Israel will 'see' Jesus for the first time as their Messiah. This time, when the stick is about to be burnt up, the Holy Spirit will break through Israel's stubborn pride and they will understand what they have done to Jesus. This time, for the first time, Israel will mourn for him; they will be genuinely sorry for what they have done to Jesus. Jesus will then return and pluck 'Joshua' out of the fire. What Satan thought would be one of his greatest victories, will turn out to be one of his greatest defeats.

Adam choosing Satan over God; rampant control of the earth by the Nephilim; hemming in Israel by the Red Sea with the Egyptian army in hot pursuit; the plague destroying 70 000 men because of David's pride; Jesus hanging humiliated and rejected on the Cross; the Jews with nowhere to go after Satan, using Hitler, wiped out 6 million of their number; Israel in the future when the Antichrist will have persuaded the whole world to destroy her. What do all of these events have in common? In each case, it appears to be a comprehensive victory for Satan. In each case, God begins a new salvation initiative.

Do you have any doubt who is in control? Unfortunately Satan's well honed denial mechanisms prevent him from acknowledging the obvious and he will eventually pay the price.

He whom they mocked and refused to acknowledge will now take up habitation for 1000 years on the very site of the threshing floor that David bought from Orman. The very site where more than 3000 years earlier David had fallen on his face before God's avenging angel, covering himself with sackcloth and ashes in repentance for taking the census. Beauty from ashes. Restoration from repentance. Not once but twice.

There, on the threshing floor where, so many years before, grain was separated from the stalk and later made into bread, the Bread of Life himself would come to rule and reign.

SUMMARY

- We have so far been looking in detail at Satan's creation, his rebellion, his temptation of man, the god-men he produced and through the example of Job how he controls people's lives and particularly their death.
- The last two times he is mentioned in the Tenakh are no less important. They are to do with his interactions with the nation of Israel.
- The first has to do with Satan inciting David to take a census.
- This is sinful because God didn't ordain it and he wanted David to trust him, rather than put his confidence in numbers. David succumbed to the second of the three Gs; glory.
- Once again, while Satan appears to win and David is punished, God trusts the heart of David, just as he trusted the heart of Job, and David moves from pride to humility.
- Satan is more interested in events and punishment. God is more interested in heart attitude and repentance.
- Out of the ashes of this mistake, God stakes a geographical claim on a tiny piece of land that will be a focal point till the end of the world. Out of despair, God brings hope.
- The last appearance of Satan in the Old Testament has a future focus. It has yet to be fulfilled completely. Satan is in the process of fulfilling that verse right now, because he is currently accusing Israel.
- Satan accuses Joshua the high priest, who is symbolic of Israel. The eight night visions in the book of Zechariah all refer to Christ's second coming. This is the fourth of the eight visions.

- Very close to Christ's return, as Israel is all but 'burnt up', God will no longer accept Satan's legal rights demands, and Israel will finally 'walk in his ways' by accepting Jesus as Messiah and then be part of those who will govern with him on earth.

- Chapter 4, the sixth night vision about the olive trees and lampstand, confirms the fifth vision and ties in with Revelation 11. We learn that the two witnesses will play an important role in bringing the fullness of the Holy Spirit to the people of Israel.

- Through the continual preaching of the two witnesses, Israel will realize that Jesus is their true Messiah. More importantly, Israel will express heartfelt repentance, just as David did.

- Because of David's pride, Satan thought he had won, but God was working on David's heart. Satan will think he had won against Israel, because of their stubbornness and pride, but God will be working on Israel's heart.

- The past event of David's repentance and the future event of Israel's repentance happen on the same spot: the Temple Mount. An Old Testament Archetype with a New Testament completion.

- There is a clear pattern that when a comprehensive victory for Satan appears assured, God uses the event to establish a fresh salvation initiative that always provides hope.

Chapter 8:
THE GREATEST STING OF ALL

"And I will put enmity between you and the woman, between your seed and her seed; he will bruise you on the head and you will bruise him on the heel". (Gen 3:15)

We have seen that the enmity between Satan's seed, the Nephilim, and Eve's seed lasted for half the total amount of time man has been on earth. It was David and his men that brought the prophecy of the first half of this verse to a close. Now we turn our attention to the second half of this verse, the part that refers to what happens directly to Satan. Where the first half of the verse referred to the collective offspring of Eve, the second half refers to a specific offspring of Eve; Jesus. The phrase Jesus used more than any other when referring to himself was 'Son of Man.' Of all the names he could have chosen, why did he emphasize that? Why not 'Son of God?' It delighted Jesus that he was *adding* our humanity to his divinity. It wasn't a chore for him to become human. He thrilled everytime he said the phrase "Son of Man." He loved being completely human. He was also making a point, one not missed by Satan, that he was the Son of Man, the son of Adam and Eve, the seed of Eve, the head bruiser.

A fly in the ointment

Having examined every direct occurrence of Satan in the Old Testament, we can see God's hand in each instance. Satan doesn't. Any time something doesn't go entirely his way, Satan sees it as a minor setback. He doesn't see it as a defeat. It is true that Satan no longer has his Nephilim, but otherwise he appears to have it all his way. The whole world is under his control. Man is under his control. There is no recorded instance in the Old Testament of anyone casting out Satan or his demons. God used Elijah and Elisha to perform some extraordinary miracles but none involved deliverance. Satan was above Elijah and Elisha. You can't cast out those who are above you in authority.

Satan can even hinder prayers. The angelic response to Daniel's prayers could be blocked because he had legal rights over the earth, which included Persia. The immediate control of the earth was under the jurisdiction of the satanic kingdom. That was the reason why the angel of God could be bailed up by the Prince of Persia. God's angel was trespassing and therefore the kingdom of darkness had a right to intervene. This is Satan's territory now and any angel trying to bring a message had better have a good reason or risk detainment. At an overview level, God is still in control and has overall ownership of his creation and has a right to send reinforcements.

Satan is relaxed. Everything is going according to plan and has been for thousands of years. He's just a little concerned about what's happening in that small town near Jerusalem. .Bethlehem presented a problem for Satan. Satan was well aware that God was up to something. He was not stupid enough to ignore the fact that this supernaturally conceived baby could be the 'head bruiser' of Genesis 3:15. Through the angelic chorus of hosannas over the place of his birth, God wasn't only sending out a message of declaration to the human world.

A puzzle

Because Jesus was fully human, in every respect, he perplexed Satan. The angelic-human hybrids that Satan's kingdom had produced were distinguishable from the average human by their size. But this child had no distinguishing characteristics. Except one. He didn't have an inherited set of legal rights from his parents, like all other humans had. He lacked those initial hooks or handles that all humans were born with; anchor points that Satan and his kingdom could grab a hold of and manipulate. Mary and Joseph and their parents certainly weren't perfect so why didn't this child inherit the usual iniquity?

Once before, a human was created without any human intervention and perhaps Satan was expecting another dust-to-man miracle. He put God in a box, which is always a dangerous thing to do. This child took him by surprise. Mary was the first surrogate mother, a living Ark of the Covenant, carrying within her womb God himself; genetically completely distinct from his earthly parents. John the Baptist leapt in his mother Elizabeth's womb when Mary arrived for a visit, just as David leapt and danced before the Ark of the Covenant as it was escorted to Jerusalem.

No human contribution

The Holy Spirit provided both sperm *and ovum* in Mary's womb. She was an incubator. Many Christians believe that Mary provided 50% of Jesus' genetic material. She provided the ovum and the Holy Spirit supernaturally provided the sperm. If that were so, Jesus would have inherited Mary's generational iniquity, stretching back several generations, and with that enough legal rights to allow the satanic kingdom direct access to influence Jesus. That is not possible. Jesus was the only man ever to exist without any legal rights whatsoever. Jesus can still be completely human without any human intervention, just as Adam was completely human without any human intervention. Making Mary sinless, as Catholics and others do, doesn't solve the problem of the iniquity of her parents, grandparents and beyond still impacting Jesus. Generational iniquity affects every human being, both then and now. Experience has taught us that generational iniquity can impact us from as far back as thirteen generations. That is why David says,

> *Behold, I was brought forth in iniquity, and in sin my mother conceived me.* (Ps 51:5)

Even if Mary was sinless and her parents, grandparents and great grandparents were sinless, it doesn't insulate Mary and her ova from the effects of Adam's sin which infects all humans since Adam; death. Everything that derives ultimately from Adam must die. If Jesus had half of Mary's genetic material, then he would have to die. The spirit of Death would have a legitimate claim on his life.

Philosophically, to be fully God necessarily means a completely unique conception without any human intervention. To be fully man simply requires God the Son to contain himself within a complete set of human chromosomes. Jesus was both fully the second member of the Trinity and fully man. Had Mary provided the ovum and the Holy Spirit provided the sperm, then Jesus would have differed little from the Nephilim. With Satan's angel-human hybrids, supernatural sperm fertilized human ova, producing offspring that were fully human but not fully angelic[1]. In like manner, Jesus would have been completely human but not completely God.

Jesus was not only the second Adam in that he spiritually succeeded where Adam failed, he is also the 'second Adam' in that he was the only human since Adam to be entirely the direct creation of God. No human intervention.

Yet still from the line of David

Although no genetic material was provided by Mary, Jesus still fulfilled the condition that the Messiah would be from the line of David in that both Mary and Joseph were descendants of David. From an earthly perspective, from the perspective of anyone observing these events, Mary gave birth to a son, who could rightly claim that he too was from the line of David because both his 'parents' were. Jesus is the issue of the womb of a woman who comes from the line of David, hence there can be no dispute that he is from the line of David. From a biological perspective, there was no genetic connection, via human intervention, back to David. It is impossible to be fully God *and* humanly linked to David.

However, Jesus did look Jewish, rather than Arabic, African or Chinese. Unlike Adam, whose genetic makeup encompassed enormous variability in order to give rise to many different races, Jesus' biological information was limited to a much narrower set of characteristics. It is highly likely that his chromosomal makeup would have been very similiar to the makeup of either Mary or Joseph, complete with all the biological markers that linked him to David's blood line. God would have made sure of that. If we had a sample of his parents blood and could do an accurate genome map, we would find it very similar to Jesus' blood, even though there was no direct biological contribution from either his earthly father or mother. In a very real sense then, Jesus could still claim be descended from the blood line of David (and therefore the seed of Eve) and he probably looked like his parents as well. The only difference is that Jesus' DNA would have been perfect; free of any chromosomal mutations that would necessarily have affected his earthly parents, due to the accumulative effect of 4000 years of decay.

A dilemma

This God-man was too dangerous. Satan's solution was really quite simple. Kill him. He couldn't do it directly because he can't find any legal rights. Herod was the man. He had him well and truly under his control. This should be a pushover. It didn't work. Egypt became a sanctuary. He tried to get the crowd to throw him off the top of a cliff. It didn't work. Jesus calmly walked through the middle of them.

A cut above

OK, so trying to eliminate Jesus didn't work. Getting him to sin would give Satan just the legal right he needed. Just one sin. After all, one sin is all it took to knock Adam from his perch. In the wilderness, he tried to tempt him with some very real temptations. Make no mistake about it; each of Satan's temptations would have been a strong temptation to Jesus. Yes, Jesus was God, but he was fully human and he could not have used his divinity in any way to diminish the impact of the temptation. Otherwise he would have made a mockery of the verse,

> *For we do not have a high priest who cannot sympathize with our weaknesses, but One who has been tempted in all things as we are, yet without sin.*
> (Heb 4:15)

Yet from Satan's perspective, the most disturbing aspect of Jesus, this fully human enigma, was that for the first time since Adam, there was a human whose sinlessness meant that he didn't slot in nice and neatly under Satan, like the rest of the human race. Instead, Jesus' sinlessness meant that Satan had no authority over him. Worse still, the reverse was true. Jesus had authority over Satan. One who is sinless will always have authority over one who has sinned. Sinlessness exempts you from the Law; sinfulness brings you under the Law. Satan was under the Law and therefore under judgment. Jesus was above the Law, and, by virtue of being beyond judgment, was able to pass judgment.

Before it was	**God**	Now it was	**God**
	over		*over*
	Satan		**Jesus**
	over		*over*
	Man		**Satan**
	over		*over*
	The World		**Man**
			over
			The World

Above but voluntarily under

However, being 'above the Law' did not mean that Jesus was in any way superior or not subject to the same laws we are. The phrase 'above the law' in modern usage is often applied to people who exempt themselves from the very laws they expect others to obey. In other words, there is a measure of hypocrisy in their actions. This was not the case with Jesus. He voluntarily submitted to every aspect of the Law. Although God created the Law, he did not exempt himself from any aspect of it and the whole legal rights system we have been alluding to in this book is based on the very laws that God subjected himself and all of us to.

Meanwhile, back in Capernaum

From Satan's perspective, it was not just disturbing; it was downright undermining! Embarrassing to boot! Jesus was doing things no human before could do. He was speaking directly to demons and they were being expelled. You can only do this when you are above and not below. This had never been done before. That is why the end of the first chapter of Mark created such a stir.

> *They were amazed at His teaching; for He was teaching them as one having authority, and not as the scribes. Just then there was a man in their synagogue with an unclean spirit; and he cried out, saying, "What business do we have with each other, Jesus of Nazareth? Have You come to destroy us? I know who You are— the Holy One of God!" And Jesus rebuked him, saying, "Be quiet,*

and come out of him!" Throwing him into convulsions, the unclean spirit cried out with a loud voice and came out of him. They were all amazed, so that they debated among themselves, saying, "What is this? A new teaching with authority! He commands even the unclean spirits, and they obey Him." Immediately the news about Him spread everywhere into all the surrounding district of Galilee. (Mark 1:23-28)

Amazing! He even commanded unclean spirits and they obeyed him! A new teaching and with authority unheard of before. It was no wonder the news about him spread like wildfire. We had never heard this done before. Elijah couldn't, Elisha couldn't, but this man could!

There is evidence that in the inter-testamental period, from 200BC to the time of Jesus, rabbis did have limited success in driving out demons. However, it wasn't done by rabbis directly commanding demons to leave like Jesus did. Rather, they would appeal or petition God directly, to free the person from the demons. The person did not necessarily need to be present. Sometimes God, in his mercy, would set the person free. This process is not unlike what happens today when one believer asks another believer to join him in a prayer request. Perhaps you ask me to pray for your sick mother. I pray for her and, if God honours my prayer, she may be healed. However, what Jesus did was to talk directly to demons as though he was God! Now that was audacious, that was authoritative, that was impressive. No rabbi had ever done that or dared to do that!

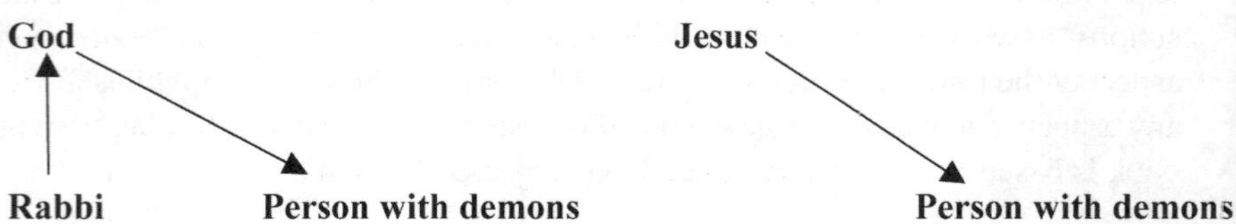

It is no wonder Satan wanted this man eliminated. He undermined the confidence of the troops. They had roamed to and fro on earth with impunity for 4000 years and now this 'upstart' was a party pooper! Satan bided his time. At last the pieces of the jigsaw finally started to come together. There was disgruntled Judas, jealous Caiaphas, and weak Pilate. Now it was his chance to strike, once and for all, and remove this nuisance.

Reading between the lines
Smart, intelligent, perceptive and forward thinking are all adjectives that could aptly be attributed to Satan. He's no fool as we have already established. But

pride, arrogance and presumption clouded his thinking and once again he had underestimated the subtlety of his opponent.

He failed to grasp the nuances and hidden indicators of what was about to happen. Satan knew that life was in the blood and without the shedding of blood there was no remission of sins. He watched the people of Israel offering their lambs, heifers and bulls as sacrifices and, from his perspective, it did them little good. After all, weren't they all still under his control after death? Locked in Sheol and he had the keys. Separated from the God they were trying so diligently to serve. What a joke. No, let them sacrifice all they like. It's a waste of time.

He heard John say, 'Behold, the Lamb of God that takes away the sin of the world!' He didn't understand what it meant but after all, he had John's number so why bother. John was a weirdo; isolated and increasingly marginalized. Herod's wife hated his guts. It was only a matter of time.

The clues were there. Satan just overlooked them. He was presumptuous. He was myopic. He had tunnel vision. He failed to step back and look at the bigger picture. He became complacent.

The power of paradox

Perhaps most important of all, he didn't understand paradox. He listened to Jesus but once again, it seemed like pie in the sky. He who saves his life will lose it and he who loses his life will save it. He who is first will be last and the last first. To be a leader, you must be a servant. Victory through surrender. None of this rang true from his perspective. After all, he was a leader and still is a leader and he has no intention of being a servant. He was first, still is first and has no intention of relinquishing this position and being last.

The greatest paradox of all, the sting to end all stings, was about to occur and Satan didn't have a clue. He would be the scapegoat. He would end up with egg on his face. The last laugh would not be his. He would be stumped, snookered, bruised in fact. And here is the paradox.

> The vilest act possible by man, that is the murder, through torture and slow death, of the most innocent man who ever existed, turns out to be the very act that saves the murderers[2].

Read it again. It bears re-reading. Doesn't that take your breath away? Only God could come up with such a paradoxical solution. Yet it bears his signature. It has truth written all over it.

SUMMARY

- Bethlehem represented the first direct challenge to Satan's complete control in 4000 years.

- Man as a trinity intrigued him; this God/man is a complete enigma. Fully human with no legal rights. Not even any inherited legal rights, like all other humans. He didn't see that coming.

- Mary couldn't have provided 50% of Jesus' genetic makeup.
  (a) All flesh linked to Adam must die.
  (b) Generational iniquity would have given satanic control.
  (c) Jesus would have been fully human but not fully God.
  (d) Jesus wouldn't have been physically the Second Adam.

- Jesus was the first human who had authority over Satan, by virtue of his sinlessness. He slots just above Satan in terms of authority.

- Sin brings you under the judgment of the Law. Satan was under the judgment of the Law. Jesus was not. Jesus was therefore above Satan.

- Jesus voluntarily submitted to the whole Law to fulfill the Law. This shows us that God submits himself to the very laws he creates so that he doesn't set a standard that he himself doesn't expect to keep.

- The people had heard and seen miracles before, but a man speaking directly to demons and these demons obeying had never been seen before. Never. Ever. No wonder it caused such a stir.

- Satan is smart but his pride, arrogance and presumption meant that he failed to read the messianic clues of what this God/man would do.

- Satan often overlooks the subtleties of paradox. Christianity is full of paradoxes. The Cross is the biggest paradox.

- The greatest paradox of all is that salvation for the murderer was achieved in the act of the murder!

Chapter 9:
KEYS AND CAPTIVES

Let's paint the scene at Calvary, from Satan's perspective. This is Satan's hour. He has waited a long time to engineer the circumstances to get to this point. This time he is going to crush this God-man. This time he is going to make him bleed, figuratively and literally. Everything is going according to plan. He has manipulated Judas well.

> *During supper, the devil having already put into the heart of Judas Iscariot, the son of Simon, to betray Him* (Jn 13:2)

In fact, Luke tells us that Satan actually entered into Judas at this time;

> *And Satan entered into Judas who was called Iscariot, belonging to the number of the twelve* (Lk 22:3)

The betrayal of Judas hurt Jesus. Within a few hours, most of the rest of the men that Jesus had invested his heart and soul into had scattered. Despite all the support he had given them over the last three years, when he needed them most, they couldn't stay awake. Added to that, when the going got tough and the chips were down, they left him. They ran for their lives, deserting him. This was an added bonus for Satan. Satan knew he could put the knife in and twist it if he got his hands on one of Jesus' closest confidants. Peter was the leader. His betrayal would hurt the most. Satan had worked on priming Peter for this moment. He had watched Peter closely. He had gathered a lot of legal rights against him. This man was brash, impulsive, presumptuous and full of pride. Now was the time to boldly approach the Father regarding Peter. He had so many legal rights, he could even be demanding in the way he requested permission.

> *Simon, Simon, behold, Satan has demanded permission to sift you like wheat; but I have prayed for you, that your faith may not fail; and you, when once you have turned again, strengthen your brothers.* (Luke 22:31,32)

Permission granted. Mission successful.

Jesus was accused, tried and condemned. Satan had groomed Caiaphas well. The religious establishment that knew the Scriptures, that should have known better, dismissed and rejected both him and his message. The scourging and crowning with thorns should be enough to make any man break. It had always worked in the past. The rejection of the crowd, many of whom he had healed, would add to the layering betrayal. Pilate had washed his hands of him. There was no one left to defend him. However, Satan was starting to get a little concerned that so far none of this carefully laid foundation appeared to be achieving its desired effect. He needed Jesus to sin just once. Only one small sin. No worries yet, there was still more to come. Let's see how he handled the humiliation as he walked through the crowd on the way to the Cross and then the shame of hanging naked in front of everyone. Add to that the pain of the nails and the difficulty of heaving himself up and down for each breath. The sarcastic comments of the crowd as Jesus was dying would be a lovely finishing touch. Satan watched closely as layer upon layer of rejection and pain took its toll. But still his eyes were too soft and loving when he forgave those who taunted him on the Cross.

Now for his master stroke. He had waited a long time for this moment. Satan was about to do something he could only do once and hasn't been able to do since. During the four millennia when he had undisputed authority over man and the earth, he had gathered an enormous amount of legal rights. In addition, the rejection of Jesus; the rejection of the Creator by those he created, increased Satan's leverage enormously. The fact that his best friends had rejected Jesus was the icing on the cake and now gave Satan the confidence to approach the Father and ask for this incredibly audacious request. God granted him his request.

Satan brought darkness upon the earth.

Supernatural darkness

Light is aggressive towards darkness. This means that when I switch on a light globe or light a candle, the light drives away the darkness. The light always overwhelms the darkness. Darkness doesn't overwhelm light. Darkness is an absence of light; light is not an absence of darkness. A shadow is formed because light is being blocked; it is absent. Light pierces the darkness. Darkness never pierces light.

Satan is keen to have Jesus as isolated as possible. Jesus is still getting comfort from John, his mother and Mary Magdalene. If there were such a darkness; a cold, clinging, enveloping darkness that Jesus literally couldn't see past the end of his nose, then Jesus would be completely on his own; then he would really be suffering.

What a celebration of victory this darkness is for the satanic kingdom. Satan has the legal rights for this spectacular show of power and he can't wipe the glee off his face as he seeks permission from God and gets it. Philosophically, darkness overpowering light is not an event the Kingdom of Light would choose, but it is an event that God allows. Now, at last, for the first and only time in history, darkness has its day.

The sun is overwhelmed by the darkness. It is a supernatural event. The Jews use a lunar calendar. In a lunar calendar, a new moon begins each month. The moon waxes until it becomes a full moon in the middle of each month and then wanes in the last half of the month. Jesus' crucifixion occurred at Passover. Passover always occurs in the middle of the month of Nisan. It always occurs, therefore, when the moon is full. In other words, the moon is receiving and reflecting the sun's light, not blocking it. Scientifically, an eclipse is impossible. Even if an eclipse were possible, full darkness during an eclipse lasts for three minutes. At the height of an eclipse, observers can still see one another easily. The darkness of an eclipse isn't like the debilitating, eerie, cold, all encompassing darkness that took place at Calvary. This darkness lasted three hours.

> *From the sixth hour until the ninth hour darkness came over all the land.* (Matt 27:45)

How do we know the darkness is so devastating? There were seven spoken sentences directed to the Cross by others and seven spoken statements that Jesus uttered from the Cross. Three of these seven utterances from Jesus occurred before the darkness. These were:

> *"Woman, behold, your son!" "Behold, your mother!"* (Jn 19:26,27)
> *"Father, forgive them for they know not what they are doing".* (Lk 23:34)
> *"Today you will be with me in Paradise".* (Lk 23:43)

In the six hours Jesus is on the Cross, three hours are in light and during this time he makes three statements. He says nothing during the three hours of darkness. The isolation that Satan intends has the desired effect. Jesus carries the sin of the world without any comfort from anyone. At the end of the darkness, in quick succession, Jesus utters four more statements and dies.

> *Now from the sixth hour until the ninth hour darkness fell upon all the land. About the ninth hour Jesus cried out with a loud voice, "Eloi, Eloi, lama sabachthani?" that is "My God, my God, why have you forsaken me?"... And when Jesus had cried out again in a loud voice, he gave up his spirit. At that moment the curtain of the temple was torn in two from top to bottom. The earth shook and the rocks split.* (Matt 27:45,50,51)

> *When the sixth hour came, darkness fell over the whole land until the ninth hour. At the ninth hour Jesus cried out with a loud voice, "Eloi Eloi, Lama sabachthani?", which is translated, "My God, My God, why have your forsaken me?" When some of the bystanders heard it, they began saying, "Behold, He is calling for Elijah." Someone ran and filled a sponge with sour wine, put it on a reed, and gave Him a drink, saying, "Let us see whether Elijah will come to take Him down." And Jesus uttered a loud cry, and breathed His last. And the veil of the temple was torn in two from top to bottom.* (Mk 15:33-38)

> *It was now about the sixth hour, and darkness fell over the whole land until the ninth hour, because the sun was obscured; and the veil of the temple was torn in two. And Jesus, crying out with a loud voice, said, "Father, into your hands I commit my spirit." Having said this, He breathed His last.*
> (Lk 23:44-46)

> *Therefore when Jesus had received the sour wine, He said, "It is finished!" And He bowed His head and gave up His spirit.* (Jn 19:30)

No one gospel rendition gives the complete picture. Combining all four accounts, we can see that the likely order was:

> *My God, my God, why have you forsaken me.* (Matt 27:46, Mk 15:34)
> *I thirst.* (Jn 19:28)
> *It is finished.* (Jn 19:30)
> *Father, into your hands I commend my spirit.* (Lk 23:46)

Torment

The demons thrive best in darkness. The torment they must have put Jesus through as he hung on the Cross, during the blackout, would have been almost unbearable.

What follows is a possible monologue from Satan to Jesus.

> 'You should have taken that temptation I offered you, Jesus; all the kingdoms of the world. If you had played your cards right, you could have set up a worldwide empire and, with you at the apex, it would have been hard for me to knock it over. There is still time. Just bow the knee to me, Jesus, and earthly glory could be yours. Look at you now. What a pathetic piece of humanity. Once again God had a plan and I have managed to thwart it; throw a spanner in the works. I did it with Adam and I am doing it with you. Too easy! Look at Peter. You chose him as leader. What a push over! No contest! Do you seriously expect him to lead your cause? You're a joke, Jesus! Such a sad excuse for a saviour. Where is your Father now? I can't see him, can you? Forsaken you has he? That wouldn't surprise me? He's supposed to be Light. Well, he obviously can't stand up to my darkness. Look around you! Who is in control? What an impotent God you serve. There is still time. Just say the word and I'll get you off this Cross. Bow the knee to me and you will be set free! You can still accept my offer of all the kingdoms of the world and this torment will end. The choice is yours, my friend. Why suffer in vain?'

His Father didn't turn away
'My God, my God, why have you forsaken me?' The commonly accepted explanation for these words exclaimed loudly by Jesus, is that God the Father rejected his Son; he had to turn away from Jesus. The reasons given are usually twofold. The collective weight of the sin of the world Jesus was carrying repulsed the Father. The sin that the Son, as the sacrificial lamb, represented was too much for the Father to face and so he had to turn his head away from his Son. The second reason is that Jesus had to bear the sin of the world on his own, without any help from his Father, because sin separates us from God. Therefore, God had to separate himself from his Son. It was the one and only time in history when the Godhead was dismantled; the communication lines broken and a barrier came between the three members of the Godhead. It was the instant in time when intimacy was destroyed.

This is a serious error. Here are six reasons why the Father didn't reject Jesus.

(1) Sin is not something that causes God to recoil in abhorrence, disgust or fear. Just as the idea that God is repulsed by demons is a human reaction that we transfer onto God, so too is the notion that God is repulsed by sin and evil. Every second of every day God is simultaneously aware of the collective sin of seven billion people and he can handle that! Whether it is seven billion or the accumulative effect of all the people who have ever existed, estimated currently at seventy billion people, there isn't a magical number that finally overwhelms God and forces him to reject his Son. God wasn't at all repulsed when he looked at the collective iniquity of mankind's sin that his Son was carrying on our behalf. He is comfortable talking to Satan, comfortable with demons. He doesn't close his eyes when evil is happening. In fact, the opposite is true. The phrase, 'did evil in the sight of the Lord' is used 56 times in the Scriptures and adds emphasis to the fact that God not only judges what is evil but sees every evil act done. His omnipresence means that it is impossible for him not to see evil. Some confusion has been caused by the NIV mistranslating Habakkuk 1:13.

> *Your eyes are too pure to look on evil; you cannot tolerate wrong.* (Hab 1:13 NIV)

The NASB translates it more accurately:

> *Your eyes are too pure to approve evil, and You cannot look on wickedness with favor.* (Hab 1:13 NASB)

It is not that God can't look on evil, but he will never look on evil approvingly.

(2) Does God ever turn away from us? Does he ever reject us? A sinful action, per se, isn't the real issue that God has with us. It is the heart attitude behind the sin that is always at the centre of God's attention. It wasn't the act of biting the fruit that separated Adam and Eve from God; it was the heart attitude toward independence that separated them from God. At a fundamental level, all sin reflects a heart attitude of independence from God. *We* separate ourselves from God. It is not that God separates himself from us but that we choose separation from God. Isaiah sums this up succinctly;

> *We all, like sheep, have gone astray,* ***each of us has turned to his own way;*** *and the Lord has laid on him the iniquity of us all.* (Is 53:6)

Adam and Eve chose to obey Satan instead of God and the consequence of that sin was separation from God, symbolized by expulsion from Eden. Adam and Eve rejected God. God didn't reject Adam and Eve. The expulsion from Eden was a *consequence* of their rejection of him, not his rejection of them. Because Jesus never sinned, there was never any reason for God the Father to ever separate himself from his Son, let alone reject him.

(3) We make the mistake of thinking that Jesus *became* sin. Jesus was the sin offering but Jesus himself didn't become sin anymore than the lambs used as sin offerings in the sacrificial system became sin. It was the blood of the lamb that made temporary atonement for sins of Israel because the life in the blood nullifies the 'death' in the sin. Similarly it was Jesus' shed blood, not his death, not his suffering, not his identification with our sins, that atoned for our sins.

> *In Him we have redemption* ***through His blood****, the forgiveness of our trespasses,* (Eph 1:7)

> *...and from Jesus Christ, the faithful witness, the firstborn of the dead, and the ruler of the kings of the earth. To Him who loves us and released us from our sins* ***by His blood****...*(Rev 1:5)

Isaiah 53 makes it clear that our transgressions and iniquities were laid *upon* him but that was quite different from believing that Jesus actually became sin. I can carry a burden but that doesn't make me the burden! Jesus bore our transgression, he was crushed for our iniquities, but all the time he was distinct from our transgressions and iniquities. All the time his loving Father was focusing on his courageous, sinless Son, not the sin his Son was bearing. God always separates the sin from the sinner and that is why he can love us despite our constant sin. How much more then was he separating the sin his Son was bearing from his sinless Son?

The following verse appears to indicate that Jesus actually *became* sin, not just a sin bearer.

> *He made Him who knew no sin to be sin on our behalf, so that we might become the righteousness of God in Him.* (2 Cor 5:17)

If Jesus somehow supernaturally morphed from a sin bearer into sin itself, then it wasn't Jesus who was crucified, it was sin that was crucified. Theologically and logically, that is not possible. Sin doesn't have a 'life' that can be killed, suffer or die. Sin is a collective term for our rebellion against God. It is not a living organism that can be personified and destroyed, like you can destroy a person. Philosophically, sin is the total antithesis of life. Sin destroys life. Hence sin cannot be crucified. Sin cannot die because it has no life to lose. Conceptually, this verse is more accurately translated;

> God made Him who knew no sin to be the sin offering, on our behalf, so that we might have the imputed righteousness of God through Him. (2 Cor 5:17)

Another perspective on this verse is that Paul is using poetic license to make a point regarding the enormity of the sin that Jesus had to carry. The sin and iniquity were so huge that it appeared to smother or absorb Jesus into itself. When I see a small ant moving a huge crumb of bread, it looks like the crumb is moving by itself, with a life of its own. The reality is that the ant is carrying the crumb but the size of crumb in comparison to the ant means that the ant appears to merge into the crumb and be almost indistinguishable from the crumb.

(4) In Semitic thinking[1], a man's life is complete when he has a son. It is as though his life's purpose has been achieved. A man lives for his son and sees his life complete in his son. Given a choice between his own life and the life of his son, a Middle Eastern man would offer himself first, instead of his son. You can understand then, that the ultimate sacrifice a father could make would be to sacrifice his son. It strikes at the very core of a man's purpose or reason for living. God demanded that of Abraham and Abraham was faithful. As a consequence, he was the only man in Scripture to be called God's friend. The ram in the thicket was the substitute sacrifice and the precursor or archetype of the Lamb who would be the substitute for every human. Abraham was faithful and now it was God's turn to show his faithfulness to the covenant with Abraham. Now God would provide his only Son as a sacrifice and this time there would be no last minute reprieve. It was almost inconceivable that a Semitic father would reject his son. Even when the son had brought embarrassment or shame upon the family, the father would still stand by his son. How much more then, would a father support his son if that son was innocent. Although Scripture doesn't record the final dialogue between Abraham and Isaac before Abraham raises his hand in the air to kill him, it is likely to have sounded something like this;

> 'Isaac, you have been such a blessing to me and my heart delights in you. I am so impressed with your trust in me and your surrender to the desire of my God and your God. You know that I would rather be on the altar and have you holding the knife over me instead of the situation we find ourselves in. I love my son. I love you so much'.

If that is likely to have been Abraham's response to his innocent son's submission, how much more tender and comforting would have been the words of our heavenly Father to his Son as he was dying? To suggest that the heavenly Father rejected his innocent Son is, frankly, abhorrent to the Middle Eastern mind and a gross misrepresentation of God's character. When Isaiah states that it pleased the Lord to crush him (53:10) this doesn't mean God took sadistic delight in Jesus' suffering but rather that the Father was pleased with his Son's intercession on our behalf.

(5) Implicit in the belief that God had to reject Jesus or leave Jesus alone to endure the suffering on his own is the belief that God is somewhere up in the third heaven looking down on Jesus but disconnected from the whole Calvary scene. God watches from afar. God is a passive bystander in the unfolding drama on earth. God's omnipresence and his intense love make that impossible. God the Father was there and involved in helping his Son in every aspect of his suffering as much as he was able to, within the legal rights system. In fact, God the Father was *in* his Son throughout the whole ordeal.

> *...that they may all be one; even as* ***You, Father are in Me*** *and I in You, that they also may be in Us, so that the world may believe that You sent Me.* (Jn 17:22)

Jesus said these words in his discourse after the Last supper, just a few hours before his cry of despair on the Cross. To re-emphasis the point, he says the same thing again in the next verse; verse 23. Would the Father have left his Son in the short time between the Last Supper and his death? Would the Father have left his Son when he needed his comfort more than ever before? Jesus is the only person in history to have had both the Father and the Holy Spirit dwelling in him at the same time. He was fully Emmanuel, 'God with us'. It was still Jesus that died on the Cross, not the Father or the Holy Spirit, but it is a mistake to think that they were disconnected in any way from the passion and death of Jesus.

(6) There is the theme[2] in the Old Testament of God hiding his face from evildoers and turning his face towards the righteous. In the priestly blessing of Numbers 6:24-26, the priests ask the Lord to turn his face towards his people.

> *The Lord bless you, and keep you; the Lord make His face shine on you, and be gracious to you; the Lord lift up His countenance on you, and give you peace.* (Num 6:25,26)

Some Christians believe that God had to 'turn his face away' from the evil that Jesus represented when he hung on the Cross. There is no scriptural basis for that assertion. This concept of God 'turning his face away or turning his face towards us' should be interpreted figuratively rather than literally. God turning away or hiding his face from evildoers means that God leaves them to their own devices. God doesn't hide where evildoers can't see him! He doesn't look away from evil or pretend that it doesn't happen. It simply means that he will not actively intervene on their behalf. God turning his face towards us means that God is pro-active in his interactions with us. When his face is turned towards us, he is revealing himself to us or intervening on our behalf.

Keep in mind that this is an Old Testament concept that was made redundant after the Cross; when God, via the Holy Spirit, took up residence in every believer. Prior to the Cross, God was external to man. He couldn't dwell in a person. Therefore, if I was someone who lived and loved God before the Cross, the best I could have hoped for would have been that God graciously 'turn his face towards me'. Today, all believers have the indwelling presence of the Holy Spirit radiating from within them and so this blessing and the concept behind it is redundant. Sadly, this blessing is still said in churches today and gives legal rights to the kingdom of darkness rather than the Kingdom of Light. Actually, the first time this concept became redundant wasn't at the Cross, but when Jesus was conceived. He was the first person to have God dwell in him. Because God was present in Jesus throughout his life, it was impossible for God to 'turn his face' away from his Son when he was on the Cross.

Why then did Jesus cry out in such despair?
Three people in history were created whose spirits were absolutely pure from the moment of their creation: Adam, Eve and Jesus. Adam and Eve lost that purity when they sinned. However, the main difference between Adam & Eve and Jesus was that Jesus had the presence of his Father and the Holy Spirit infused with his spirit from conception. Adam and Eve didn't. They walked with God in the evening but God was external to them. For all other humans, from the moment of conception, our human spirits were under the control of the satanic kingdom because of inherited generational iniquity. Very quickly, personal sin compounds these legal rights.

> *As for you, you were dead in your transgressions and sins, in which you used to live when you followed the ways of this world and of the ruler of the kingdom of the air, the spirit who is now at work in those who are disobedient. All of us also lived among them at one time,...* (Eph 2:1-3)

Only at the moment when we become believers, does our human spirit become 'recreated' and imbued with the Holy Spirit. We are 'born again' in our spirit.

> *Now we have received, not the spirit of the world, but the Spirit who is from God, so that we may know the things freely given to us by God,* (1 Cor 2:12)

> *He saved us, not because of righteous things we had done, but because of his mercy. He saved us through the washing of rebirth and renewal by the Holy Spirit,* (Titus 3:5)

From this point on, our spirit is in continuous communication with God. The primary function of our spirit is awareness of God and the supernatural realm. The primary focus of our soul is social consciousness; awareness of other people and relationships. However, our souls are not transformed at the moment we become believers. Sanctification is letting our souls increasingly come under the control of our renewed spirit so that the soul becomes more aligned with our spirit. Because our soul and spirit interconnect, the strong independence in our souls reduces our ability to hear clearly what God is saying to us in our spirit. There is a tension that exists between the will of the soul and the will of the spirit, which is why we don't always do what we want to do, as Paul so eloquently states in Romans chapter 7. Hence we sin daily even though our spirits are renewed.

Jesus never had any of these problems. Because he was conceived sinless, without generational iniquity, his spirit was completely infused with the Holy Spirit and the presence of his Father from conception. This meant that as his soul matured, it was always under the complete and total control of his spirit and so his soul maintained and retained the same purity as his spirit. Everything Jesus said and did in his interactions with others was always totally appropriate, always responsive, never reactive, never impulsive, never 'soulish'. He still had to learn all the same social skills as you and I do. He still had to study his times tables and other math concepts and learn to read and write Hebrew. He had to memorize the Scriptures and learn the history of his forebears and the world around him but he did all this with a soul and spirit in total unison with each other and the Holy Spirit and his Father. Jesus never had to 'become a believer' by saying the 'sinner's prayer' like the rest of humanity. He had the Father and the Holy Spirit in his spirit from conception. He did, however, need the baptism in the Holy Spirit to increase his effectiveness in his public ministry. This happened when John baptized him and the Holy Spirit, taking the temporary form of dove, hovered over him. When Jesus was baptized in the Holy Spirit, the Holy Spirit entered into his spirit and soul in a deeper, more profound way than when the Holy Spirit entered at his conception.

As Jesus was hanging on the Cross, increasingly his soul and body were absorbing intense negative inputs of physical and emotional pain; excruciating pain racking his body coupled with heartbreaking rejection, loneliness, isolation, debilitating darkness and torment that couldn't help but impact his spirit. His spirit was nonetheless still steady, firm and secure as he maintained his internal communication and relationship with his Father and the Holy Spirit. In his soul, it was becoming more difficult to focus but Jesus could still sense his Father's loving encouragement and affirmation as he endured the Cross. However, eventually Jesus' anguish of soul was so strong, it swamped his ability to stay connected or tuned into his Father's comfort and this overwhelmed his spirit. It is important to note that Jesus never lost his spirit to spirit connection with his Father. Only a personal sin committed by Jesus himself could break that connection. The connection was there, Jesus just couldn't find it. His soul swamped his spirit.

A rowing boat can be secured to its moorings by a rope and then swamped by a huge wave that submerges the boat. Although the boat is now submerged and the connecting rope not immediately visible from the surface, the boat is still securely connected to that steadfast mooring.

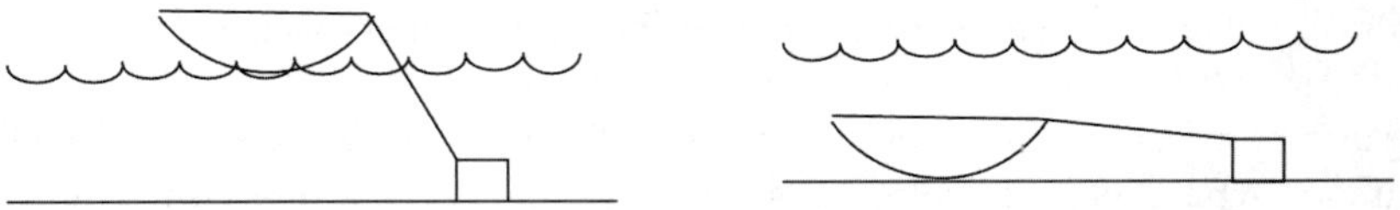

Put another way, Jesus had little difficulty remaining connected to his Father throughout his life. Jesus still had close connection with the Father in the garden of Gethsemane. As the rejection of people around him compounded, he was still connected to the Father but he was hurting. The physical pain, as it too increased in its intensity with no let up, would have had a huge distracting influence on his ability to maintain a clear connection with his loving Dad. His life was ebbing away. The pain and rejection were taking its toll. Added to it all was this enveloping darkness; an eerie demonic blackness coupled with incessant personal torment from Satan. The surrounding inputs were just too much. The static was now so strong that Jesus couldn't hear anything. Try as he might, he couldn't maintain that connection with his Father. Despite the fact that his Father was there, with him and in him, sharing his Son's pain, loving him as he stood in the gap on our behalf, it appeared to Jesus that his heavenly Dad had also deserted him. He hadn't. He was still there, closer than ever.

In a drowning situation, the person drowning progressively becomes disoriented and loses his perspective. If he loses the grip of a secure hand that he is holding onto, it appears to him that his rescuer has abandoned him; let him go. The truth is that the drowning man was unable to maintain his grip or that current was simply too strong. It was the first time in his life that this communion with his Father appeared to be broken. It may have been for an instant, but it seemed like an eternity to Jesus. Jesus may have thought the Father had left him but in reality, the Father was still there.

Did Jesus sin?

Did Satan win? Was Jesus' cry of despair the very legal right that Satan was hunting for? Is believing that his Father had forsaken him a sin when in fact he hadn't?

When trauma overwhelms us emotionally, we often absorb a belief about our circumstances that is not true. Statements such as 'I am on my own', 'No one is protecting me', 'God is not here for me' are common self talk statements that people adopt in the midst of an intense trauma. Even though the truth is that God is always there for everyone, all of the time, it is not a sin to think such thoughts in moments of anguish. God understands that. The thought itself is not a sin. It is a sin if you dwell on that thought, believe it is true and reject God, reject the help of others or make internal vows such as 'I will never trust anyone', 'I will only rely on myself in future', 'I will stop others getting too close to me'. An erroneous belief held momentarily and then rejected is not a sin. A misbelief held and absorbed and then acted on is a sin.

In Jesus' case, it is clear from his following statements that this belief was fleeting. The statements uttered afterwards were "I thirst", "It is finished" and "Father, into your hands I commend my spirit". These statements indicate a sense of task completion and reconnection with the Father and the Holy Spirit. Immediately after uttering the statement, "My God, my God, why have you forsaken me?", Jesus managed to re establish clearer communication with his Dad. The darkest point had passed and the swamped boat was rising again to the surface. Jesus had regained his perspective and the finish line was in sight. There was no sin.

Bittersweet

Despite all his posturing, all his celebration of an end finally achieved, Satan was hamstrung in one crucial area that made the victory bittersweet. He couldn't determine the point of death for Jesus as he had been able to do with every other human who had existed. The spirit of Death was the one in charge of determining when people would die; the exact moment people would pass from human life to eternal life. Satan loved that power. Satan can't create life; he can't impart soul and spirit. That is God's domain. Removing life, ending it, that's Satan's domain. It's the delicious, delectable, final touch that he enjoys every time it happens; snuffing out life that God created. Jesus would afford him no such pleasure.

No one can take it away from me

The Spirit of Death hovered around the crosses. He knew he could take each of the thieves but he couldn't touch Jesus.

> *I will not speak much more with you, for the ruler of the world is coming, and he has nothing in Me;* (Jn 14:30)

No legal rights. How frustrating! Jesus knew he was going to die. The continual loss of blood meant that death was imminent. But it wasn't going to be the satanic kingdom that would determine when this moment would happen. Jesus and Jesus alone would determine the moment of his death. For all other humans; past, present and future, the moment of our death is determined by the kingdom of darkness. This was the one and only exception in history. Jesus made this perfectly clear earlier.

For this reason the Father loves Me, because I lay down My life so that I may take it again. No one has taken it away from Me, but I lay it down on My own initiative. I have authority to lay it down, and I have authority to take it up again. This commandment I received from My Father. (John 10:17,18)

This passage has two layers of meaning. At one level, Jesus is saying that he can live forever if he chooses to; there are simply no legal rights to kill him. Death has no claim over him because there is no sin in his life. Had Jesus chosen to remain on earth, he would be 2000 years old today but not have a wrinkle on him! No plastic surgery required. At a second level, he is saying that because the whole process of his death is purely voluntary, there is no aspect that can be forced upon him; no aspect that is out of his control.

Jesus is the only man in history who could say, *"Father into your hands I commend my spirit"*. He chose the moment of his own death. There was a direct transaction between him and the Father. There was no demonic middle man.

Some readers may think I am being legalistic in stating that everyone, other than Jesus, dies when the kingdom of darkness calls them. You may know of godly people who managed, against the odds, to stay alive until all their family had arrived by their bedside and then died. Perhaps you have heard of or known others who seemed to have been told by God their time had come, and they settled their affairs, went to bed and didn't wake up. God's hand in preparing people for death or allowing last wishes to be fulfilled is not in dispute. It is the exact timing of the death of any individual that is out of his or her control. The kingdom of darkness determines the precise moment of death even if God has enough legal rights to prolong that event from occurring earlier.

After Jesus' death

What happened immediately after his death? Although he had commended his spirit into the hands of his Father, it didn't mean that he went to heaven and was reunited with his Father in the fullest trinitarian sense. It simply meant that his spirit bypassed the kingdom of darkness. The Father would simply have sent angels to escort Jesus' spirit through the transition between life and death.

The Nicene Creed states that 'He descended into hell'. Jesus' spirit didn't need to go to hell because there wasn't any sin that separated him from his Father. His purpose in going to hell was two-fold. Firstly, he went there to take back the keys of Death and Hades from Satan. Secondly, to preach to the captives.

The shocked look on Satan's face must have been priceless. He had barely stopped grinning about his great 'victory' when the 'loser' on the Cross was standing defiantly in front of him. Satan was not one to relinquish anything without a fight but before he realized it, his head was under the foot of Jesus and a mark of Jesus' authority was permanently etched on Satan's forehead. It was the greatest humiliation Satan had suffered. Under the feet of Jesus in front of all the heavenly hosts and all the people in Sheol. A public spectacle no less!

Bruised, not crushed

At this point, Genesis 3:15 was fulfilled. The offspring of Eve, the issue of Mary, had indeed bruised the head of the serpent. The very thing Satan had feared had come upon him. In that instant, there was a diminution, a reduction in Satan's personal power and his intrinsic attributes. However, it was not as much as many Christians would like to think. Satan was not some snake with his head now bashed in. He doesn't now wander around in a daze. He is not a broken, destroyed individual whose powers have been completely removed.

The Hebrew word is correctly translated 'bruised' in the NASB and incorrectly translated as 'crushed' in the NIV. Satan was not crushed, as one might crush a soft drink can or paper cup. He was 'crushed' to the extent that you might crush a fabric by squeezing it in your hands and leaving it wrinkled instead of smooth. The perfection of Satan's outward appearance and intrinsic abilities was now compromised; wrinkled. Not by much, but still compromised. Through revelation, it appears that this bruising has resulted in a reduction in his capabilities of no more than 20%. Jesus' feet on Satan's head reduced him to operating at 80% of his created capacity.

We have a car powered by both petrol and liquid petroleum gas (LPG). LPG is a lot cheaper than petrol in Australia, which is why we use it, but it can result in a power loss of up to 20% compared to petrol. If you were travelling in a small car, and you switched fuel sources, you would notice the difference. The car wouldn't have quite the same 'pep', particularly when overtaking. In a large car, you don't notice any difference at all. A large car has power to spare. In our four litre Ford Falcon, there is no perceptible change when we switch fuels. Satan is a *very* large car. His capabilities are so far above any other created being that a 20% reduction is not noticed by anyone else. Anyone else, that is, except himself…and Jesus.

The fulfillment of Gen 3:15 was not a figurative event. It did literally happen. At an instant in time, Jesus' heel was placed on Satan's forehead. Satan was humiliated. His head and hands might as well have been put in the stocks.

> *When He had disarmed the rulers and authorities, He made a public display of them, having triumphed over them through Him.* (Col 2:15)

Aside from the above scriptural support for this being a literal event, Jesus has revealed to me that this happened. Not because I asked but because it was part of his supernatural intervention in high end ministry we do to people heavily invested in the occult. I cannot elaborate further at this stage other than to say that Satan did get branded with a spiritual mark on his forehead. This mark affirmed the Lordship of Jesus Christ; the very thing that Satan has spent most of his existence trying to dispute and deny. It was humiliation beyond compare for Satan. However, one of his many abilities is that of being able to mask or cloud what others can see. Satan does not allow any of his fallen angels to see this mark. He has the ability to significantly affect the minds of his fellow fallen angels. Just as Satan can blind the minds of humans (1 Cor 4:4), he can blind or block out the memory of those under his command. Satan has erased this event from their memories so that even those closest to him cannot remember what precisely happened when Jesus took over control of Sheol.

Peter also refers to the same event:

> *Who is at the right hand of God, having gone into heaven, after angels and authorities and powers had been subjected to Him.* (1 Pet 3:22)

This verse needs to be read in the context of the preceding five verses, from verse 18 onwards, which refers to Jesus' time in hell when he preached to the captives in Sheol, immediately after his death on the Cross.

In Genesis 3:15, it also says that Satan has bruised Jesus' heel. He did this by virtue of the fact that Jesus had to die to win us back. The sinless God-man, who least deserved to die, had to endure death to free us from Satan's grip. Death, which is the domain of the satanic kingdom, would forever be part of Jesus' résumé. Death, which is the absolute antithesis of who Jesus is, is now part of his experience. He who is the Way, the Truth and the Life immersed in death! Inconceivable! Unimaginable! While Jesus wears it as a badge of honour, because through it he has set us free, Satan nevertheless gloats about the God who had to die.

It is a profound point to ponder, one that is difficult to fully grasp; the second member of the Godhead is forever and inextricably linked to our humanity. God the Son has a human resurrection body. God the Son will forever be a seamless blend of divinity and humanity. Since Jesus is both fully human and fully God, then God the Father has no difficulty adopting us as his sons and daughters. In fact the Father and the Spirit share in our humanity through their oneness with Jesus. This is one reason why we become sons and daughters of God, adopted into the Trinitarian family although obviously not part of the Trinity. Jesus has elevated our humanity to the level of divinity. While angels are called sons of God in that they are a direct creation of God, they cannot be elevated to the same level of sonship as humans can because Jesus never became an angel.

Unlocking

The keys of death and Hades now had a new owner. The former lease had expired.

> *I am the Living One; I was dead, and behold I am alive forever and ever! And I hold the keys of death and Hades.* (Rev 1:18)

The keys of death and Hades are figurative, not literal. They are not a physical entity. They refer to the one who has the legal right to control hell and the second death. The second death is eternal separation from God. Satan had the legal rights or 'keys' to control death and Hades but Jesus now has them. Keys lock and unlock. Satan had 'locked up' Hades and the second death. Jesus 'unlocked' Hades and set those captives, who were righteous, free from the second death.

Preaching and freeing

Jesus now preaches the gospel to those in Sheol.

> *...having been put to death in the flesh, but made alive in the spirit; in which also He went and made proclamation to the spirits now in prison, who once were disobedient, when the patience of God kept waiting in the days of Noah, during the construction of the ark, in which a few, that is, eight persons, were brought safely through the water.* (1 Pet 3:18b,19,20)

In the last part of verse 18, Peter is telling us that although Jesus' body was hanging dead on the Cross, his spirit was very much alive and on his way to Sheol where he preaches the good news that the penalty for their sin has just, a few seconds ago, been paid. Verse 20 tells us that the spirits in prison were people who existed before the Cross and specifically mentions those who were on earth before the flood. Jesus preaches to both the disobedient (those who will be damned because they refuse the gospel) and the obedient; Noah and his family.

> *But they will give account to Him who is ready to judge the living and the dead. For the gospel has for this purpose been preached even to those who are dead, that though they are judged in the flesh as men, they may live in the spirit according to the will of God.* (1 Pet 4:5,6)

What Peter is saying here is that Jesus will judge everyone, both those who are alive today and those who have died in the past. This is the purpose, or reason why the gospel had to be preached to those who had died. God had to be fair and give those who didn't have an opportunity to hear the gospel a chance to hear it. By the phrase, *'though they are judged in the flesh as men'*, Peter means that those who have died have already receive God's judgment by the very fact that their flesh is now dead. Death is the penalty of sin and those who have died have obviously received that penalty. You and I, who are still alive, have yet to receive that judgment but it will come! But, he says, although they have received God's judgment physically, hearing the gospel will give them an opportunity to come alive spiritually; to be set free from Sheol and finally enjoy fellowship with God.

> *The Spirit of the Lord God is upon me, because the Lord has anointed me to bring good news to the afflicted; He has sent me to bind up the brokenhearted, to proclaim liberty to captives and freedom to prisoners; to proclaim the favorable year of the Lord.* (Isa 61:1,2a)

In Luke 4:18, Jesus opened up the scroll of Isaiah in the synagogue in Nazareth and read these verses from the beginning of chapter 61 and applied them to himself. When Jesus said that he had come to proclaim liberty to captives and freedom to prisoners, he obviously didn't mean that he wanted us to set all earthly prisoners free since that would be unjust; violating society's requirement for justice to be served as well as the law of sowing and reaping. Most commonly, Bible commentaries[3] and sermons apply these verses to all of us, because we are all held captive by sin and need salvation. While there is no doubt validity in such an interpretation, the first or primary application of what Jesus was saying was that he was going to set the prisoners in Sheol free. The NIV translation lends weight to this interpretation with its emphasis on the darkness the prisoners are in.

> *...to proclaim freedom for the captives and release from darkness for the prisoners,* (Is 61:1 NIV)

The context indicates that this freedom for the prisoners wasn't linked to a continuous event of setting captives free but to a one-off event; an event linked to the favourable year of the Lord. His double emphasis, *proclaim freedom for the captives* **and** *release from darkness for the prisoners,* meant that Jesus was making an important point. He was making a declaration when he read from that scroll and it wasn't just to his human listeners in the synagogue. He was sending a message to Satan that his time as controller of the keys of Sheol would soon be over. Every person ever created had been held captive in the pit, in the darkness of Sheol, unable to see God. Jesus was saying that thousands of years of captivity for mankind was about to end. The favourable year of the Lord was upon us. Favourable not only for the living, but also for the dead. The second Adam had arrived.

Attack and counter attack

If we read between the lines, what happened next is even more enlightening. Satan was listening and knew exactly what Jesus meant with that double emphasis on freedom to the captives. He reacted by inciting the synagogue congregation to murder Jesus, there and then, by throwing him off a cliff. Jesus certainly stirred the crowd by saying that a prophet wasn't accepted in his own hometown but that was hardly enough reason to want to kill someone. Why did Satan react that way? Why did he knee jerk and put in jeopardy his own careful planning?

Earlier in the same chapter, Satan had experienced one of his worst humiliations to date. Satan chose to tempt Jesus directly and personally. He hit Jesus hard when he was at his weakest; after 40 days of fasting. Satan embodied; assumed the appearance of man by clothing himself with flesh and personally intended to take care of this nuisance. The rest of Satan's followers would have watched this confrontation with baited breath. A personal head-to-head between the raw temptation power of Satan himself, the tempter supreme, the manipulator par excellence and the physically weakened Son of God. Satan's presumption and pride meant that he would have bragged about his upcoming victory much like boxers today do in the hype before a fight. The last direct temptation between Satan and sinless man occurred in Eden and was a push over. No contest. Rather than occupying a serpent, Satan would appear in person. In case the first temptation failed, he had several others up his sleeve. This was going to be an action replay of the Garden of Eden. Finally, he would use his extra-dimensional capabilities and simultaneously show Jesus all the kingdoms of the world. Surely, this God-man will succumb to final impressive carrot that I dangle in front of him.

> *The devil led him up to a high place and showed him in an instant all the kingdoms of the world.* (Lk 4:5)

Once again, he underestimated his opposition. He failed. All the angelic hosts, from both sides, saw it. That was bad enough but this synagogue incident rubbed salt in the wound. Not only did Jesus emerge unscathed from Satan's most aggressive offensive yet, but shortly afterwards, Jesus went on the offensive himself and declared that he was going to set Satan's prisoners free; swipe Satan's precious keys! That was too much for Satan to handle. He was incensed. He had enough demons in each of those listening and enough legal rights to stir up a violent response to Jesus' words. The momentum of the masses would deal with this upstart once and for all; I just want him dead, out of my sight. Get rid of him. But Jesus calmly walked through the crowd, not unlike Moses parting the Red Sea. Failed again, Satan.

Identificational Repentance

Why did Satan choose the 40 days of fasting as the time to tempt Jesus? The obvious answer is that Jesus was at his most vulnerable physically after 40 days without food. This was clearly an important factor. Yet there was another reason. Satan was shocked at the baptism of Jesus. It was unexpected. John's baptism was a baptism of repentance (Acts 19:4). Everyone baptized by John was repenting of personal sin. Jesus didn't need to be baptized because he didn't have any sin to repent of. Then he realized that Jesus was standing in the gap and repenting on behalf of all mankind. Before God could forgive our sin, there had to be repentance. A sinless man was needed to stand in our place and pay with his life the sacrifice we could never pay. Before that could happen, a sinless man was needed to stand in the gap and repent on behalf of all of us. The high priest had done that yearly, by repenting, on behalf of all Israel and sprinkling blood on the mercy seat of the Ark of the Covenant in Holy of Holies. Now Jesus carried this identificational repentance one step further. Although he was sinless, he was still a man, and as a man, he stood in the gap for all men and repented on our behalf. Did the Father accept Jesus' repentance on our behalf? He boomed out in a loud voice that he was well pleased. The penalty for that sin still needed to be paid but the first step in the process was complete. The spiritual impact of Jesus' act of repentance reverberated throughout the earth and in Sheol. The presence of all three members of the Godhead together meant that something really, really important was taking place. Something had begun to shift in the heavenly realms. A message was sent by Jesus to Satan and Satan started to get a little agitated. He needed to do something soon, before Jesus became too confident with his new, power imparting relationship with the Holy Spirit.

Description of Hell

At this point it is worth looking at the structure of hell in more detail. Jesus gives us some clues.

At the time of Jesus, Jews believed that Sheol was somewhere in the earth. This is why the Scriptures, particularly the Psalms, use the term 'descended' when referring to hell or Sheol. This needs to be taken figuratively. Hell, being a spiritual place, is unlikely to be confined within a physical structure like the earth. It probably exists in the second heaven, that extra dimension beyond our space-time world, where Satan and his angels dwell. Nevertheless, the Old Testament is consistent in its imagery of hell being a pit and being underneath us. Perhaps there is ability for an extra dimensional reality to be contained, at least temporarily, within the physical confines of our world.

Hell had three compartments. The first compartment was for those whose heart was turned towards God; those who were considered righteous because of the faith and trust they had in God when they were alive. It was not a place of torment. This place was termed the 'Bosom of Abraham'. It is alluded to in the parable when Lazarus is described as being in Abraham's bosom.

> *In Hades he lifted up his eyes, being in torment and saw Abraham far away and Lazarus in his bosom. And he cried out and said, 'Father Abraham, have mercy on me, and send Lazarus so that he may dip the tip of his finger in water and cool off my tongue, for I am in agony in this flame. But Abraham said, 'Child, remember that during your life you received your good things, and likewise Lazarus bad things; but now he is being comforted here, and you are in agony. And besides all this, between us and you there is a great chasm fixed, so that those who wish to come over from here to you will not be able, and that none may cross over from there to us.* (Luke 16:23-26)

Another compartment of hell was for those who were damned; those whose hearts were not turned towards God. This applied to the rich man. It was a place of torment. Then there was a compartment for the fallen angels that sired the Nephilim, called Tartaros, as explained in chapter 6.

> *For if God did not spare angels when they sinned, but cast them into hell* [tartaros] *and committed them to pits of darkness, reserved for judgment;*
> (2 Pet 2:4)

As the parable indicates, both halves could see each other and there was an impenetrable barrier that separated the damned from the righteous.

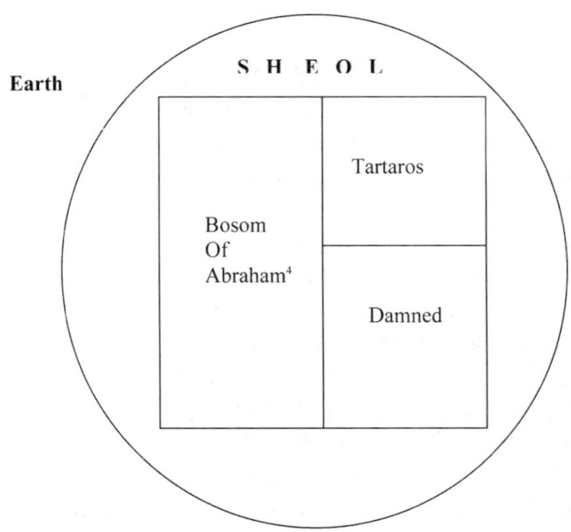

Jesus preached the gospel to all in hell but only those who were in the Bosom of Abraham accepted what Jesus said. *No one* gets to heaven without acknowledging that Jesus Christ is their Lord and Saviour.

What happens at death that divides the people so decisively into two groups? From experience that I will elaborate on in the book, *'Darkness in the Light: Satan's Trojan Horse'*, I know that the kingdom of darkness, like the Kingdom of Light, has the ability to spiritually 'scan' a person and, in an instant, see whether or not that person is saved. Not only that, they can also see how committed the heart of the person is towards God. The satanic kingdom is constantly scanning people to see who the biggest threats to their plans are. Therefore, at death, the spiritual state of a person's soul is instantly read and they are sent to either heaven or hell. Prior to Jesus' death, righteous people couldn't go to heaven. They were separated at death into two groups; those going to the Bosom of Abraham and those going to hell. Both places were in Sheol. Everyone who died went to the same place and a barrier, or chasm, separated the two groups.

Meanwhile, back on earth

The earthly parallel to these events that were being transacted in the heavenly realms provided a powerful confirmation. Let's look at these amazing three verses in Matthew in more detail.

> *And behold, the veil of the temple was torn in two from top to bottom; and the earth shook and the rocks were split. The tombs were opened, and many bodies of the saints who had fallen asleep were raised; and coming out of the tombs after His resurrection they entered the holy city and appeared to many.* (Mt 27:51-53)

The veil

The veil of the temple was a threefold symbol. Firstly, it represented the barrier that existed between the Holy of Holies and the rest of Israel; between God and humanity. It represented the blockage between God and mankind due to man's sin.

Secondly, it was protection for Israel from the glory of God. When Moses came down from the mountain, his face shone with the reflected glory of God. Moses had to put on a veil so that the people of Israel could look at him safely. In the same way, the veil of the temple protected the people of Israel from being overwhelmed by the shekinah glory that surrounded the Ark of the Covenant. This glory was intensified by the contrast between man's sinfulness and God's purity. In other words, it was both glory and judgment that emanated from the Holy of Holies. The unpaid penalty of our sin meant increased sensitivity to his glory, and this meant protection was necessary.

Thirdly, it was also a symbol of Jesus. Woven seamlessly, with purple yarn at the top and a gradual fade from purple to red with solid scarlet at the bottom, it was the perfect picture of Jesus. The purple at the top was a symbol of royalty and also divinity. Red at the bottom of the curtain was a symbol of earth and his humanity. The gradual fade in the middle, where one colour blends into the next was symbolic of the perfect blend of divinity and humanity that Jesus embodied.

The tearing of the veil

With the tearing of the veil, the barrier between God and man was removed. Israel now had unhindered access to the Holy of Holies, the dwelling place of God. No middle man; no earthly high priest was necessary. No veil, no barrier and no glaring judgment that justice demanded.

The tearing of the veil also meant there was no longer a need for protection from the glory of God. No longer was the glory of God coupled with his judgment. That judgment had just been appeased. The judgment of God, that intensified the glory, had been removed. We can now stand before the glory of God because we are wearing 'songlasses'; the righteousness of his Son means that we can now approach the Father as children; princes and princesses instead of condemned prisoners.

It is likely that the Ark of the Covenant was hidden just prior to the Babylonians invading Israel in 587BC. It hasn't been seen since. If and when it is found, it will not have the glory and judgment attached to it that it did in the Old Testament; as we see portrayed in the movie 'Indiana Jones and the Raiders of the Lost Ark'. The Sinai covenant was made redundant at the Cross. The Ark, as representative of God on Earth is no longer valid because now God indwells all believers. We are all 'Arks of the Covenant'. There is no need for one focal point.

The tearing of the veil represented the death of Jesus. The death of Jesus provided direct access between man and God.

> *Therefore, brethren, since we have confidence to enter the holy place by the blood of Jesus, by a new and living way which He inaugurated for us through the veil, that is, His flesh,* (Heb 10:19,20)

The deliberate inclusion of how the veil was torn; from the top to the bottom, indicated this was a supernatural event and that it was God who was doing the tearing. God himself removed the barrier. Had there been human intervention, it would have torn from the bottom to the top since the curtain was too high for a man to access the top without a ladder or scaffolding of some kind.

Earthquake

The covenant at Sinai was established with an earthquake and lasted for more than one and half millennia.

> *Mount Sinai was covered with smoke, because the Lord descended on it in fire. The smoke billowed up from it like smoke from a furnace, the whole mountain trembled violently,* (Ex 19:18)

That physical shaking was an earthly event with a heavenly reverberation. God was giving man a get-out-of-jail card. He was providing man with a way to obtain righteousness. It was the first hope man had received since Adam's fall. There is a way out. Keep all of the 613 commands and regulations of the Law and freedom is yours! You can bet the heavens reverberated. Satan would have taken notice, those in Sheol would have taken notice. God had provided some hope. Slim hope, mind you, but hope nonetheless. Satan would have had his 'feathers ruffled' initially but soon would have realized that there was no way anyone would be able to cash in their card. No, my inmates in Sheol are still very secure.

That covenant ended on Good Friday and the second covenant, the new and everlasting covenant, was also established with an earthquake.

> *...and the earth shook and the rocks were split.* (Mat 27:51)

In keeping with this new covenant, a covenant infinitely better than any before it, the earthquake was just one of many supernatural signs indicating that the old had gone and the new had come. Like the Sinai quake, this earthquake also had a heavenly parallel. Things were once again being shaken in the heavenlies and everyone, the angels and the dead, from both kingdoms, were on full alert. Sheol also shook, as it did 1500 years before but this time it was different. This time there was something more. This time the rocks were split! It is no accident that the phrase, *'and the rocks were split'* was added. In the heavenlies, the keys of Sheol had just been taken. The seemingly impenetrable fortress of Hell had just been penetrated; opened up. Its physical parallel on earth was the rocks splitting. Rocks, that were as old as mankind itself, as old as man's confinement in Sheol, had split; opened up. Matthew mentioning the earth shaking would have reminded his Jewish readers of the Sinai covenant event but the deliberate additional detail of the rocks splitting pointed to something else; hell split open.

Fancy meeting you, Uncle Avi, I thought you were dead!

The rocks splitting probably applied to the random cracking of rocks in the region but not limited to that. The next portion of these verses is intriguing.

> *The tombs were opened, and many bodies of the saints who had fallen asleep were raised; and coming out of the tombs after His resurrection they entered the holy city and appeared to many.* (Mt 27:53)

The splitting was also highly specific resulting in the tombstones of many graves being split open exposing the graves themselves. Others would have been moved aside with the shaking. Both the splitting and the shaking needed to have been so carefully directed that the supernatural control of this event is undeniable. The gravestones needed to be opened or rolled away without splitting or shaking the rest of the tombs to pieces. Keep in mind that most of the graves were set into the hillside so that when the stones were rolled aside, shaken ajar or split in two, a passerby could look right inside. Can you imagine the furor this must have created? It was almost the Sabbath and the Passover as well. Nothing could be done for fear of being ceremonially defiled. Everywhere, there were gaping graves. Notice that the dead in the tombs didn't come out until after Jesus' resurrection. In other words, at the instant that Jesus died, the tombs were opened but those inside were still dead.

Why did the gravestones open? The stones in front of the graves were for the physical sealing or locking away of those who had died. They also symbolized the spiritual locking away in Sheol; the hopelessness and finality of going down to the pit. This was now no longer the case. Jesus had just preached the good news! They were no longer sealed or locked in Sheol forever! They were about to be set free; to be taken up to heaven. There was now hope. The specific tombs that opened belonged to those people who were in the Bosom of Abraham and had just accepted the gospel message! They had all been given a get-out-of-jail-free card and this time they could use it!. However, Jesus was just being sealed in his own tomb and so they couldn't yet go to heaven until his stone too had been 'unsealed' or rolled away.

They didn't have to wait for long. Two days later, the inevitable happened. The sinless one, whom death had no right to hold, was set free. Just as you have to apply effort to hold a cork under water, so too it required effort to keep Jesus in the snares of death. His resurrection was simply a matter of releasing the cork. No effort on the Father's part. Jesus didn't belong in the 'waters' of death anymore than a cork can remain under water. He had to bob to the surface[5]. Now that he had resurrected, those in the semi open graves were able to resurrect and they did. Imagine the consternation in down town Jerusalem on that Sunday morning! We are not told how many were resurrected, how long they have been dead or for how long they would remain alive. Probably, like Lazarus, they simply lived out the rest of their lives. God may have limited the resurrection to those who had died recently so that they could be integrated easily back into their families and this would ensure maximum impact in the community.

Hang on a minute Mary, I've just got to drop off some friends at Dad's!
Before these multiple earthly resurrections could take place, something else had to happen. Earlier on that Sunday morning, just after Jesus had risen from the dead, he spoke to Mary Magdalene.

> *Jesus said to her, "Stop clinging to Me, for I have not yet ascended to the Father; but go to My brethren and say to them, 'I ascend to My Father and your Father, to My God and your God.' "* (Jn 20:17)

We can only imagine how surprised, elated and relieved Mary must have been to find that Jesus was alive. It is easy to picture her holding onto him like she would never let him go! Jesus, knowing that there is still part of his job to be completed, eventually has to prise her from him and tell her what he was about to do.

This ascension Jesus refers to wasn't the official welcoming of Jesus back into heaven. It would be another forty days before he would make his grand entrance into heaven as the glorified Lord and take his place at the right hand of the Father. What Jesus was referring to was a handing over ceremony. As the new mediator between God and man, Jesus still had to go back to Sheol and lead the captives, to whom he had preached the gospel two days prior, out of Sheol and to his Father. His interaction with Mary was the interlude between his resurrection and his trip back to Sheol to set the captives free. On Good Friday, Jesus told the captives that they now had a new Jailer and he would be setting them free soon but they still had to remain locked up until then. They had the promise of freedom, but not yet tasted its reality. On resurrection Sunday, Jesus simply opened up that section, called the Bosom of Abraham, and led the excited captives to the third heaven, to his Father. Almost all would have followed him to heaven but a few returned to earth to re-enter their earthly bodies, still inside the opened tombs. Like waking up out of a deep sleep, they would have stretched out, got up, walked out into daylight and wandered into Jerusalem!

Maybe he and his Father had a brief chat, but it is more likely they communicated without words. Much more would be shared between them during the formal welcome of Jesus into heaven in six weeks time. The Father was eagerly waiting, his hands outstretched in welcome to all those who had been separated from him for so long. The scene would be not unlike the parable of the father waiting for the return of the repentant prodigal.

Scriptural support

> *This is why it says: "When he ascended on high, he led captives in his train and gave gifts to men." (What does "he ascended" mean except that he also descended to the lower, earthly regions? He who descended is the very one who ascended higher than all the heavens, in order to fill the whole universe.)* (Eph 4:8-10 NIV)

These verses from Ephesians are the clearest reference to the event just described. In fact, to emphasize the point and make sure there is no confusion, Paul defines this ascension as a two part process of first descending into Sheol (The NASB is more specific *'He also had descended into the lower parts of the earth?'*) and then ascended to the highest heaven and beyond. Interestingly, the Old Testament verse Paul quotes, Psalm 68:18, talks of receiving gifts *from* men but Paul changes that to *'gave gifts to men'*.

> *When you ascended on high, you led captives in your train; you received gifts from men,...*(Ps 68:18)

Paul, under the inspiration of the Holy Spirit, is directed to this verse in Psalms and sees its messianic fulfillment in this event. His change of the wording is deliberate because although gifts have been given to Jesus, the blessings Jesus bestowed on these captives far outweighed what they could give him in return. The gifts Jesus gave to the captives were his righteousness, intimate relationship with his Father, adoption as sons and daughters of the Father, entrance into Paradise and the promise of an eventual resurrection body themselves. The gifts Jesus received from these captives was their gratitude; the depth and extent of which mankind had never before expressed to God. Can you imagine the enormous relief and absolute joy those captives in Sheol must have experienced when their utter hopelessness and despair had turned to hope. Like any prisoner who is set free from a life sentence, the gratefulness to his liberator is beyond words. In addition to gratitude, the adulation and the praises of the Lamb was a gift that kept on giving; a gift that was first sung on resurrection Sunday and will continue to be sung for all eternity.

The primary application of these verses has to be the freedom of the captives from Sheol because there is no other context in which the phrase, *'he led captives in his train'* makes any sense. The secondary application is that as a result of Jesus' ascension in heaven and being seated on the right of the Father, he gave spiritual gifts to the church; apostle, prophet, teacher, evangelist and pastor (Eph 4:11). This ties in with the gift of the Holy Spirit given at Pentecost that happened after Jesus' final ascension.

Therefore having been exalted to the right hand of God, and having received from the Father the promise of the Holy Spirit, He has poured forth this which you both see and hear. (Acts 2:33)

Another relevant reference is the following:

For Christ also died for sins once for all, the just for the unjust, so that He might ***bring us*** *to God, having been put to death in the flesh, but made alive in the spirit;* (1 Pet 3:18)

As has been mentioned, the context of the verses in 1 Peter 3:18-22 is the time period when Jesus descended into hell to take back the keys and preach to the captives. Hence, the use of the phrase 'bring us to God' is important. Peter chose that phrase because it applied *directly* to what Jesus did with regard to those in Sheol; he *brought* them to his Father. Additionally, Peter is applying it metaphorically to all believers since.

The spirit of Elijah

There are Christians today who believe that there are earthbound spirits. Earthbound spirits are human spirits that don't directly go to either heaven or hell immediately after death but remain on earth indefinitely. According to some who hold this viewpoint, these spirits can enter another human being, often a relative, and take up residence. A Christian counsellor or minister may encounter one of these earthbound spirits when counselling to a person. The counsellor can preach the gospel message to the earthbound spirit and, if the spirit accepts the message, it can be released to go to heaven. For example, suppose a grandfather, who wasn't a believer, on dying, remained on earth and entered his grandson. Years later the grandson receives counselling and the counsellor discovers his grandfather is there. The counsellor takes this opportunity to tell the granddad about Jesus. He accepts Jesus as his Saviour and the counsellor now releases him to go to heaven. The grandson is set free from his grandfather's presence and the grandfather is now in heaven. It's a win-win. Regarding earthbound spirits that don't inhabit people, the belief is that these spirits are observed by others as 'ghosts'.

The reality is that there never has been and never will be earthbound human spirits. The above scenario about the spirit of the grandfather in the grandson is a demonic deception.

However, those holding to this viewpoint justify it by referring to Saul's meeting with the medium of Ender. The spirit of Samuel is conjured up, proving, they say, that some spirits can remain on earth.

The king said to her, "Do not be afraid; but what do you see?" And the woman said to Saul, "I see a divine being coming up out of the earth." He said to her, "What is his form?" And she said, "An old man is coming up, and he is wrapped with a robe." And Saul knew that it was Samuel, and he bowed with his face to the ground and did homage. Then Samuel said to Saul, "Why have you disturbed me by bringing me up?" (1 Sam 28:13-15)

It is true that Samuel did come back from Sheol and communicate with Saul. The imagery of coming up out of the earth which is repeated several times in this passage confirms the belief that Sheol was 'the pit' or in the earth. What is overlooked is that Satan, at this stage, had control of the keys of Death and Hades. Mediums, who were working Satan's agenda anyway, as well as those in Sheol, were under Satan's control. If a medium called someone up from Sheol, Satan would willingly comply if it served his purposes. Satan knew that Saul shouldn't be trying to contact the dead so he eagerly obliged his request. Because of Satan's control, Samuel had no choice but to reluctantly comply and this reluctance is evident in the full dialogue. However, on Good Friday, Satan lost the keys to Sheol. Jesus is now in control of Sheol. No longer can a medium command a human spirit to appear and that spirit oblige. Jesus won't allow it. Despite what spiritualist mediums today believe, it is impossible to contact the dead; all that they contact are demons masquerading as dead human spirits. The mediums are simply getting in touch with demons that are familiar with the habits of the dead person.

The complete and final separation of any interaction between the dead and the living began on Good Friday and was completed on Easter Sunday.

Changed

The third heaven was invaded by human spirits for the first time. The dwelling place of God now held those created in his image. They were now reconciled to God and could freely enter his presence with the imputed righteousness of his Son. From now on, everyone who died would go immediately to one of two places; heaven or hell. Sheol was no longer a holding place for everyone. Sheol was changed forever. No longer could the damned in torment look across to those in the Bosom of Abraham. The rich man had lost sight of Lazarus. That parable was now redundant. The loneliness of hell just got lonelier.

SUMMARY

- Satan prepared well for his last and greatest assault on Jesus. He intended this event to be the one that would finally cause Jesus to sin.

- Satan was responsible for the darkness over the earth. The darkness was not an act that God would do. Darkness is not philosophically compatible with the Kingdom of Light. It is the modus operandi of the kingdom of darkness.

- The darkness was used by Satan to torment Jesus even further.

- Contrary to popular opinion, the Father did not turn his face away from his Son causing Jesus to cry out about being forsaken.
  (1) God is aware of all sin all the time. There is no set amount that repulses him.
  (2) God doesn't distance himself from us when we sin. We distance ourselves from God through our independance.
  (3) Jesus bore our sins, he didn't become our sins. God can separate the sin from the sinner and loves the sinner in spite of the sin. How much more his innocent son?
  (4) In Middle Eastern thinking, the commitment of a father to his son is unparalleled. That the Father should reject his innocent Son is incomprehensible.
  (5) The Father and Holy Spirit indwelt the Son from conception and never departed from him. It is a popular misconception that sees the Father passively looking on the Calvary scene.
  (6) There is a theme of God turning his face towards those who love him and away from those who are evildoers. Applying that to God turning away from Jesus who represented evil is errone ous in Jesus' case since God was present in him since conception.

- The physical, emotional and spiritual inputs simply over whelmed Jesus and he lost connection with the Father.

- The precise moment of every human's death is under the control of the satanic kingdom. Except for Jesus. He and he alone could commend his spirit to the care of his Father, because of his sinlessness.

- Immediately following his death, Jesus went to hell. His purpose was to take back the keys and preach to the captives.

- Gen 3:15 was fulfilled when Jesus left a mark on Satan's forehead, a stamp of his authority over Satan. Forever branded. In this transaction Satan lost about 20% of his original power.

- Sheol, or Hades, before the Cross had three compartments. One for the damned, one for fallen angels linked to the Nephilim, and one for those who were made righteous through faith but separated from God. The damned, such as the rich man, could look across and see Lazarus.

- Jesus preached the gospel to everyone in hell. Only those who were in the Bosom of Abraham accepted the message. No one, in this life or the next, gains entrance into heaven without believing the gospel message.

- The physical parallels on earth confirmed the spiritual reality of what had just happened in Sheol. The veil of the temple was torn indicating that no barrier remained between God and man. The stones of the tombs moved aside signifying that death's hold was no longer secure. Those who resurrected on the Sunday were symbolic of the resurrection bodies we would all one day receive and which Jesus had just received.

- On resurrection Sunday, Jesus took those who accepted the gospel in Sheol to his Father in heaven.

- Christians believing in earthbound spirits today defend this belief by quoting Samuel's appearance to Saul. This passage is quoted out of its context and reflects a lack of understanding of both Satan's role and containment of the dead prior to the Cross and after the Cross.

Chapter 10:
RE-EXAMINING SATAN'S DEFEAT AT THE CROSS

Satan was stunned, figuratively and literally, after that eventful weekend. He kicks himself for missing the clues. The first legal right given to Satan by Adam was now rescinded. Rendered null and void. A second Adam resisted all the temptation Satan could fling at him. Not just on one occasion, but constantly for 33 years. Jesus was the only human not to succumb. The world was bought back. The Creator ended the lease that man had so foolishly given to Satan in the Garden.

Principle of First Occurrence

One key principle concerning legal rights is a term we have coined, the *Principle of First Occurrence*. This principle has far reaching effects in a number of areas and some of these will be discussed in later books. When dealing with the layering impact of legal rights, it is important to go back to the first instance the legal right was established and nullify that. Then many of the legal rights gained from that first legal right are automatically voided.

To some extent this truth is self evident. If a person has a fear of getting into elevators, a counsellor will often go back to the first time this happened and examine the circumstances in detail. The counsellor won't spend a lot of time examining the last time the client had a problem getting into an elevator because that won't lead to root causes. Understanding the conditions that led to the establishment of the problem, and removing those, will be foundational in resolving the problem.

When Jesus talked to the father of the epileptic boy in Mark 9, he asked him, 'How long has this been happening to him?' The man replied, 'From childhood'. That response gave Jesus some important clues.

Another example

When identifying a lie or erroneous thinking pattern that a person holds regarding herself, the counsellor will try to get the client to go back to the earliest memory of when she felt this way. Let's say the client is 35 years old and her name is Crystal. The lie or misbelief Crystal struggles with is *'I am powerless when it comes to arguing with dominant males in authority'*. The client can remember a number of occasions in her life when these feelings of powerlessness were particularly strong. If the counsellor explored the latest event and brought resolution to that, it usually won't bring resolution to earlier events. Interestingly, if we go directly to the earliest memory and explore and bring resolution to that, then usually all the subsequent memories will no longer be an issue.

Two diverse examples but they nonetheless exemplify this principle. The principle of first occurrence is the basis of Jesus' role as the second Adam.

A spiritual Goliath

The first legal right that Satan gained over man was that man chose to listen to him instead of God. Adam succumbed to Satan's temptation. Every person born since Adam has similarly succumbed to temptations from the kingdom of darkness. The first legal right was given through Adam and subsequently every sin of every person since has layered further legal rights that Satan has been able to use. Satan stands before God, rather smugly, and states, 'There is no one that can resist my temptations. All of them are just like Adam, full of pride. All of them deserve eternal separation from you.' That's true. God has to agree. His justice demands it even if his mercy would like to let mankind off the hook. Satan is not unlike Goliath who constantly challenged Israel to take him on, winner take all. 'Give me a man that can resist my temptations,' says Satan.

Where is the person who will nullify that first legal right and restore the balance? He has to be fully human just as Adam was and he must resist every temptation that Satan can throw at him. Every temptation, every time. No exceptions. Not one.

Jesus was the second Adam, fully human and unable to use his divinity in any way to influence his humanity. Like the first Adam, who walked closely with God, this second Adam also walked closely with God. Unlike the first Adam, who caved in at the first temptation, this second Adam didn't crumble at all. He took Satan on. Every temptation that was thrown at him he resisted. The first legal right was rescinded. Just as Adam was our representative and we all reaped the consequence of his sin, so Jesus was the new representative and we all reaped the consequence of his righteousness. The Principle of First Occurrence in action. The First Occurrence had been nullified and the healing flowed down to the rest of mankind.

Jesus' death is necessary to *complete* the role

The role of Jesus as the second Adam wasn't formally completed until he died. While Jesus remained alive, his role as the second Adam was not, could not, be complete. There was always a chance that Satan might still be able to tempt him. Had Jesus not died but still been alive on earth today, we would all still be locked in Sheol, Satan's first legal right still valid. The victory over Satan in this temptation contest could only be finalized by the death of Jesus. This defeat of Satan wasn't achieved by the Cross; it was achieved by Jesus remaining sinless second after second, minute after minute, hour upon hour, year upon year for more than thirty years. The Cross simply formalized the end of the temptation period.

Why did Satan send Jesus to the Cross if he knew that Jesus' death would formally end his chance of tempting Jesus and he would lose the contest? Satan had tried every means he could think of for more than three decades to tempt Jesus. Money, sex, power; none of them worked. Satan took a gamble. He had observed man for a long time. He knew how humans hated physical pain. Slow torture would get a man to sin every time. He also knew how humans invariably made a sinful response to the sinful rejection of others. Rejection, alienation and isolation were powerful emotional motivators to move a victim into self pity, discouragement, despair and a host of other subtle sins. If he could get a combination pack of intense physical pain, coupled with the extreme emotional pain that accompanied comprehensive rejection, then this paragon of virtue was bound to fail. 'Let's see him resist what I am going to throw at him. The temptation in the wilderness was a stroll in the park in comparison to what I have in store this time,'

Satan's 'defeat' and the Cross

Satan wasn't defeated at the Cross! Satan was defeated every time he tempted Jesus throughout his life on earth and failed. The Cross was Satan's greatest temptation attempt and the Cross formalized the end of the contest. That's all. The Cross was merely the last and toughest round of a fifteen round boxing contest. Yet theological treatises, biblical commentaries, Bible dictionaries and countless sermons imply that the Cross achieved some amazing comprehensive victory over Satan and his followers; that Satan now wanders around dazed, defeated and powerless. They believe he is dejected and forlorn because he knows he can never win. Nothing could be further from the truth. Rather than being defeated, in the sense of being made powerless, all that Satan lost was the challenge to get Jesus to sin. In that sense, and only in that sense, has Satan been defeated.

It happened ages ago

Satan was comprehensively defeated once. That happened soon after the creation of the world when he rebelled against God and lost. He and his followers were thrown out of heaven but that didn't mean they were out of God's sight. He has never escaped to require re-capturing or re-defeating. Once you are defeated, you are defeated unless you can somehow marshal your troops and rebuild your army. In regard to the angels who fell with Satan, that has never happened. The angels of the kingdom of darkness are not in constant battle against those of the Kingdom of Light, as some Christians believe. That happened once. God won, Satan lost. The battle has ended. The satanic kingdom's angels are still servants, albeit reluctant ones, but servants nonetheless of the Kingdom of Light. Servants don't do battle with their masters. Sometimes intercessors wrongly believe that their prayers are enabling God's angels to gain 'battle' advantage over the enemy angels. They imagine a physical confrontation in the heavenlies regarding the issue they are fervently interceding for. Such is not the case. As stated previously, the only 'swords' used are legal rights that each side gains and these are provided by us. How these legal rights are allowed to be used has been outlined by God, and both parties abide by those rules. Where there is doubt, Satan brings accusations. Rather than a battlefield, it is a courtroom where heavenly confrontations are resolved. Satan is out to destroy what God wants to establish, and thinks he can outwit God. God uses Satan's attempts to outwit him as tools to advance his own kingdom among men. God is in control and his sovereignty means he is never out of control. Satan was comprehensively defeated once and doesn't have to be defeated again.

To state this more emphatically: It wasn't the Cross that defeated Satan. It was his initial rebellion and loss of the battle against God's angels that defeated him. The Cross simply removed the legal right he has gained from Adam.

What about the Scriptures?

Here is the most popular verse quoted to imply Satan was soundly defeated and rendered completely powerless by the Cross.

> *Therefore, since the children share in flesh and blood, He Himself likewise also partook of the same, that through death He might render powerless him who had the power of death, that is, the devil.* (Heb 2:14)

Context is always important in the interpretation of Scripture, both in regard to the surrounding verses and within a verse. Within this verse, the word 'powerless' can only be applied to that which Satan has power over. The verse makes it clear the power Satan held was *power of death* or *power over death*. More specifically, power over our second death. Paraphrasing verse 14:

> Since Jesus was fully human, flesh and blood just like us, his death completed his role as the second Adam and enabled him to remove from Satan the legal right Satan gained from Adam. That legal right enabled Satan to keep us in Hell forever. This is the second death. Satan is now powerless over our second death. (Heb 2:14 Paraphrased)

It applies to Satan holding power over man's eternal destiny. Jesus has rendered him powerless by removing the keys. Not powerless personally, not powerless in his ability to influence mankind and keep operating as usual; only powerless to keep man in Hades forever. Hades as a place of separation from God is now removed.

The author of Hebrews confirms this interpretation in the next verse, verse 15, which is about freedom from Sheol.

> *and might free those who through fear of death were subject to slavery all their lives.* (Heb 2:15)

This verse refers to all those people, made righteous through their faith (Rom 4:2,3), who existed before the Cross and were in Sheol. Prior to the Cross, death was something to be feared. Not that people were individually frightened of dying but rather that death held no hope for anyone; death was confinement to Sheol, separation from God. They were subject to slavery while alive; both slavery to sin because sin's penalty hadn't yet been paid and slavery to the devil, who still controlled the world because of Adam's sin.

The mistake commonly made by Christians is to apply these verses universally to every aspect of Satan and the kingdom of darkness. Satan is only powerless to control the destiny of the righteous after death. Satan himself is not powerless. Satan's kingdom is not powerless. He hasn't gone from hero to zero. If he was powerless, then he certainly isn't a 'roaring lion seeking whom he may devour' as this and many other post resurrection Scriptures clearly state. We will look at these in a later chapter.

Christian ministries have built their whole ministry model on Hebrews 2:14 and have dismissed the satanic kingdom as totally defeated and not to be engaged with because that would admit that the devil and his angels still have power. Sadly, this limits their overall effectiveness in bringing complete healing and plays right into the hands of the kingdom of darkness. The satanic kingdom will willingly oblige such misconceptions and be more passive if it means that they can fly under the radar and continue undermining without detection or direct confrontation.

Unfortunately, the NIV has inaccurately translated the Greek phrase 'render powerless' as 'destroy' and this has changed the whole point of what the writer of Hebrews was trying to make. This error has reinforced the notion that Satan was 'destroyed' by the work of the Cross.

> *Since the children have flesh and blood, he too shared in their humanity so that by his death he might* ***destroy*** *him who holds the power of death—that is, the devil.* (Heb 2:14 NIV)

The second most quoted verse

What about the verse that says Jesus made a public spectacle of Satan? Doesn't that indicate that Satan was defeated? I have heard several sermons based on this verse and the preacher implied that Satan was thoroughly and comprehensively defeated at the Cross.

> *When He had disarmed the rulers and authorities, He made a public display of them, having triumphed over them through Him.* (Col 2:15)

This question was dealt with in the previous chapter when we looked at this verse in the context of Jesus' descent into hell and the removal of the keys from Satan. However, let's expand on what has already been said. The preceding two verses make it clear that the context of verse 15 is the Cross. The use of the linking word, 'when' confirms this.

> *When you were dead in your transgressions and the uncircumcision of your flesh, He made you alive together with Him, having forgiven us all our transgressions, having canceled out the certificate of debt consisting of decrees against us, which was hostile to us; and He has taken it out of the way, having nailed it to the cross.* ***When*** *He had disarmed the rulers and authorities, He made a public display of them, having triumphed over them through Him.* (Col 2:13-15)

Verse 15 refers to what happened to Satan when he resisted handing over control of Sheol to Jesus. Satan and his inner circle were humiliated in front of Jesus. From Satan's perspective, having his head trapped firmly under Jesus' foot wasn't a good look. The rest of the fallen angels and all in Sheol, both saved and unsaved, must have gasped at the spectacle. Embarrassment and humiliation for Satan beyond belief! The phrase 'rulers and authorities' can't refer to humans since Jesus' death didn't have any direct impact on earthly rulers. Pilate and Herod still reigned in Judea and Caesar still ruled the Roman Empire. Jesus didn't make a public display of these rulers and authorities in front of men on earth. Rulers and authorities refer to the upper echelons of Satan's kingdom, including Satan himself. This verse can't apply to what physically happened at Golgotha because it was an apparent victory for the powers of darkness on that Friday afternoon. The 'public' referred to in this verse were those in Sheol and all the heavenly hosts who were watching. Jesus made a 'public' display of Satan in front of all the other rank and file fallen angels and those from both sides of Sheol.

Jesus 'disarming' the rulers and authorities refers to the 'legal right weapon' the kingdom of darkness had held until that point. The weapon they had held for so long was that man had voluntarily come under Satan's authority through the transaction at Eden. Physical death didn't end Satan's authority. He still controlled men after death. That is why he had the 'keys' of death and Hades. Man would remain under his authority until that first legal right was rescinded; until a man lived a sinless life and resisted all temptation. This moment had just arrived. This verse does not mean that the satanic kingdom has been totally disarmed of all abilities to tempt man or influence mankind. We just have to look around at the world today, both Christian and non-Christian, to realize that. This verse only refers to the removal of the authority to hold man in Sheol.

Let's look at further references that indicate that we have overcome Satan; verses that are used to show that Satan is a has-been, defeated and dejected and that we have nothing to worry about anymore.

Over all the power of the enemy

> *Behold, I have given you authority to tread on serpents and scorpions, and over all the power of the enemy, and nothing will injure you.* (Luke 10:19)

Jesus anticipated the completion of his role as the second Adam. The reclamation of authority from Satan back to man would soon be completed and Jesus was giving the seventy a foretaste of that authority. Without that authority, there was no way whatsoever that the apostles could cast out demons. Satan would laugh in their faces because, positionally, he still slotted above man. If they had attempted to do that without Jesus giving them authority, they would have most likely been physically injured. In Acts 19, we saw the sons of Sceva, who were not believers, and therefore did not have the authority of Jesus, trying to take on demons and were 'chewed up and spat out' by the kingdom of darkness. God gave Jesus permission because he knew the apostles needed to be trained. They had a formidable task ahead of them after Jesus would eventually leave. Like eager kids, the apostles returned from their mission and were so excited about their newfound authority, *"...even the demons obey us"*. This verse merely talks about the positional authority of man over the satanic kingdom that was established after the Cross. In this context, the emphasis is on deliverance and not on demons always being obedient to mankind. It doesn't mean that Satan is powerless in his ability to influence the day to day lives of the apostles, or any other believer. We see this graphically illustrated later on when Satan enters into Judas and sifts Peter like wheat, both ultimately betraying Jesus.

Overcoming the evil one

Twice in John's first letter it says that we have overcome the evil one.

> *I am writing to you, young men, because you have overcome the evil one.* (1 Jn 2:13 & 2:14)

If we look at the surrounding verses, we see that John is writing to children, young men and fathers. His statements are words of encouragement to each group. He reminds the children that their sins have been forgiven and that they know their heavenly Father, probably because of the good example of their earthly fathers. Twice he tells the fathers that they 'know him who has been from the beginning'. This most likely refers to Jesus, the Alpha and Omega, as well as the Father and John is indicating that the fathers have a mature understanding of God. Twice he tells the young men that they have overcome the evil one. In addition he reminds them that they are strong and that the word of God abides in them. Why does he do that? Probably because he realizes the temptations that young men are exposed to and this is why he immediately follows his statement to these younger men with the warning not to love the world with all of its lusts.

> *I am writing to you, little children, because your sins have been forgiven you for His name's sake. I am writing to you, fathers, because you know Him who has been from the beginning. I am writing to you, young men, because you have overcome the evil one. I have written to you, children, because you know the Father. I have written to you, fathers, because you know Him who has been from the beginning. I have written to you, young men, because you are strong, and the word of God abides in you, and you have overcome the evil one. Do not love the world nor the things in the world. If anyone loves the world, the love of the Father is not in him. For all that is in the world, the lust of the flesh and the lust of the eyes and the boastful pride of life, is not from the Father, but is from the world.* (1 Jn 2:12 -16)

John is not saying that the devil is totally powerless, helpless and rendered null and void in his influence on all Christian young man but rather that Jesus, who abides in them, has overcome the enemy and that they too can overcome Satan's attempts to derail them.

Destroying the works of the devil

Here is a commonly quoted verse used to indicate that the devil is totally defeated.

> *The Son of God appeared for this purpose, to destroy the works of the devil.* (1 Jn 3:8b)

The argument used is that Jesus has thoroughly destroyed all the works of the devil, hence the devil is powerless in the life of the believer. That is a huge extrapolation. 'The works of the devil' is a non-specific statement. It could mean a number of things. It may mean reversing the work of Satan in Eden. It may apply to Jesus physically healing 'all who were oppressed by the devil' (Act 10:38). It could mean the believers ability to resist the devil. That is why the context of any verse is always important. Let's look at the surrounding verses.

> *Everyone who practices sin also practices lawlessness; and sin is lawlessness. You know that He appeared in order to take away sins; and in Him there is no sin. No one who abides in Him sins; no one who sins has seen Him or knows Him. Little children, make sure no one deceives you; the one who practices righteousness is righteous, just as He is righteous; the one who practices sin is of the devil; for the devil has sinned from the beginning. The Son of God appeared for this purpose, to destroy the works of the devil. No one who is born of God practices sin, because His seed abides in him; and he cannot sin, because he is born of God. By this the children of God and the children of the devil are obvious: anyone who does not practice righteousness is not of God, nor the one who does not love his brother.* (1 Jn 3:4-10)

Notice that verse 5 is very similar to verse 8.

> *You know that He appeared in order to take away sins;* (1 Jn 3:5a)
> *The Son of God appeared for this purpose, to destroy the works of the devil.* (1 Jn 3:8b)

Verse 8 is a restatement or re-emphasis of verse 5. Destroying the works of the devil, in this case, is taking away sin. Jesus, through the Cross, has dealt a blow to Satan's stranglehold over us through our slavery to sin. Now we can be set free from that stranglehold. It is in this sense that Jesus has destroyed the work of the devil. The context doesn't allow us to apply this verse universally to *everything* that the devil does.

The theme of these verses is clear: it is about whether or not you are practicing sin. The word 'practice' appears six times in these verses. John is saying that practicing sin means you are of the devil and if you are born of God, you don't practice sin. Common sense tells us John doesn't mean that we do not, or cannot, sin after we become believers. Everybody, Christian and non-Christian, sins many times daily. Christians simply have their sins forgiven when they confess them. John himself states that earlier in his letter

> *If we say that we have no sin, we are deceiving ourselves and the truth is not in us. If we confess our sins, He is faithful and righteous to forgive us our sins and to cleanse us from all unrighteousness. If we say that we have not sinned, we make Him a liar and His word is not in us.* (1 Jn 1:8-10)

The phrase 'practices sin' has a deliberate aspect to the sin committed. God always judges the heart so if we genuinely try not to sin but sin despite our efforts, or if we sin through ignorance, God gives us grace. If we *choose* to keep on sinning, indulging in sin that we know is wrong, then we fool only ourselves and, in the long term, God's grace will be thin on the ground. The writer of Hebrews confirms this.

> *For if we go on sinning willfully after receiving the knowledge of the truth, there no longer remains a sacrifice for sins, but a terrifying expectation of judgment and the fury of a fire which will consume the adversaries.*
> (Heb 10:26, 27)

Not touched by the evil one

The final verse from John we will look at is one that can be used to imply we are totally untouchable with regard to the devil.

> *We know that no one who is born of God sins; but He who was born of God keeps him, and the evil one does not touch him.* (1 Jn 5:18)

What does this verse mean? The surrounding verses, in this case, don't give us many clues. On the contrary, they provide a puzzle to scholars.

> *If anyone sees his brother committing a sin not leading to death, he shall ask and God will for him give life to those who commit sin not leading to death. There is a sin leading to death; I do not say that he should make request for this. All unrighteousness is sin, and there is a sin not leading to death. We know that no one who is born of God sins; but He who was born of God keeps him, and the evil one does not touch him. We know that we are of God, and that the whole world lies in the power of the evil one.* (1 Jn 5:16-19)

There are some ambiguities in this passage. John talks about a sin leading to death but nowhere in his writings does he tell us what this sin is. Is it one particular sin or an attitude to sin or the concept of willful sinfulness that John talked about in chapter 2 which we have just been discussing? No one knows for sure. Whatever the case, he appears to be saying that believers should intercede on behalf of other believers who are sinning and God will honour that intercession except in the case of this sin leading to death. The implication is that believers could commit this sin that leads to death and if a believer does, then no amount of intercession will help. There seems to be finality about this sin. It appears to be a salvation-losing sin. More about the possible nature of this sin in *"Darkness in the Light: Satan's Legal Rights"*.

So let's look at this verse as a stand alone verse. 'But He who was born of God' is another way of saying 'Jesus'. Rewritten, this part of the verse becomes,

> '...but Jesus keeps him, and the evil one does not touch him'.

'The evil one does not touch him' does not mean 'Christians are Kevlar coated and impervious to absolutely any attack from the satanic kingdom' any more than 'no one born of God sins' means 'Christians don't sin'. Within the context of the verse, what John probably means is that the devil can't touch a believer's new birth. Once a person is 'born of God' or 'born again' his sin is covered by the imputed righteousness of Christ. In that sense he doesn't 'sin'. The Spirit of Jesus now indwells the person and 'keeps' him: the transaction of salvation is not one that Satan can interfere with or touch. Satan can try hard to stop the person in the lead up to salvation but once the person has chosen Jesus, the actual process of being born again is totally independent of satanic interference.

Submission and resisting required

> *Submit therefore to God. Resist the devil and he will flee from you.* (Jam 4:7)

The devil fleeing is predicated on our submission to God and resisting him. Resisting the devil is linked to standing firm which has to do with the armour. We will talk in detail about the armour in a later chapter. Implicit in this understanding is that we *recognize* that the devil is tempting us. We have to know the devil is tempting us to be able to resist him. The problem lies in the fact that most Christians, most of the time, don't realize that the devil is tempting them and so he doesn't flee. Instead we give him a foothold, as Paul has stated:

> *Be angry, and yet do not sin; do not let the sun go down on your anger, and do not give the devil an opportunity.* (Eph 4:26)

Therefore, I want younger widows to get married, bear children, keep house, and give the enemy no occasion for reproach (1 Tim 5:14)

How much protection?

But the Lord is faithful, and He will strengthen and protect you from the evil one. (2 Th 3:3)

Once again it is so easy to take a verse like this and preach a sermon about how God has promised to protect us from the devil, so we have nothing to fear. It talks about protection. The question is how much protection? Does this mean that you will be protected completely from all that the kingdom of darkness has to throw at you? Are you exempt from every temptation, every calamity, all verbal, emotional and physical abuse directed to you by others? The answer is no. Common sense once again tells us that this verse and others, such as Luke 10:19 which we have already looked at, do not mean total and complete insulation from the satanic kingdom. It is ambiguous then as to how much protection these verses are talking about. It probably means that God won't allow Satan to overwhelm us to the point of us losing our salvation. It means that God will provide a measure of protection beyond which the devil cannot trespass. These verses must be balanced with all of Paul's other warnings about the devil and our need to be wary.

A measure of frustration arises when reading such verses because there is no objective standard we can apply. How do I know whether I am exercising enough faith, resisting enough, submitting enough to be able to stand firm against the devil? The truth is that our success in resisting, submitting and maintaining the armour in our lives lies on a continuum and equally then, the access and influence of the devil to our lives must also lie on a continuum. We have found this to be true in our counselling experience. Clients who have a closer walk with the Lord and exercise self discipline are less affected by demonic influence than clients who lack self discipline (See Graph).

Only four changes in Satan's function since the Cross

There are four areas that the Cross has changed, from Satan's perspective.

(1) Satan knows that he no longer has any control of the righteous after they die. They go straight to the Father.

(2) He no longer has default control over the world. He no longer retains complete and absolute control of mankind due to Adam's sin. Now to gain control he must work with each person or people group separately. Jesus makes this point clear when referring to his upcoming death.

Godly Relationship versus Satanic Influence

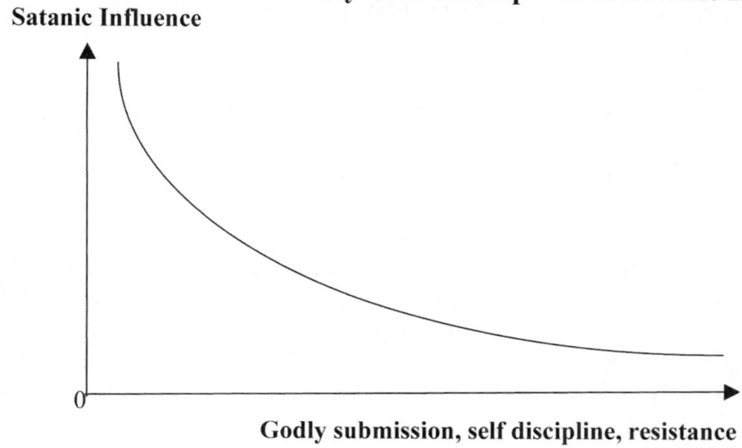

Now judgment is upon this world; now the ruler of this world will be cast out. (Jn 12:31)

Jesus can't be referring to Satan being cast out from heaven because that was a past event. He can't be referring to his second coming and the 1000-year reign when Satan is locked up because the context of all the surrounding verses is Jesus' death. He can't be referring to Satan being completely removed from the earth after the Cross because there are many post-resurrection Scriptures that indicate that this never happened. The only possible application of this verse is that Satan's position as official ruler of this world will be removed. Instead of slotting in above man in authority over the world, he is removed from the equation altogether. It doesn't mean he can't gain control of sections of the world through man's free will choices. It means he is no longer the recognized ruler of the world, like he was before the Cross.

Before the Cross	**After the Cross**
God	**God**
over	*over*
Satan	**Man**
over	*over*
Man	**The World**
over	
The World	

(3) He knows that people who choose to believe in Jesus now have the Spirit of Jesus, the Holy Spirit, dwelling in them. These people, individually and collectively, have authority over his kingdom, if they use it properly.

(4) He has been bruised. Not crushed but bruised. He knows he is not quite as powerful as he was.

Eleven factors that remain unchanged for Satan since the Cross

Both before and after the Cross:

(1) Satan uses the spirit of Death and Hades to control the moment when people die.
(2) Satan controls the length of people's lives.
(3) People are all born with inherited generational iniquity.
(4) More men are damned than receive eternal life.
(5) The whole of creation is still in the process of decay.
(6) Satan acts within the legal rights system set up by God.
(7) He is free to roam around.
(8) He is the accuser.
(9) Satan is a very real and active enemy of the righteous.
(10) He has a lot of control over human physiology and psychology.
(11) Satan has the ability to control the elements.

Satan wasn't defeated at the Cross. He simply had the first legal right he gained in the Garden taken back. When you get something you weren't expecting and it gets taken away again, that is hardly a defeat. A loss? Yes. A defeat? No. Was Satan devastated? No, not at all. Although his authority was removed at the Cross, immediately after the Cross Satan still had complete control of all humanity except eleven apostles and a few other followers. After Pentecost and the period following, he lost a significant measure of control of a few thousand more. In comparison to the millions on earth at the time, that was a drop in the ocean. Even John, fifty years after the Cross, acknowledges that the world is under the control or power of Satan.

> *We know that we are of God, and that the whole world lies in the power of the evil one. (1 Jn 5:19)*

Over the ages that followed, the widespread acceptance of the gospel by the Roman and Byzantine empires, followed by the European nation states, increased the number of believers. However the millions of Chinese, Hindus, Africans, Aztecs and other dispersed people groups still meant Satan controlled the destiny of the majority of humanity. The advent of Islam and Buddhism added to Satan's control. Today, as the world becomes more atheistic and other religions increase their influence, Satan is satisfied with the current situation. Before the Cross, he controlled the world absolutely. After the Cross, he controls mankind by deception and, as the third graph illustrates, his position hasn't changed that much.

Graph 1: Satan's Authority in the Heavenly Realms

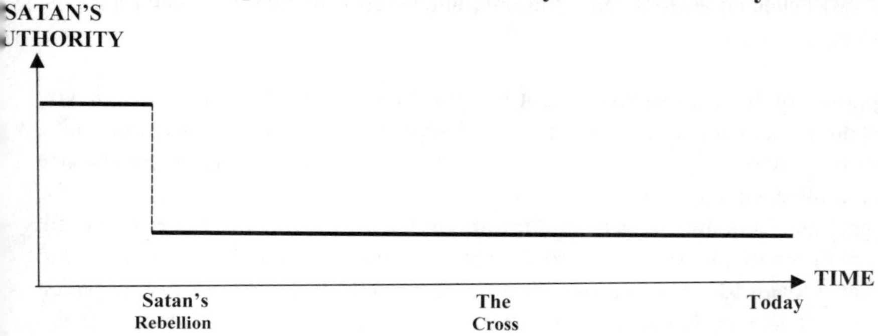

Graph 2: Satan's Authority on Earth

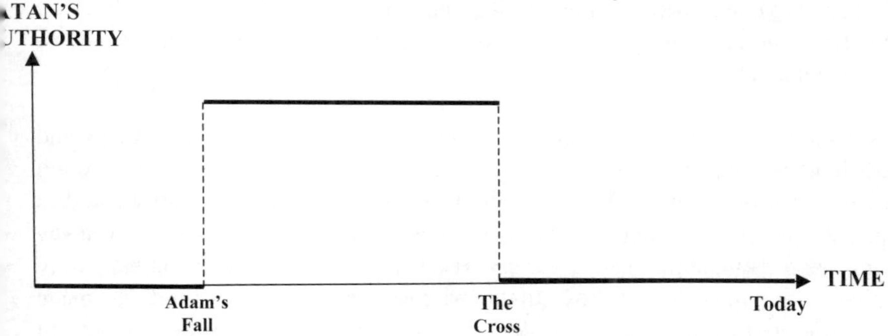

Graph 3: Satan's Control on Earth

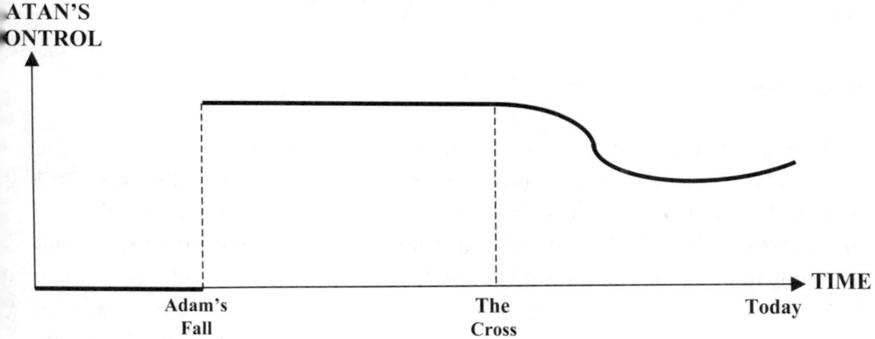

Pikes and Minnows
The difference between Satan's authority and control can be seen in the following analogy.

Suppose you have an aquarium that is full of small fish called minnows. If you introduce into that aquarium a larger fish that likes eating minnows, such as a pike, very soon there will be no minnows left. If you now take the pike out and place it in another smaller aquarium, by itself, and place this aquarium back into the bigger aquarium, the pike will see the minnows, try to get them, but won't succeed. Every time the pike sees a minnow swimming in the surrounding aquarium, and makes a lunge for the minnow, it hits the glass wall of its own aquarium, which the pike can't see. Try as he might, he can't get the minnows. Eventually he gives up. If you now take the smaller aquarium away and put the pike back into the big aquarium with the minnows, like it was originally, an interesting thing happens. Even though there is now no barrier between the pike and the minnows, the pike will starve to death, with minnows all around him and bumping into him, because he believes he can't get them. The pike is deceived into believing the minnows are unattainable[1].

If the minnows represent Satan's kingdom and the pike represents Adam and mankind, then before Adam's sin, Adam could have 'eaten' Satan up. Adam had authority over Satan. After the fall, Adam and the rest of humanity couldn't touch Satan. The smaller aquarium represents the authority Adam gave away to the satanic kingdom. There was an invisible barrier that prevented man from dealing with Satan. At the Cross, that barrier was removed. However, that made little difference to the pike. After 4000 years of no control over the kingdom of darkness, almost all of humanity didn't realize that the barrier was no longer there. The few pike that do know the barrier is gone are busily eating up minnows, but most of humanity is deceived into believing that they can't deal with the enemy, and are slowly dying.

Satan wonders what all the fuss is about the Cross. He argues,

> 'Although my authority is gone, most of mankind doesn't know it. The Cross has opened a way for them to make inroads into my kingdom but they don't believe they can. Before the Cross, they had no choice regarding my authority over them. After the Cross, they voluntarily give me their authority. That suits me fine. I don't care how I get it'.

For 4000 years, the emperor paraded in his regal garments, his crown and scepter; symbols of his authority. The people *had* to line the streets and cheer. For the last 2000 years, the emperor has been stripped of his garments, crown and scepter, but he still parades and most people still line the streets and cheer.

Dejected? Hardly!
We make a big mistake by thinking that Satan realizes what a big mistake he made at the Cross!

It is a dangerous misconception to think he simply wanders around dejected, knowing that he is defeated and that his end will come. Yes, he realizes that he lost the challenge to get Jesus to sin. Satan now understands the sacrifice Jesus has paid with his own blood to restore our relationship with God. He doesn't see that as defeat. He sees it as a minor setback. He simply moves to plan B. More about Satan's plan B in the book, *'Darkness in the Light: Satan's Trojan Horse'*. Extreme pride sees every defeat as a minor setback. Extreme pride doesn't allow for dejection or self-pity. Extreme pride never admits defeat, never gives up. Never. Ever.

From Satan's perspective
If I were Satan right now, at the beginning of the third millennium of the Common Era, I would be pretty pleased with myself. I still have complete control over the exact time of death of every human being. My kingdom still decides the length of life of most non-believers and Christians. I roll the dice. I say when their number is up. I can manipulate the weather, the direction of a Tsunami, the impact of an earthquake; I can wipe out large sections of humanity if I so choose.

True, I have lost my default control of the world but I still have control of huge portions of the earth. I have control of large sections of the world's population through false religious beliefs and therefore I control the territory in those countries where those false beliefs predominate. In fact, I even control large sections of so called Christian countries because of their compromised Christianity.

Far more people die who are not reconciled to God than those who are. So I still have a wide and well-trodden highway to hell. As each decade passes, I gain more and more legal rights as the world becomes more selfish, egocentric and self-absorbed. Gold, glory and girls/guys mean I have most people, including Christians, eating out of my hand. Many Christians blindly think their salvation is secure and their presumption and complacency places them on shaky ground. Of course I have read the book of Revelation and I know what your Bible says about what will happen to me in the end but I know that it is never going to happen. Wake up and look around you! My kingdom is in control!

In fact, would you like to come on board?

SUMMARY

- The principle of first occurrence means that if we are to nullify any behaviour or accumulated set of legal rights, we need to go back to the event that first established the problem and nullify that. Then the following layered legal rights will automatically be dealt with.

- To be freed from the grip of the second death, to end our eternal separation from God, we needed another Adam that would go back and nullify the first legal right. Nullifying that legal right meant resisting every temptation throughout his life.

- Just as Adam was our representative and we all reap the consequence of his sin, now Jesus is our new representative and we all reaped the consequence of his righteousness.

- Jesus had to die to formalize the end of the temptation period and therefore the completion of his role as the second Adam.

- Satan thought that the horrendous emotional and physical agony of the Cross would cause Jesus to sin. It didn't. Only in that regard has Satan been defeated. He tried to tempt Jesus to sin and he failed.

- The popular misconception is that as a result of the Cross, Satan was comprehensively defeated and rendered powerless, and became just a former shadow of himself.

- Satan wasn't defeated at the Cross. Satan was defeated when he first rebelled.

- In heaven today, there is no ongoing battle between opposing angels. The Kingdom of Light serves God. The kingdom of darkness serves God. The kingdom of darkness also serves Satan. The 'courtroom' is the battleground.

- The universally accepted weapon is legal rights. In various instances, Satan has to make a case to God before he can use his legal rights. God may or may not grant permission. When the satanic kingdom uses these to serve Satan and thwart God's apparent will, it indirectly serves to train and strengthen God's kingdom.

- The two verses most often quoted to indicate that Satan was conquered at the Cross are Colossians 2:15 and Hebrews 2:14,15. Interpreted in context, these verses don't support this belief.

- Verses used to indicate that Satan is no longer an issue for Christians are often quoted out of context. The context of these verses is our positional authority over Satan. They cannot be applied in an all encompassing sense that Satan and the kingdom of darkness has no influence whatsoever over any Christian.

- There are four consequences of the Cross that have an impact on Satan.

Satan before the Cross	Satan after the Cross
Satan had absolute authority over the world; the dominion mantle he received from Adam.	Satan no longer has absolute authority over the world but gains authority through legal rights.
Satan had authority over the eternal destiny of man. Hell is for everyone.	Satan's authority over the destiny of man has been removed. People can now go to heaven.
Satan's intrinsic abilities were at 100%.	Satan's intrinsic abilities are slightly diminished. Approx 80%.
Satan had authority over every human. He could not be resisted.	Satan has no authority over believers. He can now be resisted.

- There are eleven areas that remain unchanged since the Cross.

Satan before the Cross	Satan After the Cross
He used the spirit of Death and Hades to control the moment when people die.	He uses the spirit of Death and Hades to control when people die.
He controlled the length of people's lives.	He controls the length of people's lives.

People were all born with inherited generational iniquity that enables the K of D to have immediate control.	People are all born with inherited generational iniquity that enables the K of D to have immediate control.
More men were damned than will eventually receive eternal life.	More men are damned than will eventually receive eternal life.
The whole of creation, in all areas, was in the process of decay.	This process of decay has deteriorated further and, in all areas, continues to deteriorate.
He acted within the legal rights system set up by God.	He acts within the legal rights system set up by God.
He was free to roam around.	He is free to roam around.
He was the accuser.	He still is the accuser.
Satan was a very real and active enemy of the unredeemed righteous.	Satan is a very real and active enemy of the redeemed righteous.
He had a lot of control over human physiology and psychology.	He has a lot of control over human physiology and psychology.
Satan had the ability to control the elements.	Satan has the ability to control the elements.

- Satan's control over mankind didn't suddenly drop to zero after Jesus, took back Satan's automatic authority over mankind.

- Despite the Cross, most of the world continues to give Satan voluntary control over their lives. If you are not following Jesus, you are still under the control of the kingdom of darkness.

- John, writing fifty years after Jesus' death, acknowledges that the unbelieving world is under the control of Satan. (1 Jn 5:19)

- From Satan's perspective, globally, both back then and today, little has changed. The Cross hasn't affected him that much. It's business as usual.

- Extreme pride never admits defeat, never gets dejected, never gives up. As we enter the third millennium, Satan is quite confident that the predictions of the book of Revelation will not come to pass.

Chapter 11:
SATAN'S CAPABILITIES AFTER THE CROSS

> We don't need to focus on the devil; we just need to focus on Jesus. Don't give him any more attention than he already gets. Jesus has defeated him on the Cross and so he is not an issue. He may be a roaring lion but he hasn't got any teeth. If we resist him, he will flee. The IRS doesn't focus on counterfeit dollar notes but they study the real thing and so they recognise the counterfeit bill because they know the real thing so well. So too as we concentrate on Jesus, the devil will be recognized as the counterfeit that he is. Greater is he who is in me than he who is in the world, so I have nothing to fear.

This was quoted in the introduction to this book but it is worth repeating. It is so common in so many churches and a foundational premise in many Christian ministries. It is dangerously deceptive. We have developed a case, contrary to popular Christian understanding, that Satan hasn't lost that much since the Cross. The common Christian cliché is that 'Satan was defeated at the Cross' whereas the only defeat Satan experienced was that he failed to get Jesus to sin and, as a consequence, his keys to death and Hades were taken back and he lost his power to control our second death; our eternal separation from God. The keys were a bonus, the bonus has been removed. That's hardly a defeat.

In this chapter, we will look at a range of post-resurrection Scriptures to see if my assertion, that Satan is still a powerful force to be reckoned with, has any backing.

Bruised not crushed

We have said that Satan wasn't crushed at the Cross, only bruised. The following Scripture confirms this assessment.

> *The God of peace will soon crush Satan under your feet. The grace of our Lord Jesus be with you.* (Rom 16:20)

If Satan was crushed at the Cross, then this verse from Paul to the Romans is redundant. Paul says 'soon', because he was expecting Jesus' second coming within his lifetime or at least in the not too distant future. Since Jesus hasn't yet returned, Satan is *still* to be crushed. Paul could have been using the phrase 'crushed under your feet' in relation to Satan being locked up for 1000 years in Sheol, which is considered under the earth and therefore under our feet. He could alternatively be referring to Satan's final judgment. In his first letter to the Corinthians, he makes the point that Christ's enemies, which obviously include Satan, won't finally be put under Jesus' feet until he has completed his reign on earth.

> *But now Christ has been raised from the dead, the first fruits of those who are asleep. For since by a man came death, by a man also came the resurrection of the dead. For as in Adam all die, so also in Christ all will be made alive. But each in his own order: Christ the first fruits, after that those who are Christ's at His coming, then comes the end, when He hands over the kingdom to the God and Father, when He has abolished all rule and all authority and power. For He must reign until He has put all His enemies under His feet. The last enemy that will be abolished is death.* (1 Cor 15:20-26)

As Paul states in the last verse above and John confirms in the following passage, the Angel of Death is indeed the last member of Satan's army to be placed under Christ's feet; to finally be thrown into hell (Rev 20:14). Satan found himself under Jesus' feet immediately following the Cross. At that time, he was bruised. He will be crushed finally when he is exiled to hell. He will receive that punishment shortly before the angel of death receives the same punishment (Rev 20:10).

> *And the devil who deceived them was thrown into the lake of fire and brimstone, where the beast and the false prophet are also; and they will be tormented day and night forever and ever. Then I saw a great white throne and Him who sat upon it, from whose presence earth and heaven fled away, and no place was found for them. And I saw the dead, the great and the small, standing before the throne, and books were opened; and another book was opened, which is the book of life; and the dead were judged from the things which were written in the books, according to their deeds. And the sea gave up the dead which*

were in it, and death and Hades gave up the dead which were in them; and they were judged, every one of them according to their deeds. Then death and Hades were thrown into the lake of fire. This is the second death, the lake of fire. (Rev 20:10-14)

Satan's control over death

In the Old Testament we saw that Satan had control over death. In the New Testament, after the Cross, is there scriptural support for the assertion, in the previous chapter, that Satan has control over the length of our lives and death? We have just read in 1 Cor 15:26 that the last enemy to be destroyed is death. Since death is considered an enemy, it is logically still under the control of the satanic kingdom.

Do not fear what you are about to suffer. Behold, the devil is about to cast some of you into prison, so that you will be tested, and you will have tribulation for ten days. Be faithful until death, and I will give you the crown of life. (Rev 2:10)

I know where you dwell, where Satan's throne is; and you hold fast My name, and did not deny My faith even in the days of Antipas, My witness, My faithful one, who was killed among you, where Satan dwells. (Rev 2:13)

These two verses attribute the death of the saints to the direct influence of Satan. The two witnesses in Revelation 11 are killed by Satan (the beast). Satan's control over death was obviously not relinquished at the Cross.

I looked, and behold, an ashen horse; and he who sat on it had the name Death; and Hades was following with him. Authority was given to them over a fourth of the earth, to kill with sword and with famine and with pestilence and by the wild beasts of the earth. (Rev 6:8)

In this passage, during the tribulation, just before Jesus returns, God exercises his judgment against a quarter of the earth. He gives authority to the satanic kingdom, more specifically to the two principle angels in control of death, allowing them to kill and destroy in this wholesale manner.

A roaring lion

Be of sober spirit, be on the alert. Your adversary, the devil, prowls around like a roaring lion, seeking someone to devour. But resist him, firm in your faith, knowing that the same experiences of suffering are being accomplished by your brethren who are in the world. After you have suffered for a little while, the God of all grace, who called you to His eternal glory in Christ, will Himself perfect, confirm, strengthen and establish you. (1 Pet 5:8-10)

There is no animal analogy more frightening than a roaring lion. An angry apex predator is not to be ignored. Not only is a prowling lion far from powerless and defeated, the context of these verses indicates that Satan is capable of inflicting suffering. This suffering is not explained but suffering is usually associated with sickness, oppression, calamity or other negative circumstances in our lives. Either way, it indicates considerable control.

The sentiments regarding Satan as a roaring lion are echoed in the phrase, 'having great wrath'. The context of this phrase is the period of time from the Garden of Eden to the end of the tribulation, before he is locked away for 1000 years.

For this reason, rejoice, O heavens and you who dwell in them. Woe to the earth and the sea, because the devil has come down to you, having great wrath, knowing that he has only a short time. (Rev 12:12)

Very deceptive

The use of the word 'snare' in the following two verses implies a trap that is carefully set. A snare is a device that the victim is unaware of. The implication is that the enemy is very deceptive.

And he must have a good reputation with those outside the church, so that he will not fall into reproach and the snare of the devil. (1 Tim 3:7)

And they may come to their senses and escape from the snare of the devil, having been held captive by him to do his will. (2 Tim 2:26)

There's nothing more deceptive than appearing as a convincing imitation of your enemy. Keeping in mind Satan's majestic appearance, that wouldn't be too difficult for him.

No wonder, for even Satan disguises himself as an angel of light.
(2 Cor 11:14)

Knows when we are vulnerable

Be angry, and yet do not sin; do not let the sun go down on your anger, and do not give the devil an opportunity. (Eph 4:26)

Stop depriving one another, except by agreement for a time, so that you may devote yourselves to prayer, and come together again so that Satan will not tempt you because of your lack of self-control. (1 Cor 7:5)

Both these verses indicate that Satan and the kingdom of darkness are aware when we are angry and when we are sexually vulnerable. These two areas are merely examples of sins that the kingdom of darkness tempts us in. This is not meant to be an exhaustive list. There are few sins, if any, that the satanic kingdom is not aware of and cannot tempt us in.

God uses or allows Satan to continue to discipline the saints

Because of the surpassing greatness of the revelations, for this reason, to keep me from exalting myself, there was given me a thorn in the flesh, a messenger of Satan to torment me—to keep me from exalting myself! Concerning this I implored the Lord three times that it might leave me. And He has said to me, 'My grace is sufficient for you, for power is perfected in weakness.'
(2 Cor 12:7-9)

Paul had been given extraordinary revelations from God. In the last section of the previous chapter, dealing with God's judgments, the case was made that the tolerance limits of God's grace are narrowed in proportion to the extent of the revelation we receive from God. It means then that Paul was walking on very thin ice! It appears that Paul's pride was growing and, if left unchecked, the consequences could have been dire.

A messenger from Satan can only be a demon. Either Satan sent the demon or God sent the demon. Perhaps Satan was acting on his own initiative and exercising his legal right to afflict Paul because of Paul's pride. Alternatively, God brought a preliminary judgment against Paul and commanded Satan to send a demon. God would do this to keep him humble and prevent him from suffering the same fate as Herod or Ananias and Sapphira. Either way, these verses show that God was quite comfortable with a demon being sent to torment Paul. This is another example of God using the satanic kingdom to achieve his purposes.

From experience, not directly from Scripture[1], as far as we are aware, there are eleven levels within the demonic hierarchy. If Satan is number one, Messengers, or Consorts, are at level 4, just under Princes. If this premise is correct, Paul was sent a very capable and powerful demon to torment him.

These verses are no different from the Old Testament verses we have already looked at where God sent or used demons to achieve his purposes. Angels were created to serve God and their fallen state does not alter this. The Cross has not made any difference in this regard. Consider the following verses.

> *I have decided to deliver such a one to Satan for the destruction of his flesh, so that his spirit may be saved in the day of the Lord Jesus.* (1 Cor 5:5)

> *Among these are Hymenaeus and Alexander, whom I have handed over to Satan, so that they will be taught not to blaspheme.* (1 Tim 1:20)

It looks like Paul was playing pass the parcel! The affliction in the flesh Paul received to keep him humble, he then sent to the man in Corinth who was sleeping with his father's wife, so that his soul might be saved. He did it again with Hymenaeus and Alexander. Satan had to act within clearly set parameters so that these people were not broken to the extent of losing their salvation. Satan was being used by God to discipline the members of God's kingdom here on earth.

These three scenarios are essentially no different from the example of Job. Paul, the man from Corinth, Hymenaeus and Alexander, as well as Job, were all disciplined by God. Like the Corinthian man, God had delivered Job 'to Satan for the destruction of his flesh'. God allowed this to happen to these men because he knew that their hearts were in the right place. All five men were considered 'blameless', four of them having the imputed righteousness of God because of the Cross. Despite Job 1:1 describing Job as blameless, he was still a sinner, like his New Testament counterparts. An example of this is that his trust in God was not complete, because he feared that calamities would come upon him. All fear is sin; its foundation is a lack of trust in God.

> *For what I fear comes upon me, and what I dread befalls me.* (Job 3:25)

As we mentioned earlier, he was also fearful that his children would offend God with their partying, so he offered sacrifices on their behalf (Job 1:5). Since they were adults, he appeared to carry more of their guilt than he should have and perhaps overfunctioned by presenting sacrifices on their behalf.

These verses below refer to the same Corinthian man mentioned above.

> *But one whom you forgive anything, I forgive also; for indeed what I have forgiven, if I have forgiven anything, I did it for your sakes in the presence of Christ, so that no advantage would be taken of us by Satan, for we are not ignorant of his schemes.* (2 Cor 2:10,11)

After Paul's severe admonishment to the Corinthians in his first letter regarding this man's sexual behaviour, the Corinthians followed through with his command.

At the beginning of his second letter, he told them to forgive and re-establish the man in the community lest the punishment overwhelm him (2 Cor 2:6-9). Paul said that he too had forgiven the man and he pointed out that they shouldn't give any advantage to Satan through harsh punishment and an unforgiving heart. Unforgiveness, then, gives an advantage or legal rights to Satan. These verses reaffirm the point made in Ephesians 4:26 and 1 Corinthians 7:5 that Satan gets an advantage from personal sin areas and attitudes of our heart.

By saying that we are not ignorant of Satan's schemes, Paul was not implying that he had exhaustive knowledge of all of Satan's movements, intentions and entire modus operandi. Satan exists and operates in dimensions outside of our space-time world in a way that no human could possibly comprehend. Paul couldn't read Satan's mind! Paul was simply saying that, unlike others, such as those who are unsaved, Christians are aware of the kingdom of darkness and some of the schemes and snares that are laid to trap us.

Satan influences man's thinking and controls unbelievers

> *In whose case the god of this world has blinded the minds of the unbelieving so that they might not see the light of the gospel of the glory of Christ, who is the image of God.* (2 Cor 4:4)

This verse indicates that Satan has the capacity to blind people's minds, preventing unbelievers from recognizing the truth of the gospel. That is a powerful capability. In the previous verses, we have seen Satan as reactive to the sin opportunities that present themselves in our lives. Now we see him in a more pro-active role; actively blinding the minds of people so that they are unable to receive the truth.

If you have presented the gospel to unbelievers, you may have been frustrated at times by their total indifference, lack of interest or arguments that are really very shallow or even irrational. You may have wondered what was happening in their minds. It is as though there are layers of reinforcing mesh that block the Word from even making it into their minds. It can be very disheartening. Satan has done a good job of blinding them to the truth. Based on the verse just quoted, we asked Jesus for a more effective way of praying for such 'blinded' people, and he gave us the following prayer. We have found it effective in praying for the unsaved, particularly relatives and close friends. The prayer goes:

> 'Jesus, can you please send a shaft of your light into the darkness of __________ *(person's name)* mind and illuminate the truth so that __________ *(person's name)* can clearly see the options laid before him/her'.

You can't ask Jesus to *make* the person choose him or change her mind from her current thinking. Jesus can't do that. He cannot and will not violate people's freewill choice. If he could, then there would be no one in hell because God could then change every person's mind to follow him. All you can do as a concerned believer for a non-believer that you love, is to ask God to make the choices as clear as he can for the person and then hope that the person makes the right decision. The reason we ask God to send a shaft of light is because the unbeliever has been blinded to the *light* of the gospel. Another reason is that John uses the metaphors of light and darkness throughout his gospel and epistles. Jesus is the Light of the world, and his Light has come into the darkness of the world. Light pierces the darkness, light illuminates.

Once again, based on experience of dealing with the kingdom of darkness, unfortunately it is not just unbelievers that Satan can blind the thinking of. Depending on the extent of the legal rights that the satanic kingdom has over the believer's life, he can affect our ability to recall and block our understanding so that we don't absorb all that God wants us to. We plateau far too soon.

Note that the phrase, 'god of this world' in the above verses doesn't indicate default authority of the whole world, like he had before the Cross. The 'world' in this context is the 'unbelieving world'.

The god of unbelievers
The following verses from John's first letter lend further weight to this interpretation that the term 'world' refers to the unbelieving world.

> *We know that no one who is born of God sins; but He who was born of God keeps him, and the evil one does not touch him. We know that we are of God, and that* ***the whole world lies in the power of the evil one.*** (1 John 5:18,19)

John is at pains in the first verse (v18) to say that believers are not under, in an authoritative sense, the deceptive power of the evil one, so the 'whole world' in the next verse must logically refer to unbelievers.

Satan, then, is the god of all who are unbelievers. Paul confirms this in the verse below:

> *In which you formerly walked according to the course of this world, according to the prince of the power of the air, of the spirit that is now working in the sons of disobedience.* (Eph 2:2)

Walking 'according to the course of this world' is 'walking according to the prince of the power of the air'. Paul is using the common writing technique of parallelism; restating the same thing more than once, or paraphrasing. This tool is used often in the Psalms. Here he restates the first part of the verse two more times within the same verse; each restating carries a slightly different nuance.

The following two verses reinforce the principle that those who oppose the truth are held captive by the devil.

> *with gentleness correcting those who are in opposition, if perhaps God may grant them repentance leading to the knowledge of the truth, and they may come to their senses and escape from the snare of the devil,* ***having been held captive by him to do his will.*** (2 Tim 2:25, 26)

This next verse also makes the same point.

> *...to open their eyes so that they may turn from darkness to light and* ***from the dominion of Satan*** *to God, that they may receive forgiveness of sins and an inheritance among those who have been sanctified by faith in Me.*
> (Acts 26:18)

Below, Paul echoes what Jesus called the Pharisees; sons of Satan, reinforcing the assumption that if you are not in the Kingdom of Light, then you are under the control of the kingdom of darkness. 'To make crooked the straight ways of the Lord' is another way of saying, 'putting darkness in the Light'.

> *And said, "You who are full of all deceit and fraud, you son of the devil, you enemy of all righteousness, will you not cease to make crooked the straight ways of the Lord?"* (Acts 13:10)

Satan's dominion is absolute over unbelievers. But he still has significant sway in the lives of Christians. Being able to lie to us and affect our heart decisions is a sobering reminder to believers not to become complacent.

> *But Peter said, "Ananias, why has* ***Satan filled your heart to lie*** *to the Holy Spirit and to keep back some of the price of the land?* (Act 5:3)

This is a clear example of Satan piercing through the breastplate and striking right at the heart of Ananias with unrighteous thoughts and deeds.

Thwarts God's plans

> *But we, brethren, having been taken away from you for a short while— in*

person, not in spirit—were all the more eager with great desire to see your face. For we wanted to come to you—I, Paul, more than once—and yet Satan hindered us. (1 Th 2:17,18)

If Satan was actively hindering Paul, we can assume Paul was hearing from the Holy Spirit regarding going to the Thessalonians. Why didn't God intervene?. There were obviously enough legal rights for Satan to thwart Paul's intentions.

We often ignore Satan's ability to block God's plans for our lives today. Ironically, Christians often attribute to God what is actually the work of Satan. We fall into the same trap as Job. When we think we have heard from God, and pursue the direction we believe God is leading us in, and then obstructions come, we frequently say, 'God must have closed the door.'

Does God close the door?
Only once in Scripture is there any reference to God opening or closing doors.

He who is holy, who is true, who has the key of David, who opens and no one will shut, and who shuts and no one opens, says this: (Rev 3:7)

It appears that this action of opening and closing a door has a certain finality about it. It is not something God does often, and it is irrevocable. The phrase, 'God closed the door' is not used anywhere else in Scripture. The only thing God 'closed' in the Bible is the flesh around the gap where Adam's rib was, the door of the Ark, the elements, such as the rain and the waters, and the wombs of women. That's it!

Behind the phrase 'God closed the door' is the thinking that God has shut off an opportunity that he had previously made available and that he did so simply for his own reasons. 'The mission was running well but then God closed the door on the finances'. 'I dated several men with the intention of getting married and none of the relationships worked out. God was closing the door on marriage'. Underlying this thinking is passive fatalism. 'I wanted to do something that was in accord with God's will but he changed his mind. Oh well, it's a shame, but he's God, he can do that'. This is not scriptural at all. God doesn't change his mind after he has told you to do something. If he tells you to do something and you fail, then God moves to another person or another plan to fulfill his purposes. The reason God changes his plan is because of our failure, not his unpredictable whims.

There are probably many reasons why the finances of the mission dried up and all of these will be related to the sinful actions of man and the legal rights they gave Satan. It has nothing to do with God suddenly deciding that he wants to end the mission and stop all the money flowing. God didn't close the door on this girl's desire to get married. God gives us the desires of our heart when they are in accord with his will and it is his will that man should not be alone. If someone wants to get married, they don't have to pray and fast to find out whether it is God's will or not! Having decided that she would like to get married and having several failed relationships is not a sign that God doesn't want her to get married. It is a sign that she has issues regarding her ability to choose suitable men or to maintain relationships. The demise of her relationships should be used as an indicator of sinful attitudes and dysfunctions in her, rather than an indicator that God doesn't want her married.

If King Saul was writing his autobiography using today's 'Christian speak', he would probably say, 'God opened the door for me to be become King and I thought that, overall, I did a good job but then God closed the door and gave the job of King to David'. Today, many Christians would translate 1 Thes.2:18, just quoted, as,

> 'For we wanted to come to you—I, Paul, more than once—and God has closed the door'.

We have had people go to a lot of effort to fill out all the forms necessary to come to our three month training school. In these forms, they explain why they believe God has led them to attend the school. Even their pastors have had to fill out a form and confirm that, in their opinion, this person is suitable to do the school. When they cannot make it to the school because the money hasn't come or there has been a problem in their domestic circumstances, they invariably say, 'God has closed the door'. The truth is that the kingdom of darkness has successfully distracted or thwarted them. If God told them to go, which option is more likely; that God has changed his mind or that Satan has successfully blocked God's intentions through affecting finances and family relationships? We serve a double-minded God if the former is correct!

When circumstances appear to be favourable, lining up and meshing with the direction in which we are heading, we can quickly assume it is God's signal or approval to go ahead. It may be. Too often we don't exercise the necessary caution and question whether it is the satanic kingdom that is making the way smooth so that it can achieve its own ends. A common example is when Christian ministries or churches grow at a rate far faster than the leaders have the experience and maturity to handle. Satan has a vested interest in seeing a Christian endeavour peak too early and then collapse. God is always more interested in character development than in numbers and outcomes achieved. God is more concerned with slow and steady growth that is grounded in love and intimacy between the members than he is with outward appearances or a high profile. It is in Satan's interest to engineer smooth sailing in a certain direction if that direction is God's second best. Timing is very important and we often pay too little attention to it.

There is an example of poor timing regarding evangelism in the life of Paul.

> *They passed through the Phrygian and Galatian region, having been forbidden by the Holy Spirit to speak the word in Asia; and after they came to Mysia, they were trying to go into Bithynia, and the Spirit of Jesus did not permit them; and passing by Mysia, they came down to Troas.* (Act 16:6,7)

The Holy Spirit clearly told Paul not to preach the gospel in Asia Minor. The four regions mentioned are in Asia Minor. It appears that Paul was blatently disobedient. Alternatively, he may have been so eager to spread the gospel that he forgot what the Holy Spirit had said. Maybe Satan tempted him: 'After all, isn't spreading the gospel *always* what God wants. Maybe you heard God wrong, Paul. God *surely* loves them as much as anyone else'. The point is Paul failed and God had to intervene. Nice idea Paul, good motive, bad timing. Notice that this is not an example of God closing the door. The door was never opened by God to begin with. This could have been the legal right Satan later used to stop him entering Thessalonica when it was God's will. It was obviously important enough to God for him to block Paul's disobedience and you can be sure that Satan took note.

In my opinion, the phrase, 'God opened/closed the door' should be banned or used extremely cautiously among believers. In many or most cases, it is likely to be untrue and God will subtly be blamed; once again, darkness in the Light. The real offender will more frequently be the kingdom of darkness and our own sinful responses. A changing circumstance is more likely to reflect a blockage from Satan or a lack of tenacity on our part than it is God closing the door. Of course, many God-directed projects or ventures will naturally run their course and finish but again that is quite different from God closing the door. Similarly, what we interpret as a green light to go ahead could reflect presumption and a lack of forethought and wise caution rather than God opening the door.

What underlies this kind of thinking are the foundational assumptions of Calvin, who has had a lot of influence on Christian thinking. The base assumption is that God's sovereignty and control is so absolute that anything that happens must be God's own direct doing. As we have been at pains to point out throughout this book, such a viewpoint often attributes to God what is the work of the kingdom of darkness and non-believers, as well as sincere believers are left disillusioned and angry with a God who appears so cruel and whimsical.

Still does signs and wonders

In Exodus, we see Satan mimicking some of Moses miracles such as staffs turning into snakes. After the Cross, we still see him active in this way.

> *That is, the one whose coming is in accord with the activity of Satan, with all power and signs and false wonders,* (2 Th 2:9)

A spiritual termite

The scriptural references quoted in this chapter confirm the theme of this book; that Satan is alive and well. The Cross hasn't rendered him impotent and he still has all of the capabilities he had prior to the Cross. The major change is that in his daily interactions with believers, he can be resisted, if they recognize him. Although they can do this because of the indwelling presence of the Holy Spirit, the sad truth is that most Christians are unaware of the subtle attacks of the enemy and daily fall victim to his carefully laid snares. We think we are victorious and we develop a blasé verbal swagger that proclaims we are victorious but all the while the enemy is slowly eroding the very platform on which we are standing.

Satan cannot alter the fact that we stand on the platform of the finished work of the Cross. That platform is only as strong and secure as the foundations that support it. These foundations are; an open and receptive heart; a humble, non-judgmental attitude; a teachable and tenacious spirit. He can however gnaw away at the supporting structure so that over time our pride, self-righteousness, presumption, legalism, complacency, self-justification and self-satisfaction become more prominent in the platform's support. Left untreated, the increasing brittleness that these sinful attitudes bring, means the platform will eventually collapse. Instead of the rock-like virtues predominating, these shifty acidic vices eventually take over and turn the rock into sand.

> *Everyone who hears these words of Mine and does not act on them, will be like a foolish man who built his house on the sand. The rain fell, and the floods came, and the winds blew and slammed against that house; and it fell—and great was its fall.* (Matt 7:26,27)

SUMMARY

- Satan wasn't crushed at the Cross, simply bruised. Scriptures from Romans, Corinthians and Revelation confirm this assessment.
- The assertion of Satan's control over death has scriptural support in Revelation 2 and 6

- A roaring lion is an angry apex predator and is hardly powerless.
- He is deceptive, he sets snares.
- He knows when we are vulnerable.
- God uses or allows Satan to continue to discipline the saints. God allowed Satan to send a high level demon to Paul so that Paul's pride would not incur God's judgment.
- In like manner, Paul delivered others to Satan, for a time, to be disciplined by him.
- Satan can blind minds. In our experience, he is not limited exclusively to blinding only unbelievers.
- An effective prayer when praying for unbelievers is:
  'Jesus, can you please send a shaft of your light into the darkness of (name) mind and illuminate the truth so that (name) can clearly see the options laid before him/her'.
- Satan is the god of unbelievers. The phrase, 'The god of this world' refers to the unbelieving world. Unbelievers are under Satan's control.
- Satan can lie to believers and influence their hearts.
- Christians today frequently attribute to God what is actually the work of Satan. They do this by using the phrase, 'God closed the door' when in reality 'Satan blocked them'.
- Satan did signs and wonders in the Old Testament and he still does them today. The Cross hasn't changed that.
- Ironically, the more we dismiss Satan as a non-event and the more we proclaim our victory over him, the more likely we are to be increasingly under his control. When we are proud, dismissive, arrogant, brash and presumptive toward him, we play right into his hands because we are just like him.

Chapter 12: THE ARMOUR

You may have done it. I went through a brief phase of doing it because everyone was doing it. You may still be doing it. The practise of daily putting on the armour of God has been widely adopted by Christians around the world and many go through the motions of physically placing each piece of the armour on. It is perhaps the most popular passage of Scripture that is used to show that we are in a battle with Satan. It is probably one of the most misunderstood.

In the previous chapter, we looked at many post-resurrection Scriptures that built a profile of Satan still being an effective and dangerous adversary for Christians. Below we will look at just one passage of Scripture and see whether this adds to our understanding.

Too often, we follow what others are doing without stopping to think carefully through our responses. We don't apply reason and logic and therefore we adopt a formalized set of actions that we hope will magically protect us. Daily putting on the armour is really no different from the common Catholic and Orthodox practice of making the 'sign of the Cross' with my hands on head, shoulders and chest. It is no different to putting on a St Christopher medal around my neck for protection. It is a waste of time at best and superstitious at worst. It is an ineffectual exercise that has no spiritual impact on the satanic kingdom whatsoever and doesn't protect Christians from the enemy at all.

None of the items Paul exhorts us to put on are ever officially taken off so why do we bother to put them on each day? If they are never taken off, then they never need to be put back on. If we are to apply in a literal sense the 'Put ons' of Eph 6, then logically we should be daily doing the other 'Put ons' that the Bible also exhorts us to do. *'Put on the new self...'* is mentioned twice (Eph 4:24, Col 3:10) and *'..put on a heart of compassion, kindness, humility, gentleness and patience'* (Col 3:13) and two verses later *'..put on love...'* (Col 3:14). We don't hear of Christians daily putting on the new self and all these other character attributes!

> *Put on the full armor of God, so that you will be able to stand firm against the schemes of the devil. For our struggle is not against flesh and blood, but against the rulers, against the powers, against the world forces of this darkness, against the spiritual forces of wickedness in the heavenly places. Therefore, take up the full armor of God, so that you will be able to resist in the evil day, and having done everything, to stand firm.* (Eph 6:11-13)

Paul's use of the word 'struggle' means that we are not taking a nonchalant stroll down Easy Street when we deal with the devil! It is clear from Paul's soldier analogy he uses in the verses following these, that we are in a battle. How can we be in a battle if we have Jesus dwelling in us now and if greater is he that is in us than he that is in the world (1 Jn 4:4)?

Not position but outworking

The battle, or struggle, is in regard to the legal rights each Christian gives, on a daily basis, to the kingdom of darkness or the Kingdom of Light. Every action, whether active or passive, gives greater leverage to the satanic kingdom or the Kingdom of Light to affect our lives. While we fight from the *position* of being saved, because of the finished work of the Cross, what Paul is emphasizing is the daily struggle we all endure in the outworking of this salvation in our lives. This is the process of sanctification. Every day, many, many times a day, we have to make a choice to act against our natural inclination towards self-centeredness and choose selflessness. It is a battle! It is not easy! We fail a lot. Each time we fail, we give the satanic kingdom greater leverage to bring destruction and death into our life and family. Each time we succeed in dying to self, in being intimate and relational with each other, we give the Kingdom of Light greater leverage to bring to life, grace, blessing and peace. It is a two way street. It is the law of sowing and reaping.

Notice that our battle is not against earthly rulers and authorities. Paul doesn't mean that we shouldn't be fighting against pro-abortion legislation, euthanasia, gay rights, dictators etc. He means that *people* are not the issue; the issue is the principalities and powers influencing the people. Too often we make our battle with others a personal one; focusing on the individual, not separating the sin from the sinner, having a revenge focus, rather than stepping back and taking a look at the bigger picture. Paul wants us to take our focus off our brother and keep it firmly fixed on the bigger cosmic tussle that is affecting all our lives. He is exhorting us to look at ourselves and the way in which each of us gives leverage to the satanic kingdom, rather than concentrating on the splinter in our brother's eye. In this context, the verses regarding the armour make more sense.

> *Stand firm therefore, having girded your loins with truth, and having put on the breastplate of righteousness, and having shod your feet with the preparation of the gospel of peace. In addition to all, taking up the shield of faith with which you will be able to extinguish all the flaming arrows of the evil one. And take the helmet of salvation, and the sword of the Spirit, which is the word of God. With all prayer and petition pray at all times in the Spirit, and with this in view, be on the alert with all perseverance and petition for all the saints.* (Eph 6:14-18)

Paul means that if I want to protect myself against giving too many legal rights to the kingdom of darkness, I need to be paying attention to these nine areas: truth, righteousness, peace, faith, salvation, the Word, prayer, petition and perseverance.

A point not emphasized in any sermon I have heard is that the virtue or discipline mentioned is specific to the part of the body it is referring to.

Loins girded with truth

Loins refer to our sexual organs and their function.

> *All the persons who came from the loins of Jacob were seventy in number* (Ex 1:5)

To gird your loins literally means to protect your sexual organs. Cricketers today gird their loins with a protective box in case they are hit in that area with a speed ball. To a lesser extent, most people daily gird their loins with underpants! When Paul says, 'Gird your loins with truth' he means be truthful in the sexual area. The best protection sexually is to be truthful. Be open and honest. Seek help. Don't conceal and hide. This is a huge issue for most Christians, especially men. There is a lot of deception surrounding sexual sin. Surveys indicate that 85% of people lie about their sexual history to their partners and that more than half of regular church-attending men struggle with porn and masturbation. People often present an image of purity on the outside but it is quite different in reality. It is the sin we are most pharisaical about. We often don't walk what we talk. Sexual sin is the sin that is most frequently closeted. It is hard to find men, in particular, who have sexual purity and truthfulness. It is hard to find men that God can truly trust in this area. I am amazed at how many Christian women have been sexually abused as little children by their Christian fathers or relatives. Many of these dads scrub up well in the outward appearance stakes. From counselling experience, I can say without any doubt, it is the single biggest area of deception in people's lives. No wonder Paul's opening salvo is about sexual truth.

The covering of our loins is more than just truth in the sexual area. It applies to every area of our sexuality. It is truth in our identity as men and women; it is being truly masculine and feminine. The role of a male is to stand in the gap, to defend, to initiate, to be the first line of defense. He is to be the spiritual umbrella for his family, to provide secure leadership through servanthood, encouraging and calling each of his children into the security of their own masculinity and femininity, and laying down his life for his wife. Many men are not true to their calling; they are passive spiritually and underfunction emotionally. They dictate rather than serve and criticize rather than encourage. Because of this, women try to compensate and fail to express their femininity as God intended. Rather than providing the emotional security for the family, women then overfunction and carry far more of the family anxiety than God ever wanted them to. Because of their husband's passivity, which is sinful, they respond by taking more initiative than God intended and therefore sin through their over-reaction. They fail in their role as responder. Rather than being supportive of their husbands, they frequently align themselves with the children and leave their husbands isolated. Notice we are not talking about tasks. God is into flexibility regarding breadwinning and couples maximizing each other's strengths. He has no issues with women breadwinning or handling the family finances and men doing the cooking and cleaning. The roles related to our sexuality are independent of the tasks each partner does but are more about our attitude and focus.

Although the emphasis is on sexual truth, Paul doesn't mean that truth in our lives should be limited to the sexual area exclusively. God wants truthfulness in every area of our walk with him and, through Paul, he is drawing attention to our Achille's heel; sexual truth.

Girding your loins with truth is about sexual honesty and being truly masculine and feminine.

The breastplate of righteousness

The breastplate covers the heart and lungs. It covers the area that symbolizes *life*; our heartbeat and our breath. The heart also represents the seat of our emotions and symbolizes our deepest attitudes, drives and desires. The breastplate of righteousness refers to the heartfelt desire to serve God and pursue him. A person 'with a heart after God' is a person who wants to please Jesus with her whole being, to offer him her life. She is someone who really cares about what Jesus might think of a particular attitude; who won't do an action that she can get away with because she knows Jesus is watching and she doesn't want to break intimacy with him. Such a person speaks the truth, in love, and doesn't people-please. She truly desires the very best for others. Her heart rejoices in another's success and is not envious. She wants to see people and situations from God's perspective, with his eyes. She has a heart of compassion that can separate the sin from the sinner and give grace without rescuing. Now that is a truly righteous person; a person with no self-righteousness. Because her heart is in the right place, she doesn't condemn or judge or distance from others. It is easy to see righteousness as only something that is given to us because we are believers rather than it being also a heart attitude that must be developed. If God has our hearts, he has us. Sadly, among Christians, these people are rarer than most of us would like to think. For many, there is no protective breastplate.

Putting on the breastplate means checking our heart attitude.

Our feet and the gospel of peace

Feet symbolize our walk, the direction we are going in life. Uniquely, Christianity is a gospel of peace. A gospel of peace between man and God, peace between man and man.

> *For He Himself is our peace, who made both groups into one and broke down the barrier of the dividing wall, by abolishing in His flesh the enmity, which is the Law of commandments contained in ordinances, so that in Himself He might make the two into one new man, thus establishing peace, and might reconcile them both in one body to God through the Cross, by it having put to death the enmity.* (Eph 2:15,16)

It is so radically different from other belief systems in that its emphasis is on forgiveness instead of revenge. It is not about getting even, an eye for an eye; justice done from my perspective. It is about choosing to release my right to judge another, even though I have every right to judge the person because he has offended me. There are many Christians for whom bitterness is a big issue. Bitterness is accumulated unforgiveness and there is no peace. You hold on to the situation and replay it in your mind. This leads to an internal tension that expresses itself in a variety of ailments such as arthritis. Paul knew how important this issue was and how the enemy would use it to sidetrack our walk.

But the gospel of peace is more than forgiveness, much more than racial harmony. The gospel of peace is not passive. The feet move. It is the feet that carry us into the heat of battle. It is about facing issues head on and wrestling with them until they are resolved. It is not for wimps! Our feet shod with the gospel of peace is about a walk characterized by *peacemaking* and not *peacekeeping*. Peacekeepers keep warring factions apart, with the pretense of peace. Peacemaking engages in the difficult aspects of conflict resolution so that a true peace can be formed. Peacekeepers patrol the borders of hostile countries preventing these warring nations from destroying each other. Peacemakers meet for joint discussion to resolve outstanding issues that separate these nations. True peacemakers will wrestle and debate the issue, listen to the other party, compromise or approach the problem from another perspective, until there is a resolution. Peacekeeping leads to the pretence of intimacy, peacemaking leads to true intimacy. Unfortunately, we are very good at being peacekeepers. Peacekeeping means that at family gatherings we don't talk about *that* issue because it will offend so and so. Satan knows true intimacy between believers is their greatest weapon against his kingdom. He also knows fear of conflict is one of the biggest phobias people have.

Being shod with the gospel of peace is about being a true peacemaker.

The shield of faith

The first thing the enemy sees in battle is your shield. It is your largest piece of equipment and your first and greatest line of defense. You are most vulnerable when the enemy has got past your shield. The first thing that the satanic kingdom sees when it evaluates a believer is her faith. A strong faith makes penetration difficult. The words 'faith' and 'trust' are interchangeable. Christianity is all about trust. I *trust* God when he said that Jesus was his Son. I *trust* God when he said Jesus died on the Cross and rose from the dead. I *trust* God when he says the Holy Spirit lives in me. I *trust* God when I ask him for guidance that he will speak and I will hear his voice. I *trust* God when I exercise the gifts of the Holy Spirit that he will speak and move through me The shield of faith means exercising the faith described in Hebrews, chapter 11, following the examples described and realizing that I can't please God without faith.

> *And without faith it is impossible to please Him, for he who comes to God must believe that He is and that He is a rewarder of those who seek Him.* (Heb 11:6)

Satan's arrows then are attacks targeting our trust and confidence in God; in who God is and what he says. 'Did God really say…' is what Satan said to Eve and still says to us every day. Once he gets us doubting God, then we only have ourselves to rely on, and because deep down we know we fail, this leads eventually to fear. The opposite of faith is fear, and fear always portrays a lack of trust in God. There are so many fears and phobias that hinder Christians from completing God's will for their lives, hence Satan's arrows are more successful than most of us would like to admit. Perhaps the biggest reason for people failing to complete God's will for their lives is not the mistakes they make but the fear of making the mistakes. It is not the sins of commission but the sins of omission.

The shield of faith, then, is a bedrock trust in God that does not give in to fear.

The helmet of salvation

Where the heart represents our attitude and desire toward God, the head represents our ability to remain true or steadfast to the heart's commitment. Double-*mindedness* leads to instability. Double-mindedness undermines. The helmet of salvation means having a balanced understanding regarding our salvation. It is being comfortable with the tension that exists between both *being saved* and *working out* our salvation. Satan is very successful at casting doubt in the minds of so many Christians regarding their salvation. This double-mindedness reduces their effectiveness as a tool in God's hands. Many Christians struggle with a confidence that they are saved. While God doesn't want an arrogant presumption of our salvation that leads to pride and passivity, equally he doesn't want fear and unbelief to lead to a manic drivenness or a sense of giving up. He wants us to be plumb-lined, straight down the middle, not on the extremes of the pendulum swing.

SALVATION PENDULUM

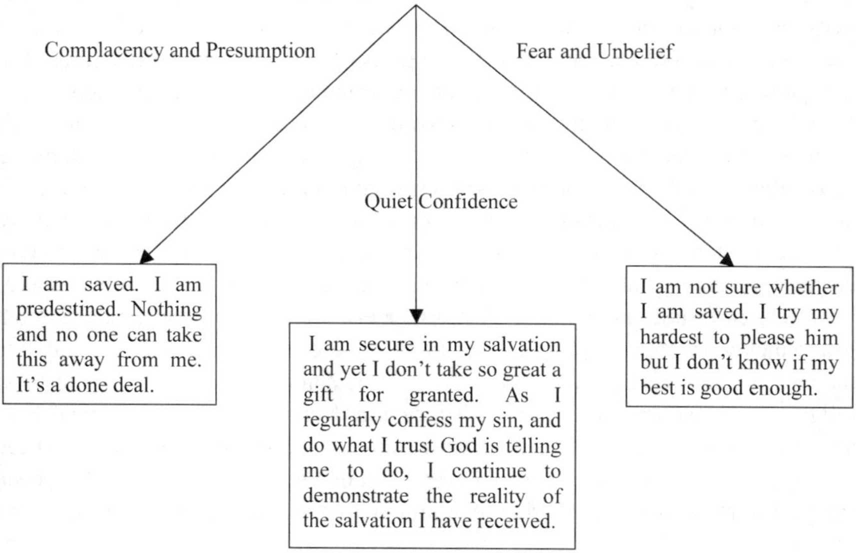

The helmet of salvation is about confidence in our salvation without presumption.

The sword of the Spirit

The sword is the offensive weapon. It is what attacks and does damage. It is held by the hands. Hands represent work and service. The sword of the Spirit represents works done that are Holy Spirit directed, not self-effort driven. Following on from the previous paragraph, often our work and service is anxiety driven or done in our own strength. We may verbally give God the glory but in reality he has had little to do with it. *We* did it. There wasn't really a partnership. We weren't really listening to what he wanted to do. We did it our way and asked him to rubber stamp it at the end. That is why all our works will be tested by fire and only those that were truly Holy Spirit directed will stand the test.

> *Each man's work will become evident; for the day will show it because it is to be revealed with fire, and the fire itself will test the quality of each man's work. If any man's work which he has built on remains, he will receive a reward. If any man's work is burned up, he will suffer loss; but he himself will be saved, yet so as through fire.* (1 Cor 3:13-15)

Too often, we think of the sword of the Spirit as the written Word of God. We think it is memorizing and quoting Scripture. While these can be useful disciplines, what Paul means in this context is the *whole word of God.* It is everything God says. It is awareness of his total revelation of himself to us without getting pedantic and making majors out of minors. It is getting the balance right. The difference between a good sword and a bad sword is usually in its balance. Chef's knives are the same. A well-balanced knife is easier to handle and cuts more efficiently. It is not quoting Scripture in a legalistic manner to bring condemnation on others. It is a knowledge and understanding of God's word, that contributes to our work and walk through a balanced maturity. There is gratitude, grace, compassion, understanding, reconciliation and peace when the sword is used to protect and defend. Yet there is an incisive thrust, as necessary, to bring conviction and deal swiftly, but thoroughly, with sin in all its forms; in our own lives first and then in the lives of those who give us permission to speak. Minor components of the sword of the Spirit are prayer, intercession, fasting and tongues. Unfortunately, we so often associate these four disciplines with spiritual warfare and think we are making incisive inroads into the enemy's ranks when we use them. Satan is happy with us engaging in these religious exercises provided we don't look too deeply at our own personal lives and sinful heart attitudes. It is not that we shouldn't pray, intercede, fast or speak in tongues. These all have their place and can be very effective tools. However, spiritual warfare is less about what we *do* but more about our heart attitude and who we *are*.

The sword of the Spirit is about a balanced maturity in our lives. It is recognizing that God's word is much more than the Bible. It is not just what is said but *how* it is said, *when* it is said, if it needs to be said and the heart attitude behind the words.

An effective Christian

The following are features that characterize a Christian who will be effective as an instrument against the kingdom of darkness:

(1) Must truly love God; be soft and teachable, have a heart of compassion and yet fear offending God more than man.
(2) Needs to be secure in her salvation.
(3) Must trust God and be sure, acting quickly when God speaks. Exercises faith with a firm assurance but not a blasé presumption.
(4) Keeps short accounts, forgives easily and extends forgiveness without rescuing and people pleasing. A true peacemaker who is not afraid of conflict.
(5) Waits on the Holy Spirit for guidance and direction without being driven by the task. She has a mature and balanced understanding of the word of God.
(6) Is discreet, but open to enquiry, about every aspect of her sexuality - masturbation, porn, thought life, affairs, sexual activity. These have been worked through to a point that they are not an issue. One who doesn't make the opposite sex feel uncomfortable, is aware that masculinity and femininity are far more encompassing than a strictly sexual emphasis and who functions in this role sensitively.
(7) Prays frequently but it is not obvious because she is too busy being present in the moment and yet she is in close connection with God. Perseveres when the going gets tough and persists when others give up. Yet she knows the difference between tenacity and stubbornness. She has a sober realization of how easy it is to move into self-satisfaction and complacency and let the enemy in.

Each of the first six points represents one of the pieces of armour. In the order above, they are (1) the breastplate, (2) the helmet, (3) the shield, (4) shod feet, (5) the sword, (6) the loins. Each of these six points are major areas of attack where Satan is highly effective.

Such an individual is a rare commodity. It shows you just how effective the enemy is in doing what he does.

Challenge
We need to move away from treating this passage as an exercise we must do; a set of hoops to jump through, some magical means of protection. Instead, we need to see this as a very sober warning of important attitudes and reactions that require constant guarding, lest we give the enemy too much of a foothold and fail to persevere. We might paraphrase it as: Be true, pure, peaceful, faithful; know the fullness of your salvation; wield the Word in a balanced manner, sensitive to the Spirit's leading.

Finally Paul says,

With all prayer and petition, pray at all times in the Spirit, and with this in view, be on the alert with all perseverance and petition for all the saints. (Eph 6:18)

This last verse is not separate from the previous six pieces of armour and is the seventh characteristic mentioned in the list above. This last verse describes the attitude God wants us to have towards these six pieces of armour. He wants us to be alert for defensive lapses in any of these areas. He wants us to persevere in these attitudes and behaviours and to intercede, asking for his grace, not only for ourselves but for others. In my own personal life, Satan usually 'gets me' after I have had a victory against him, let my guard down and relax. He never relaxes. He will counteract and take advantage of my slackness. Paul uses the word 'all' four times in this last part of the armour passage. There is no sense of complacency or bravado in this last sentence. It is hardly the exhortation of a person who has a dismissive approach to his enemy.

On the contrary, Paul is only too well aware of Satan and what he can do. Keep in mind that Paul was in prison awaiting his execution at the time he wrote Ephesians. It was towards the end of his life. There is no doubt that he was constantly being reminded of the demon Satan had sent him and that God had refused to remove.

He knew only too well how the enemy could penetrate our armour.

SUMMARY

- The armour of God cannot and should not be physically 'put on'.
- It is a passage of Scripture emphasizing that it is the kingdom of darkness, not people, that are our real enemy.
- So often we want to make *people* the issue, not the spiritual agenda driving the people.
- The need to wear the full armour of God is redundant if Satan is powerless.
- The applications of the verses on the armour are best interpreted

in the context of legal rights. The battle, or struggle, is in regard to the legal rights each Christian gives, on a daily basis, to the kingdom of darkness or the Kingdom of Light.

- While we fight from the *position* of being saved, what Paul is talking about is the outworking of this salvation in our lives. This is the process of sanctification.

- The part of the anatomy that the armour is linked to has a spiritual parallel.
  e.g.: Loins – sex and sexuality
  Breastplate – heart
  Helmet – mind
  Feet – walk
  Hand (holding the sword) – work
  Shield – covers everything

- The spiritual parallel coupled with the associated virtue is where the focus needs to be.
  Gird loins with truth – sexual honesty, not deception.
  Breastplate of righteousness – a heart that really wants to please God, a heart that is righteous in God's sight.
  Helmet of Salvation – no double-mindedness regarding our salvation. Confidence without presumption.
  Shield of Faith – our strong faith and trust in God is our first and best defense. It is also the first area Satan will attack. 'Did God really say…?'
  Feet shod with the gospel of peace – our walk through life needs to be characterized by forgiveness not bitterness, peacemaking not peacekeeping.
  Sword of the Spirit which is the Word of God – our work for the kingdom is balanced, Holy Spirit led, without the Word being used inappropriately. God's word is much more than the Bible.

- Alertness, perseverance and petitioning are the attitudes that should accompany the implementing of the armour. The use of the word 'all' four times implies no complacency, no excuse for slackness, otherwise Satan wins. If he pierced Paul's armour, where do you stand?

Chapter 13:
SATAN'S CONTROL OVER HOW LONG PEOPLE LIVE

This is a tough chapter. Already the title has raised the hackles of some of you! Fasten your seat belts, this could be a rough ride!

In the example of Job, we saw how Satan had sufficient legal rights to kill Job's servants and children. Job incorrectly attributed these actions to the Lord but they were directly attributable to Satan. Satan, however, was acting within the legal rights system God had created.

In the New Testament, Jesus acknowledges that Satan has the ability to steal, to kill, to destroy. Using the analogy of himself as the Good Shepherd, Jesus' reference to the thief is commonly interpreted as symbolic of Satan.

> *The thief comes only to steal and kill and destroy; I have come that they may have life, and have it to the full.* (Jn 10:10)

That Jesus has come to give us life doesn't mute or nullify Satan's efforts. Satan continues, to this day, in his capacity to rob, kill and destroy. Jesus, in response, has given us tools, such as his indwelling presence, his authority, gifts, grace and the exchanges he made on our behalf at the Cross, so that we can counter Satan's actions. Satan *continues* to steal, kill and destroy and Jesus *continues* to give his life to believers, provided they draw on these resources he has made available. One important aspect of Satan's agenda is to kill us prematurely, robbing us from completing the full life God had intended for each of us.

We have seen that the Cross hasn't affected the fact that we all die. Hence, the same legal rights that enabled Satan to cause the death of people before the Cross still apply after the Cross. Except for the instances where God's judgment falls directly upon man, God is not directly responsible for when any of us die. Satan is. Satan and the kingdom of darkness are directly responsible for the deaths of most humans today, including Christians.

When a baby dies of SIDS (Sudden Infant Death Syndrome), it is because Satan has decided to end her life. When a young child dies of leukemia, it is the satanic kingdom that has decided he should die. Satan's kingdom, not God's, is the one that activates the sickness that ends the child's life. When the young mother, who loves Jesus, dies of cancer leaving behind a distraught husband and three young children, it is Satan who decided that she would die. Not God. Anyone who dies early in life, dies prematurely. It is not God's intention that the person die. Anyone who says that the person fulfilled God's plan for his short life is not speaking from God's perspective. This may come as a shock to many Christians but it makes a lot of sense when we think this through. Satan wants us to blame God for early deaths and, in so doing, keep his ability to kill and destroy very quiet as well as create confusion in our minds. How often have we heard of people becoming disillusioned with Christianity because they can't believe in an 'all loving God' who would 'take a baby home to himself' or allow famines, earthquakes, tsunamis and the bloodshed of war?

It answers one of the most perplexing questions; why does God choose to end the life of little babies, young children, young mums and dads? He doesn't. It is such a relief to realize that he doesn't! He doesn't call them back to himself because they have achieved their purpose on earth. It is God's desire that all people reach a ripe old age. If they die before this, it is because there are sufficient legal rights for Satan to take their lives. If we adopt the belief that God decides when we die, we are left feeling powerless and out of control of our lives. We just have to wait till our number is up. We have nothing to hope for but a fatalistic resignation that we could die at any moment. It is written in the stars, so to speak. It appears to be some random act of God, for reasons known only to God. We can't answer the question, 'Why does God choose to take this young father who loved the Lord and was such an evangelist but not take this other person who is doing so much damage to God's kingdom?'

Is my lifespan set in concrete?

Part of the fatalism common in Christian thinking is due to the misconception that God has ordained an inflexible number of days for each person. Psalm 139 is often quoted to support this notion.

Your eyes have seen my unformed substance; and in Your book were all written the days that were ordained for me, when as yet there was not one of them. (Ps 139:16)

The most popular interpretation of this verse is that each person has a unique number of days assigned to him; each person's allotment is different from the next person's. Before any of us were created, God allotted a set number of days for each person. This allotment is a sealed, done deal.

Such an interpretation contradicts many other verses which imply that each of us has control over the length of our lives. A more accurate understanding, one consistent with the rest of this Psalm and other Scriptures, is that this verse is simply highlighting God's foreknowledge; God knows the beginning from the end and everything in between. The Psalm begins by David saying that God knows my coming in and my going out, when I sit and when I rise, because God knows everything about me from the moment I was fearfully and wonderfully created in my mother's womb to the time when I die. Knowing what happens to us is quite different from *determining* what happens to us. God knows what the outcome of every person's life will be but that is quite different to believing God fatalistically assigns the set number of days each of us will live. The context of the rest of Psalm 139 does not allow that conclusion to be drawn. God has the same number of days allotted to *every* human. The number of days that God wants us all to live are not ordained in the sense that God *planned* for some to live short lives and others to live long lives. There is not a set-in-concrete, immutable, unchangeable predetermined aspect to them.

Scripture is very clear that the days of our lives may be shortened or prolonged dependant on our obedience to the Lord. In other words, the length of our lives is flexible; dependent on the weighting of legal rights given either to the Kingdom of Light or the kingdom of darkness.

A leader who is a great oppressor lacks understanding, but he who hates unjust gain will prolong his days. (Pr 28:16)

But You, O God, will bring them down to the pit of destruction;
Men of bloodshed and deceit will not live out half their days. (Ps 55:25)

Honor your father and your mother, that your days may be prolonged in the land which the Lord your God gives you. (Ex 20:12)

He has weakened my strength in the way; He has shortened my days. I say, 'O my God, do not take me away in the midst of my days'. (Ps 102:23,24)

For by me your days will be multiplied, and years of life will be added to you. (Pr 9:11)

If you listen carefully to what he says and do all that I say, ... none will miscarry or be barren in your land. I will give you a full life span. (Ex 23:22a,26 NIV)

My son, do not forget my teaching, but keep my commands in your heart, for they will prolong your life many years and bring you prosperity. (Pr 3:1,2)

So that you and your son and your grandson might fear the Lord your God, to keep all His statutes and His commandments which I command you, all the days of your life, and that your days may be prolonged. (Deut 6:2)

If you walk in My ways, keeping My statutes and commandments, as your father David walked, then I will prolong your days. (1 Ki 3:14)

When these verses are collectively interpreted within a legal rights context, they support the major premise of this chapter. The more legal rights we give to Satan, the more likely we are to have our lives shortened. The more legal rights we give to the Kingdom of Light, the greater the leverage for God to fulfill our allotted days and even prolong them. Therefore, the length of our lives, to a large extent, is really under *our* control. The key point to keep in mind is that it is never *God's intention* that any of us should die before we reach a ripe old age.

'Prime Minister Satan'

It appears from some of these Scriptures quoted above that it is God who lengthens and shortens our lives not Satan.

We has seen that it was never *God's desire* or *intention* that Satan's angels come down to earth and have sex with women, but there were enough legal rights in Satan's favour that God *allowed* this to happen. God's final consent must be given before Satan can act and in that sense and only in that sense is God responsible for what Satan does. Like the Queen in England, the Governor General in Australia must give his consent before parliamentary legislation comes into force. The Governor General may not personally agree with a particular decision of parliament, but he acknowledges that it is the desire of the people through their elected representatives. Officially, the Governor General is responsible for the new legislation but in reality it is the people who have decided. In the same way, God is officially responsible for the lengthening and shortening of our lives, which is what these verses above are saying. What really happened is that Adam elected 'Prime Minister Satan' and his large 'house majority' to govern us and it is Satan that makes the real decisions concerning the length of our lives. While the Cross overturned Adam's official vote, we still individually cast votes for Satan daily and his power base is almost as strong as it was before the Cross. At times the Governor General can and does override parliament as Australia experienced in 1975 when John Kerr, the then Governor General dismissed Gough Whitlam, the serving Prime Minister. Similarly, God can and does override Satan's desires concerning the lives of particular individuals. Unlike parliament, where such overrides are rare, he does intervene and exercise his sovereign authority often. Nonetheless, it is still important to remember that these vetos are much less frequent than we would like to believe.

Although these human analogies are helpful, they all commit the error of reductionism; reducing a complex issue into a form that is too simple. The legal rights system is a spiritual, multi-level concept. In reality, God is not as passive as the Governor General or the Queen is in the human process. He is actively working in 'parliament' on our behalf and helping us as much as he is able, within our freewill choices, to store up enough good legal rights that he can use to influence the final decision in the legislature. At the same time, he is the Governor General and again wants to influence that final decision, in our favour, if he can.

'I have called you back to myself'

Let's refrain from saying, at funeral services in particular, that God was well pleased with a life ended early or that the person had fulfilled God's call for her life. This, sadly, is no more than wishful thinking. Some readers may feel affronted. Perhaps you had a child who died early and you asked the Lord why and you honestly believe you heard God reply,

> 'I called him to myself.'
> 'Her life was complete.'
> 'He achieved my purposes.'
> 'Her time was up.'
> 'Only the good die young.'

You think you must have heard the Lord since this response has given you a measure of comfort and solace in the midst of your grief. The truth is you have simply provided your own solution to your own anxieties. It's an understandable reaction that all of us are guilty of doing, from time to time, as we try to hear God's voice. Nail this as an absolute somewhere:

> God does not and will not call a young child, teenager or person in their prime to himself. It is never his *intended* will that people die early.

No child has ever completed God's will for her life. God always wants each and every person to live a full life. It is God's desire that we remove legal rights so that he can bless us with long lives. Of course there are some children that are born with severe physical and genetic disabilities and as a consequence will only live a matter of months or a few years. In such cases it is impossible for them to live out a full life and their early death is inevitable. Nonetheless, it is important to keep in mind that it was never God's intention that the child should be born so grossly compromised in her ability to live. As we saw in chapter 1, the world is in an increasing state of decay with genetic mutations multiplying and generational iniquity compounding. *We* are responsible for the mess we are in.

How long should we live?

So what is the number of days ordained for us? There are two Scriptures on this matter.

> *Then the Lord said, 'My Spirit shall not strive with man forever, because he also is flesh; nevertheless his days shall be one hundred and twenty years'.* (Gen 6:3)

> *As for the days of our life, they contain seventy years, or if due strength, eighty years,..* (Ps 90:10)

Which of these two apparently contradictory statements do we take? The Genesis version is a direct decree of God, whereas the Psalmist appears to be basing his statement on his observations on the length of life of those around him. From our observations today, more people are reaching 100 years of age than ever before and the upper limit appears to be 120 years. If you want to be diplomatic and take the average of 120 and 80, we get a nice round 100 years! For our current dispensation, prior to Christ's return, we can assume it is God's intention that everyone lives to be about 100 years old. However, this will change during the millennial reign. It will not be unusual for people to live many hundreds of years, like the pre-flood patriarchs. God, then, sets the upper limits of human lifespan for each dispensation but our personal actions and other legal rights will determine whether each of us will reach God's intended allotment.

A whimsical God?

A God who appears to act randomly is not the God that I have come to know. He is not one of the capricious gods from Greek mythology who manipulates men like pawns, in some big cosmic joke; deciding which one he will wipe out and which one he will leave. He is not the god of Islam where whatever happens is the 'will of Allah'. He is not the god of Hindus where I fatalistically subject myself to the whim of the particular god I am worshipping. It is easy to fall back on the safe reply that God's ways are mysterious. This is really just an excuse. It is a lame response that doesn't earn us any credibility with unbelievers. Are God's ways mysterious? Yes, many of them are. That is why he exhorts us to have faith; to trust him even when we don't understand. We will never get the full picture here on earth. Nevertheless, there is a whole lot more we can understand, that is reconcilable with Scripture, if we approach problems from a different perspective. We must do this if we are to provide a considered explanation to the unbeliever. Let us not commit intellectual suicide with fob offs that leave unbelievers thinking we are just as confused as they are.

A kingdom divided

God is for us! He is for life! He is the Way, the Truth and the Life. Scripture refers to death as an enemy of the Kingdom of Light.

> *The last enemy that will be abolished is death.* (1 Cor 15:26).

If God is for death and decides when we die, then death is not an enemy. If God decides when we die, it logically follows that he is in control of the sickness that leads to death. If that is the case, then he is working against himself when God acts as a healer. Jehovah Rophe, the 'God who heals', is the first aspect of his character he chose to reveal to the Israelites in the wilderness (Ex 15:26). When we open the gospels, we find Jesus invariably going to a healing, in the middle of a healing or coming from a healing. If Jesus was known for anything in his earthly ministry, it was his healing of disease and sickness.

> *You know of Jesus of Nazareth, how God anointed Him with the Holy Spirit and with power, and how He went about doing good and healing all who were oppressed by the devil, for God was with Him.* (Act 10:38)

He destroyed the devil's work in the Garden of Eden by his sinless life. He destroyed the devil's work whenever he encountered sickness in people's lives. Jesus made the point that a kingdom cannot be divided against itself (Mat 12: 26). If sickness were from God, why would God want to destroy the very thing he created? Many of the sicknesses Jesus healed had a demonic component. It is clear that sickness emanates directly from the satanic kingdom or as a result of the fact that all creation is in a state of decay due to the Fall. It doesn't come from the Kingdom of Light.

If God is responsible for when we die, then we all die according to God's will. That necessarily means that Martha and Mary's brother, Lazarus, as well as Jairus' daughter and the son of the widow of Nain, all died according to God's will. If this was the case, Jesus was working against God's will in raising these people from the dead! The Kingdom of Light becomes a kingdom divided against itself.

It's logical!

If sickness is established in our lives by the satanic kingdom, the logical follow-on is that our deaths are also under the control of the kingdom of darkness. A sickness that leads to death means the satanic kingdom can control when we die. We know that Satan can only act with the legal rights system God has set up. Therefore, he can only establish sickness in our lives if there are enough legal rights. The big question is how many legal rights are required to establish sickness? Much more about that in later books.

Some Christians believe that Jesus destroyed *all* the works of the devil when he died on the Cross. If that is the case, why do Christians get sick today? Why are they just as sick as non-believers? Why do Christians live no longer than non-Christians? We need to face these realities in our lives and try to reconcile them with the gospel message, rather than hold dogmatically to a theological viewpoint that doesn't reflect reality. We simply remain in denial; we bury our heads in the sand. We commonly believe that if we confess our sins, God forgives our sins and so there are no legal rights for the devil to use. If this were true, we would never get sick. But it can't be true because we do get sick. Hence, there must be legal rights that the satanic kingdom is able to use that are not removed by merely confessing our sins. We need to work backwards from our life experiences and read Scripture in that context.

Satan's control

Let's tease apart the application of Satan's control over our lives and the length of time we will spend on the earth. The next book will explore the seven categories of legal rights the devil uses to gain considerable control over our lives. Suffice to say that it doesn't take very long before Satan has sufficient legal rights to cause our death.

When a baby dies of SIDS, it can be because of a combination of some or all of the following legal rights: inherited generational iniquity; trauma in the womb and the baby's accompanying reactive vows; trauma at birth or in the weeks and months following; genetic predisposition (the fact that all of creation is in decay); the environment and the life style choices of the parents[1]. As we get older, other legal rights, such as the cumulative impact of personal sin, increase considerably the leverage Satan has over our lives. Further trauma compounds these legal rights. When a teenager suddenly dies of a brain haemorrhage, or gets cancer and dies, these additional factors come into play. Most deaths that result from sickness are the direct result of the satanic kingdom having sufficient legal rights to activate that sickness. If the truth were known, in most people's lives, there are enough legal rights for Satan to activate a wide variety of sicknesses and to kill most babies through SIDS if he chose to. Why doesn't he?

Why choose her?

Why does Satan target one person and not another? Why does he target *that* particular young mother of three young children to kill through cancer and not another mother? When dealing with an incredibly complex personality like Satan's, there is no formula or easy answer. Satan looks at the big picture. He is always looking at possible future ramifications. We have discovered, through counselling, that the kingdom of darkness has the ability to see the heart of a person and know how soft, teachable and committed to Jesus that person is.

Consider the example of a young mother who dies leaving three young children. Let's say Satan looks at the family of the young mother and sees one of her children with a tender heart towards Jesus, a strong faith with determination and a focus that impresses him. He sees the potential damage she could do against his kingdom as she matures and he is justifiably concerned. Looking at her father, he sees a somewhat passive, codependent person. The mother is well liked and the pillar of the family. Satan chooses to give her cancer, knowing that this may be the best way to derail this girl who has so much potential. With a weaker father left to hold the fort on his own, perhaps he will rail against God, just as Job's wife did, and the impressionable girl might be inclined to join her dad in giving up on God. Perhaps the girl will have difficulty reconciling how God could take her mummy, and become disenchanted with Christianity.

Let's assume there is no amazing child among the three children but instead Satan is concentrating on the church the family attends. The church is a young, growing church with a pastor who has a love and zeal for God, and a congregation that is open and teachable. The mother may be an important member of the church, well liked with a wonderful peace and grace about her. She has a mature stability that provides, for many others, a sort of anchor in the midst of all that is happening. Satan is aware that if she gets cancer, the whole attention of the church will be on her. He has a well developed set of legal rights regarding the establishment of cancer and he knows God will be unlikely to miraculously intervene because of how extensive the legal rights are. He knows that there will be some well-meaning, but ultimately presumptuous people in the church who are likely to use the gifts of 'prophecy' and word of 'knowledge' to declare that she will be healed. Everyone's hopes will be raised and they all agree that it will be a wonderful testimony for God and the church when she is healed. More prayer will be sent up as her health deteriorates and the declarations about her miraculous healing will continue. Of course, she will die and then, the part that Satan loves best, the internal questioning of many of the parishioners will begin.

> 'If God didn't answer those prayers, those earnest, heartfelt prayers, what prayers does he answer?'
>
> 'Where is God? Doesn't he care? Those poor children and their lonely, lost dad. How could God be so indifferent, so callous?'
>
> 'With all the prayer that went up for her that God didn't answer, what hope would there be for me if I get sick? I wasn't as well liked as her'.

Some will be stunned. Those who declared she would be healed will be embarrassed at best and devastated at worst. The father and his children, whose hopes were raised, will be bitterly disappointed. No, they will be shattered. The rest of the people will be confused. 'Didn't we hear from God?' 'Perhaps this is all a big game that we are playing'. Satan is quite happy with the results. One strategic death and the church has been dealt a body blow to their faith.

Aside from these two reasons, there can be any number of other scenarios; some obvious, some more subtle that Satan has in mind when he chooses to kill *this* young mum as opposed to *that* young mum. From Satan's perspective, she is little more than an expendable pawn in a cosmic chess game.

God is not passive

From God's perspective, she is a dearly loved member of his Body for whom his Son bled and died on the Cross to redeem. It is not his intention that this young mother should die so soon. Make no mistake; he is not passive in all of this. If Satan's focus is on the child with the extraordinary faith, God will be doing all he can, within the freewill choices the child exercises, to use this incident to build an internal resolve and steadfastness that will backfire on Satan. Rather than derailing her, God wants it to be a fire of refining that will temper her into an even more effective weapon against Satan in the long term. God wants her to turn to him and trust him in the midst of all the confusion, loss and pain.

If Satan's focus is the church, God will be using this to get the church to ask the hard questions and dig deeper to find the answers, rather than be satisfied with the glib fob offs that are so often given. What Satan intends for evil, God will turn around and use for good, *provided* people keep their focus on him. It was true for Job then, it is true for us today. What God really wants is the church to respond to the challenge of adversity and still remain true to him. Not in a manner that doesn't question or wrestle with him. He wants us to be Jacobs and Davids that argue, question, wrestle and even get angry with him. God wants us to be honest with him and not offer him religious platitudes that reflect a resignation and lack of thought. Instead, he wants us to be tenacious, to grapple, to use critical, incisive thinking that looks beneath the surface. If the church can do that, then there is hope. If they see Satan as the culprit and understand the legal rights system, they will then be able to minister far more effectively to the next person who is seriously ill. They will methodically eliminate the legal rights linked to that disease so that God can extend his grace more easily and heal.

Legitimate actions

A misconception common in Christianity today is that many or all of Satan actions are illegitimate. This belief assumes that everything Satan does has no legitimate basis and therefore he simply needs to be put in place or challenged and he will walk away 'with his tail between his legs.' The truth is that almost everything Satan does *has* to be legitimate. Satan cannot act on a capricious impulse and destroy or kill without having the necessary legal rights to do so. God would not allow that. Satan must act within the legal rights system God has ordained and, as a supreme legalist, you can be sure he will petition God whenever he can, to maximize these legal rights. If Satan could act illegitimately, then there is no doubt he would have wiped out all the apostles and associated followers immediately after the resurrection and thus torpedo the efforts of the early church to get established. If I was Satan, that is what I would have done.

Satan had legitimate control of the earth for 4000 years because Adam chose to obey Satan instead of God. The satanic kingdom had a legitimate right before the flood to have intercourse with women because all mankind was under his control. It was not what God wanted to happen but man had made his choice and that was an unfortunate consequence of choosing a malevolent dictator. Satan had a legitimate right to enter Judas, to sift Peter, to darken the earth for three hours. When Satan chooses to end the life of the much loved mother of the three young children mentioned above, he has the legitimate legal rights to do so. If he could act illegitimately, whenever he wanted, the world would be truly chaotic.

Satan is not in complete control all of the time

While sickness is the killer of most people, there are many other ways people die where the influence of the kingdom of darkness is not as direct. Some deaths result from our own freewill choices to behave recklessly. If I drive my car carelessly, crash it and die, it is not the direct intervention of the kingdom of darkness that caused my death. I *chose* to sin by driving recklessly. Extreme sports with high risk, such as BASE jumping, come into the same category. Deaths resulting directly from the freewill choices of others, whether accidental, such as medical mishap, or deliberate, such as murder, can have far less of a demonic component. Equally, such incidents could have a high degree of demonic control.

Suicide is more complex. More suicides than people realize are controlled by dissociative parts, some of which have been explained in my first book, *'The Forgotten Factor in Healing.'* In these cases, the person himself has diminished responsibility for his actions. In other cases, the dissociative control can be so strong that the person bears no moral responsibility for their own suicide. This will be explained in far more detail in the book, *'Darkness in the Light: Satan's Trojan Horse.'* In further cases, suicide is strongly driven by a demonic agenda, although the person retains the final decision as to whether or not to take his own life. Sometimes suicide is more knee jerk, reactionary and almost entirely under the control of the person's freewill choices. In such cases, the demonic factor is minor.

Do you mean the devil could miraculously save me?!

Although not in complete control in the situations mentioned above, Satan and his minions can still exercise a surprising degree of control even in apparently random accidents. In circumstances where the kingdom of darkness wants to keep a person alive, they have the ability to do this. Just as God can send his angels to protect and miraculously intervene in situations where one of his saints might otherwise die, the satanic kingdom can do likewise. If you were about to die in an accident or unforeseen tragedy, and the satanic kingdom deems that you would do more damage against God's kingdom by being alive, they can intervene to 'miraculously' save you when others around you die. If you are a believer, you will naturally attribute your escape to the powerful, rescuing hand of God when the opposite is actually true! Ironic, really. Your pride, presumption, arrogance, self-righteousness and judgmental attitude may well be heightened as a result of this escape and that is exactly what Satan wants to see happen. Satan's best weapons are not raving atheists but hypocritical Christians that inadvertently lead others astray.

When you make the paradigm shift in your thinking and recognize just how much influence the satanic kingdom has over death, it makes you question exactly which kingdom is at work when someone miraculously survives. You become a little more circumspect about quickly giving God the glory when you hear that another Christian survives in unusual circumstances. Because it is only God and the kingdom of darkness that can truly see the heart of a person, we often judge incorrectly on outward appearances. Sometimes it will be the Kingdom of Light that intervenes, sometimes the kingdom of darkness, sometimes it can be both.

How could both intervene? When a person is sitting on the fence spiritually but has a strong potential for either kingdom once they make a decision, then both kingdoms will have a vested interest in keeping that person alive. Both God's angels and fallen angels could be involved in keeping this person alive in circumstances that would ordinarily have killed him. At times, because God knows what Satan is thinking, he will use Satan's intervention to keep someone alive that he also wants alive. All the while Satan thinks this action is solely working his agenda. However, this situation happens rarely. Because of the strong legal rights that the kingdom of darkness has over all of us, God has limited ability to move in our lives to save us. Much more limited than most Christians realize.

Engineering circumstances

Alternatively, it is possible that if the satanic kingdom wants me dead quickly, demons could do this in a number of ways. They could distract me when driving and the crash causing my death would be directly due to their intervention rather than any reckless driving. This distraction could be a supernatural flash of light that temporarily blinds me. It could be the *appearance* of an animal or person in the middle of the road causing me to swerve. The distraction possibilities are numerous and varied. Most will look natural. Of course, no one else will know that.

Alternatively, they are able to engineer situations more often than we realize. They have limited, but still significant, control of external factors so that the load of timber on a truck travelling in front of you is compromised and an item falls off and smashes through your windscreen killing you. The satanic kingdom also has a measure of control over the direction of the falling timber. It is not totally a matter of gravity and natural forces.

When there are circumstances that appear unusual or freakish, don't discount the influence of the demonic. Recently we went on a bush walk to a waterfall and at the base of the falls was a plaque relating to several people who were killed by a falling tree. On the plaque it said that on a clear, windless day, a large tree toppled over and landed directly on these people; the only people in the area, and killed them. Highly unusual occurrences need to be questioned. Sometimes we may be too quick to write off such incidents as bad luck or coincidence.

Steve Irwin

The kingdom of darkness can take control of animals. Satan's use of the serpent wasn't limited to the Garden of Eden. While animals have a measure of unpredictability, when they act completely out of character and someone is killed, consider the influence of the demonic as a factor. A high profile example that most readers will have heard about is the death of Steve Irwin, the crocodile hunter. He was swimming with stingrays in a quiet, non-intrusive manner and the stingray below him arched its tail and the barb directly pierced Steve's heart. As a keen snorkeler, I have encountered stingrays several times. They are non aggressive animals whose first instinct is flight rather than fight. Injuries from stingrays happen when you directly stand on them, not when you merely swim above them. Reports repeatedly used the phrase, 'a freak accident'. Those who viewed the video footage said there was no provocation by Steve of the stingray at all. Stingrays don't attack without a reason. It is completely uncharacteristic for the stingray to do what it did. However, if the kingdom of darkness wanted Steve Irwin eliminated for whatever reason, then inhabiting a stingray and carefully directing the barb to his heart is not difficult for them to do. Step back, question and consider another alternative instead of simply going with the standard stock explanations or calling it a freak accident.

Despite the fact that it wasn't God's intention that Steve Irwin die when he did and in the manner that he did, it doesn't mean that God has been passive throughout all of this. What has come to light since his death, is how well liked he was world-wide and how influential, for good, his life has been. There is a congruence with Steve, regarding his public persona and who he was naturally, that is rare among celebrities. He loved life and all aspects of it. He was a wonderful example of a family man who put family first despite all the demands on his time. Whenever his family needed him, no matter what he was doing, he made them the priority. Television crews would have to wait while he gave his attention to Bindi or Bob. This has spoken volumes to many men around the world. Steve Irwin has left a legacy far beyond that of man with a good rapport with animals.

Peter Brock

A few days after Steve Irwin died, another famous Australian was also killed. Peter Brock, Australia's most well known motor racing driver, known as 'Peter Perfect' for his almost machine like consistency when driving, was killed in a rally in Western Australia. He lost control on a bend, and the car moved sideways into a tree, the car absorbing the impact on the driver's side. The interesting thing was that the corner on which he was killed was not particularly difficult to negotiate. Other drivers of lesser renown and skill had handled it easily. The accident was totally unexpected. In the car was the equivalent of an aircraft's black box that recorded speed and driving patterns. It didn't indicate that Peter was speeding or driving in a manner that would make the car behave in the way it did. His performance throughout the race and at this particular bend was as measured and consistent as it always was. In fact, his co-driver, Mick Hone, said Peter had been driving 'brilliantly' before the crash. There was no mechanical failure that contributed to the accident. The accident is a mystery. Demons can take the momentum of the car and exert force to swing it hard to one side. In trying to correct and regain control, the demons can now exert pressure in the opposite direction, making the car leave the road and they can direct the momentum quite specifically, steering the car so that Peter takes the full brunt of the tree and is killed. Two famous Australians; household names, killed, three days apart. Coincidence?

Some readers may react to the last two examples, thinking that demons are used as the cause or explanation for everything! That is not the case. Many accidents have plausible explanations free from overt demonic interference. But when an accident defies adequate explanation or has highly unusual aspects to it, then we need to think outside of the square. Not to consider the satanic kingdom is to buy into the usual Christian bravado that Satan is no longer an issue. Such thinking is presumptuous and dangerous. The kingdom of darkness *is* an issue in almost every aspect of our lives, whether we are Christians or not.

Haphazard

Sometimes demons can incite other people to kill a person they want removed. In Job we saw how Satan incited the Sabeans who attacked and put Job's servants to the sword. Major catastrophes such as tsunamis, earthquakes, the collapse of the World Trade Centre in New York and the atom bomb dropped on Hiroshima, are all examples of people dying in large groups without being individually selected. Satan may have initiated a tsunami, but he couldn't be as selective as he would have liked regarding who lived and who died.

Is long life a blessing from God?

Another aspect of Satan's ability to control the length of our lives that is overlooked by Christians, is the issue of longevity. Frequently we assume that if a person lives to a ripe old age, relatively free from sickness, that they are enjoying the blessing of God. Sometimes that is the case, but more often than Christians realize, longevity is the result of Satan choosing to keep these people alive for his purposes.

Take the issue of non-believers first of all. Non-believers live just as long as believers. There is no statistical support for the premise that Christians live longer than non-Christians. There is evidence that religious beliefs have a positive effect on our health and may have an impact, to a limited extent, on longevity but that includes *all* religious beliefs, not specifically Christianity[1]. If long life is predominantly a sign of God's blessing on a person, a blessing resulting from a righteous Christian life, then logically there should be far more old people who are Christian than non-Christian. Statistically, the population on the Japanese Island of Okinawa have the highest ratio of people living beyond 100 of any group in the world. These people are predominantly non-Christian. The obvious conclusion is that longevity, in the main, is not the result of the favour of God. Either God equally blesses believer and non-believer with long life *or* longevity is not under God's control. We have made the case, scripturally, that God wants us to live long lives and that our lives can be prolonged by righteous actions. It is not logically consistent that God will similarly bless non-believers with long lives if they don't keep these conditions. Solomon recognized this and he couldn't make sense of it!

Although a wicked man commits a hundred crimes and still lives a long time, I know that it will go better with God-fearing men, who are reverent before God. Yet because the wicked do not fear God, it will not go well with them, and their days will not lengthen like a shadow. There is something else meaningless that occurs on earth: righteous men who get what the wicked deserve, and wicked men who get what the righteous deserve. This too, I say, is meaningless. So I commend the enjoyment of life, because nothing is better for a man under the sun than to eat and drink and be glad. Then joy will accompany him in his work all the days of the life God has given him under the sun. (Ecc 8:12-15)

As you can see, it led Solomon to make contradictory statements (v12 contradicts v13). You can almost get inside his head. He knows the theory; it should be that the wicked live short lives and that the God-fearing man should be blessed but he records his observations that wicked live long lives and good men get the punishment the wicked deserve. He wants the theory to be true but is confused by the facts! At least he is more honest than most Christians. We cling tenaciously to the erroneous theory that God is in control of the length of our lives and live in total denial of the reality that faces us each day. Solomon didn't have the understanding of the Cross that we have, or the knowledge of legal rights and the potency of the kingdom of darkness, so he came to the wrong conclusion. His solution to this dilemma is that life is meaningless and we should live for the moment!

The source of longevity then, must reside elsewhere. What alternatives are there other than the kingdom of darkness? It can be in Satan's interest to keep some non-believers alive for a long time because they are doing such an effective job of discrediting the Kingdom of Light. There will be enough legal rights for Satan to activate any number of fatal diseases if he chose to, but he chooses not to, so that the impact of this person's actions against God's people can be maximized. Even more so if the person is a so called card-carrying Christian!

Regarding believers, he may keep a professing Christian alive for a long time, because that person is so full of self-righteous and pharisaical attitudes that he misrepresents the Kingdom of Light extremely effectively. All the while, the person believes he is enjoying the blessing of God. This is why it is not in Satan's best interests to immediately cause the death of people when they become Christians. Satan knows that people can lose their salvation if they are not diligent in moving forward in their relationship with God. He knows that pride is man's Achilles' heel and that it eventually leads to self-satisfaction and complacency. He also knows that a slack or hypocritical Christian is much better ammunition against the Kingdom of Light than an atheist's direct attack.

A master manipulator

You might be an effective witness for Jesus, doing damage to the kingdom of darkness and you come to Satan's attention as a consequence. He is not necessarily going to wipe you out just because you are a nuisance or current public enemy No 1. No, he is far more experienced with human nature than that. Having observed and interacted with us for six millennia, he is more of an expert on us than we are on ourselves! He knows that being effective for God today doesn't mean you will be effective for God in ten years time. He maintains a long term view. If he were to kill you now, at your evangelical prime, the possibility that you may be considered a 'martyr' could stir up others to step into your shoes and that would be a counterproductive move. But if you slacken off and he can work on weaknesses in your character, tweak a potential addictive behaviour, distract you with money or a pretty girl, then he can undo many years of good work very quickly and he has won. There are numerous well known Christian leaders and role models who have fallen from grace because of sexual sin. Discrediting them in front of the unbelieving world is far more effective than killing them at their prime.

You see, from Satan's perspective, killing you off is too crude. He takes far more delight in a gung-ho Christian gone wrong. He takes delectable pleasure in putting in the knife and turning it slowly. He knows that other Christians are often his best allies against a truly effective Christian. Jealousy, gossip and rejection from those you thought you could trust, are the cruelest wounds to a person; the most demoralizing blows. David expresses this well.

> *If an enemy were insulting me, I could endure it; if a foe were raising himself against me, I could hide from him. But it is you, a man like myself, my companion, my close friend, with whom I once enjoyed sweet fellowship as we walked with the throng at the house of God.* (Ps 55:12-14)

Satan knows that when Christians put fellow believers on a pedestal and they fall; they will be buried as deep as the pedestal was high. No, there are far more subtle ways to bring a man down than killing him directly.

Weighed in the scales and found wanting

What about legal rights that obedient Christians give to the Kingdom of Light? Don't these nullify the other legal rights we give to the satanic kingdom? Is it possible to gain sufficient legal rights so that the satanic kingdom cannot kill us, even if they want to?

It is theoretically possible for a Christian to reduce the number of legal rights the kingdom of darkness has, so that even if they wanted to, the enemy could not kill that person. Jesus, as we have seen, was a case in point. Unfortunately, for almost all Christians, if not all Christians alive today, the balance is firmly in the favour of the kingdom of darkness. Most of us are unaware of the extent and cumulative effect of sin in our lives. We erroneously believe the blood of Jesus covers all the legal rights Satan may have against us, or that a general prayer of confession for our sins is all that is necessary to deal with these legal rights. Personal and generational sin is far more complex than this and will be explored further in the next book in this series. These two categories aside, the five other categories of legal rights add further weight to Satan's already hefty claims[2]. The truth is, at the moment, Satan can take out virtually every person alive today whenever he wants to. Unpalatable as that may be, it is true. Despite the inflated opinion we may have of ourselves as individuals or collectively as the Body of Christ, the church today is only in its infancy in terms of the growth in maturity and understanding God wants us to develop before he can return. In the future, when people fully grasp the nature of legal rights and diligently work at removing them, there will be the possibility of people being free enough from their influence to the extent that God won't need to exercise over-riding grace to protect us from dying prematurely.

Watch out for presumption!

Despite what we have said, there are Christians who have been saved out of almost impossible situations due to God sending angels or by his direct intervention. These are circumstances in which the kingdom of darkness wanted the person dead but God intervened. God is sovereign, and although Satan may have legal rights, God's grace can override the legal right balance against us. Although God can do this, as we have said, it is the exception rather than the rule. In such cases, where we hear of miraculous escapes from death, we need to be careful not to assume that this person is now 'bulletproof'. For his own reasons, God has chosen to intervene *in this particular situation at this particular time.* In another situation, at another time, the same person may have died.

To reiterate, we are talking about getting to the stage where a person is so in tune with God that there are not sufficient legal rights to kill him, no matter how many times the satanic kingdom tries. In my opinion, there *probably* isn't anyone, any Christian alive on earth today, who has reached that stage yet. There is no person who can confidently and humbly stand and say that the kingdom of darkness cannot kill him even if it wanted to. Restated, there is no one alive who is so sure he has eliminated sufficient legal rights that, at any time, if an enemy puts a gun to his head, he can confidently say, 'Pull the trigger, God will stop the bullet!' Perhaps there are Christians that may have been in such a situation and God did stop the bullet, but that is quite different from being confident that God *always will* stop the bullet.

Is God anaemic?

God is still sovereign. God is still in control. He can say to Satan that Satan cannot kill a particular person even if the legal rights are there. God's own purposes and plans for a strategic individual means God can put a temporary cover over a person and Satan cannot kill him during that period. All of us would like to believe that God will make a special exception for us. In reality, that won't happen. Currently, there are simply not enough good legal rights available for God to use. Conversely, and only very occasionally, God can command the satanic kingdom to take a righteous individual early to spare him suffering. Josiah's righteousness meant that God spared him from being part of the judgment to come.

> *Therefore, behold, I will gather you to your fathers, and you will be gathered to your grave in peace, and your eyes will not see all the evil which I will bring on this place. So they brought back word to the king.* (2 Kings 22:20)

> *The righteous man perishes, and no man takes it to heart; and devout men are taken away, while no one understands. For the righteous man is taken away from evil, he enters into peace; they rest in their beds,* (Isa 57:1,2)

It is wishful thinking to take these verses from Isaiah and make a global statement that God will spare all righteous men from evil and suffering. Looking around us, we know this is not the case. Such examples are the exception rather than the rule. There are far fewer King Josiahs than we think there are.

God can also warn people people about impending death. Some readers may have prayed for someone who was sick and God told you that the person was going to die. Sure enough the person died. Doesn't that mean that God was responsible for that death? No, God simply used his fore knowledge of what Satan was going to do and he told you.

God's judgments

From a legal rights perspective, what is happening when God intervenes and brings his judgment on individuals or groups? Satan thinks he is in control of the earth because he can cause sickness and is largely instrumental in the length of life and time of death of most people. His tunnel vision stops him from seeing that he in fact is a pawn in a much bigger picture. God allows Satan his myopic freedom of movement provided it doesn't interfere significantly with his own big picture. There is obviously a delicate balance between Satan's freedom to act given man's wrong choices and Satan serving God's purposes as a defeated foe, reluctantly under God's command. There are times when Satan's freewill actions, based on legal rights given to him by man, go beyond what God is comfortable accepting. We have seen that the tremendous corruption on the earth as a result of Satan's half breeds meant God had to intervene with the judgment of the flood to redress the imbalance. Keep in mind, God was never out of control when the Nephilim were on the earth. Some of the other times that God exercised judgment against man were Sodom and Gomorrah, the ten plagues against Egypt, rebellious Israel in the desert, the complete destruction of the Canaanite nations by Israel, Herod Agrippa and Ananias and Sapphira. Let's look at some of these.

God's judgment of groups

When Satan, who is in control of death, looks at Sodom and Gomorrah or at the Canaanite nations that occupy the Promised Land, he is pleased with himself. They are full of sexual sin and corruption, worshipping false gods and offering their children as sacrifices to these gods. He has no intention of wiping them out. They are jewels in his crown. Satan knows the huge impact of generational iniquity and he knows that he has full control of these people groups for generations to come because of his demons passing from father to son and perpetuating the sins of their fathers.

God, seeing the bigger picture, realizes the future impact these cities and nations will have on the nation of Israel if they are not wiped out. He cannot simply wipe out the fathers and mothers because the generational iniquity will be continued through the children. If he is to establish the nation of Israel as a beacon to the world, if he is to give this fledgling nation a chance, then these corrupting influences must be removed completely. A complete spiritual antibiotic must be administered to the system to eliminate any chance of re-infection with the spiritual bacteria of these nations. God, using the huge legal rights built up against these Canaanite nations, employs Israel to destroy every man, woman and child. We can tend to be overly compassionate and, looking through a magnifying glass at the poor innocent children that are killed, we exclaim, 'How could a loving God destroy those innocent lives'. We don't consider the bigger picture. Although not ideal, these children will be in heaven[3], which is a better outcome for them than if they had matured to continue their father's corruption.

God's judgments of individuals

With individuals that bear the brunt of God's judgment, such as Moses (Numbers 20), Korah and his family (Numbers 16), Ananias and Sapphira (Acts 5), and Herod Agrippa (Acts 12), his judgment fell upon them because of the extent of the revelation each had received and their disobedience to that revelation.

If we take Moses, who hit the rock in anger instead of speaking to it as God commanded, God's judgment was that he could not enter the Promised Land. Moses should have known better. Having spent almost three months in the presence of God (two periods of 40 days) on Mt Sinai, Moses was without excuse. Had God given the command to Joshua, and Joshua had struck the rock instead of speaking to it, God would have given Joshua grace. Why? Because Joshua hadn't received the same revelation as Moses had.

Similarly with Korah, he should have known better than to be disobedient and keep some of the booty. After all, he had seen God work mighty miracles in Egypt; he was there when they crossed the Red Sea on dry land. He picked up the miraculous manna and quail in the desert. He was given an express command not to keep any of the spoils. He had no excuse. Judgment came.

Herod Agrippa heard John the Baptist, he heard and knew about Jesus and would have been aware of the miraculous circumstances surrounding his death and resurrection. He was aware of the commotion surrounding Pentecost. He had no excuse to passively accept the status of a god. God's judgment fell and it fell swiftly.

Likewise with Ananais and Sapphira; it is highly likely they were directly involved in many aspects of those miraculous formative New Testament events. Such revelation and privilege brings with it a narrow tolerance limit regarding God's grace. They overstepped the mark. His judgment fell and Satan implemented that judgment.

Denial

This is a hard chapter for many readers. It is not comfortable to dwell on the thought that the length of your life and time of your death is largely under the control of the kingdom of darkness. Yet, for all the reasons stated in this chapter, it is more discomforting to believe God is responsible. Blaming God provides too many logical inconsistencies. Some of you will be in denial. How could Satan have so much power? I thought he was a has-been since the Cross? That's not what we are told in church. You may be struggling now, but as you re-read this chapter and others, ask the Holy Spirit about what you have read and wrestle with him. It is a paradigm shift in your thinking and such a 180 degree turnaround won't be absorbed overnight. It requires us to humbly confess that we have attributed to God that which is Satan's work. We have placed darkness in the midst of God's pure Light. Like all truth, you will see that this new understanding actually brings freedom. Rather than operating from wishful thinking and presumption, such as "I'm in the centre of God's will, he will protect me", you will come to a more sober and realistic assessment of the tenuous nature of your existence. You will act with greater deliberation and less fatalism. There will be a little less swagger and bravado in your declarations against the kingdom of darkness lest Satan decide to make a fool of you. A greater humility and deeper reliance on God will characterize your walk.

Hope

Some of you may think that all this new understanding has done is to swap the fatalism of God's control for Satan's control. Really we are no better off because Satan could wipe us out at any time. Not true. We are much better off. With God in control of when I die, there is nothing I can do about that. Who are you and I to argue with God? He knows everything. He doesn't make mistakes. He decides, that's it, no discussion! With an enemy whose control of my life is largely based on *my* decisions and a God who wants to partner with me in fighting that enemy there is no fatalism. There is hope. Such an understanding is empowering. God actually wants me to live a long life! He is on my side. He is my encouraging coach, my biggest fan and he is always ready to work with me in making the right decisions. He wants me to get it right. He doesn't want me to die prematurely. He doesn't want me to die before I get to triple figures! If I can understand the legal rights that are in my life and work at removing the negative ones and gaining Godly ones, then I actually have some tangible control over the direction and length of my life. My actions, each and every day, will either shorten or prolong my days on earth. That's empowering. That is life giving. That gives me a game plan. That makes me *over* the circumstances, not under them. Being passively resigned to dying when God 'calls me' is demoralizing. It is fatalistic. It breeds complacency and hopelessness. It is shrugging my shoulders and waiting till my number is up. This new understanding means I am now no longer just another lemming heading for the cliff, blindly following the lemming in front of me. I have been given the tools to take charge of my destiny. I am in the process of removing darkness from the Light.

SUMMARY

- Except for the instances where God's judgment falls directly upon man, God is not directly responsible for when any of us die. The kingdom of darkness is.

- God sets upper limits for the length of human life for each dispensation and he can and does stop Satan killing people that Satan would like removed but these instances are rarer than people think.

- God doesn't choose the *length* of our lives, the satanic kingdom does.

- A popular misconception is that the length of our lives is uniquely assigned by God to each person and is fixed. Scripture clearly indicates that the length of our lives is flexible and dependent on legal rights.

- Scriptures indicating that God shortens our lives means that God gives the final consent, not unlike a Governor General officially recognizing an Act of parliament. It doesn't mean that it is God's intended will.

- God wants everyone to live to be around 100 years old. Any death before this is premature from God's perspective.

- If God controls when we die, then we serve a whimsical God. We have nothing to look forward to other than the same fatalism of those in the rest of the world's religions.

- If God decides when we die, it logically follows that he is in control of the sickness that leads to death. If that is the case, then he was working against himself whenever Jesus healed someone.

- If sickness is established in our lives by the satanic kingdom, the logical follow-on is that our deaths are also under the control of the kingdom of darkenss.

- There are a large number of legal rights that quickly accumulate enabling the kingdom of darkness to have more control over our lives than we realize.

- Satan has a number of different reasons as to why he chooses one person to die prematurely and not someone else. It is not as random as we may think.

- Human freewill choice can be a factor in when we die. Careless or dangerous activities will be factors. I can choose to kill myself with a shot gun and there is little the kingdom of darkness can do about it even if they don't want me dead.

- Miraculous escapes can be engineered by either kingdom. Don't necessarily assume it is God's angels who have protected a Christian in dire straits.

- The satanic kingdom can engineer a variety of physical circumstances to cause a person's death that onlookers would consider coincidental.

- Long life is not necessarily a blessing from God.
- Killing an effective Christian that does damage to the kingdom of darkness can be counterproductive to Satan. Knowing human nature and working on a long term view, Satan's best strategy is often to let the person 'destroy' himself. eg. complacency, self-satisfaction, sexual sin.
- Based on our understanding of legal rights, it is highly likely that all humans alive today have sufficient legal rights for the kingdom of darkness to kill them when it chooses. While God can intervene, this is the exception rather than the rule.
- There is a popular belief that Satan has no legitimate basis for doing what he does. Just declare this 'truth' and he will leave you alone. The truth is that, as a defeated foe, the only way Satan can do anything is to have a legitimate right to do so. He cannot act illegitimately.
- If Christians seriously pursue an understanding of legal rights and work diligently at systematically removing those given to the kingdom of darkness, then it is theoretically possible that God won't need to extend much grace over us because the satanic kingdom will have difficulty accumulating sufficient legal rights to kill us, even if it wanted to.
- God's judgments on individuals and groups are the only exceptions when he intervenes and destroys people. God's judgments fall and Satan implements those judgments, whether he likes it or not. These are relatively rare occurrences.
- Uncomfortable as it is to hold this new viewpoint that Satan is in control over how long we live, it is actually empowering. The truth always liberates. Knowledge is power, ignorance leads to presumption.
- The church today is largely unaware of the extensive control the satanic kingdom has in our lives resulting from the daily free will choices we and others make. The church is still immature. Satan can and does act with relative impunity. Once we understand and make a conscious effort to remove legal rights, we gain the control over our lives and destiny that God always wanted us to have.

Chapter 14:

EARTH, WIND AND FIRE

You were shocked. I was shocked. None of us could comprehend the enormity of the tragedy that happened on December 26, 2004. An extremely large earthquake (9 on the Richter scale) out at sea generated a tidal wave, a tsunami, which devastated coastal Indonesia and parts of Thailand and Sri Lanka. Not 2 000 fatalities, not 50 000 fatalities, not 150 000 fatalities but over 280 000 people died! Entire communities were completely obliterated. It was the worst natural disaster in living memory and the second worst natural disaster in recorded history.

Whenever a major tragedy occurs, the inevitable question is asked, 'How could a loving God destroy so many innocent people?' A disaster of this magnitude makes the question all the more pointed. It begs for an answer. Like me, you probably heard or read a variety of replies over the following weeks on TV, radio, in editorial columns and from pulpits. The responses basically fitted into one of the following categories:

> 'It simply proves that there is no God because a loving God would not randomly destroy so many people.'
> 'It is the will of Allah.'
> 'God's ways are mysterious and we will never know the answer in this life.'
> 'It is God's judgment for mankind's sins.'
> 'It is God's judgment against Islam.' (Indonesia is 98% Moslem)
> 'It is Satan that caused it.'
> 'It's nature, it's random.'

As always, the answers don't satisfy because nobody really seems to know. It is all conjecture. There is no quantitative proof, no hard evidence to back up any of the above responses.

Don't despair, there is an intellectually satisfying answer that is backed up by hard evidence and supports the premise of this book.

Basic Probability

Assume I toss a coin four times and get four tails. I could wrongly assume that I will always get a tail when I toss the coin. A small number of tosses doesn't necessarily give me an accurate indicator that the true probability of getting a tail is 50% or ½. If I toss a coin 400 times, I expect to get close to 200 tails. Tossing a coin 400 times will give me a more accurate measure of the true probability of a tail occurring than tossing it four times. In other words, the greater the size of the sample, the closer to the actual probability we get.

Suppose I toss the die 600 times, I would expect to get roughly 100 of each number. Let's say I get the following results.

50 ones, 98 twos, 103 threes, 94 fours, 105 fives, 150 sixes.

There is a surprisingly low number of ones and higher than expected number of sixes. I could reasonably assume that some other factor besides random chance was involved. It could be that the die was weighted heavier on the face where the number one is. When it was tossed, the die would land with the number one against the table surface more than any other number and therefore the six would be uppermost. (Note: the number 1 is always opposite the number 6 on a die).

If I toss a coin, I have a 1 in 2, or 50%, chance of getting a tail. It is not unusual to toss a coin four times and get four tails. It is more unusual to toss a die four times and get four sixes. Why? Because the chances of a six occurring on any throw is 1 in 6, or 16.7%. The chance of getting four tails in a row is only 1 in 16; the chance of getting four sixes is 1 in 1296. A dodecahedron is a 20 sided die, each face is the same. If the faces were numbered from 1 to 20, and I tossed it four times, the chance of the die landing with the number 20 uppermost, four times in a row, would be 1 in 160, 000. The conclusion we can draw is that if the chance of an event occurring is very low, then the chance of it occurring several times in a small sample is remote.

To summarize the last two paragraphs; where the probability of an event occurring is high, (like tossing a three on a die or a tail on a coin) we need a large number of trials to determine whether there is any bias. If the probability of an event occurring is very low (like getting a 20 on a dodecahedron) we only need a small number of trials to determine if there is a bias.

A puzzling anomaly

What does this have to do with the Indonesian tsunami? Below is the list of the world's most serious earthquakes[1], in terms of people killed, that can be verified with a reasonable degree of accuracy. This list spans almost 1200 years. Those that resulted in fatalities of more than 30 000 people are the ones included below.

DATE	PLACE	FATALITIES
January 23, 1556	China, Shansi	830 000
December 26, 2004	Sumatra	283 106
July 27, 1976	China, Tangshan	255 000
August 9, 1138	Syria, Aleppo	230 000
May 22, 1927	China, Xining	200 000
December 22, 856	Iran, Damghan	200 000
December 16, 1920	China, Haiyuan	200 000
March 23, 893	Ardabil, Iran	150 000
September 1, 1923	Japan, Kanto	143 000
October 5, 1948	Turkmenistan	110 000
December 28, 1908	Italy, Messina	100 000
September 1290	China, Chichi	100 000
October 8, 2005	Pakistan	86 000
November 1667	Caucasia, Shemakha	80 000
November 18, 1727	Iran, Tabriz	77 000
May 12, 2008	Sichuan, China	70 000[2]
November 1, 1755	Portugal, Lisbon	70 000
December 25, 1932	China, Gansu	70 000
May 31, 1970	Peru, Chimbote	66 000
January 11, 1693	Italy, Sicily	60 000
February 4, 1783	Italy, Calabria	50 000
June 20, 1990	Iran, Western	50 000
December 26, 1939	Turkey, Erzincan	32 700
December 26, 2003	Iran, Southeastern	31 000
May 30, 1935	Pakistan, Quetta	30 000

One would expect that if the earthquakes were random, then the dates on which they occurred should be evenly spread throughout the year. However, of the 25 events, we notice that six occurred in December. We should expect, randomly, only two occurrences. December is more than twice as much as the next highest month, November. If we look at the December dates they are all grouped together; 16, 22, 25, 26, 26, 26, 28.

January 11, 1693	Italy, Sicily	60 000
January 23, 1556	China, Shansi	830 000
February 4, 1783	Italy, Calabria	50 000
March 23, 893	Ardabil, Iran	150 000
May 12, 2008	China, Sichuan	70 000
May 22, 1927	China, Xining	200 000
May 30, 1935	Pakistan, Quetta	30 000
May 31, 1970	Peru, Chimbote	66 000
June 20, 1990	Iran, Western	50 000
July 27, 1976	China, Tangshan	255 000
August 9, 1138	Syria, Aleppo	230 000
September 1, 1923	Japan, Kanto	143 000
September 1290	China, Chichi	100 000
October 5, 1948	Turkmenistan	110 000
October 8, 2005	Pakistan	86 000
November 1, 1755	Portugal, Lisbon	70 000
November 18, 1727	Iran, Tabriz	77 000
November 1667	Caucasia, Shemakha	80 000
December 16, 1920	China, Haiyuan	200 000
December 22, 856	Iran, Damghan	200 000
December 25, 1932	China, Gansu	70 000
December 26, 2004	Sumatra	283 106
December 26, 1939	Turkey, Erzincan	32 700
December 26, 2003	Iran, Southeastern	31 000
December 28, 1908	Italy, Messina	100 000

Whenever there are anomalies in a group of data, we need to determine whether they are within the bounds of random occurrences or if they are statistically significant. Mathematicians use the phrase, '*statistically significant*', to apply to results which are outside of the range of random, but acceptable, variation. In other words, there are other factors behind these results that need to be considered. Mathematicians have tests that can measure whether the results are statistically significant. Applying these tests to the results above, we find that they are statistically significant. This means there are other factors behind why December has more earthquakes than other months. Not only that, but the dates are not randomly spread through December as we would expect. This means there is another underlying reason why the dates are concentrated together.

Rolling a very large die

Instead of a dodecahedron, imagine that you have a die that has 365 faces. It would look like a many faceted diamond and its shape would almost be that of a smooth ball. Let's say you number the faces and you roll it. You would not expect to get the same number twice unless you did a large number of throws. So you would be really surprised if in 25 throws, you got one number three times and three other numbers very close to that same number! You would have to suspect that the die was biased in some way, and mathematicians would agree with you. In the 25 earthquakes listed, there are three December 26s and four other results very close. It is statistically significant. Highly significant. The secular world, of course, cannot explain why the world's most lethal earthquakes occur around these dates.

The answer

Thinking outside the box, there is a plausible explanation. If the kingdom of darkness can and does influence the elements, then it becomes clear why there is a concentration of lethal earthquakes around Christmas.

Satan hates Christmas.

He hates Jesus. He hates so much of the world celebrating the birth of Jesus. It is the biggest single celebration in the world. He hates the fact that the build up to and emphasis on Christmas is increasing worldwide and is becoming more accepted in non-Christian nations. Satan gets his revenge by destroying the season of peace and goodwill for as many people as he can. God enjoys people celebrating his Son's birth[3]. Satan is so jealous that he does his best to spoil God's enjoyment. He does it because he has the legal rights. Satan is the real Grinch who loves to steal Christmas!

He doesn't get all the blame!

These earthquakes are not entirely demonic in nature. The whole world is in a state of continual decay. Creation groans, as Paul so aptly puts it in the book of Romans (8:22). The tectonic plates push against each other and internal stresses and tension in the earth's plates need release and this release is often through earthquakes. The satanic kingdom is aware of the build-up of these forces and, if it has the legal rights, it can affect the timing of the quake, the intensity of the event and the direction of the release of the pent up energy. In other words, it carefully directs and applies the energy that is naturally already there.

Let's look more closely at the Indonesian earthquake that caused the tsunami. Satan would have seen the sheer pressure in the earth's crust building and, knowing how a tsunami forms, he had a choice. If the earthquake had happened without his intervention, it may well have been an underwater event where the two plates slide over each other and there is minimal movement of the water. But if he could use the locked up energy and affect a more vertical sheer, then he will set off a displacement of water that would send a pressure wave that would gather momentum and, if carefully directed, will have maximum impact when it reached land. Because he has so many demons at his disposal and can collect energy, he had enough leverage to direct the plate movement in the manner and direction that he wanted. Yes, Satan *can* collect energy. More about his abilities will be explained in *'Darkness in the Light: Satan's Trojan Horse'*.

Major destruction, major influence

Even the world's most horrific earthquake in China, 500 years ago, was less than a month from Christmas. It is likely that Satan's fingerprints were all over this event, given the enormity of the death toll. It could be that he didn't have the necessary energy to manipulate the timing to be closer to Christmas. Keep in mind that death is the currency of the kingdom of darkness, not the Kingdom of Light. Because God is for life, it is his desire that we all live to a ripe old age. We have already mentioned the relatively rare occurrences when God brings down his judgment. These events aside, when disasters happen, God will be trying to minimize the destruction and death. The decay of creation and the legal rights given to Satan by man mean that God's hands are often tied in the amount of intervention he can do. Because of the incredibly destructive nature of the earthquakes in the above list, most will have a strong demonic component, even if they didn't occur near Christmas. When Satan's careful plans are thwarted, he often reacts immediately instead of taking a more considered approach. When he doesn't get his way, sometimes he can throw quite a tantrum. Because his pride prevents him from taking the blame, his knee jerk reaction is to blame or punish someone or some group of people. This explains why the other earthquakes are spread through the year. If we could see what was happening in the heavenly realms, there would probably be some event that Satan was not happy with that corresponded to each of the above dates.

I am not saying that every quake that has ever happened has a demonic component. Of the many thousands of tremors and quakes that happen around the world on a yearly basis, most of them will be free from demonic interference. Most of them will be purely the result of natural forces and pressures that need to be released. Most of them are minor and don't cause much destruction. We would expect the pattern of occurrence of these minor quakes to be spread evenly throughout the year and they are.

Over a five year period, from January 1st 2001 to December 31st 2006, there were 188 fatality-free earthquakes worldwide that were of magnitude 3.3 or higher on the Richter scale. A statistical analysis of the dates when these occurred indicated a random pattern. There is no statistically significant correlation to indicate any other factor which needs consideration as to why these events occurred. Satan was not involved.

In summary then, the more destructive the quake is, both in terms of property and lives lost, the greater will be the influence of the satanic kingdom.

The range of earthquakes we have looked at are those of 30 000 or more casualties. This range was chosen simply because the list becomes too large if all the earthquakes with lower fatality rates were included. However, anyone wishing to carry out the same study with a wider fatality range will find a similar correlation.

Not just Christmas

In fact, when you choose a wider range of earthquakes, another interesting anomaly occurs. Aside from the very obvious peak around the November, December, January period, there is another peak around the March, April, May period. If you list all the recorded earthquakes with a death toll of 1000 or more and take any three month period, the next highest grouping is the March, April, May period. It is not as strong as the Christmas peak but it is there. This is the period around Easter. We shouldn't be surprised since Satan also hates the world celebrating Jesus' death and resurrection. Forty days before Easter we have Ash Wednesday which marks the beginning of the Easter period and 49 days after Easter we have the celebration of Pentecost, marking the end of the Easter period and, more specifically, the time when the Holy Spirit was given in power to believers. Since Easter weekend occurs predominantly in April, that puts Ash Wednesday usually in March, and Pentecost usually in May or early June. Satan hates Pentecost just as much as he hates Easter. Easter freed us from eternal separation from God but Pentecost gave us the gifts of the Holy Spirit and a bold confidence in dealing with the kingdom of darkness that Satan has no defense for. Satan doesn't mind a fearful Christian without many weapons. He hates a bold Christian armed to the teeth! It could explain why May overall, in the earthquakes listed above, has the next highest peak after December.

It is no surprise then that the latest earthquake, prior to this book going to print, to enter the 30 000 plus category is the Sichuan earthquake. It occurred on Monday, 12 May 2008, one day after Pentecost Sunday!

The worst earthquake in US history happened on April 18th, 1906 in San Francisco. 3000 people died. It was three days after Easter Sunday. The three May earthquakes listed above are all within two weeks of Pentecost Sunday. The same is true for the worst earthquake in 2006, which killed 5749 people in Java, May 26th. In 2005, the worst earthquake occurred in Sumatra, Indonesia, killing 1313 people. It happened a day after Easter Sunday. In 2004 and 2003, the worst earthquakes, included in the list above, both occurred on December 26th. In 2002, the worst quake occurred in Afghanistan, killing 1000 people. It occurred on the

Monday of Easter week, six days before Easter Sunday.

Like the Indonesian tsunami, New Zealand's worst disaster of natural origin, in terms of lives lost, was a tsunami, a fresh water tsunami; a 6 metre high wave of two trillion litres of water released from the crater lake of Mt Ruapehu, NZ's most active volcano. The lahar, as it is officially called, contained rocks, ice and debris and wiped out a bridge over the Whangaehu river. An approaching train plunged into the water, killing 151 people. The date, Christmas Eve, 1953. Queen Elizabeth was visiting NZ for the first time. Maximum publicity was assured.

We can't say, 'Fascinating information but it could be all coincidence'. Mathematics won't allow us to say that! Mathematics accounts for coincidence and very strictly states that the above statistics are more than coincidental. It is evidence that demands a verdict; a satisfying explanation.

Wind

Did Satan have control over the elements before the Cross? Yes. Satan has a measure of control of the elements based on the legal rights given to him by man. God has overall sovereignty of the earth and that includes the weather. Satan can control different aspects of the weather for brief periods of time but not the whole global weather system for any length of time.

The most well known example in the New Testament was the storm on the Sea of Galilee.

> *Without warning, a furious storm came up on the lake, so that the waves swept over the boat. But Jesus was sleeping. The disciples went and woke him, saying, 'Lord, save us! We're going to drown!' He replied, 'You of little faith, why are you so afraid?' Then he got up and rebuked the winds and the waves, and it was completely calm. The men were amazed and asked, 'What kind of man is this? Even the winds and the waves obey him!'* (Matt 8:24-27)

Indicators that this storm was likely to have a strong demonic component are in the first few words of verse 24. The storm was freakish, without warning. Storms usually build and these are seasoned fishermen. The lake was their livelihood and they no doubt knew it intimately. It might have caught a Sunday sailor unawares but not these men of the sea. They would have read the signs if a natural storm was brewing and warned Jesus. Matthew uses the metaphor 'furious' to describe the storm. The storm was not just a regular storm. It had a particularly furious or violent aspect to it. The impression is of something suddenly whipped up that is very intense, even angry. This had all the hallmarks of demonic control. It was designed to destabilize seasoned fishermen. It worked. It was designed to catch

Jesus off guard and hopefully get him to sin. It didn't work.

Demonic storm

The defining aspect of this passage, pointing to the demonic, was the way Jesus spoke to the storm. If it was a natural storm, Jesus would not have rebuked it. You rebuke an angel, a person or animal. You don't rebuke inanimate objects or events such as the rain, fire or wind. You rebuke a person or an animal that has done something 'wrong'. You rebuke something that has the capacity to listen and change. The weather can't do that. Jesus knew that this storm was demonic and he made it very clear to the demons creating the havoc that they had to stop. A further indicator that it was demonic was that it stopped immediately. If the storm was a natural event, the result of normal air pressure differences, then it would have subsided much more slowly. While Jesus recognized that it was demonic, verse 27 shows us that the apostles, at the time, didn't pick this up.

Does Satan still exercise control over the elements on this side of the Cross? There are no post-resurrection Scriptures that are as clear as the Sea of Galilee example just quoted. However, I think it is more than coincidental that Paul had to endure three shipwrecks. Satan was likely to be involved in some or all of these, given his desire to destabilize Paul at every opportunity. We are given no information about these wrecks except the one mentioned in Acts 27. It is inconclusive whether it was entirely demonic, had a strong demonic component or was entirely natural. My guess is that it had a significant demonic component. It could be argued that since it was the stormy season, storms were to be expected. Nevertheless, the sudden nature of this storm has the kingdom of darkness' fingerprint on it.

> *When a moderate south wind came up, supposing that they had attained their purpose, they weighed anchor and began sailing along Crete, close inshore. But before very long there rushed down from the land a violent wind, called Euraquilo; and when the ship was caught in it and could not face the wind, we gave way to it and let ourselves be driven along.* (Acts 27:13-15)

Satan is very good at using the existing natural forces and whipping them up. It is likely that the Euraquilo wind would have been manageable by the sailors had the satanic kingdom not stirred it into a fury and a shipwreck resulted. As has been established, the Cross did not impact Satan as much as we think it did. We detailed, in chapter 10, the four things that changed for Satan as a result of the Cross.

(1) Satan no longer has any control of the righteous after they die.
(2) He no longer has a default control over the world.
(3) He knows that people who choose to believe in Jesus now have the Spirit of Jesus, the Holy Spirit, dwelling in them and they, individually and collectively, have authority over his kingdom, if they use it properly.

(4) He has been bruised. Not crushed but bruised.

Everything else has remained the same. Satan's automatic authority over the world is now rescinded, but the legal rights system means that he still gains considerable control over mankind; both Christian and non-Christian, and the world in general. He can still control the elements, as he did before the Cross, provided mankind gives him the power through their freewill choices. We know that he has control over the non-believing world (1 John 5:19), and that the enormous legal rights he gains from these unbelievers, give him considerable influence over the weather and micro climates around the world.

Personal experience

From a personal perspective, the following example is convincing enough to me to indicate that Satan still has influence over the weather. In late February 2007, Heather and I were travelling by car from Queensland to Victoria. We had just had a powerful breakthrough against the satanic kingdom and reclaimed someone that Satan thought he had. We knew that he would not be happy. On Saturday February 24th, we left Sydney on a glorious day and spent the morning on a beautiful South Sydney beach. As we travelled south, in the Wollongong region, during the early afternoon, a localized storm came out of nowhere. The sky was suddenly filled with dark, ominous clouds and lightning soon followed. As we were travelling along, lightning was striking the fields directly beside the car. It was eerie, as though the lightning was following us. First, it was parallel to the car but some distance away, and then it came closer and closer, striking the ground just metres from the car as we travelled along. The rain was torrential, so strong that even the top speed of the wipers barely coped. Cars were stopping at the side of the road. We decided to stop at a McDonalds. As soon as we pulled into McDonalds, lightning struck the restaurant and it lost all its power. Huddled in the entrance, we talked to a local, who said he had never seen weather like this down here. We got drenched, literally soaked to the skin, trying to get back into the car, a distance of 10 meters (30 feet) away. We continued on, driving at about 20 km/hr (13 miles/hr).

O.K, I get the message!

We needed fuel so we stopped at a petrol station and as we did, a lightning strike removed all power to the station and none of the pumps would operate. We continued driving down the road and stopped at the next service station. Just as we pulled in, guess what happened? You guessed it! It too was rendered powerless by lightning. As we pulled up to the pump, the attendant said that no pumps were operational. At this point, I asked Jesus to send his ministering angels to get the pump going. Immediately, the pump became functional, we filled up with gas and as soon as we were finished, the pump was no longer functional. I went inside to pay the bill and the cashier said, 'You were lucky to get that gas. It was knocked out with the others and came on just for you and it's out of action again'. I responded, 'It's not luck, mate, I said a prayer and God answered!' He looked at me as if to say, 'We've got a weird one here' but I knew that this was not a coincidence. As we drove on, the storm intensified with large hail stones. We stopped under a tree for shelter while lightning was still striking the road. The hail abated, we drove on and, just as fast as the storm had come on, it stopped and we were once again in clear skies.

Why did Satan do that? Because he wanted Peter and Heather to know that he was not happy with what had happened and to intimidate us with a show of strength. It worked to some extent because when lightning strikes the ground following your car and Satan knows that you know what this is all about; you are unsettled to say the least. When you understand the legal rights system, you are also aware that Satan has sufficient legal rights to kill almost anyone, including us. Equally, giving into fear plays strongly into his hands and is sinful so we were careful not to do that but to place a quiet trust and confidence in God's protection. We knew we were in the centre of God's will which brings with it a large number of legal rights for the Kingdom of Light. We had a strong sense that, posture though he might, Satan wasn't going to, or wasn't allowed to, eliminate us yet.

I can understand if you think I suffer from 'delusions of grandeur'. If someone told me that a certain storm was designed for them, I would certainly be skeptical. Unfortunately it is beyond the scope of this book to detail how important this victory in the heavenly realms was. This is an introductory book designed to challenge the popular misconception that Satan is a 'has been'. In subsequent books, we will go into more detail about the structure and operation of the satanic kingdom. Consequently, we were anticipating a strong and immediate reaction. The specific nature of the events outlined above; the way the lightning followed us up the road and knocked out each of three venues when we stopped at them, reduces significantly the probability that it was just coincidence.

Australia's worst cyclone is still 'Cyclone Tracy'. It destroyed over 70% of the city of Darwin, killing 71 people. It began on Christmas Eve, 1983.

Fire

Fire is Satan's calling card. He uses fire a lot in coven ceremonies. In Job, we saw how Satan was able to send down fire that consumed Job's servants and sheep.

> *While he was still speaking, another messenger came and said, 'The fire of God fell from the sky and burned up the sheep and the servants, and I am the only one who has escaped to tell you!'* (Job 1:16)

As stated earlier, the servant wrongly attributed to God what was actually the work of Satan. We know that this is the case because of the preceding dialogue in heaven.

The general rule of thumb to determine whether the weather or other physical phenomena, such as earthquakes or fires, have any satanic component is to look for aspects that appear abnormal, freakish or strange.

'Diabolical'

Aside from Antarctica, Australia is the world's driest continent. Not surprisingly, it is frequently plagued with forest, bush and scrub fires. Australian firemen are well seasoned and the dry summer months can be taxing. On Friday, January 17th, 2003, the Canberra skies came alive in the late afternoon with a fiery glow never seen before in the nation's capital. We lived in Canberra at the time and the unusual darkness in the afternoon was eerie. It was a fire storm that no one anticipated, the likes of which even the most experienced fireman had never seen before. By Saturday afternoon, over 500 houses were destroyed. Fortunately, there was little loss of life. There were numerous news reports. It was not uncommon for both newspaper, radio and television to use phrases like, 'the fire had a mind of its own' and was 'diabolical'. Many commented on the unusual highly selective nature of the fire in choosing some houses and sparing others. Firefighters commented that the intensity that the fireball generated was unlike anything experienced before.

There were obviously natural factors that contributed to the fire. The conditions were dry and there was a large pine forest planted very close to residential housing. The wind conditions were a factor but nothing out of the ordinary. There was a fire already burning prior to that dreadful Friday holocaust but it was in bush land some distance from residential housing and not considered a threat to Canberra. What remains a mystery is how the fire jumped from so far out to so close to the residential area so quickly. Even if there was an adequate explanation, the clincher is in the incredible ferocity of the fire once it got close to the residential area. It whipped into a frenzy from nowhere. It formed into an all-consuming fireball so quickly that it defied the usual patterns of fire development. As we have seen with the Sea of Galilee incident, the kingdom of darkness has the ability to whip up the air into a frenzied wind very quickly. Add fire to the equation and we have a whirling vortex of intense heat and destruction that has 'a mind of its own'.

To a secular world, and unfortunately to most Christians, the fire was extreme, unprecedented with several unexplained and unusual aspects but nature is nature and we are always learning something new. The fire will be examined from a purely naturalistic perspective and patterns duly noted but the possibility of any demonic component will be overlooked. To make such a suggestion that there could be a strong spiritual component to the fire would be considered medieval thinking.

Another example, not unlike the Canberra fires, only much more intense, was Australia's worst fire, in terms of human lives lost. This occurred on Feb 7th, 2009. The day has become known as 'Black Saturday'. Extremely temperatures (46°C or 116°F), high winds, several years of drought, uncleared undergrowth and debris, all combined to form a lethal combination. More than 200 people died and the final toll is likely to never be known. The ferocity of the blaze was such that people were burnt to ash with no trace, in one case a titanium hip joint being the only identifying feature. Car engines melted, forming a river of alloy. The feature that overwhelming distinguishes and characterizes this fire compared to others, apart from its intensity, was the speed at which it spread. In many cases those who perished had no warning the fire front was even near. There wasn't any apparent danger and then, within a minute or two, literally, a wall of flame was at your doorstep. The fire was stealthy. The greater percentage of the fire's ferocity was due to the factors already mentioned but the influence of the satanic kingdom was not minor. Just like in Canberra, 'demonic' was a word used by some CFA workers, volunteer firemen, with 30 years experience.

Timing

Australia's worst fire experience, in terms of destruction, occurred in 1983. The fires swept across Victoria and South Australia, killing 76 people and causing widespread damage. 3,700 buildings were lost, including around 1,000 farms. Over 2,400 families and individuals lost their homes. Around 340,000 sheep and 18,000 cattle died. The date? They began on Ash Wednesday, the first day of the Easter period, 16th February, and are referred to by everyone in Australia as the 'Ash Wednesday' fires. It's a pun that I'm sure Satan's takes some delight in!.

On 7th February 1967, during a time of considerable drought, 264,270 hectares were burnt in southern Tasmania in the space of five hours. Of the 110 fires raging on that fateful morning, the worst was the Hobart fire. The fire made its way over Mt Wellington, destroying many homes in its path, and encroached on the city's western suburbs. The fires resulted in the death of 62 people and the destruction of 1,400 dwellings and other buildings. At the time, it was the largest loss of life and property on any single day in our history. The date? Shrove Tuesday, the day before Ash Wednesday. Is it coincidence that this is the same date as the 2009 'Black Saturday' fire mentioned above?

In countries throughout the world, there are numerous earth, wind and fire phenomena that have a demonic component. The two large scale fires in San Diego, USA in Oct 2003 and again four years later in the same month in 2007 have a strong demonic influence. In the 2007 disaster, 500 000 people were evacuated,

1500 homes were destroyed and over 2000 square kilometers of land burned (200 000 hectares or 500 000 acres). Once again, the San Ana winds were the natural template that Satan used and he simply increased their ferocity. The land was tinder dry. The timing of the two fires is not as coincidental as people may think.

Some storms will be as dramatic as the examples cited, most won't. Some will be localized, as happened to Heather and me, others will be global. Whether it is a tornado that seems to 'coincidently' choose a specific path ensuring maximum destruction or an earthquake that kills an inordinately large number of people, demons can be more than 50% of the driving force behind the destruction. However, it is usually very difficult to prove a smaller localized natural disaster has a strong demonic component because it won't show up statistically.

Christian foundations help

You might have noticed that of the three and a half million people destroyed in the earthquakes listed, only 346 000 or 10% are from Christian countries (Italy, Sicily, Peru, Portugal). If we exclude Antarctica, over 80% of the world's land mass is occupied by Christian countries[4]; traditionally Christian in foundation, statutes, ethos and adherence. Logically we would expect 80% of the earthquake casualties to occur in these countries, not 10%. Since Christian countries also have their fair share of fault lines and geological instability, why aren't more Christians killed? It is another anomaly that defies an adequate non-spiritual explanation.

All non-Christians are under the control of the kingdom of darkness. Satan gets huge legal rights over countries that are not Christian; Hindu, Buddhist, Moslem, Shinto, Sharman, Atheist etc. When he is angry, when his goals are blocked, when it comes to Easter, Pentecost or Christmas, he can react and move with relative impunity and destroy large groups of people in such countries. The fact that these countries are indirectly worshipping him doesn't save them from his wrath. He disdains humans. When they are helpful to his cause, he spares them. When he reacts in a fit of pique and needs a scapegoat, they are dispensable. Being faced with the raw power of Satan's control over large sections of humanity is both frightening and sobering. Sometimes, Christians want to believe that the contrast between themselves and non-Christians isn't as stark as these statistics indicate. We would like to believe that people who are not Christian will be let off the hook, given another chance. Peter's statement in Acts 4:12 rings loud and clear and there is no escape clause.

> *And there is salvation in no one else; for there is no other name under heaven that has been given among men by which we must be saved.* (Acts 4:12)

Obviously, the greater the number of true believers that make up a Christian country, the greater the collective legal rights the Kingdom of Light has to protect that country from Satan bringing the same wanton destruction he inflicts on those under his control. Nevertheless, for those of us in pre-dominantly Christian countries, there is no place for complacency. Increasingly, many traditional Christian countries are having their foundations eroded with more and more worship to foreign gods, as well as growing indifference and secular humanism, taking its toll.

God and weather

God created the earth and the dynamics that control the weather. He has always controlled and still controls these elements. Scripture is full of examples of God using the weather to achieve his purposes.

Earth destroyed by flood *(Genesis 6:5-9,19)*
Burning sulphur rained down on Sodom *(Genesis 19:24)*
Hail and fire from heaven on Egypt *(Exodus 9:23-29)*
Rainless sky, parched earth *(Leviticus 26:19-20)*
Rain as reward for obedience *(Deuteronomy 11:13-15)*
Drought punishment *(Deuteronomy 28:24)*
Hail on the Amorites, etc. *(Joshua 10:11)*
Thunder disperses the Philistines *(1 Samuel 7:10)*
Drought and famine *(2 Samuel 21:1)*
Good weather reward *(1 Kings 8:35-36)*
Rain withheld and given *(1 Kings 16:30-18:45)*
Judgment with whirlwind and drought *(Nahum 1:3)*
Dry weather *(Hosea 13:15)*
Rain given and withheld from certain cities *(Amos 4:7)*
Jonah redirected by a sea storm *(Jonah 1:4,10-15)*
Rain withheld as judgment *(Zechariah 14:17)*
Hailstone punishment *(Revelation 16:21)*

Just because God controls the weather and can use it to bring both blessing and judgment, doesn't mean that he has *exclusive* control. Like everything else on earth, the weather is subject to the legal rights system and can be influenced by Satan to bring his judgment when he has sufficient legal rights. To hold that all weather is controlled by God is to blame God for many of the calamities and disasters mentioned in this chapter and we are left with an impetuous God who acts with no apparent logic, using humans as pawns. As we have clearly established, the majority of weather based calamities that result in high loss of life have Satan's fingerprints all over them, not God's.

Man's impact on the environment through clearing trees and burning fossil fuels had increased carbon dioxide levels, in turn increasing global temperatures making worldwide weather patterns far more erratic. This plays right into Satan's hands as he can use this unstable template to manipulate the weather more easily than before. God isn't going to miraculously step in and change things. God honours the legal right system and although he may not agree with the way Satan wreaks his havoc, he equally recognizes that what man sows, he reaps.

Is God on holiday?

Hard as it is to fully grasp, the premise that Satan is predominantly involved in mass destruction is the only intellectually satisfying and consistent explanation that reconciles a loving God with such apparently random carnage. It is consistent with our premise that Satan is in control of death and has sufficient legal rights to wipe out almost anyone he chooses, whenever he chooses.

Some of you are still not satisfied. You think I am letting God off the hook too easily. There may be an internal anger at God, a sense of injustice, a deep resentment at God's indifference. God just lets it all happen! He is a casual bystander watching Satan wreak havoc with impunity. The satanic kingdom wipes out lives, huge numbers of people, with complete disdain and an utter contempt for the sacredness with which God holds human life. Where are you, God? Is there anybody up there?

Your anger at God's apparent impotence is understandable but it is more a reflection of a failure to grasp how important and all pervasive the system of legal rights is. Man makes choices. Every day we make choices. Choices for good and choices for evil. Choices that result in blessing, choices that result in curse. It can't happen any other way. It wouldn't be fair. Justice demands it. It is sowing and reaping. Joshua reminded the people that the Lord would fulfill both good and evil promises depending on their choice. (Joshua 23:14-16 cf. Deuteronomy 28.) The currency of the heavenly realms is man's freewill choices to follow God or reject God. Every God-rejecting action, whether you are a Christian or not, gives more power to the kingdom of darkness. Just like accumulated credit card points that enable you to have a free plane trip or purchase an item, so too the accumulated legal rights give Satan and his helpers enormous freedom as to how they will spend their 'points'. An earthquake here, a localized tornado there, a pseudo miracle elsewhere. The choice is largely theirs because the legal rights they have are so strong.

Passionate

Don't make the mistake of thinking that God is passive throughout what happens. If we could see how many people were saved from that Indonesian tsunami, we would be amazed. The death toll would have been many thousands more without his intervention. His angels worked overtime during those devastating moments when the waves hit the land, doing whatever they could to save as many as they could within the legal rights system. God's omnipresence means that he was with every person when they were struggling to come to the surface, struggling to take a breath, struggling for their lives. He was helping as many as he possibly could to live. Whether they are Moslem or not isn't an issue for God. He created them, he loves them, he wants as many as possible to live as long as possible and have more opportunities to choose his Son. God is passionate about people. He is passionate about people not dying prematurely. He is passionate about people being saved eternally. How do we know that? Because he died a slow and painful death on a Cross to set us free from ourselves. That is passion. That is commitment! And you think God doesn't care?! Let's not react so judgmentally when we can't make sense of a disaster. Let's reclaim a more balanced perspective of the Kingdom of Light. Let's take back another area of darkness that we have mistakenly placed in the Kingdom of Light.

SUMMARY

- There is statistical evidence to support the belief that earthquakes are not a random event.

- The Kingdom of Light wants people to live as long as possible. It is against God's nature and character to randomly destroy people. Sometimes God exercises his judgment on individuals and peoples but these are rare events and always for specific reasons.

- The only plausible explanation for the statistical anomalies is that the satanic kingdom is responsible. It is consistent with the character and nature of the satanic kingdom to inflict random and wanton destruction.

- It also supports the premise that Satan and his demons control when we die. He can wipe out large numbers of people at any time he chooses and for whatever reason he chooses.

- Satan's control of the elements is demonstrated scripturally in the examples of fire that destroys Job's servants and the storm on the Sea of Galilee.

- The Cross has reclaimed Satan's overall control of the earth but hasn't affected his ability to use legal rights gained to affect the elements as he is able.
- The more destructive a natural event is, the stronger the demonic component is likely to be.
- The more unusual, coincidental or freakish a natural event is, the more likely it is that there is a demonic component involved.
- Dates of natural disasters that coincide with significant Christian celebrations such as Ash Wednesday, Easter, Pentecost and Christmas and the associated build up to these events are likely to have a strong demonic influence.
- Satan's fingerprint can be seen in small localized events as well as major catastrophes although these smaller events lack statistical support.
- God is passionately committed to us and does all he can to save as many as he can when catastrophes happen. God has to nonetheless honour the legal rights system he has set up.

Chapter 15:
THE CROSS AND THE FIRST AND SECOND DEATH

We have progressively built up a picture of a formidable foe that we underestimate at our own peril. We have seen that he wasn't defeated at the Cross in the way we are commonly taught. In fact, his capabilities after the Cross are almost as impressive as they were before the Cross. Physical attempts to put on the armour indicate just how ineffectual we are in dealing with him and how easily he manages to pierce our defenses. Satan's control over the length of our lives, the time of our death and even over major disasters seems so hard to believe that we would rather remain in denial; with our heads buried in the sand or looking the other way. It's easier. Our world view has been challenged to its foundations. We can see more clearly what a large part presumption has played in our thinking and what a perilous position it places us in. In this chapter, we will look at another aspect of presumption, less prevalent but nonetheless still dangerous.

The manner of his death

If Jesus' death was the completion of his role as the second Adam, why was it necessary for Jesus to die on a Cross? Couldn't he have died by being stoned to death or perhaps strangled? For Jesus to fulfill the role of the second Adam, surely how he dies is academic? Couldn't he have died in any number of ways and wouldn't man still have been set free from hell?

The death of Jesus was a multi layered event. Aside from Jesus needing to fulfill the role of the first Adam, he also had to fulfill his Father's requirements for man to be reconciled to him. The penalty for man's sin couldn't be satisfied without the shedding of blood.

> *For the life of the flesh is in the blood, and I have given it to you on the altar to make atonement for your souls; for it is the blood by reason of the life that makes atonement.'* (Lev 17:11)

> *And according to the Law, one may almost say, all things are cleansed with blood, and without shedding of blood there is no forgiveness.* (Heb 9:22)

God's mercy wanted to let man off the hook. God's justice demanded a penalty for man's sin. God had decreed a legal right that without the shedding of blood, there was no remission of sin. A final, perfect, sinless, once and for all, sacrifice was needed for God's justice to be satisfied. A perfect 'lamb without blemish' was necessary to complete God's demand that the penalty for sin be fully paid. John the Baptist summed this up when he proclaimed,

> *The next day he saw Jesus coming to him and said, "Behold, the Lamb of God who takes away the sin of the world!"* (Jn 1:29)

Blood must be shed. Therefore stoning and strangling were not options. Another aspect of the crucifixion that will be examined in our forthcoming book, *'Darkness in the Light: Satan's Trojan Horse'*, is the need for the Cross to be 'staked' in the ground to complete the reclamation of the earth from Satan's control.

It is important to see our salvation occurring on at least at two levels. Jesus was simultaneously both the second Adam and the perfect sacrifice. Jesus as the second Adam set man free from hell's control, but it was Jesus as the perfect sacrifice that reconciled us with God. Jesus as the second Adam unlocked the captives. Jesus as the penalty payer led the captives into heaven.

But we still die!

Why then do we still age and die? If the legal rights given to Satan by Adam have been removed, why aren't we now living forever just like Adam was before he sinned? The consequence of the legal rights given to Satan through Adam's sin were twofold: the first death and the second death. The first death referred to the *physical* consequences of Adam's sin. The second death referred to *spiritual* consequences of his sin. The first death affected the body, whereas the second death affected the soul and the spirit.

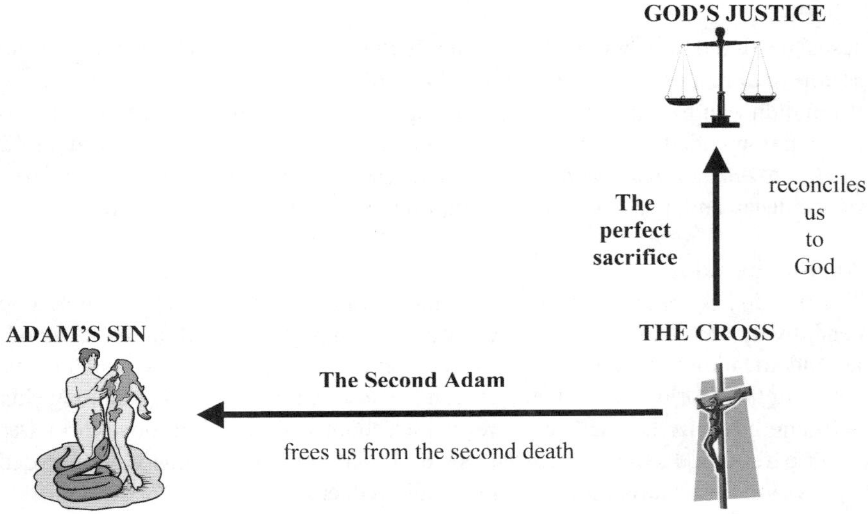

The first death

The first death meant that everything physical would now decay. Flesh was no longer eternal. It was now temporal. It now had a 'use by' date stamped on it. The unique triune creation of man was now compromised. Instead of the body being eternally linked to the soul and spirit, as God had intended, the body would eventually wear out. The tri-unity was now shattered. The soul and the spirit wouldn't wear out, but the body would. Like three runners in a race where one falls away, the body won't eventually be able to hack the pace. It will get tired and won't be able to continue. The other two will have to continue on their own.

A logical consequence of the body's decay, and in fact the decay of all creation, was that the earth could no longer be the final dwelling place of man. Adam's sin automatically meant that the earth was no longer a viable option for the eternal habitation of man. Designed to be an eternal dwelling, man's sin changed it to a temporary dwelling. There was no turning back. For from dust man was taken (made) and to dust he must now return (Gen 3:19). God's first plan had been *irreversibly* corrupted.

Plan B

Once Adam's sin was committed, God had to restore man's trinitarian nature differently. He would have to give us a new body. Our soul and spirit would now need to be housed in a body not of this world. This new body would have to exist in a dimensional realm different to this earth. He would need to create a new heaven and a new earth to accommodate our new resurrection body. Our spirit and soul will wait in heaven, after we die, until our resurrection bodies are created, and then our spirit and soul will once more be united with new flesh, eternally.

Jesus' death did nullify the impact of the second death. We have been freed from Sheol. We are now reconciled to God. We will now live forever with God. Jesus' death didn't nullify the first death, as it applies to this world, because this earth is no longer intended as our final dwelling place. He did nullify the first death, *as it applies to our new resurrection bodies,* because these new bodies will never experience decay and die. They are incorruptible bodies that will last forever.

Another paradox

The paradox is that we can only reap the rewards of freedom from the second death by dying! We can only enjoy freedom from physical death in our new bodies and an eternal relationship with God by experiencing death in our old bodies. Death in this world, for the believer, can be seen as jumping from a sinking ship onto another ship that will sail forever. Freedom from death in this world was never part of God's plan after Adam's sin. It was never something God intended to redeem. It was never something he could redeem.

Earthly death still under Satan's domain

How can death be still under Satan's domain if Jesus has the keys of death and Hades?

Jesus having the keys of death and Hades meant that he had the right to remove those who were righteous through faith and take them to his Father. He couldn't do that without the keys. He has done that. Man is reconciled to God. Man will never die again once his trinity of spirit, soul and resurrection body is finally reunited. But having the keys of death and Hades has nothing to do with the legal right to control our physical death on this earth. That is something that could never be changed once Adam sinned, for the reasons already stated. God moved from plan A to plan B but plan A has to work out its natural course.

Because death, decay, disease and deformity are not fundamental aspects of the Kingdom of Light, God assigned the consequences of Adam's sin to the jurisdiction of those who specialize in it; the angels of the kingdom of darkness. The spirits Death and Hades were assigned to that task. Although the spirits, Death and Hades, will *eventually* cease their function because of the Cross, they continue to call all humans into eternal life or eternal death until this earth passes away.

Mission Impossible

In his role as the second Adam, Jesus was able to nullify the legal rights Adam gave to Satan. These were Satan's control over the earth and the containment of our spirit and soul in Sheol. However, Jesus' death can't go back in time and stop Adam taking a bite of the fruit!

He can't undo Adam's freewill choice to know the difference between good and evil and as a consequence come under the Law. Once that event took place, there was no way of reclaiming the lost innocence. Every human being would be born under the Law and consequently sin and continue sinning throughout their lives. Therefore, daily we invite death into our lives through our sinful choices. The *spiritual penalty* of sin has been paid for by Jesus but the *physical consequence* of our sin in our bodies can never be reversed. That is part of the law of sowing and reaping.

Earthen vessels

Let's say, through carelessness, I break a precious Ming Dynasty vase of yours. It is worth a small fortune. I am really sorry and apologize profusely, especially when I find out that it wasn't insured. Let's say you choose to forgive me and let me off paying you anything to replace it. While I am relieved that I have been pardoned by you, both of us are still sad that the beautiful and precious vase is lying on the floor in pieces. Nothing can be done to restore that vase to the state it was before it was broken. It doesn't matter if I painstakingly glue all the pieces together; it is still a broken vase. The action of the breaking is irreversible, even if the action itself has been forgiven. My sinful act of carelessness has an irreversible impact on the Ming vase, even if the owner has chosen to nullify any 'legal rights' that she might rightly claim.

Adam was a perfect 'Ming' vase, but he broke. Each of us, as a consequence of coming under the law, break. We apologize to our owner, God, for our careless handling of ourselves, 'his earthen vessels'. Because of his Son's sacrifice he forgives us, but that doesn't stop the fact that we are broken. The law of sowing and reaping means that what we sow in carelessness or sin, we must reap in brokenness or death. Like living sacrifices that wriggle off the altar, we are constantly breaking ourselves, breaking into smaller and smaller pieces. Death's grip on our lives increases daily.

Death must continue to be outworked in our bodies as long as we continue to sin. Every human sins daily, hence death is part of every human until we stop sinning. Jesus' death on the Cross doesn't stop us sinning; hence Jesus' death has no impact on our earthly deaths. Jesus' death removed the spiritual consequences of our sin, not the physical consequences. We saw in chapter three how death entered the world because of sin. Sin came first, then death. Death didn't exist before sin. Sin is the cause and death is the effect, just as clouds are the cause and rain is the effect. An absence of sin is a prerequisite for an absence of death.

Presumption

Hence the curses that accompany death, mentioned in Genesis 3, still apply.

Pain in child birth, the domination of man over woman, sweat, toil, thorns and thistles and our bodies decaying back to dust are all a consequence of the first death and won't be removed while this earth exists. Daily, our sin, both individually and collectively, reinforces each of these curses. However, the mistake some Christians make is in believing that Jesus' second Adam role also applies to these physical consequences of Adam's sin.

For example, some believe that women should no longer experience pain in childbirth. This has led to the erroneous belief that a Christian woman, if she has enough faith, should be able to experience pain free childbirth. Correct physical exercise and preparation, practicing relaxation techniques, not giving into fear, watching the words we speak and a quietly confident trust in God throughout the whole birth process will no doubt alleviate a lot of pain. Nonetheless, to expect a totally painless birth experience is unrealistic. While some women may have had a totally painless experience in giving birth, these are the exceptions rather than the rule. Claiming the finished work of the Cross in this regard is both a misrepresentation of the Cross and a misappropriation of grace that is not available. In addition, it could provide a doorway for the demonic to remove the pain as a means of re-enforcing the lie.

'Healing' disease

This thinking is not limited to painless childbirth. There are Christian ministries that believe because Jesus completed the second Adam role, we are restored to the state prior to Adam's sin. Since Adam and Eve were without sickness, poverty and sin, should we expect anything less? This is dangerous because claiming healing for sickness and disease based on the false premise that we are now partakers of the same conditions Adam and Eve first enjoyed plays right into Satan's hands.

Giving Satan a foothold

Think about it. Who controls the onset of sickness? Satan does. Who then can equally stop a sickness getting worse and even diminish or 'heal' it. Satan can. The satanic kingdom is more interested in reinforcing wrong beliefs and will allow 'healings' to cement those beliefs. Hence a ministry having success with healing based on this false premise will all the more believe the error because of the 'healings'.

Therefore, we need to make the distinction between true healing, that Jesus does, and symptom removal that Satan can do. For example, just because a person's cancer decreases and disappears doesn't necessarily mean it was a true healing in the biblical sense.

The satanic kingdom can initiate a disease, accelerate that disease, make it plateau, diminish it, stop it and restart it. Hinduism, Buddhism, Taoism and the various

New Age healing therapies that radiate from these philosophies claim healing of every kind of ailment, including cancers[1]. Satan is comfortable providing temporary 'healing' if it keeps people locked into the worship of foreign gods that will ultimately lead to their eternal death. Such pseudo-healing can happen in Christianity *if* the foundational premise is flawed and the impact of the demonic ignored.

Note that I am not saying that all Christians have to have correct theology for God to heal. God can still heal and genuinely does heal us even if our beliefs or foundational premise for the healing is wrong. After all, who is perfect?! We are all learning and refining our understanding. God gives grace and looks at our heart. Hence, such ministries can and do have genuine miracles and I believe that many or most of the healings, in the name of Jesus, are genuine New Testament style healings. However, if we are basing our reason for painless childbirth or freedom from sickness on the false premise that we are entitled to a pre-Fall existence, then it does give more leverage for Satan to confuse the situation, muddy the waters and ultimately allow him more access than God would like.

If we claim a pre-sin Adamic lifestyle as a right that has been won back for us by Jesus' death on the Cross, why do we still die? Why are we still sick? Why do we still contend with weeds? The absence of sin is the only way we can enjoy a pre-Fall Garden of Eden existence and we all sin daily.

Can God's angels sin?

Since an absence of sin is a prerequisite for an absence of death, it raises the interesting question of how we can remain sinless for all eternity and still retain our ability to make freewill choices. If Adam was sinless and managed to sin at the first temptation, then how do we manage to last for all eternity if we retain our knowledge of good and evil and the ability to choose evil if we so desire?

Perhaps a clue is found in what happened to the angels that chose to continue following God instead of Satan. We know that Satan's angels have sown in sin and therefore will reap eternal 'death' in hell. What about God's angelic followers? Can they still sin and make the switch to the enemy camp? Scripture doesn't specifically answer that question, although the overall impression is that God's angels remain on his team forever. This must mean they don't sin. Yet they still must retain their freewill. Just as they could have chosen to join the kingdom of darkness, they can still choose to join the kingdom of darkness but none do. Why not? Conjecture perhaps, but after the angelic rebellion, after the angels had all made their choices, is it possible that God came into the angels that chose him for the first time? Before the rebellion he was external to them, just as he was external to Adam. After the rebellion, not only does he come into them but his presence is deeper, more powerful, and more complete than we, here on earth, are currently experiencing. They are aware of his presence in them every millisecond that passes. There is never any doubt that it is his voice they are hearing. Having made the right choice, they were rewarded with deeper intimacy and connection with him than they had ever imagined.

His presence in them, in a manner so tangible and continuously 'there', means that they simply wouldn't think about sinning, even though the possibility exists. They continually refer to him in every decision that they make. His instructions are crystal clear and his love for them so intense that it is almost palpable. Who would want to sin in those circumstances? Who would want to betray so great a lover?

Doesn't that get you excited about eternity?! Beam me up, Scotty!

SUMMARY

- There is a horizontal aspect to Jesus' death in that he was the second Adam. He went 'back in time' and nullified the legal right Satan gained from Adam. Hence nullifying the impact of the second death and setting us free from hell's grip.

- There is a vertical aspect to Jesus' death in that he was the perfect sacrifice. As the perfect sacrifice, he satisfied God's demand for justice. The penalty of sin was paid through the shedding of blood.

- The first death referred to the *physical* consequences of Adam's sin. The second death referred to the *spiritual* consequences of his sin. The first death affected the body; the second death affected the soul and the spirit.

- Jesus, as the second Adam, dealt *immediately* with the spiritual consequences of Adam's sin but the physical reclamation can't become a reality until this earth passes away. In other words, it is a two stage process. The first stage happened at the Cross; the second stage will happen in the future.

- This world is a 'death star'. It will eventually be destroyed. The paradox is that the only way to escape from it and enter into the promised freedom from death is to die.

- While the consequences of Adam's sin, both physical and spiritual, were nullified by Jesus, the sin itself, choosing to come under the Law, cannot be nullified. The fruit can't be put back onto the tree.

- The law of sowing and reaping means that the consequence of coming under the law, which is death, must continue to be outworked in our bodies as long as we continue to sin. Every human sins daily, hence death will be experienced by every human until we stop sinning.

- Jesus' death on the Cross doesn't stop us sinning; hence Jesus' death has no impact on our death.

- Death entered the world because of sin. Sin came first, then death. Death didn't exist before sin.

- An absence of sin is a pre requisite for an absence of death.

- Be careful not to apply the work of the Cross to the physical consequences of Adam's sin. In particular, to an expectation of totally painless childbirth or thistle free farming!

- Sickness is often initiated by the kingdom of darkness, so it stands to reason that they can control the course of the sickness, even to'healing' it. Most New Age philosophies claim healing for a wide variety of ills.

- Some Christian ministries pray for healing based on freedom from the physical consequences of Adam sin. There is a belief that we should be enjoying a Garden of Eden existence because of what Jesus did on the Cross. This can lead to 'healings' being manipulated by the kingdom of darkness to enforce these erroneous assumptions.

- Perhaps when the angelic rebellion was over, those angels that remained true to God experienced a far greater presence of God in them than they had before. This enables them to effectively never sin even thoughtheir freewill choice is still intact.

Chapter 16:

GREATER THINGS THAN ME YOU WILL DO

Brian has epilepsy. He's around 30 years old. He's had it all of his life. He came seeking help for a number of issues, epilepsy being one of them. We had addressed some of these and came to the epilepsy. I began by commanding the demons linked to epilepsy to manifest. There was an immediate response; a tenseness in Brian's face. I set the parameters for the interaction with the demons and asked Jesus to appoint a spokesman from among them to speak on behalf of all them. Commanding the spokesman to speak the truth that the true Lord Jesus recognizes as truth, I asked the following questions;

Peter: When did you enter?
Demon: At birth.
Peter: How?
Demon: Through high forceps delivery.
Brian: (holding his temples) Wow! There's a strong pain on both sides of my forehead.
Peter: Speaking to the spokesman that Jesus has appointed, what legal right do you have to remain?
Demon: The trauma.
Peter: Brian, do you know anything about your birth? Has your mother told you about what happened?
Brian: No, not really. But I get the pain I am currently getting often prior to epileptic attacks and it feels like someone has put a G clamp across my forehead, on my temples and is tightening the screw.

Peter: Jesus, could you please come and unlock the trauma that was caused by the high forceps. *Brian's face grimaces slightly.* Jesus, could you please lift off the trauma. *A stronger grimace. I anointed Brian's temples and laid my hands on them.* Jesus, could you please restore any damage to his soul and spirit as a result of that trauma. *Pause.* Jesus, can you now bring physical healing to the head region that was damaged by the forceps.
Brian: Amazing, it feels as though my head is being pulled out by both temples. It's as though what the G clamp was doing is being reversed.
Peter: We will need to break all ungodly soul ties between you and your mum, the doctors and nursing staff, the forceps and the territorial spirit involved.
Brian does this.
Peter: Speaking to the demon. Do you have any further legal rights to remain?
Demon: No
Peter: Go directly, completely and immediately to the true Lord Jesus Christ and he will deal with you as he sees fit.

Brian has been free from epilepsy since then. That was six years ago. The whole process took as long as it took to type up. About 15 minutes. Under his doctor's directions, he came off his medication shortly afterwards.

Throughout the counselling, Brian sat comfortably on the chair in front of me. Aside from relatively minor facial expressions, there were no overwhelming manifestations.

Contrast this with the deliverance Jesus did with the epileptic boy.

> *They brought the boy to Him. When he saw Him, immediately the spirit threw him into a convulsion, and falling to the ground, he began rolling around and foaming at the mouth. And He asked his father, "How long has this been happening to him?" And he said, "From childhood. It has often thrown him both into the fire and into the water to destroy him. But if You can do anything, take pity on us and help us!" And Jesus said to him, "If You can? All things are possible to him who believes." Immediately the boy's father cried out and said, "I do believe; help my unbelief." When Jesus saw that a crowd was rapidly gathering, He rebuked the unclean spirit, saying to it, "You deaf and mute spirit, I command you, come out of him and do not enter him again."* ***After crying out and throwing him into terrible convulsions, it came out; and the boy became so much like a corpse that most of them said, "He is dead!"*** *But Jesus took him by the hand and raised him; and he got up.* (Mk 9:20-27)

Demonic theatrics

The symptoms fit epilepsy and this deliverance was 'messy'. The demon does finally come out of the boy but not without making a big show and the boy was left lying lifeless. In fact, in other gospel accounts of the same incident, the apostles first had a go and couldn't get past first base. Jesus later explained that prayer and fasting were necessary for this deliverance (Matthew 17:21).

A puzzle

Why did the deliverance from epilepsy for Brian proceed so smoothly? His dignity wasn't in any way compromised. It was over very quickly and there was no need for prayer or fasting. Other people have received freedom from epilepsy through our counselling in similarly non-dramatic circumstances. Yet when we read about the way Jesus did deliverance, it was often dramatic, messy and the people receiving deliverance were hardly dignified and composed.

The solution

The reason that deliverance was messier in the pre-resurrection examples is that Jesus was trespassing on Satan's territory. Although Jesus was sinless and spiritually above Satan, at the same time, he was under the territorial demonic Prince over Israel. There was a juxtaposition. On the one hand, Jesus' sinlessness meant that Satan was underneath him because there were no legal rights against Jesus. There were legal rights against Satan because Satan sins. Because of this, Jesus could and did speak directly to demons and they had to obey. On the other hand, Satan was in authority over the world and that meant *everything* in the world. Jesus, as the man who walked and taught in the Galilean countryside, was in the world and so Jesus was under Satan. Jesus had dared to come right into the middle of Satan's territory. He had parachuted behind enemy lines[1]. Any landowner has the right to evict a trespasser from his property. Adam had that right when Satan tempted him in the Garden but he didn't exercise it. Satan had the right to tell Jesus to go but he has the additional problem of lacking the power to remove him because of Jesus' sinlessness. Removing Jesus means killing him and he couldn't. No legal rights. This created the tension between Satan and Jesus.

POSITIONAL AUTHORITY Jesus as the sinless Son of God	**TERRITORIAL AUTHORITY** Jesus as the Son of Man
God	**God**
over	*over*
Jesus	**Satan**
over	*over*
Satan	**Man (including Jesus)**

To complicate matters further, Jesus had not yet completed his role as the second Adam. This wasn't completed until he died. The show isn't over till it is over. Jesus had done well to date, but he still had a way to go. 'I've got a few tricks up my sleeve to spoil the party and Judas and Caiaphas are two party poopers I'm currently working on. So far so good, Jesus, but let's not count our chickens just yet'. Satan had every right to 'sock it to Jesus' with maximum impact because the contest hadn't reached the end of round fifteen. Satan's thinking went along the lines; 'If I can cause maximum reaction and impact when Jesus tries to deal with my army, maybe he will be discredited in the eyes of onlookers.'

Defiant demons

Encounters between Jesus and the kingdom of darkness often reflected this underlying tension. The demon's didn't mildly lie down, belly up. When Jesus dealt with the demon in the synagogue, it came out shrieking. Hardly etiquette for a synagogue!

> *Just then there was a man in their synagogue with an unclean spirit; and he cried out, saying, "What business do we have with each other, Jesus of Nazareth? Have You come to destroy us? I know who You are— the Holy One of God!" And Jesus rebuked him, saying, "Be quiet, and come out of him!" Throwing him into convulsions, the unclean spirit cried out with a loud voice and came out of him.* (Mk 1:23-26)

Notice that the demons didn't do as they were told. Jesus told them to be quiet and they cried in a loud voice. They disobeyed. Jesus, the Creator of the universe, the Creator of angels, spoke to them and gave an instruction and they only partially obeyed. Yes, the demon did leave but not quietly. Yes, it did stop talking about who Jesus was but through the convulsive display made sure its exit was anything but quiet and orderly. Why? Because of the clash of legal rights; their territorial position over Jesus meant they could disobey, to a limited extent.

A greater level of disobedience came from the demons in the Gerasene demoniac.

> *Then they sailed to the country of the Gerasenes, which is opposite Galilee. And when He came out onto the land, He was met by a man from the city who was possessed with demons; and who had not put on any clothing for a long time, and was not living in a house, but in the tombs. Seeing Jesus, he cried out and fell before Him, and said in a loud voice, "What business do we have with each other, Jesus, Son of the Most High God? I beg You, do not torment me."* ***For He had commanded the unclean spirit to come out of the man.*** *For it had seized him many times; and he was bound with chains and shackles*

and kept under guard, and yet he would break his bonds and be driven by the demon into the desert. And Jesus asked him, "What is your name?" And he said, "Legion"; for many demons had entered him. They were imploring Him not to command them to go away into the abyss. Now there was a herd of many swine feeding there on the mountain; and the demons implored Him to permit them to enter the swine. And He gave them permission. And the demons came out of the man and entered the swine; and the herd rushed down the steep bank into the lake and was drowned. (Lk 8:26-33)

The order of events appears to be as follows:

1. Jesus commands the demons to leave.
2. The demons don't leave.
3. The demons say, "What business do you have with us".
4. Jesus asks, "What is your name?"
5. Demons reply, "Legion".
6. Jesus strikes a deal with the demons and they go into the swine.

Notice that they didn't respond to Jesus' initial command for them to leave. After some dialogue, a deal was brokered and they went into the swine. Again we have the Son of God speaking to the demons and they don't do as they are told. That wouldn't happen in heaven but it did happen on earth because of the legal rights Satan still had, due to Adam's sin.

Meek and mild demons

We can see that Jesus had to put up with a lot more defiance than I have to put up with today. Not all of Jesus' interactions with demons were testy. It appears that some or even a lot of the time, the process went relatively smoothly.

When evening came, many who were demon-possessed were brought to him, and he drove out the spirits with a word and healed all the sick. (Matt 8:16)

The point is not that Jesus could sometimes deal with demons effectively and efficiently, but that there were times that the demons disobeyed. There were times when bargaining was required and the dignity of the person was compromised. Over the last eight years of doing deliverance with a post-resurrection understanding, I have had only two instances, in thousands of hours of deliverance, where the demons made a 'show' that has embarrassed the person and been totally unexpected. These two instances were very mild in comparison to what Jesus had to put up with. In a post-resurrection model of deliverance, demons should *not* make a fuss. Jesus cares too much about the individual to see them act in an undignified manner during the process of deliverance but sometimes he had no choice in the matter before the Cross. Unfortunately, many Christians are put off from receiving deliverance today for this very reason.

Whether I am dealing with demonic princes or lower level minions, I never tolerate demons taking the limelight, distracting or manifesting in any way that embarrasses my client. If I were to deal today with the same demons Jesus had to deal with in the synagogue, they would come out of the man as meek and mild as a pussycat. If I dealt with the Gerasene demoniac today, there would be no bargaining with any demons regarding them going into pigs. There would be no destruction of the local pork industry! The demons would leave quietly and without fuss. Jesus had no choice because of the strength of the kingdom of darkness at the time. Bargaining was his only option.

Why the difference? Is Peter Toth better at deliverance than the sinless Son of God? Far from it! I am as sinful as any other human. The difference is that the battle is now over. Jesus was the conqueror, I am more than a conqueror.

> *No, in all these things we are more than conquerors through him who loved us.* (Rom 8:37 NIV)

Jesus went those 15 rounds with Satan and won. He conquered. Like a boxer's wife, I get to spend the winner's purse without any of the agony! The struggle is over. The world that was under Satan's control is no longer under his command. Jesus went into enemy territory for 33 years and had continuous forays with Satan that often wasn't pretty. However, he reclaimed the territory and now the backup troops, you and I, move effortlessly over the same territory that Jesus struggled to subdue. Fasting was necessary at times before the Cross when dealing with demons due to their territorial strength but it is no longer necessary after the Cross. I repeat that it is no longer necessary for anyone on this side of the Cross to fast as an aid to expelling demons. Having dealt with top level Princes in highly complex demonic infestations that make the case of the boy with epilepsy or the Gerasene demoniac look like a walk in the park, I can say categorically that fasting is *never* a pre-requisite for any deliverance anymore. I am not saying that there is no value in fasting, I am saying that there is no value in fasting as a way of hastening, streamlining or concluding the deliverance process.

This is some of what Jesus meant when he said that we would do greater things than he did.

> *Truly, truly, I say to you, he who believes in Me, the works that I do, he will do also; and greater works than these he will do; because I go to the Father.* (Jn 14:12)

A Recap

To summarize the three fold impact of the Cross.

(1) Jesus, with his death on the Cross, becomes the perfect sacrifice and restores the vertical relationship between man and God. Jesus, as the Lamb of God, makes the final and complete payment to satisfy his Father's demand for justice. Man is now reconciled to God.

(2) Jesus, with his death on the Cross, brings closure to his sinless life and therefore finally completes his role as the second Adam. Jesus, as the second Adam, goes 'back to the future' and undoes the mistake made by Adam 4000 years earlier. He restores man's positional authority over the earth.

(3) Jesus, with his death on the Cross and subsequent resurrection and ascension into heaven, enables man to be inhabited continually with his Holy Spirit. For the first time, we can receive the fullness of the life of Christ in us. We are living, breathing, walking, talking 'Arks of the Covenant'.

Hence Satan and his minions have no legal right to kick up a fuss during deliverance. He has to present in my clients in a manner that does not compromise the person's dignity. When the demons are commanded to do something, they have to co-operate. When I command them to go to Jesus, they must go directly, immediately and completely. There is no bargaining. There are no pigs jumping over cliffs. Defiance is not tolerated.

Post resurrection scriptural support

The premise that deliverance today, deliverance after the Cross, is less confrontational and less dramatic compared to how Jesus did it should be confirmed in the New Testament. Does the New Testament support the effortless, drama-free, master-servant style of deliverance we have just been talking about? Let's look at the relevant post resurrection Scriptures.

> *Philip went down to the city of Samaria and began proclaiming Christ to them. The crowds with one accord were giving attention to what was said by Philip, as they heard and saw the signs which he was performing. For in the case of many who had unclean spirits, they were coming out of them shouting with a loud voice; and many who had been paralyzed and lame were healed.* (Acts 8:5-7)

This is the first recorded case of deliverance after the resurrection. This event happened not long after Pentecost. The first mission field after the immediate preaching of the gospel to the Jews was their nearest neighbours and distant relations, the Samaritans. In this case, there was little evidence to indicate that anything had changed from the way Jesus did deliverance. The demons were still putting on a show, still making a loud noise. A possible explanation is that, being so soon after the resurrection, Phillip was still doing what he saw Jesus do and from what he learnt during his training session when Jesus gave the apostles temporary authority over demons (Matthew 10). The theological understanding of what happened at the Cross wasn't yet fully appreciated. Phillip had the authority to tell the demons to leave quietly but because he wasn't aware of this fact, the demons did their usual 'song and dance' and Phillip allowed it, because that's what he expected to happen. Even today, demons will play up if you let them.

> *It happened that as we were going to the place of prayer, a slave-girl having a spirit of divination met us, who was bringing her masters much profit by fortune-telling. Following after Paul and us, she kept crying out, saying, "These men are bond-servants of the Most High God, who are proclaiming to you the way of salvation." She continued doing this for many days. But Paul was greatly annoyed, and turned and said to the spirit, "I command you in the name of Jesus Christ to come out of her!" And it came out at that very moment.* (Acts 16:16-18)

Here we see Paul firmly commanding the demon to leave and the demon doing so immediately and apparently silently. Luke, the writer of Acts, mentioned the screeching in Acts 8, so one would assume that he would have mentioned it here if it had happened. The use of the word 'we' in verse 16 indicates that Luke was an eye witness to this interaction between Paul and the slave-girl. This event occurred many years after Phillip's deliverance in Samaria and it is likely that the Church, or at least Paul, had grown in an understanding of the believer's increased authority and the diminished authority of the satanic kingdom.

> *So that handkerchiefs or aprons were even carried from his body to the sick, and the diseases left them and the evil spirits went out.* (Acts 19:12)

Later still in Paul's ministry, probably around 50AD, we see an example of the subjection of the satanic kingdom to the power and authority of the Kingdom of Light that is quite astounding. Paul isn't even present and demons leave! Deliverance by proxy, deliverance by auto pilot! The context would indicate that, once again, the demons are leaving passively, without fuss. The handkerchief touches the person and the spirits leave. Such an event didn't happen when Jesus was on earth. Such an event *couldn't* happen when Jesus was on earth for the reasons stated. Paul was doing greater things than Jesus.

These are the only three post-resurrection passages we have that are related to deliverance; to believers dealing with evil spirits. Based on such a small sample, we can't say with categorical certainty that these prove my assertions. Nonetheless, they appear to lend considerable support to the premise that, as the Church grew in its understanding of its authority, it moved away from deliverance as it was conducted when Jesus was on earth. As the New Testament church matured, there was an increasing authority over the kingdom of darkness by believers and a decreasing reactivity by demons during the deliverance process.

Deceived for too long

For fifteen years, I did deliverance the way Jesus did it in the gospels. After all, if it was good enough for Jesus, it was good enough for me! Other pastors and ministers were doing the same thing and books on the subject at the time confirmed this approach. In these cases, I would expect a dramatic manifestation and I would often get one. People would cough, splutter, scream, choke, slide, roll around, posture and act in a number of other ways that compromised the person's dignity. We would sometimes spend hours with a person trying to get a demon to leave and the person would often become highly stressed. Nonetheless, we would persist and at the end of a session, frequently, everyone was exhausted. Sometimes, we dealt with legal rights without realizing it and there was a noticeable positive change. Other times, we didn't deal with any significant reasons for the demon's presence, and there was still a change. In such cases, it was more a matter of God's grace than our good management. Sadly, too often, too much time was spent making the demon the issue without any lasting effect.

I first saw the current method I use demonstrated in a seminar I attended in 2000. I have used it ever since. Later, I found out that Charles Kraft, a prominent Christian author and teaching Professor, has advocated a similar approach and demonstrated this for a long time. There are, no doubt, other Christian ministers around the world who are doing the same thing.

Unfortunately, the pre-resurrection, the-way-Jesus-did-it model is still the most common method of deliverance used today, which is one of the reasons for this series of books. Even though their legal right has been removed, if the satanic kingdom knows that we expect to get a strong manifestation when we do deliverance, they are is only too happy to oblige. This approach wastes time, doesn't deal with the root issues, can feed the ego of the person ministering, centres attention of the demon, embarrasses the client, puts off tentative believers and unbelievers that may be observing, and often achieves little. The new legal right we give the enemy in such circumstances is our own ignorance. We should know better. We should be doing deliverance from the standpoint of a resurrected Jesus, not the stand point of an earth-bound Jesus. We should no longer be modelling our deliverance on the way Jesus did it in Matthew, Mark and Luke.

The Brian's of the world deserve no less.

SUMMARY

- When Jesus drove out demons often there were no problems. However sometimes it was 'messy': the person's dignity was not maintained as the demons threw the person to the ground, demons were loud and distracting and didn't do as they were told.

- The reasons for this were threefold:
  (1) Jesus was trespassing on Satan's turf.
  (2) Jesus hadn't yet completed his role as the second Adam.
  (3) Satan was trying to discredit Jesus in the eyes of those around him.

- A post resurrection model for deliverance means that anyone doing deliverance using this approach can do deliverance more effortlessly than Jesus.

- There are two main reasons deliverance today should be more effortless;
  (1) The earth is no longer under the complete, undisputed control of the kingdom of darkness. The demons have lost their authority.
  (2) Satan no longer has anything to gain by putting on a show, other than distraction value. The Cross has happened.

- Most Christians doing deliverance today base their approach on the way Jesus did it and therefore deliverance is cumbersome, protracted and frequently negatively affects unbelievers or new believers. In addition, the demons become the 'stars' by putting on a show and the dignity of the person being delivered is often compromised.

- Having personally dealt with similar deliverance situations as those recorded in the gospels, I haven't encountered the strong reactions Jesus encountered. Demons should *never* play up in using a post-resurrection paradigm.

- The approach advocated by Anazao is part of the fulfilment of the prediction Jesus made that we would do greater things than him.

Chapter 17: CAN CHRISTIANS HAVE DEMONS?

This question causes so much division and uncertainty within the Body of Christ and yet it is one that is so easy to answer.

Because of the surpassing greatness of the revelations, for this reason, to keep me from exalting myself, there was given me a thorn in the flesh, a messenger of Satan to torment me—to keep me from exalting myself! (2 Cor 12:7)

As we have already stated in an earlier chapter, the great apostle Paul was sent a demon. A messenger from Satan can only be a demon. There is no other satisfactory explanation. This demon appeared to produce some *internal* physical discomfort. It wasn't just oppressing him from outside. Paul was, without doubt, a Christian at the time he was sent a demon. Paul had a demon *in* him. Christians, therefore, can have demons in them. End of argument.

Can evil and good co-exist in harmony?

The argument above, unfortunately, is not proof enough for many Christians. Deep down they can't reconcile the idea that demons and the Holy Spirit can cohabit. It seems contradictory. In their thinking demons and the Holy Spirit mutually exclude each other. You can have one or the other but you can't have both. After all, what fellowship does darkness have with light?

The thinking behind this reasoning is that the Holy Spirit and demons are mortal enemies of each other. How could two enemies be in the same bed together! As this book has gone to considerable lengths to point out, such dualistic thinking is not scriptural. There are numerous Scriptures that debate this 'us against them' approach and show that the Holy Spirit is comfortable in the presence of demons and vice versa (See chapter 5). God created the angels and he loves them just as God loves all his creatures, whether or not they are fallen and disobedient. He doesn't agree with their choice to follow Satan instead of himself but he honours their right to do so. God created demons, has ultimate control over the demonic realm, uses demons to fulfill his will and is comfortable in their presence and demons are 'comfortable' in God's presence. Whether God is interacting with demons in heaven or in a human body makes no difference to the relationship.

When the person becomes a Christian, it is like a house finally being returned to its rightful owner or creator. It is like the master of the house returning home to his castle and setting back in order the mess that was created by rebellious servants. The Holy Spirit allows demons to remain because they create upheaval or dysfunctions in the person's life and the Holy Spirit uses these as a way of highlighting for the person that there are intimacy issues with God that need addressing. For example, when demons exaggerate a fear of flying in the person, the Holy Spirit is hoping that the person will turn to him and realize that this fear is really a lack of trust in God's ability to protect him. Remember, demons work with a myopic, close range view and the Holy Spirit always has the bigger picture in mind. Because of Paul's pride, God allows a demon to be sent to him to keep him humble. Paul asks God to remove it and God doesn't. The demon is clearly achieving God's purposes by remaining. The demon is causing some kind of physical discomfort and he thinks he is winning. Paul's pride is the legal right and the demon is hoping it will discourage Paul further through this fleshy agitation and provide an even greater platform for more damage. God, however, is using the demon to train Paul to rely on his grace and God knows that this affliction will more likely push Paul to even greater dependence on the Holy Spirit.

Out of context

Let's look at the verse sometimes quoted to show that light and darkness can't have fellowship together and therefore Christians can't have demons.

> *Do not be bound together with unbelievers; for what partnership have righteousness and lawlessness, or what fellowship has light with darkness?*
> (2 Cor 6:14)

The context here is that Paul is exhorting Christians to marry Christians because it is difficult to have a close and intimate relationship with a non-believer since one has the light and life of Christ and the other doesn't. This verse can't be applied to the Holy Spirit and demons because they do not marry each other! There is no intimate one flesh relationship between the Holy Spirit and demons, so there is no problem with them cohabiting. Demons are not in fellowship with the Holy Spirit. They once were but they chose to rebel. It is now a master-servant relationship, not a husband-wife relationship.

The discrete model

For those still uncomfortable with the concept of the Holy Spirit and demons cohabiting, perhaps the following diagram will help. Humans are unique in that we are created in God's image and one aspect of this mystery is that we are also a trinity too. Our body, soul and spirit are considered a trinity because they are simultaneously distinct and yet one. There are various models that are used to describe the interconnection of our body, soul and spirit. In my previous book, *'The Forgotten Factor in Healing'*, I looked in detail at three different models. One of these models is called the distinct model; where body, soul and spirit are seen as distinct from each other.

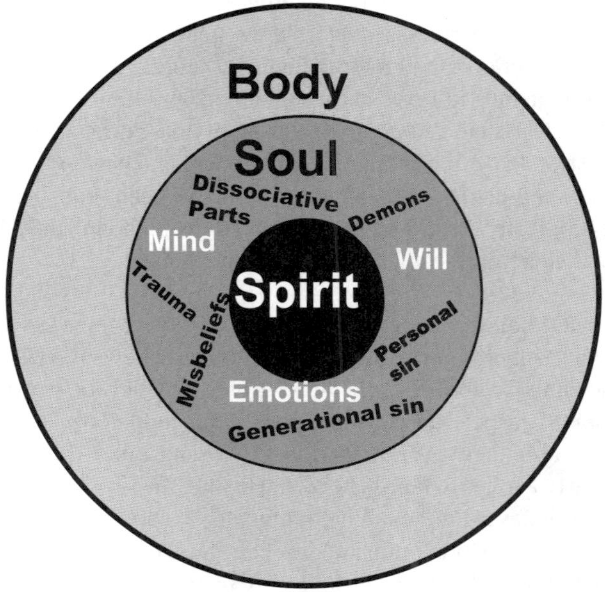

In this model, when we become a believer, the Holy Spirit occupies our spirit. Our spirit, which prior to salvation was dead to God, is now infused completely with the fullness and life of the Holy Spirit.

Therefore if anyone is in Christ, he is a new creature; the old things passed away; behold, new things have come. (2 Cor 5:17)

This verse refers to our justification; which occurs the moment we ask Jesus as Lord and Savior into our lives. Justification happens in an instant, our spirit becomes new. Justification doesn't affect the soul, it remains unchanged. Sanctification, however, doesn't happen in an instant. It takes the rest of our lives and it is the process of allowing the Holy Spirit into every area of our soul. Justification happens in our spirits, sanctification happens in our souls. Demons occupy our soul and so when the Holy Spirit enters our spirit, they are not perplexed because they are happily compartmentalized in our soul. They have significant strongholds in our soul; in our mind, will and emotions, in our finances, our work and family life, our sexual expression and our leisure time. They work well through our personal sin, our inherited generational iniquity and the trauma that has afflicted our lives. It is like the master of the castle living in the castle with the servants living close by but elsewhere; in the basement or surrounding housing.

Deliverance ministry designed for believers

Let's approach this question from another perspective. Aside from a few exceptions that will be discussed shortly, the general rule is: you can only remove demons from believers; from Christians. Demons in non-Christians won't respond to commands to leave because the person doesn't recognize the authority of Christ. A Christian can go up to a random non-Christian and demand demons to manifest or leave and nothing will happen. God won't violate the freewill choice of a non-Christian to remain a non-Christian and therefore to keep his demons. Logically then, deliverance ministry is predominantly for Christians. It must mean, therefore, that Christians have demons.

Deliverance is not a specialized ministry. God expects all of us to be dealing with the demonic as it presents in ourselves and other believers. There are three exhortations given to the apostles, and indirectly to all believers, that are common to all three synoptic gospels These are to preach the good news, heal the sick and cast out demons (Matthew 10:7,8, Mark 6:12,13 and Luke 10:9,17). Preaching the gospel clearly applies to non-believers. Healing the sick can apply to both believers and non-believers, although predominantly it applies to believers. Casting out demons is a ministry predominantly for believers, for reasons already stated. Baptizing (Mat 28:19, Mk 16:16) is done only to believers, usually new believers.

What about people in the gospels, who weren't Christians, and yet Jesus and the apostles cast their demons out? Casting out demons was part of the declaration of the kingdom of God. Most of those in the gospels that Jesus ministered to were Jewish people who approached him for help. They were the believers of that time, sons and daughter of Abraham. Jesus makes this point in his rebuttal to those who thought he shouldn't heal on the Sabbath.

> *And this woman, a daughter of Abraham as she is, whom Satan has bound for eighteen long years, should she not have been released from this bond on the Sabbath day?* (Luke 13:16)

In coming to Jesus they were implicitly acknowledging his authority and therefore the demons had to go. While they weren't officially Holy Spirit filled believers, because Jesus hadn't yet died on the Cross, their submissive heart attitude and trust in Jesus to help them, was sufficient at the time.

Today, when evangelizing in other countries, Christians have seen demons leaving Hindus, Buddhists and Moslems when they have lined up to receive prayer and these people weren't Christians. Once again, like when Jesus was on earth, this is an example of God's grace towards people who are searching for the truth and have the courage to ask for prayer. The demonstrated power of God to release people from demons in the name of Jesus leads to people becoming believers.

Exceptions

The exceptions to this principle are when a person interferes with what a Christian is trying to do. For example, when Jesus was in the synagogue and a disruptive person was yelling out, Jesus dealt swiftly with the interference and the demon left (Mark 1:23-28). When Paul was being harassed by the slave-girl, he finally turned around and commanded the demon to leave. In these cases, the kingdom of darkness has overplayed its hand and not kept within its territorial limits so the Kingdom of Light can then exercise its authority. Had the girl been minding her own business and Paul gone up to her and commanded the demons to leave, nothing would have happened. In this case, Paul would have been overstepping the boundaries and trespassing on the territory of the satanic kingdom.

This is an important principle because Christians often move in presumption in this regard. I cannot simply go to a Psychic Expo and bind all the territorial spirits over the tarot card readers and fortune tellers. Nothing will happen because I am trespassing on their territory. Through their freewill choices, they have given the satanic kingdom strong legal rights and the territorial spirits will laugh in my face. Now if a fortune teller were to come up to me and chat, I could temporarily bind the demons in her while I talk to her because she would now be in my space. However, I could not bind them permanently because she gives them the legal right to be there. When she walks away from me, the bound spirits would become unbound. If she were to challenge me regarding the power of the Kingdom of Light versus the power of the kingdom of darkness and if she were genuine in her challenge, then I could bind the territorial spirit related to her fortune telling. She would not be able to provide the usually accurate information that fortune tellers often give to clients at the beginning of a session to establish credibility.

Personal example

Very occasionally, if a non-Christian is open and teachable, I have commanded demons to manifest in them and the person has come to the Lord as a result. One man, in my counselling room, wasn't sure whether Jesus and the demonic realm were real as described in the New Testament. I could see that he was genuine in his inquiry and I asked him whether he would seriously consider becoming a believer if God showed him that demons were real. He responded, 'Definitely!' Because this man struggled with the same sexual issues that his father had, I knew that generational legal rights would be strong, as would the accompanying demons linked to this generational iniquity. I commanded these demons to manifest in a way that would leave the man with no uncertainty regarding their presence. Immediately, the man's neck went very tense and he had difficulty breathing, as though suspended by the neck. I asked him whether that was convincing enough. His face was very anxious and he gave several short, quick nods. I commanded the demons to stop and immediately all the symptoms ceased and he relaxed. He gave his heart to Jesus there and then!

Note that this is not a procedure I would recommend to be used with any regularity with a non-believer. It is an exception rather than a rule. If you try to do this whenever people want a demonstration of the demonic, it simply won't happen. God is not into performing tricks to satisfy our curiosity, as Herod found out.

No evidence to support the claim that Christians don't have demons

If it is true that non-Christians have demons, and Christians don't have demons, then the only logical conclusion is that all the demons must leave at the instant the person becomes a believer; when the person says the sinner's prayer and invites in the Holy Spirit. If that were the case, we would expect some manifestation or sensation related to this event, however slight. We would expect the person to report some change in their emotions or physiology as all the demons left. Their heart rate might increase, a subtle change in their eyes, which often occurs during deliverance, should be observed, or perhaps a tension or sharp localized pain for an instant. This doesn't happen. I have led a number of people to the Lord and observed in church services, large meetings and through para church organizations, many hundreds of people come to salvation through Jesus. Sometimes there is no change at all that the person notices. However the most common response that people report is a feeling of relaxation, peace, calmness and inner joy. There are no manifestations that one would normally associate with deliverance. There is simply no evidence to indicate that demons all leave at salvation.

Another solution: outside but not inside?

There is a vast amount of evidence regarding wonderfully dedicated believers who love the Lord but who have had demons and have needed deliverance. To get around this dilemma and, at the same time, to reconcile the 'impossible' situation that demons can coexist in the presence of the Holy Spirit, there is a school of thought that holds the belief that Christians can be *oppressed externally* by demons but that demons cannot *dwell internally* in a believer.

There is no biblical evidence to suggest that this is so but there are many Scriptures supporting the idea that demons indwell people.

There is only one verse in the Scriptures that mentions demonic oppression and the context indicates that it is used to apply to internal oppression by the devil rather than external oppression. In other words, oppression *from the inside out* rather than from the outside in. The use of the word 'healing' implies that the oppression was related more to sickness and disease, and these relate to internal physiological disruption by the satanic kingdom, not external harassment.

> *You know of Jesus of Nazareth, how God anointed Him with the Holy Spirit and with power, and how He went about doing good and* ***healing all who were oppressed by the devil,*** *for God was with Him.* (Acts 10:38)

Scripture speaks of *casting out* demons, implying that the demons come from within the person. If the demons were predominantly external, the appropriate phrase would be *cast off*. Similarly, demons *come out of* a person not *come off* the person.

> *And He healed many who were ill with various diseases, and* ***cast out*** *many demons.* (Mk 1:34)

There are 14 such references to 'casting out' demons in the New Testament. There are no references to 'casting off' demons.

> *Throwing him into convulsions, the unclean spirit cried out with a loud voice and* ***came out*** *of him"* (Mk 1:26).

There are eight references, like the one above, referring to demons 'coming out' of a person. There are no references to demons 'coming off' a person.

Jesus implies that demons don't like wandering around but prefer to *inhabit* people ('go in and live there') and will bring others with them if the place is swept clean.

Now when the unclean spirit goes out of a man, it passes through waterless places seeking rest, and does not find it.... seven other spirits more wicked than itself, ***and they go in and live there;*** *and the last state of that man becomes worse than the first.* (Mk 12:43-45)

When doing deliverance, I look predominantly for changes in the eyes of the person as an indicator of the presence of demons. The demons use the person's eyes to look at me. They are looking at me from the inside out. Under an oppression model, they wouldn't be able to use the person's eyes.

Perhaps the most convincing Scripture is when Satan entered into Judas.

Then Satan entered Judas, called Iscariot, one of the Twelve. (Lk 22:3)
As soon as Judas took the bread, Satan entered into him. (Jn 13:27)

If Satan, who is a majestically created being, can enter into and be contained within a human, then it is easy to imagine large numbers of lesser fallen angels inhabiting humans with ease. Rarely in our counselling has Satan himself manifested through a Christian client although it has happened. In higher, more specialized counselling, we have encountered and employed God's angels during the deliverance process and these angels seamlessly enter the client and help as necessary.

Although external oppression, as a modus operandi of the demonic, has no direct scriptural support, it doesn't mean that demons can't oppress people from the outside. The fact that Scripture doesn't comment on a possibility doesn't mean that possibility can't happen. In our experience, demons and demonic energy can and often does oppress a person from the outside.

Nevertheless, just because they can oppress doesn't mean that this is what they exclusively do.

Demon possession

Having settled the question concerning Christians having demons and demons indwelling believers, the next most commonly asked question is, 'Can someone be totally possessed by demons?'

The notion of 'demon possession' derives from the mistranslation of the Greek word, 'diamonizomai', which means 'to have a demon' or 'with an evil spirit'. Many translations, including the KJV (King James Version), NIV (New International Version), the GNB (Good News Bible) and the NASB (New American Standard Version) do translate it, in some places, as 'having a demon' but also translate the same word, in other places, as 'possessed by an evil spirit'. This is a digression from the original intent and the source of the confusion. In addition, different versions translate the same verse differently.

> *Just then a man in their synagogue who was* ***possessed by an evil spirit*** *cried out,* (Mk 1:23 NIV)
> *Just then there was a man in their synagogue* ***with an unclean spirit;*** *and he cried out,* (Mk 1:23 NASB)

'To have a demon' is quite different from 'possessed by an evil spirit'. The phrase 'demon possessed' carries with it the connotation of ownership. To possess something is to have ownership of it. We can see the strong link between ownership and possession more clearly in real estate[1]. The day a buyer settles on a property is the day when his money is exchanged for the title, and at that point he is said to have taken *possession* of the property. You possess something because you pay a price for it, because you now own it. It was not the intent of the gospel writers to convey to the reader that demons possessed or owned them. Demons have not paid any price for us and therefore can never possess us. Jesus has paid a price for us and so it would be more accurate to call a believer, 'Jesus possessed'. In fact, Paul uses this concept of God's possession of us in his letter to the Ephesians.

> *In Him, you also, after listening to the message of truth, the gospel of your salvation—having also believed, you were sealed in Him with the Holy Spirit of promise, who is given as a pledge of our inheritance, with a view to the redemption of* ***God's own possession,*** *to the praise of His glory. (Eph 1:13,14)*

If the question means '*Can someone be totally under the control of demons against their will?*' then the answer is no. God never allows the demonic to take complete control of a person against their will. Freewill choice can never be totally subjugated. Even the Gerasene Demoniac could still come to Jesus, despite having thousands[2] of demons. The demons in anyone have power and influence in proportion to the legal rights in that person's life. While some legal rights are generational and trauma related and therefore outside of the person's direct control, usually the majority of the legal rights are related to personal sin and therefore directly under the person's control. If I lead a life characterized by self-indulgence and a lack of self control, then the demonic will have more of an influence than if I lead a life marked by self control and a heart after Jesus. Although demons can fluctuate in their influence, no matter how many I have, I still can exercise final control over my decisions. For example, I could have an anger problem and demons, recognizing this, will overlay the anger so that it *seems* that I am losing control or have lost control in the middle of an anger tirade but the reality is that I could stop the anger if I chose to. It might be harder to do so, when I am right in the middle of an anger explosion, but it is still possible.

Possession and surrender

If someone consciously chose to surrender their freewill to the demonic, then there would be periods of time when the demon could be said to *possess* the person. Not possess as in permanent ownership but possess as in temporary ownership. In these situations, the person joins his freewill with the will of the spirits and the spirits take over. If you consciously choose to hand over your own self-control to demons, they will gladly accept the offer and take over. This happens when mediums surrender totally to a familial spirit to be used as a channel. Edgar Cayce did likewise when he went into a trance and visited 'past lives'. There have been instances when heavy metal and punk singers have invited a demon to take over when on stage and they relate afterwards, that while they were aware of what they were doing, they had lost control of their playing or their actions or both[3]. Even in these cases, Jesus would not allow the demonic complete control for protracted periods of time and I would question whether the person had lost absolute ability to exercise any control at all during this time of possession.

Only one demon-free man

In all the years of full time 40 hour-a-week counselling Christians, I have yet to counsel a Christian who hasn't needed deliverance. It doesn't make any difference whether they are priests, pastors or children. It doesn't matter whether they are eight years old or eighty years old, whether they have been a Christian for a few months or many decades. Even if they have had a deliverance ministry themselves, they will still have demons. I have yet to find a demon-free man; non Christian or Christian. The only demon-free man to ever exist was Jesus Christ and no human will ever be demon-free while alive on this earth, no matter how much work they do trying to remove them all. For some readers, this might be too much to accept. The thought of a demon inside of you right now is hard to handle. If that is the case, I would suggest you suspend your judgment for the moment until you have completed this book and read the second book in this *Darkness in the Light* series, *'Satan's Legal Rights'*.

Ironically, demons are the most helpful aids we have in the process of sanctification and the faster the church can make this shift in its thinking, the sooner will we walk in the wholeness and victory that Jesus intended for us.

SUMMARY

- The apostle Paul was sent a messenger from Satan to keep him humble. A messenger from Satan can be none other than a demon. If we move out of denial, here is biblical proof that a Christian can have a demon.

- The reason many Christians have a problem with demons cohabiting with the Holy Spirit is because they see the kingdom of darkness and the Kingdom of Light as opposing enemies rather than in a master-servant relationship, which is a better description.

- God created angels who fell (demons), has ultimate control over the demonic realm, uses demons to fulfill his will and is comfortable in their presence and demons are 'comfortable' in God's presence (Judges 9:23, 1Samuel 16:14, Jeremiah 51:1, Job 1:6-9, 1 Kings 22:19-23, 2 Kings 19:6,7). Whether God is with demons in the heavenly realms or in a human body makes no difference to the relationship.

- Demons occupy our soul. When we become believers, the Holy Spirit occupies our spirit. The discrete model of body, soul and spirit allows for a separation of soul from spirit and hence a separation of the Holy Spirit from the demonic.

- At salvation, my spirit is renewed, not my soul. Consequently, the demons I had before I was saved are still there after I am saved because they reside in my soul. Sanctification is the process of allowing the Holy Spirit into every area of my soul and progressively removing the demons.

- Apart from rare exceptions, deliverance ministry can only be carried out with *believers* because demons won't leave non-believers. In the pre-resurrection New Testament examples, although not true born again believers, people coming to Jesus were putting their trust in him; *believing* in him.

- In the rare instances when deliverance can be done in non-believers, the non-believer must be 'a nuisance' to the believer. In other words, trespassing in the believer's space or territory. Other instances include when a believer is challenged by a non-believer regarding the power of the Kingdom of Light and when a non-believer makes a genuine inquiry regarding salvation.

- If all our demons are supposed to leave instantly at salvation, we would expect some manifestation or sensations related to this event, however slight. This does not happen.

- The argument that demons oppress believers externally but can't dwell internally has no scriptural support.

- There are plenty of Scriptures that support demons indwelling people. There is no scriptural support for the belief that demons can indwell people before salvation but not after.

- In my experience, demons can 'oppress' from outside a person but just because they can doesn't mean it is exclusively what they do.

- Is it possible for someone to be totally possessed by a demon? If the question means 'under total control of demons' then the answer is no.

- In thousands of hours of counselling Christians, I have yet to minister to a Christian that hasn't needed deliverance. It doesn't make any difference whether they are priests, pastors or children.

- The only demon-free man to ever exist is Jesus. Every other person is born with demons and will never be completely free from having demons as long as they are alive on earth. More explanation as to why this is the case will be given in the next book in this series.

- The phrase 'demon-possession' is a mistranslation of the original Greek word which means 'to have a demon'. Possession implies ownership. Demons cannot own us because they haven't paid a price for us. Uniquely, Christians are 'God possessed'.

- God never allows the demonic to take complete control of a person. Freewill choice can never be totally subjugated. Even the Gerasene Demoniac could come to Jesus despite having a legion of demons.

- A conscious choice to hand over your freewill to the control of the demonic is the closest event to complete demonic control or possession, but even in such circumstances, it is debatable whether all ability to regain control is totally relinquished.

Chapter 18:
TALKING TO DEMONS: ARGUMENTS AGAINST

The beginning of chapter 16 may have surprised some readers with the dialogue between myself and the demon responsible for the epilepsy. Not only was this person healed of epilepsy but many others have been healed from a variety of ailments, mental and physical, through myself and Heather talking directly to demons. You may have been told that you shouldn't talk to demons. After all, they are the enemy and they will only deceive you.

Those who oppose the idea of talking to demons use some, or all, of the following arguments.

(1) Jesus didn't have conversations with demons so we shouldn't.
(2) Demons only tell lies so there is no point talking to them, you *will* get deceived.
(3) You don't waste time and effort paying attention to what the devil has to say, you deal with demons as quickly as possible and get rid of them.
(4) You shouldn't be talking to the enemy to get your information about legal rights. Ignore the demon and rely on the Holy Spirit to tell you what the problem is.
(5) Talking to demons is just another form of 'channelling'. You are acting like a New Age medium.

I have used some of these arguments myself, so I can understand why readers would think that way. I modelled my deliverance work on the above, taught to me by others and those regarded as experts in this field at the time. It was commonly accepted then, in the '70s, '80s and '90s that you didn't talk to demons. Many people still believe this to be the case. Who was I, back then, to argue with those that were more experienced? As I have already stated, such an approach meant that deliverance was often protracted, and exhausting for both parties. Although God granted grace and people were often set free, the niggling thought remained, 'Jesus, there has to be a better way. This needs to be quicker and, less exhausting, because there is no way we can meet the huge demand that is out there'. Jesus answered my prayer. There is a better way, a much quicker and far less exhausting approach. It is by talking to demons. Let's examine each of the above arguments.

(1) Jesus didn't have conversations with demons so we shouldn't.

Not true. Jesus had a considerable chat with the arch demon of them all when he was confronted by Satan in the wilderness, after 40 days of fasting. Jesus didn't say to Satan, 'I can't trust you. You are out to deceive me so I'm not going to listen to you and I'm definitely not talking to you!' The dialogue went back and forth till eventually Satan, not Jesus, gives up and walks away. Jesus is quite comfortable throughout this process.

Let's say a Pastor and some elders are ministering to a parishioner in the prayer ministry room of the church. Let's assume that in the midst of the session, Satan materializes, physically taking the form of a human and starts speaking. The majority of Pastors would probably say, 'Stop, Satan, we are not listening to anything you have to say. You are a liar and the father of lies. I bind you and command you to leave immediately in Jesus' name'. Yet the most biblically accurate response, based on what Jesus did, is to listen to what Satan has to say, dialogue with him, perhaps find out why he is there and how he can help the parishioner and when Satan eventually leaves, the Pastor resumes the deliverance.

In addition to this desert interaction, as we have already seen, Jesus talked with the demons in the Gerasene demoniac asking them the question, 'What is your name?'. However, that's not all he said.

> *They were imploring Him not to command them to go away into the abyss. Now there was a herd of many swine feeding there on the mountain; and the demons implored Him to permit them to enter the swine. And He gave them permission.* (Luke 8:31-33)

Like a group of attorneys for the defence, the demons plea bargain with Jesus and eventually the two parties strike a deal; they will go if he lets them go into the swine. He agrees. Jesus agrees, not because he is a Jew and against pork; he is not even in Israel so that's clearly not an issue. He agrees because they have too much power and this is his best option. Remember that before he asked them what their name was, he had commanded them to leave and they didn't budge. Jesus had a problem on his hands. Through talking, he skilfully negotiated a good deal for his client. Notice that the context makes it very clear that there was dialogue between Jesus and the demons, even if the sentence by sentence interchange is not recorded.

In other situations he also told demons to be quiet and come out without any fuss. Again, elsewhere he told them not to spout off about who he was. He talked to demons. Remember that the gospels only contain snippets of what Jesus said so it is highly likely that he interacted with demons much more than the few comments actually recorded. It is important that we don't become legalistic about what is recorded in the Bible and limit our theory about interaction with demons to *exactly* and *only* what Jesus is recorded as saying. That is moving into legalism and would be akin to you limiting your evaluation of me and my counselling to exactly and only what I have said in this book! Put another way, you would end up with a very narrow perspective if your judgment of me was based only on what you saw in our family photo album and what you heard and saw on a stilted home video.

You may retort and say, 'That's all very well, but Jesus is the sinless Son of God and that is quite different to you and me talking to demons'. Yes, in one sense that is true, in that Jesus possesses a clarity and perceptiveness, because of his absolute purity, that you and I don't have. Nevertheless, as believers, we are filled with the same Holy Spirit that Jesus had to rely on. In addition we have even greater authority than Jesus had when he was on earth for the reasons stated in chapter 16. Keep in mind, that although Jesus was the Son of God, he was also fully human and consequently he couldn't let his divinity be an extra aid to his humanity. If Jesus was, at any stage in his life, less human than we are, he would have failed to redeem us in that aspect of our humanity where he 'cheated'.

Being absolutely pure and sinless is a wonderful advantage but it is still no guarantee that you won't be duped by the devil. Adam and Eve were pure and sinless and they were very quickly checkmated by Satan. Jesus had one crucial advantage over Adam and Eve; the Holy Spirit. We have that same advantage. As stated previously, in the Garden, Adam and Eve walked with God but he was external to them; God wasn't always with them. He wasn't there when they were tempted and that made all the difference. However, we have the indwelling presence of the Holy Spirit in us and he never leaves us. To summarize: if Jesus, who is just as human as you and me, and who had the same Holy Spirit dwelling in him as you and me, can dialogue with Satan and the rest of the kingdom of darkness, so can we.

Incidentally, God never reprimanded Eve for dialoguing with Satan. It is not a sin to talk to the enemy.

(2) Demons only tell lies so there is no point talking to them, you *will* get deceived.

It is true that demons tell lies. But nowhere in Scripture does it say that demons *only* tell lies. What is more common is that there is a mixture of truth and lies. Scripture supports this belief when we look at Satan's dialogue with Eve in the Garden.

> *Now the serpent was craftier than any beast of the field which the Lord God had made. And he said to the woman, "Indeed, has God said, 'You shall not eat from any tree of the garden?'" The woman said to the serpent, "From the fruit of the trees of the garden we may eat; but from the fruit of the tree which is in the middle of the garden, God has said, 'You shall not eat from it or touch it, or you will die.' " The serpent said to the woman, "You surely will not die! For God knows that in the day you eat from it your eyes will be opened and you will be like God, knowing good and evil."* (Gen 3:1-5)

Satan's first statement is couched as a question so it isn't a lie. He generalized God's specific command to see if Eve fully understood what the prohibition really was about. She responded correctly so he knew that if she succumbed to his temptation, she did so fully aware of what she was doing. Satan needs to know this because it gives greater legal right leverage with God if he succeeds in his temptation.

The first part of his second response, when he said, 'You surely will not die!' contained both a lie and a truth in the same statement. Satan was telling the truth in that Adam and Eve will not and did not drop dead the moment they made this choice. In fact they lived for almost 1000 years. Satan was telling a lie in that spiritual death happened immediately, due to broken relationship with God, and physical death followed later. His next sentence was true. If they ate it their eyes would be opened and they would know the difference between good and evil and in that respect, they would be like God, because God knows the difference between good and evil. While he hadn't told a lie, he had been deceptive in the phrasing of the last part because the implication could be taken that this tree would *elevate* Adam and Eve to the status of God. Truth and lies were carefully interwoven.

Humans tell lies. Does it mean that humans *always* tell lies? Obviously the answer is no. The same logic that we apply to ourselves, we need to apply to the satanic kingdom. Jesus makes the human/demon analogy with regard to murder and lying.

You are of your father the devil, and you want to do the desires of your father. He was a murderer from the beginning, and does not stand in the truth because there is no truth in him. Whenever he speaks a lie, he speaks from his own nature, for he is a liar and the father of lies. (John 8:44)

In this verse he associates the lies and murderous intent of the Pharisees with the lies and murderous intent of the satanic kingdom. Yes, the Pharisees told lies but they didn't always lie. Yes, the satanic kingdom tells lies but they don't always lie. Jesus confirmed this in the last sentence of this verse. '*Whenever* he speaks a lie…' means that there are times Satan doesn't speak a lie. If Satan always told lies, Jesus would have begun the sentence, 'He always speaks lies and these he speaks from his own nature,..'

When Jesus says that Satan does not stand in the truth because there is no truth in him, it doesn't mean that he therefore must always tell lies. It means that his heart has become so wickedly deceitful that there is no truth, no righteousness at all in any of his intentions, attitudes and behaviours. Jesus is the truth and so when he says that Satan has no truth in him, Jesus is saying Satan no longer has any of Jesus' qualities. This doesn't mean that Satan can't speak the truth; it means that the truth he speaks doesn't come from a heart that believes what he says. There is no integrity whatsoever in what he says. He can talk the talk but there is absolutely not one iota of him walking the talk!

(3) We don't waste time and effort paying attention to what the enemy has to say. We deal with demons as quickly as possible and get rid of them.

The mistake behind this kind of thinking is that the demon becomes the issue rather than the reason, or legal right, it has to be there. Demons are almost always there for a reason. They have a right to be there. The mistake we made in the past was to make the demon the issue and try to remove it from the person as though it was some cancer that had to be cut out. To paraphrase Charles Kraft, it is similar to driving rats away from a rubbish dump. You may succeed but as soon as you go away, they will come back. To get rid of the rats, you need to get rid of the rubbish. Much more about this will be discussed in the next book.

(4) You shouldn't be talking to the enemy to get your information about legal rights. Ignore the demon and rely on the Holy Spirit to tell you what the problem is.

You knock at my door. I answer the door. You would think it strange, silly perhaps, even absurd if I said to you, 'Look, I'm sorry, I can't speak to you. You are a human just like me, and humans can tell lies. I don't know whether you are telling me the truth or not, so I will just ask God to tell me why it is you are here'.

Now God might be gracious and supernaturally tell me why you are here but the obvious first course of action is to ask *you*, not God. It's common sense! Once you have given your response, I will weigh up what you have said based on several factors: my discernment or intuition; my observation of your attitude, tone of voice, and body language; my experience and accumulated wisdom gained from many decades of living life. Then I will decide whether or not to believe you. The process is no different with demons. Why then do we act so strangely with demons?

When the demon is there, ask the demon why it is there. Deal with what is in front of you! Don't ask the Holy Spirit. Of course, the Holy Spirit knows why the demons are there but he is your second line of defence, not your first line. If you have difficulty getting information from a demon, then you can ask the Holy Spirit. It is not the Holy Spirit that has suddenly presented himself, it is a demon.

There are several other reasons why it is important to get the legal rights from the demons and not primarily from the Holy Spirit.

(1) Most people are in denial that they have demons. Many still labour under the misconception that Christians can't have demons. Acknowledging the presence of a demon forces a person to face the fact that demons are a reality. Training the person to listen to the legal rights the demons have further reinforces this truth.

(2) Commanding the demons to speak the truth and putting the appropriate parameters in place reinforces the master-servant relationship that God wants us to have with regard to the kingdom of darkness. They are servants. Their job description is to supply us with their legal rights. The majority of people in the church still believe that demons are the evil enemy and our over-cautiousness in engaging with them plays right into their hands.

(3) By commanding the demons to place the legal right directly into the person's mind, we are simply asking them to do in a formal sense what they are doing all the time anyway. Daily, demons accuse us, often subtly, sometimes more aggressively, by sowing seeds of doubt regarding our competence, sexuality, salvation, God's love for us, our self worth and a host of other things. They feed our self pity and victim thinking, encourage self indulgence, help us to self-justify and plant seeds of doubt by saying, 'Did God really heal you? Does God really care? Is he there for *you*?' They bring back to our memory hurtful words of curse spoken over us by significant others in our lives. Every demon is a powerful defence attorney in the legal rights or reasons they have to be there. There is no need to ask the Holy Spirit to do a job that the demons are expert at doing!

(4) The presence of a demon, particularly if there is some discomfort, is a powerful motivation to listen carefully for the legal rights and not to overlook those legal rights that are unpleasant. If we just relied on the Holy Spirit, the lack of discomfort would lead to the deeper issues being overlooked. For example, a pastor who had a demon manifest reported that it was causing considerable tightness in his chest. He thought he had mentioned all the legal rights but the pain intensified. To relieve the pain, he finally admitted that there was one legal right *that the Holy Spirit had been earlier prompting him to share but he didn't want to* because he was embarrassed. It concerned making a covenant with Satan as a young man so he could get a girl he was attracted to. The important point to note is that we can ignore the prompting of the Holy Spirit, however it is harder to argue with pain and discomfort caused by the demons. Relief from demonic discomfort can be a powerful motivator.

(5) Relying simply on the Holy Spirit is a more haphazard way of getting legal rights. No one hears the Holy Spirit perfectly, all the time, so often legal rights will be missed. Because the Holy Spirit is always present in the believer and doesn't make us feel uncomfortable, it is hard to know if all the legal rights have been addressed. With demons present, there will be some mental, emotional or physical indication of their presence that acts as a cue regarding whether all the legal rights are dealt with. In addition, demons are highly territorial. This means they won't leave until *all* the legal rights are gone. In fact, we have found that Jesus won't allow them to leave when legal rights are being directly addressed. They must remain. They cannot simply hive off during the process. As long as the manifestation is there, the demons are there. Frequently, the physical or emotional symptoms will abate during the legal rights process particularly when it takes some time to work through all the legal rights. Even during these times, the person will often have an internal sense of the demon's presence and if they don't, the demons can simply be commanded to make their presence felt again. The presence of the demon heightens our perception and we are likely to be more persistent and get most or all of the reasons they have to be there. To clarify: the fourth point concerned avoiding some of the *deeper* legal rights, this fifth point is about getting *all* the legal rights.

(6) Relying solely on the Holy Spirit is obviously not going to be as thorough as listening to what the demons are saying, exercising the gift of discernment of spirits *as well as* both counsellor and client listening to the Holy Spirit. Why have one arrow in your quiver when you can have three? The person sensing the discomfort, the counsellor exercising the gift of discernment of spirits, and both parties checking with the Holy Spirit to see whether the legal rights are relevant or that the demons have

gone is a more secure method than simply relying on the Holy Spirit.

(7) When we shift the focus from hearing what the demon has to say, to hearing what the Holy Spirit has to say, the client will often rely on the counsellor to hear, since the counsellor is often deemed to be more spiritual. The client can become too passive in his own healing and the counsellor can overfunction by hearing on behalf of the client. The client is the one who should be doing the work of hearing what the legal rights are. He has the demon, the counsellor doesn't! Jesus is more interested in training the counsellee to listen, not the counsellor. If the counsellor is the primary source of revelation regarding legal rights, it can open up the whole process to the counsellor manipulating the situation, whether she recognises it or not. God primarily speaks to us directly, not second hand. It can also increase the chance of co-dependency with the counsellor.

(8) I am always amazed at how often the demons bring up legal rights that I, as the counsellor, would never have thought of. Asking the Holy Spirit for the legal rights would result in some of the legal rights. However, I would never have discerned some of the more subtle legal rights that the demons bring up. One reason could be that I don't hear the Holy Spirit well enough. I suspect that the deeper issue is, once again, that I don't have the problem, and the Holy Spirit is not going to rescue the client through me. Yet, if I encourage the client to rely on the Holy Spirit, a similar situation would occur; we would miss legal rights. It is not that the Holy Spirit *can't* reveal all the legal rights the demons have, it is that he wants us to go to the source first and only rely on him when in trouble.

(9) If we just rely on the Holy Spirit to reveal the legal rights, without any reference to the kingdom of darkness, the subtle assumption can be that the Holy Spirit has brought upon our lives the problems and calamities that beset it. Our erroneous thinking is that if the Holy Spirit has revealed these sin areas, then the Holy Spirit must be responsible for the effects of these sins in our life. It is possible that we become just like Job; attributing to God what is the work of the kingdom of darkness. The Holy Spirit doesn't want to take the blame for how the kingdom of darkness chooses to use their legal rights in our life. He wants us to see, as clearly as possible, how our actions have given leverage to the enemy.

(10) It is surprising how many mature Christians admit to having difficulty hearing God's voice. Actually, they don't have difficulty hearing the Holy Spirit, they just *think* they do! Asking them to hear what the Holy Spirit is saying will often put them on the back foot and their self talk becomes, 'I don't think I will be able to hear'. Strange as it may appear, I have found that one way to increase people's ability to hear God's

voice is to learn how to hear demons speak. Most clients haven't had to listen internally for how a demon speaks so they are attentive and intrigued as to how this is achieved. After identifying a few legal rights, they become adept at hearing the next legal right. Then when I tell them that the discernment they have used to listen to demons is the same as they use to listen to God, they are much more confident in hearing what the Holy Spirit is saying. Whether you are listening to demons or the Holy Spirit, the *process* is the same. That is why people, who become Christians, after having been involved in the occult and therefore used to listening to the satanic kingdom, often have a greater sensitivity to the Holy Spirit and use the gifts more effectively. The same applies to cultures that see and hear demons easily, such as African and Polynesian people groups.

Some readers may still have a deep seated caution regarding talking to demons instead of the Holy Spirit. This is due largely to decades of indoctrination that it is an absolute no-no to talk to demons. Consequently, they will usually ask, 'Can you do deliverance by just speaking to the Holy Spirit alone without interacting with the demons?' The answer is yes. 'Do many clients who come for counselling hear the Holy Spirit well?' Again, the answer is yes. 'Together, with the collective wisdom of both client and counsellor listening to the Holy Spirit, won't this bring freedom from the demon's legal rights?' Yes, although more difficult, it is possible to get all the legal rights this way. 'So why bother talking to demons?'

Being practical

Here is a practical counselling example of why relying on the Holy Spirit alone will sometimes fail. Frequently, when a person has come to me with a fear or phobia and I have asked the Holy Spirit to take the client to a memory[1] linked to the origin of this phobic reaction, he does. We get to an important memory, work through it, Jesus is seen in the memory, speaks, brings peace and it makes a difference to the phobia. The phobia is either less intense or gone completely.

At other times, using the same process, we draw a blank. Nothing happens. I can't get to a memory. Asking the Holy Spirit hasn't helped. Frequently demons are blocking access. I then command demons linked to blocking access to this memory to present themselves. They duly present and I command them to reveal their legal rights. They do. We work through each of their legal rights and then send them on their way. I then ask the Holy Spirit to take us to the memory linked to the phobia and this time, because blockages have been removed, we get in touch with the memory and it is resolved, often with a measure of healing following. On still other occasions, I ask the Holy Spirit to take us to a memory and nothing happens. I command the demons blocking the memory to present and still nothing happens. There are no demons blocking the memory. But we still can't get to the memory. The Holy Spirit isn't apparently helping. I then command the demons directly linked to the phobia to present themselves. There are *always* demons linked to phobias. We progressively move through the legal rights the demons have to be there. Almost invariably, along the way, we come to a legal right where the demons reveal the memory linked to a foundational event that helped establish that phobia. We move through the memory and bring resolution to it as described above.

The point is that if we had only relied on the Holy Spirit, we wouldn't have reached this important memory. Why didn't the Holy Spirit reveal it when I first asked him, particularly when there were no demons blocking access? Possibly because he wanted the client to deal with the preceding legal rights first. In addition, it could be for any of the ten reasons listed above. I hope you are beginning to see the subtle and complex interactions between demons and the Holy Spirit that the counsellor needs to be aware of. The Holy Spirit works *with* the demons in such instances to reveal the memory. This will only be a problem for you if you hold onto dualistic thinking; an 'us against them' approach.

Anazao is an organisation that is primarily involved in counselling and secondly, teaching. Each year, Heather and I do at least 1000 clinical hours of counselling on the topics we teach and write on. I began my deliverance counselling in the '80s, making the demon the issue and focused on getting the demon out of the person. My deliverance became more effective when I focused on the reasons the demons were there. Following the trend at the time, I didn't allow demons to talk or interact with me and instead I have relied on the Holy Spirit to hear what the legal rights were. The current approach to deliverance, where the demons speak into the person's mind the reasons they have to remain, has been by far the most efficient, thorough, client-empowering method of all. For all the reasons listed above, talking directly to the demons is the best method I have encountered to date. I am always looking for faster ways of doing ministry without compromising thoroughness and the client's connection with Jesus. Having looked at many different ministry approaches to healing, there is nothing I have seen, currently, that has the swift incisiveness and thoroughness of dealing with demons and bringing healing as the above approach.

(5) Talking to demons is just another form of 'channelling'. You are acting like a New Age medium.

Channelling is a term used in New Age literature. Channelling means being a 'middle man'; a connection, a conduit, a channel between the spirit world and the person seeking help. A person who does channelling is called a medium. The medium consciously tries to contact the dead or 'the other side', acting as a go-between for the person asking for information about a dead loved one and the spirit giving the information. The demonic spirit speaks to the medium and the medium in turn interprets and relays the information to the inquiring person.

The reality is that the spirits of all humans who die are either in hell or heaven and both places are uncontactable by humans. Therefore, when a medium says that they are contacting your dead uncle Ernest, all they are contacting is a demon who knows about your uncle. The medium tells you that your uncle Ernest used to put his false teeth in a whiskey glass with a 'Johnny Walker' monogram on it, as he got into bed each night. You may get excited but this information simply comes from a demon who knew your uncle's habits intimately. This demon is called a familiar or familial spirit. Channelling, in this sense, is always wrong.

Using the Anazao model for deliverance, the counsellor commands the demon to speak the legal right, the reason they have to be there, *directly* into the mind of the person. The counsellor is not an intermediary or channel between the demon and the client. The counsellor is the last person to know what the legal right is. The client will share with the counsellor what he thinks the demon is saying and, using the experience of the counsellor, the two discuss together what the specific aspects of the legal right might be.

If the counsellor insisted that the demon speak through him and tell him what the legal right was, then the counsellor would be channelling and acting like a medium.

CHANNELLING:

Demon ⟶ Counsellor ⟶ Client

ANAZAO DELIVERANCE:

Demon ⟶ Client ⟶ Counsellor

Sadly, there are well meaning Christian 'intercessors' who are channelling more than interceding. It is beyond the scope of this book to explore the whole area of intercession but, in a nutshell, to intercede in a truly Christian sense is to ask God to help the person. Intercessors move onto dangerous ground when they believe they need to receive information from God that must be passed on to the person for that person's good.

> 'As I was praying and interceding for you, the Lord told me that your son is in particular danger today and that you need to be praying for his safety'.

This is an example of the type of intercession that is more closely linked to channelling than true intercession. It violates the fundamental principle that God will always speak directly to the person first, because he indwells every believer and requires no intermediary. Frequently, because we don't trust our own ability to listen to God's voice, we listen to those we deem more spiritual than ourselves and we give these people greater power to speak into our lives than God ever wanted us to. If the intercessor thinks that he is more spiritually in tune with God than the person he is interceding for, then the satanic kingdom will use this to speak to the intercessor and, because of the intercessor's pride, he will think it is God he is listening to and will inadvertently be channelling. The statement in speech marks above is a statement God is highly unlikely to make through another person. It is fear-inducing at best and manipulative and controlling at worse. If my son is in danger and God wants to warn me, he will do so by prompting me through his Holy Spirit. A true intercessor participates with me, joins with me in petitioning God over an issue currently affecting me. Being in agreement with me over a particular matter lends weight to my petition (Matt 18:19).

Please note: I am not saying it is wrong to get a direct prophetic word for another person. I am saying that when we are passive, bypassing our own relationship with God to rely on others to hear from him on our behalf, we tread on thin ice and allow the process to be highjacked by the satanic kingdom. We need to exercise common sense and wisdom with all prophetic words we receive. The potential for manipulation is huge.

CHANNELLING

'God' ⟶ Intercessor ⟶ Person

CORRECT INTERCESSION

Intercessor ⟶ God ⟶ Person

Not logically consistent

Philosophically, we shouldn't have any problem talking to demons. Demons are fallen angels. Their intrinsic nature hasn't changed just because they no longer choose to worship God. The fact that they have rebelled against God doesn't mean they can no longer talk, reason, argue and give valuable information like any of God's angels. Humans who rebel against God are obviously just as intelligent and articulate as humans who love Jesus!

Scripture is full of examples of humans dialoguing with angels. Lot entertained angels and chatted with them in Sodom, Abraham cooked for his angelic visitors and they told him about his future son. Jacob spent the night wrestling with one. Some of the Old Testament prophets dialogued with angels as they received and recorded their visions. Mary talked with and asked questions of the angel Gabriel regarding the conception of Jesus. So too did Zechariah, the father of John the Baptist. The person mentioned in chapter 4, who smuggled Bibles into Albania, chatted with an angel in his Bible laden VW.

If we have no problem talking to angels, we should have no problem talking to fallen angels. We just have to be more cautious because they are likely to be deceptive.

SUMMARY

- Talking to demons to gather legal rights has resulted in a variety of healings. These healings have been achieved with less effort than the alternative; not talking to demons.

- Five common reasons are given for not talking to demons:
  (1) Jesus didn't.
  (2) They always lie.
  (3) Don't interact, just get rid of them quickly.
  (4) Talk to the Holy Spirit instead.
  (5) You could end up channelling so don't take the risk.

- Jesus had extensive dialogue with Satan in the wilderness. He also bartered with the demons who went into the swine. Eve wasn't admonished for talking to Satan.,

- Demons don't *always* lie. Satan's dialogue with Eve contains both truth and lies. They can tell the truth, they can tell lies, they can tell a mixture of truth and lies. Just like humans.

- The demon is not the issue, the reasons they are there, is the issue. Rats are not the issue; the garbage that attracts them is the issue.

- Talking solely to the Holy Spirit
  (1) reinforces denial about the existence of demons.
  (2) doesn't allow us to be trained in the master-servant relationship God wants us to have with regard to demons.
  (3) bypasses what is naturally happening in our minds on a daily basis. Demons are always accusing us so listening to them to give us the legal rights makes more sense than going to the Holy Spirit as a 'third party'.
  (4) doesn't cause the discomfort necessary for the release of deeper legal rights.
  (5) doesn't allow for definitive completion of *all* the legal rights in the same way that the presence and then the absence of demons does.
  (6) will be less accurate than commanding demons to share what they know *as well as* listening to the Holy Spirit.
  (7) can lead to passivity in the client and over functioning by the counsellor.
  (8) doesn't get the same thoroughness as talking to the demon because the counsellor doesn't have the problem, the client does.
  (9) means that demons don't get the blame they rightly deserve for the problems in a person's life. Subtly we become like Job and attribute to God what is the work of the enemy.
  (10) can intimidate people because listening to the Holy Spirit is a problem for many Christians but training them to listen to demons inadvertently trains them to listen to the Holy Spirit.

- Channelling occurs when a person is a conduit between the spirit world and the human world. Talking to demons in the way I have outlined doesn't put the counsellor as an intermediate step in the process. The counsellor is the last one to know what is happening.

- Christians who intercede on behalf of others need to be careful that they don't become mediators of God's will for other Christians. This can, inadvertently, become channelling and leave the intercessor open to deception by the kingdom of darkness. There is only one mediator *between* God and man and that is Jesus Christ (1 Tim 2:5).

- Talking to God's angels is commonplace throughout the Scriptures. Talking to demons should be no different; we just need to exercise more caution. God does it. We have the Holy Spirit. We can do it.

Chapter 19:

TALKING TO DEMONS: THEY ARE JUST LIKE US!

All books written on deliverance over the past thirty or forty years, that have shaped our understanding of demons and how to deal with them, have been written without the authors[1] having made mention of dissociation. Since our awareness of dissociation is relatively recent, over the last two decades, many of these authors simply had no knowledge of its impact on deliverance. The authors of the more recent books make no significant reference to dissociation and consequently one would assume lack extensive experience interacting with demons in people who are highly dissociative. A whole new world opens up when dealing with demons in those who are at the far end of the dissociative scale. In these circumstances, the growth in understanding the kingdom of darkness is exponential. It is as if all books written to date on deliverance have been like books written about the surface of the sea. They have taught us a lot about waves, tides, currents, seabirds, polar ice etc. None of them, however, have dealt with what is under the sea. No one has put on a mask and put their heads under the water. Dissociation is like the mask and aqualung that for the first time introduces the reader to the life under the sea. For the first time you go behind the 'surface presentation' of demons. Your whole perspective changes.

I have, on more than a few occasions, had to deal directly with demonic princes. Talking directly to a demon, without human influence, occurs when dealing with clients who are highly dissociative and invariably have suffered comprehensive ritualistic abuse. The satanic investment in such people is immense and hence encountering high level Princes is not unusual. When a well differentiated alter, or 'part', takes over, the client himself is not cognitively present; he is totally unaware of what is happening or able in any way to influence the proceedings. When demons interrupt at such times, which they often do, the interaction between the counsellor and the demon is as 'pure' as it can be. In such situations, when I talk to them, it is like talking to an intelligent person. It is just like dialogue I would have with any other rational person. Even demons lower down in rank can talk intelligently, articulately and perceptively.

This is quite different from normal deliverance, where the demon presents himself through a person who is well aware of what is happening and the counsellor is a third party in the process. Often in these situations, demons appear to speak using cryptic, monosyllabic one line statements, uttered in deep, raspy guttural voices and we can wrongly assume that this is the only way they can communicate. In fact, demons prefer us to think they are one dimensional and unintelligent because it enables their true nature to remain in darkness and they thrive best in darkness. They also gain more legal rights through our false assumptions.

The scriptural account of God's interaction with Satan regarding Job, and Satan's interaction with Eve illustrate both intelligent and deceptive dialogue. The lying spirit in Micaiah's vision (1 Kings 22) talks clearly and concisely to God. There is nothing unintelligent about what the demons said to Jesus, speaking through the man in the synagogue (Luke 4:34). Demons can be arrogant, dismissive and shallow. Demons can also be thoughtful, logical and responsive, speaking in a soft, modulated voice. They can be subtly cunning and disarmingly deceptive, just like a crooked salesman. In a word, they can be just like you and me!

Demons and fallen angels are the same

Some Christians believe that demons are different from fallen angels. This has not been my experience. Whether I am dialoguing directly with a Prince, the equivalent of an army general, or the lowest level demon, a minion or army private, the nature of the interaction is the same. There is no fundamental difference. A demonic Prince knows more, as you would expect, is not as myopic as a minion and generally is more cautious in communication; more considered in the responses he gives. That is no different from the earthly parallel of the dialogue difference we would expect when talking to an army general compared to an army private.

As mentioned, few people have had the experience of interaction between demons and highly dissociative parts that manifest in *complex* satanic ritualistic abuse victims. Most, if not all, Christians who have written on the topic of whether or not demons are fallen angels do so from ministry experience when the person is to a greater or lesser extent co-conscious with all that is happening. Based on this limited experience, it is understandable that there is a measure of conjecture about this issue. Yet, the truth is, there is no difference.

Some conjecture that demons were the spirits of those belonging to a pre-Adamic race; a race of people that existed before Adam but died out. A pre-Adamic race is not theologically tenable. God created the world perfectly. Adam was the first man. There was no death until after Adam's sin. Death entered *because* of Adam's sin. A pre-Adamic race implies that death entered the world before Adam's sin and therefore renders the temptation in the Garden of Eden as irrelevant. This contradicts Scripture and nullifies Jesus' role as the second Adam.

Others conjecture that demons are the spirits of the Nephilim because these creatures were an angelic-human hybrid, not fully human and therefore couldn't receive the same salvation as we receive. However, despite their unorthodox paternity, Scripture makes it clear that they were human. The Nephilim are called '*the mighty* ***men*** *of old,* ***men*** *of renown' (Gen 6:4)*. Had they been considered other than human, then the words 'creatures, creations, beings' would have replaced the word 'men'. This issue has been explored in detail in chapter 6.

One of the reasons we have difficulty believing that demons could be angels is because of the popular perception of demons as the antithesis of angels. Mention the word 'angel' and the average person, including Christians, think of purity, holiness, beauty, female, wings, clouds, harps, singing. Mention the word 'demon' and the associated words and images are evil, ugly, revolting, gargoyles, scary, deceptive, warty, red. The reality is that angels are male, masculine, strong, protective, more like Arnie Swartzenegger than Miss World! Our connection of angels to females is so strong that we would think nothing of naming a girl 'Angel' or 'Angela' but most English speaking people wouldn't name a son 'Angel'. Yet naming a boy 'Angel' is the most appropriate application of the word and people of Spanish and South American extraction do. Demons, fallen angels, are also male, masculine, strong, protective of their own and with all the capabilities of God's angels. They can also act in a devious, deceptive and scary manner.

Hypothetically, let's assume an outer space alien is only given an album cover of a young, fresh faced Britney Spears and one of Gene Simmonds from the heavy metal group KISS, with the jagged black and white makeup, the scary look with the long extended tongue. The alien may well conclude it was looking at two different earthlings. The truth is both are equally human, but the presentation is vastly different.

Still other Christians argue that demons didn't exist before the heavenly rebellion but God made some of the fallen angels into demons, lesser beings, as a punishment after the rebellion. Firstly, there is no Scriptural backing for this assertion. Secondly, when God creates a being, he doesn't diminish that individual's intrinsic attributes and capabilities simply because that creature chooses to rebel against him. We can clearly see this in God's interactions with humans. If a person becomes a Christian and then chooses to reject Jesus, that person still retains all his physical and mental faculties after the rejection. The person doesn't suddenly get zapped by God and change his appearance or become mentally challenged.

It is stating the obvious but a Christian who later becomes a Buddhist or Hindu doesn't change physically or intellectually. God's principle that what a man sows he will reap means that God wants the same cognitive, capable individual who made both good and bad choices to be the same cognitive, capable individual who will reap the reward or curse of those choices. Why? So he will learn wisdom. If God mentally or physically diminishes us when we rebel against him, then we are equally diminished in our ability to truly learn from these mistakes and our future mistakes. If I had a genius IQ and was devastatingly good looking when I choose to reject God and then God punished me for this by changing me into an ugly moron, I now won't truly reap what I have sown. Why? Because I can no longer fully appreciate the gravity of my offence due to my diminished mental capacity to comprehend what I have done. Furthermore, God is nothing if he is not consistent and reliable. If he zapped the fallen angels and changed them into 'toads' back then, what is to stop him from doing the same to us now when we commit a similar sin? As has been stated, he is not one of the impulsive, reactionary, vindictive gods that the ancient Greeks believed in.

Scripture doesn't support a distinction between fallen angels and demons. The 'New International Encyclopaedia of Bible Words' states:

> "The devil and his fallen angels are the only evil spiritual beings about which we have any information in Scripture. Surely if the demons of the Gospels were different from the fallen angels, there would be some mention of them when Jesus describes hell as *'the eternal fire prepared for the devil and his angels'* (Mt 25:41)

'Demons', 'evil spirits', 'fallen angels', 'sons of God' are all interchangeable terms just as the words 'humans','people' and 'mankind' are interchangeable. God created angels and God created humans. There is no mention in Scripture of a third spiritual being distinct from these two and conjecture is unwarranted if both Scripture and experience indicate that no such entity exists.

An inconvenient truth

As we first mentioned in chapter 5 and has been a theme throughout the book, the big mistake we make is seeing ourselves as somehow radically different from demons. We are not. Consider the following similarities:

THE KINGDOM OF DARKNESS	HUMANS
Satan was created sinless.	Adam was created sinless.
Satan walked with God.	Adam walked with God.
Satan's downfall was wanting to be like God.	Adam's downfall was wanting to be like God.
Chose Satan over God.	Chose Satan over God.
Pride and Satan's sin was adopted by all his followers.	Pride and Adam's sin has been adopted by all humans since Adam.
Expulsion from the third heaven, God's presence, was the immediate consequence of Satan's sin.	Expulsion from Eden, God's presence, was the immediate consequence of Adam's sin.
Hell is the place of final punishment.	Hell is the place of final punishment.
Satan and his fallen angels exercise freewill choice.	Humans exercise freewill choice.
Wicked and deceitful in their intentions.	Wicked and deceitful in our intentions. (Jer 17:9)
Loved by God because he created them.	Loved by God because he created us.
Loved by God despite their constant sin.	Loved by God despite our constant sin.
God can use their sinful choices to further his plans.	God can use our sinful choices to further his plans.
Can tell the whole truth.	Can tell the whole truth.
Can mix truth and lies together.	Can mix truth and lies together.
Can tell nothing but lies.	Can tell nothing but lies.
Can argue very persuasively and logically to make their point.	Can argue very persuasively and logically to make our point.
Can physically, emotionally and mentally destroy humans.	Can physically, emotionally and mentally destroy each other.
In disembodied form, have a human shape. In addition, some have wings.	After death, in disembodied form, have a human shape.

Spirit and soul but able to clothe themselves with flesh for a limited period of time and look like humans.	An integrated trinity of spirit, soul and flesh. Humans wouldn't be able to recognise a demon in flesh that might walk past them.
In disembodied form, capable of having sexual intercourse with humans.	Capable of having sexual intercourse with disembodied demons.
Able to embody and participate in complete physical sexual intercourse with humans.	Able to participate in physical sexual intercourse with embodied demons and be unaware of it.
Can produce sperm that fertilizes a human ovum to produce viable human offspring.	Can receive demonic sperm and produce viable human offspring.
The offspring produced from intercourse with humans are themselves able to reproduce. This indicates a high degree of genetic compatibility.	The humans formed from intercourse with demons are not sterile but capable of human reproduction themselves. Giganticism is a distinguishing feature of male offspring.

The list is disconcerting and compelling. It faces us squarely with the truth that there is very little that separates us from the satanic kingdom.

To reiterate, just because humans are capable of telling lies, we don't stop talking to humans! We should always be cautious and exercise wisdom and discernment. Particularly so if we are unsure of the person's trustworthiness. Just because demons are capable of telling lies, we don't stop talking to demons! We should always be cautious and exercise wisdom and discernment. Particularly so because of demons' untrustworthiness.

Servants

Demons are still angels that were created as servants of God and that job description has never changed. They chose to rebel and were defeated. That makes them even more servile than before. They are still servants but they don't have the privileges of the other angels. They don't have automatic access to the third heaven anymore. Their sin, just like our sin, separates them from intimacy with God. Yet, as we have clearly demonstrated from Old Testament Scriptures, when God commands them to appear before him, they dutifully appear. He sent them to do his bidding, whether to torment Saul or be a lying spirit in the mouth of prophets. God is in control. He commands and they obey. They may be reluctant to obey, but obey they must. God commands them to speak and report to him and they report. They dare not tell a lie. The Cross hasn't changed that. The Cross hasn't made them any more servile. The Cross did, however, transfer God's authority over demons to us, believers. If God is comfortable talking to demons, why shouldn't we be? If we talk to our human servants, why are we so reluctant to talk to our spiritual servants?

In fact we have more reason to *talk* to demons, to find out the truth regarding why they are there, than we have to talk to humans.

It is a self-evident truth to say that I am on par with other humans. Other people are my equal. They can be just as deceptive as I am. However, I can't command a human to tell me the truth. I can *command* a demon to speak the truth. Jesus in me has authority over the demonic realm. That means *I* have authority over the demonic realm.

When I command demons to speak the truth, and I do so outlining the severe consequences of disobedience, I am much more likely to get the truth. Just like humans, really. If I am going to be punished for telling a lie, I am much more likely to tell the truth. The greater the severity of the punishment for lying, the greater the likelihood of me telling the truth. A gun held at my head or the head of a loved one is a strong motivation for me to tell the truth! A punishment that is no more than a slap over the wrist with a wet bus ticket will make me consider telling a lie.

During a deliverance session, when I talk to demons, I place strict parameters regarding how they will speak the truth, and explain clearly that there will be consequences for disobedience.

> 'I speak with the authority of the true Lord Jesus Christ and you will speak the truth that he recognizes as truth. If you defy me, you defy the blood and the authority of the true Lord Jesus Christ and he will deal with you severely for doing so'.

The first sentence reminds the demons that I am Jesus' representative and they had better speak nothing but the truth because it is just as though he is standing there talking to them.

Won't lie to Jesus

It is interesting to note that in the New Testament, in *every* interaction with demons, they *always* told the truth. When confronted with Jesus, they told the truth. While they could be disobedient by not leaving immediately or making a loud noise, they never told a lie in Jesus' presence. They could have lied, but they didn't. Why not? Because they knew it was futile. They knew that Jesus would instantly see through a lie. Jesus, as the sinless Son of God, confronted demons with an absolute purity they had never seen before in a man. There was an internal integrity in Jesus that matched everything he said and did. His truthfulness, in thought, word and deed meant that any lie told to him would stand out like the smallest black dot on an absolutely snow white piece of paper. Jesus just doesn't tell the truth, he *is* truth. Demons are not stupid; it was pointless trying to tell a lie to Jesus.

Does that mean that if you say the first sentence in speech marks on the previous page, the demons will never lie to you? No. Although you have the presence of Jesus in you as a believer, demons will try and lie to you. Why? Because you are not Jesus! Although Jesus, through his Holy Spirit, indwells you, your sinfulness fogs and clouds your ability to accurately discern them and their intentions all of the time. Your sinfulness means that you are not a perfect representation of Jesus. Your discernment, as a consequence, will not be as sharp. Yes, even with these parameters, demons will try to deceive you. Sometimes they will succeed. At the beginning of my deliverance ministry, they succeeded far more than they do today. Yet they still succeed in deceiving me today. They know me far better than I know them. Without Jesus in you, it would be no contest. Demons would win every time. Like taking candy off a kid! The sons of Sceva found that out the hard way. Nevertheless, adding the second sentence about the consequences of defying Jesus will make them think twice. You straight jacket them, so to speak. From a large amount of personal experience, I know that Jesus does deal severely with demons who lie, when these parameters are put in place.

When a demon presents itself, I command the demon to give an account for itself, to tell me why it is there. In other words, to give me its legal rights. I do this from the position of a master talking to a servant, never from the position of a person talking to his enemy. Never from the position of one antagonist talking to another. I am relaxed, firm, with clear boundaries that limit the servant's ability to deceive. I get the information that I need to set the captive free. I then send the servant on his way.

Controlled, collaberative, composed, concise, clipped, clinical, complete!

SUMMARY

- All books written on deliverance to date had been based on observations of the demonic through individuals who are co-conscious with the process. Dealing with demons without human interference is like putting a mask on and putting your head underwater for the first time. A whole new perspective is revealed.
- All demons are angels. We have no issue with talking to God's angels; we shouldn't have any issue talking to fallen angels. We just need to be more cautious.
- Demons can talk lucidly, coherently and intelligently. They are often characterized as only talking in a harsh guttural manner speaking with cryptic statements. This is simply part of the deception the kingdom of darkness is trying to perpetuate. Scripture shows us that fallen angels certainly don't talk like that in front of God.
- In at least 22 ways, we are quite similar to demons. Uncomfortably so. In particular, we can be as deceptive and cunning as they can be. If we talk to humans and can sift through what they say, then we can do the same with demons.
- Demons are, first and foremost, servants. Old Testament Scriptures are clear that God treats demons as servants. God has no problem talking to his servants.
- The Cross transferred God's authority to us. We now have the same authority and, similarly, shouldn't have any problem talking to demons.
- Demons can and will deceive us as we interact with them, just as humans can and will deceive us. However, placing clearly defined boundaries on them when they do talk to us constrains them significantly in their desire to deceive.
- The misconception responsible for the fear of talking to demons is dualism; believing that our relationship with demons is characterised as 'us' against 'them'. Dualism is the biggest barrier to overcome in getting the church more comfortable with notion of interacting with demons in a relaxed, clipped manner that extracts necessary information efficiently.

Chapter 20:
FROM NOW TO THE END

We are in the final phase of the dispensation that will end with Jesus' second coming. Unfortunately, we are heading towards the most cataclysmic events our planet has seen since the flood. The deterioration of the earth will reach its peak when each of the seven seals, trumpets and bowls (Revelation 6 onwards) are opened and executed upon the earth. The events of the book of Revelation are not that far away. For example, the seventh seal has seven trumpets and the sixth trumpet involves an army from the East, 200 million strong (Revelation 9:16). Through the ages, people thought the apostle John had his figures wrong; 200 million was an inconceivably large group of people, let alone an army. With a world population of now over 6 billion, an army of 200 million only represents 3% of those currently alive. Such an army, gathered from many nations of the world, is well within the realms of possibility.

In Matthew 24, Jesus talked to the apostles about the end times that would precede his return and he painted a bleak picture. It ties in with what John outlines in Revelation. Although no one knows the exact time of his return, he does give a clue as to when that time is near.

> *Now learn the parable from the fig tree: when its branch has already become tender and puts forth its leaves, you know that summer is near; So, you too, when you see all these things, recognize that He is near, right at the door. Truly I say to you, this generation will not pass away until all these things take place.* (Mat 24:32-34)

The fig tree is a symbol for Israel[1]. When Jesus cursed the fig tree in Mark 11, he was acting out a parable regarding his judgment against Israel. If this wasn't the case, it wouldn't be fair to curse a fig tree for not bearing figs when it wasn't the season for figs! Immediately afterwards, when he upturned the tables and drove out the sellers in the temple, he enforced the point that judgment would come upon Israel. Why? Just prior to Jesus cursing the fig tree, he was given a triumphant welcome into Jerusalem but he knew that within a week they would be crying out for his blood. Judgment would come upon Israel for rejecting their Messiah. Judgment did come upon Israel and relatively quickly. The Romans completely destroyed the nation in 70AD and the people of Israel were dispersed amongst the rest of the world. The fig tree was without leaves. The land was occupied by foreigners. In 1948, Israel again became a nation; the fig tree put out leaves for the first time in almost 2000 years. Summer is near. The events of Revelation will soon be upon us.

Jesus was saying that the generation *alive at the time of Israel's rebirth* will not pass away before he returns. A generation can be as little as 20 years or as much as 120 years. Twenty years is the lower limit because that is standard time given for the time it takes to reproduce the next generation and 120 years is the upper limit because that's how long it takes for those alive on earth, *at any one point in time,* to completely pass away. The latter interpretation is what Jesus meant. That is, until the last person alive in 1948 dies. Consequently, if this interpretation of these verses is correct, we can expect Jesus to return some time before 2068.

It will happen soon but not tomorrow. No doubt you have heard a sermon at some stage in your Christian walk exhorting us to be prepared for the return of Jesus because it could be tomorrow. The truth is that Jesus won't be returning for at least the next thirty years.

There are a number of reasons why Jesus won't be returning in the next few decades.

> *For I say to you, from now on you will not see Me until you say, 'Blessed is he who comes in the name of the Lord!'* (Matt 23:39)

This verse was Jesus' last public utterance. He was saying to the nation of Israel that they will not see him again until they collectively say, 'Blessed is he who comes in the name of the Lord.' Satan knows this and is doing everything he can to stop Israel from embracing Jesus, or J'shua, as their Messiah. Israel, as a nation, is a long way off becoming followers of J'shua. More humanistic and atheistic than anything else, religion is not high on the agenda of the average Israeli. Jewish believers in J'shua are less than 2% of the population and there is still a strong historical skepticism to things Christian. It is unlikely there will be a significant shift in this thinking in the foreseeable future.

A second reason that Jesus will not be returning tomorrow is that the gospel has to be preached to every people group.

> *And they sang a new song, saying 'Worthy are You to take the book and to break its seals; for You were slain, and purchased for God with Your blood men from every tribe and tongue and people and nation'.* (Rev 5:9)

According to the Centre for World Evangelism in Pasadena, California, there are still 10 000 people groups out of a total of 24 000 people groups that are unable to access the gospel without outside help. While there may be individuals within some of these 10 000 groups that are Christians, the task to reach every people group with the gospel is still enormous. It certainly won't happen tomorrow or within the next few decades. Because the task is so huge, God will provide supernatural help in completing the task in time.

> *And I saw another angel flying in mid heaven, having an eternal gospel to preach to those who live on the earth, and to every nation and tribe and tongue and people.* (Rev 14:6)

However, just because God will provide help in the end, it doesn't mean he will come tomorrow. God will provide grace but he won't rescue us from our responsibility to spread the gospel.

A third reason that Jesus is not coming back soon is because he is coming back for a bride with its lamp primed and ready.

> *Let us rejoice and be glad and give the glory to Him, for the marriage of the Lamb has come and His bride has made herself ready."* (Rev 19:7)

The church still has a long way to go before she is ready for her bridegroom. We still have little knowledge of how the kingdom of darkness operates, and deliverance is still in its infancy within the church. We are superficial in our approach to physical healing, and have no answers to the mental problems that beset our society. We are often more concerned with the music in our churches or the charismatic appeal of our sermons than truly exercising the gifts of the Spirit to bring deep healing to a hurting Body. We are fractured and bleeding and the sad part is that we think we are doing okay; that God would give us a high score on a report card right now. No, Jesus won't be coming tomorrow. It will take a few more decades of purifying, through persecution, before we are ready for our bridegroom.

The fourth reason, one that I am aware of from counselling, with a high degree of certainty but cannot objectively prove, is that the Antichrist has yet to be born. That being the case, if he was born tomorrow, it would take at least 30 years, if not longer, for him to gain the personal and political stature to convince the world to follow him. Satan is doing all he can at the moment in preparation for his birth.

All of these reasons combined make it highly unlikely that Jesus will return before the year 2040 at the earliest.

Agendas

How does Satan's role change from now until the end? The book of Revelation shows us Satan flexing his muscles as he grooms a charismatic leader for world domination. Yet, it is also about God's judgment that will be poured out on the earth. As Jesus says in Matthew 24, the world in the end days will be similar to the world in the time of Noah. Due to the perversity and collective extent of man's sin, God's judgment fell then and it will fall again. This final Antichrist, along with his right hand man, the false prophet, will control the world for seven years[2]. This is when evil, and the direct influence of Satan on the earth will reach its peak. More about how Satan will accomplish this is explained in the third book, *'Darkness in the Light: Satan's Trojan Horse'*. We are living in the time when the kingdom of darkness is beginning its buildup towards increasing control of the world. Evil will continue to build in all areas of society and the environment. As we look around us at the alarming rate of change that mankind and the world is undergoing on every front, it is unlikely that Christ's return can be delayed for another century. Global warming is a small but potent example of the law of sowing and reaping. In a few decades, we have succeeded in overturning the delicate balancing mechanisms that have stabilized the earth for thousands of years.

The legal rights we give to the satanic kingdom on a daily basis have a twofold effect. They both increase the leverage the satanic kingdom has over mankind and build up God's judgment against us. The cup of God's wrath is being filled. When it is full, it will be poured out against us. When people whom God has committed himself to, such as Christians and the nation of Israel, give legal rights to the kingdom of darkness, they receive a double impact; Satan's revenge and God's judgment. That is why, when we look at the nation of Israel, we wonder where the blessing is for them. They don't seem to be a good advertisement for God! It is also why Ananias and Sapphira dropped dead and why Paul, for all his hard work for the Kingdom of Light, still had to endure a 'thorn in the flesh'. However, when people who are under Satan's control give him legal rights, they may escape Satan's revenge but will still eventually incur God's judgment. Satan wants them to continue because they are doing his will, so he will 'bless' them. For example; Sodom and Gommorah, the Nephilim and the Canaanite nations surrounding Israel. Sometimes, however, he acts in a fit of pique and will annihilate large numbers of people under his control. He uses natural disasters predominantly for this.

It would be simple if it was an either-or situation; if any calamity was either God's doing or Satan's doing. However, it is not; it lies on a continuum. Sometimes Satan does what he wants because he has the legal rights and God has to allow it but it is not his intended will. For example, the 2004 Tsunami and other natural disasters. Other times, Satan thinks he is working his own agenda but God is also using it to bring his judgment or work out this purposes. For example, Satan used Pharaoh to subjugate the Israelites in the hope of crushing fledging Israel, and God used the situation to demonstrate his power and to bring his judgment on Egypt. Still other times, God brings down his judgment and Satan is eager to implement it. For example, God's judgment against David for taking the census. Satan willingly implemented it by wiping out 70 000 of God's chosen people. Finally there are situations where God's judgment falls and Satan has to implement it, whether he likes it or not. For example, in the flood that saved Noah, Satan would have been disappointed that his plan to corrupt the earth completely, which had almost succeeded, was being thwarted. Satan hated it as he watched his god-men drown and had to call each one from life to death. He would rather have tried to save some of his spectacular engineering but wasn't allowed.

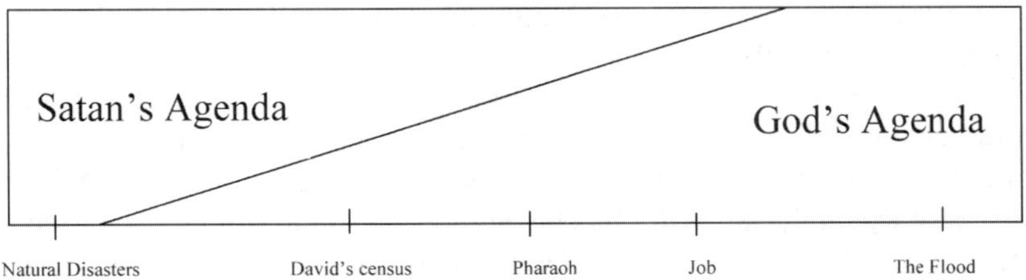

CALAMITIES

I realize that the placement of events on this graph is arbitrary and it is debatable how much of whose agenda is being worked out in each situation. The point is that calamities, both personal and global, are likely to have a combination of both agendas being outworked. The same is true for the book of Revelation. It is a complex interaction and outworking of the will of Satan and the will and judgment of God. The example of the salvation of Israel via the two witnesses, when the Antichrist is at his peak (Revelation 7), is a good illustration (see chapter 7). Satan, through the Antichrist and the rest of the world gathered against Israel, thinks he is about to crush her once and for all. However, that intense persecution actually softens Israel to finally hear the words of truth that the two witnesses speak and at last, at long last, embrace Jesus as their Messiah.

Jesus' return

When Jesus does return, the devil will be bound for one thousand years.

> *Then I saw an angel coming down from heaven, holding the key of the abyss and a great chain in his hand. And he laid hold of the dragon, the serpent of old, who is the devil and Satan,* ***and bound him for a thousand years;*** *and he threw him into the abyss, and shut it and sealed it over him, so that he would not deceive the nations any longer, until the thousand years were completed; after these things he must be released for a short time.* (Rev 20:1-3)

It is partly because he is bound and unable to directly impact the world, that the earth can begin to regenerate, as outlined in chapter one. However, it is important to realize that the rest of the kingdom of darkness is still free to tempt man. It is only Satan himself who is thrown into the Abyss. We know this because Scripture only mentions Satan being bound for 1000 years in hell and the spirits Death and Hades are not finally thrown into hell until the last judgment (Revelation 20:14). These two spirits and their helpers are active during the period of the 1000 year reign because people still die during this period.

> *No longer will there be in it an infant who lives but a few days, or an old man who does not live out his days; for the youth will die at the age of one hundred and the one who does not reach the age of one hundred will be thought accursed.* (Isa 65:20)

Unfortunately for the kingdom of darkness, but fortunately for the rest of the world, Satan's removal from the helm will leave his kingdom in considerable disarray. One would think that the next highest demon would simply step in and take over. It is not quite so simple. To the demonic kingdom, Satan is like God. He is not merely the top dog, the apex of a pyramid of similar bricks. He is untouchable, in a class of his own, as we have established. He rules absolutely, undisputedly, completely, and contrary to popular opinion, he has the loyalty and respect of all others in his kingdom. When he is gone, there will be no other demon who can step into his shoes. There is no other that would command the respect of the rest. The hole he will leave is enormous, cavernous, gaping. Satan's dictatorship is so complete that even his closest lieutenants have only very limited knowledge of the big picture. The confusion, disarray and developing internal discord will reduce considerably the efficiency of the satanic kingdom during this thousand year period. At the end of the one thousand year reign, Satan will be released.

> *When the thousand years are completed, Satan will be released from his prison, and will come out to deceive the nations which are in the four corners of the earth, Gog and Maggot, to gather them together for the war; the number*

of them is like the sand of the seashore. And they came up on the broad plain of the earth and surrounded the camp of the saints and the beloved city, and fire came down from heaven and devoured them. And the devil who deceived them was thrown into the lake of fire and brimstone, where the beast and the false prophet are also; and they will be tormented day and night forever and ever. (Rev 20:7-10)

One can imagine how pleased the kingdom of darkness will be when Satan returns from his captivity. It won't take too long for the regimented discipline and efficiency to return to this previously well oiled machine. Despite a thousand years under the prosperous reign and rule of Jesus, there will be many who will still choose rebellion over compliance, pride over humility, independence instead of interdependence and intimacy. These will succumb to Satan's enticements and a large army will arise against the Lord in Jerusalem.

Notice that those who rebel are described as numerous as 'sand on the seashore'. This is no exaggeration. With 1000 years of peace and prosperity and people living till they are several hundred years old, it won't take very long before there is massive exponential population growth. It is likely, that by the end of the 1000 years, there could be more than a trillion people on earth. Today there are six billion. At the end of the 1000 year reign of Jesus on earth, there could be 100s of times that number! The earth could easily sustain such large numbers since it will be quite different to the decayed state it is now in. The earth will increasingly become more like Paradise was at the time of Adam. There won't be deserts and everywhere there will be amazing fertility. As time passes, we will be more and more vegetarian in our food choices. Hence the food resources will easily cope with the growing population because the amount of food, or biomass, it takes to support one meat eater can support ten vegetarians!

This time there will be no battle. This time God will not allow the harmony of his kingdom to be disrupted. For a thousand years there has been no war. Swords have long since been beaten into plow shears. This time, he has one thousand years of accumulated legal rights on his side and now his judgment will be swift and effective. He will destroy his enemies with supernatural fire. Fried on the spot. End of story. Literally.

The final judgment will happen soon after and Satan will be thrown into hell for all eternity. Hallelujah! At long last!

In chapter 1, we looked at the ten periods, or dispensations, of God's dealings with us. From chapter 2 onwards, we have progressively traced the nine dispensations of Satan, emphasizing his relationship to us and our ability to deal with him.

Dispensation	Satan	Man's relationship with Satan	Man's ability to deal with Satan
Creation of Satan and the Angels	Satan is second only in authority and power to God.	Not Applicable.	Not Applicable.
Creation of Man	Satan observes a being that has qualities he doesn't possess; not a clothing of flesh but flesh seamlessly interwoven with soul and spirit.	Man has a triune nature. This puts him above the angels, including Satan. Man has authority over the earth.	Although intrinsically less powerful than Satan, Adam has the ability to resist Satan should Satan trespass on his territory, earth.
Satan's Rebellion	Satan loses his authority in heaven. He is also condemned to the first and second heavens. His created abilities are unaffected by his defeat. Satan serves God as a defeated foe.	Man is unaffected by Satan's rebellion.	As above
The Fall of Man	Satan now has the authority over the earth.	Man is now under Satan's authority	Mankind is powerless to deal with Satan. No Old Testament deliverance is possible
Jesus becomes Man	For the first time since Adam, there is a human that is above Satan. Satan tries hard to tempt Jesus to sin. He just needs one sin.	Jesus, as a sinless man, is over Satan positionally but, as a human on earth, under Satan territorially. This sets up a tension.	Jesus is the first person to be able to speak directly to demons and they must obey. However, because of a lack of territorial authority, when Jesus does deliverance, it can at times be 'messy'.

The Death and Resurrection of Jesus	Satan fails in tempting Jesus to sin. He loses his automatic authority over mankind and the earth. He still exercises control but now has to gain authority through individual legal rights. Most of humanity obliges. His created power has been marginally reduced. Evil will continue to build as this period progresses.	Believers in Jesus now have both power and authority over Satan. Non-believers are still under Satan's control. At the end of this period, a man highly invested with the kingdom of darkness will take control of the world.	Satan's lack of territorial control and that he no longer has anything to gain through a display means that man can now cast out demons more effortlessly than Jesus could when he was on earth. Greater need for effortless deliverance as evil increases toward the end.
Jesus returns and reigns on earth for 1000 years	Satan is bound and confined to hell for 1000 years. The rest of the satanic kingdom is still free to roam but they are far less effective without Satan.	There is a significantly reduced impact of the satanic kingdom upon the earth. A time of increasing peace and prosperity as the earth is restored.	Man continues to deal with the enemy using a post resurrection deliverance model. This is made even easier with the absence of Satan.
Satan is released	Satan rallies his kingdom and, with new vigour, the satanic kingdom wins many people over.	Despite unprecedented blessing and prosperity for 1000 years, many people still choose to follow Satan.	Nothing has changed but during this time the influence of the kingdom of darkness is more evident everywhere.
Satan's defeat and the final judgment.	Satan experiences his last comprehensive defeat. He is condemned to hell for all eternity	There is no battle. Accumulated LRs by the KOL means that those who rebelled are destroyed.	After Satan's defeat, there will never be a need for deliverance again.

Wrap Up

As previously stated, this book is part one of a three part series on dealing with the kingdom of darkness. It is designed to help us understand how the kingdom of darkness operates; to help us comprehend the way Satan thinks, to understand how and why the enemy does what he does. Underestimating Satan's capabilities is possibly the biggest mistake the Church has made and, attributing to God what is the work of the enemy, is the next biggest. This book outlines in detail the progressive development of the satanic kingdom from the creation of Satan to his eventual judgment and eternal damnation. It tries to illuminate for the reader the delicate balance that exists between the two opposing kingdoms. The satanic kingdom is, at one and the same time, a servant of the Kingdom of Light, under its direct control *and* acting to thwart God's plans based on accumulated legal rights. The Kingdom of Light uses what Satan intends for evil to hone, train and purify his Church. The satanic kingdom has a relatively short term view, the Kingdom of Light a long term view.

Like so many Christians, the kingdom of darkness *thinks* its relationship with the Kingdom of Light is dualistic. It thinks it has the upper hand and is winning. It thinks it is fighting a battle against the Lord of Hosts but the *reality* is that the Kingdom of Light is always in control, always knows exactly what is happening with the kingdom of darkness, and as necessary, can command the kingdom of darkness to report and give an account for its actions. The kingdom of darkness however, doesn't know what is happening with the Kingdom of Light.

The paradox is that the kingdom of darkness is in the light to the Kingdom of Light and the Kingdom of Light is in darkness to the kingdom of darkness!

The angels of the Kingdom of Light can see the angels of the kingdom of darkness but the reverse is not true. Hence the kingdom of darkness thinks that they are only ones manipulating a situation whereas, all the time, the angels of the Kingdom of Light are also involved and, in addition, Jesus, via his Spirit, is always present.

I have tried to establish a theology of Satan that best fits the facts from personal counselling. These three books, like a phoenix, have arisen out of many hours of interaction with the satanic kingdom and a realization that the current theology of Satan is underdeveloped and inadequate. It has meant re-reading many passages of Scripture and challenging existing interpretations. These are books formed at the coal face of counselling, not based on one-off experiences but repeated interactions, often in a professional setting with carefully recorded notes. I am as confident as I can be that what I am saying is the truth, although I fully appreciate that without such personal experience a reader may be skeptical. For this reason I have tried to be as thorough as I can be in quoting Scripture because such a paradigm shift in our thinking needs to be well backed up. I am acutely aware that personal experience as a basis for new theology can be a dangerous foundation because of its subjectivity. Yet the New Testament was written out of the personal experiences of a handful of men, inspired by the Holy Spirit, and it changed the world. Thus, it is not so much the personal experience that is at issue but rather the impact of this experience on others who reap its fruit. Does it lead to increased intimacy with Jesus? Does it bring greater understanding, deeper healing and long term settled peace? Is it in accord with reality? Does it have that special something that has truth written all over it? These are the acid tests.

The next book, *'Darkness in the Light: Satan's Legal Rights',* will look at legal rights and the process of deliverance closely. I will examine in more detail the seven categories of legal rights to enable you to gain a greater awareness of when you break them. There will be many personal examples of how the legal rights process works in the counselling room and practical illustrations about how to go about deliverance using a post-resurrection model. *'Darkness in the Light: Underestimating Satan'* is largely theoretical but none the less foundational. It paints a bigger picture, in broad brush strokes, of the satanic kingdom and how it operates, and in so doing, attempts to answer the hard questions the Church often avoids. In contrast, *'Darkness in the Light: Satan's Legal Rights'* is more personal, practical and will help anyone who wants to do deliverance in a more clinical, effortless manner.

The third book, *'Darkness in the Light: Satan's Trojan Horse'* will take the reader to the next level of understanding regarding how the kingdom of darkness operates. If you thought this first book was stretching regarding Satan's influence in our lives, you will find the third book even more so. First we need to walk before we can run. It will unravel the DNA of the satanic kingdom and just how much control it exercises over individuals, Christians in particular. We will look at some major changes Satan made in the way he treats humans as a result of the Cross and how understanding this hidden agenda is crucial for the end-time church to grasp. It will be a combination of both theory and practice and will tie in closely with my first book, *'The Forgotten Factor in Healing'.*

> *So then let us not sleep as others do, but let us be alert and sober.* (1 Th 5:6)

Closing Comments

Congratulations! You have made it. There was probably a range of emotions you went through at various stages as you read this book. You may now feel overwhelmed, unsettled, angry, cheated perhaps. Some of you will be excited because you now have a framework that enables you to tie up many strands that have been dangling for so long. All of you will benefit from reading this book again. Readers who have some experience doing deliverance, a tendency towards legalism, coupled with a gung-ho attitude, could use the information in this book as a weapon. Seeing the enemy as the issue without due consideration for the person you are ministering to will lead to a representation of Jesus that is harsh, task-oriented and clinically disconnected. Doing deliverance using the Anazao model is highly collaborative, client empowering and the goal is always, always, greater intimacy between the client and Jesus and the Holy Spirit. A client should never leave feeling condemned or feeling that they have just been 'processed'. I don't suggest you attempt deliverance based on the brief description in this book until you have read '*Darkness in the Light: Satan's Legal Rights'* or attended our training school.

Some of you are shell shocked, right now, in regard to how much influence the satanic kingdom has in our lives. It is easy to let the pendulum swing to the opposite extreme and become paranoid about the possibility of Satan ending your life tomorrow. Readers who have a tendency towards anxious or depressive thinking could take sections of this book out of context and dwell on them, letting their circular thinking patterns paint themselves into a corner that will remove what little hope they have. Don't let the enemy do that. He is an expert at that. I began this book with a chapter on God's desire for intimacy with us and the extraordinary lengths he has gone to since the Fall to re-establish close connection with us.

God is absolutely besotted with you, *yes you,* and although he wants you to be aware of the enemy and how he operates, his purpose is to make you more dependant and reliant on him. God wants your focus to be fixed firmly and securely on his tender, loving gaze and allow him, in the security of his acceptance of you, to reveal the areas in your life that need addressing. There is no rush. There is no need to fear. Jesus is firmly in control and he wants you to relax; to keep listening to his still small voice as he both comforts you and prompts you. Above all, he wants you to enjoy the journey with him, sometimes laughing and joking together about something frivolous, other times chatting about some of deeper issues in life and always taking time to smell the roses along the way.

> *Even though I walk through the valley of the shadow of death, I fear no evil, for You are with me; Your rod and Your staff, they comfort me. You prepare a table before me in the presence of my enemies;* (Ps 23:4,5)

SUMMARY

- From now on, things only get worse before they get better. We are heading towards the events outlined in Revelation 6 and beyond, at a rate faster than most of us realize.

- Jesus gave us a clue as to when he will return. It is predicated on when the fig tree comes back into leaf. Israel, the fig tree, again became a nation after almost 2000 years of exile in 1948.

- A generation, in this context, is 120 years. If interpreted correctly, Jesus will return some time before 2068.

- Jesus' return is unlikely to occur within the next 30 or 40 years for the following reasons:
  (a) Israel is not ready to ask him back.
  (b) The church has a long way to go to be a bride whose lamp is primed.
  (c) The gospel has still to be preached to a large number of unreached people groups.
  (d) The anti Christ hasn't yet been born.

- The events of Revelation are a complex interplay between Satan exercising accumulated legal rights and God exercising accumulated judgments. Any calamity, personal or global, will lie somewhere on this continuum.

- Satan will be locked up for 1000 years but the kingdom of darkness will still operate, though much less effectively.

- On his return Satan will raise up an army against God. Due to the enormous legal rights God has accumulated over 1000 years, he won't allow a battle to ensue and Satan's army will be consummed on the spot.

- The Final Judgment will take place soon after and Satan will be thrown into hell forever.

- There are nine dispensations or periods for Satan. This book chronologically follows these. One period is delineated from another in terms of any change to Satan's power and/or authority.

- The purpose of this book has been to challenge foundational premises regarding Satan.

- The purpose of the next book, '*Darkness in the Light: Satan's Legal Rights*', is to give practical detail concerning legal rights and how to deal with them.

- The purpose of the third book is to peel away a deep layer of the satanic kingdom and expose an agenda aimed at the church that must be exposed if we are to have our lamps primed for his return.

- All three books are based on a large amount of practical experience.

- Keeping a relaxed, close relationship with Jesus, without moving into fear or hoplessness is the best way to cope with all you have read.

How God Reveals Himself to Mankind

In writing this book I have emphasized a strong scriptural basis for most of my assertions. I have also relied heavily on experience. In addition I have used reason and logic as appropriate to fill in the gaps, make conjectures that best fit the facts and read between the lines of Scripture. It is a mistake to assume that God's revelation of truth to mankind is limited to Scripture only.

There are six ways God interacts with humans; six methods of communicating with the pinnacle of his creation. These are: Scripture, personal revelation, experience, reason, the whole of creation itself and knowledge. God doesn't exclusively limit himself to one of these but he uses all six. A balanced understanding of God, his nature, character, the way he interacts and his creation is obtained only by considering all six aspects.

1. Scripture

By Scripture, we mean the 39 books of the Jewish Tenakh, which Christians call the Old Testament, and the 27 books of the New Testament. Collectively, Christians call these 66 books, the Bible. We believe this book is inspired by God, and is his undisputed revelation of himself to us. It contains information that we could not get by any other means; the creation of the world, the first man and woman, their sin and its consequences, God's complete salvation plan to redeem fallen man. All are revealed uniquely in the Bible and without such direct divine revelation we would be unable to steer a clear pathway through the myriads of conflicting philosophies about the world and its purpose. God's fundamental nature, his character, the tension between justice and mercy are powerful foundational truths that only the Bible can give us. Scripture is the most important of the six strands in the rope that connects us to God. It is the central core from which all others radiate and coil around. It is the reference point with which all other ideas and concepts must harmonize.

2. Personal Revelation

By personal revelation, we mean God's personal revelation of truth to an individual that cannot be known by any other way. It is not from experience. It is simply because God told them. It is revelation that is extra to the Bible. Christians throughout the centuries have used this form of revelation, often via the prophetic gifting, to deliver warning, admonition and encouragement to individuals and the church in general. A more recent example would be Rick Joyner's book, 'The Vision' detailing visions Joyner says he has received from God. The plethora of Christian books available today are often a combination of varying degrees of personal revelation and the experiences that resulted from that revelation. Sometimes this revelation re-emphasizes a truth already detailed in the Bible. Sometimes it is an extension or fresh perspective of an existing truth. Still other times it is drawing together different strands within the Bible to bring a greater collective understanding. Occasionally, it is completely new material that adds to our spiritual knowledge.

Definition of the Trinity

An example of personal revelation that results in knowledge and understanding greater than we can get from Scripture is the formal definition of the Trinity. This involves drawing together different strands from Scripture to build a complete picture of the nature of God that is nowhere explicitly stated in the Bible. This is contained in the first half of the Nicene Creed. To clarify the understanding that God was three and yet one, and to avoid the misconception that Christians believed in tri-theism (three distinct Gods) the early church fathers came up with the following.

> We believe in one God, the Father Almighty, Creator of heaven and earth, and in Jesus Christ, his only Son and Lord. Eternally begotten of the Father, God from God, Light from Light, true God from true God, Begotten, not made, of one being with the Father, through Him all things were made….We believe in the Holy Spirit, the Lord, the giver of life, who proceeds from the Father and the Son. Equally with the Father and Son, he is worshipped and glorified....

This understanding adds to, but does not detract or contradict what Scripture says. That the Son is 'eternally begotten' of the Father is nowhere in Scripture. Neither is the notion that the Holy Spirit proceeds from the relationship between the Father and the Son. Wow! What an amazing statement. What a profound revelation! This definition of the trinity has become the yardstick that churches who call themselves Christian must be measured against. The Mormons and Jehovah Witnesses are not considered Christian faiths because they don't acknowledge the Nicene Creed and in particular the Trinitarian definition. The leaders within the early church, headed by Athanasius, discussed at length the precise wording of this definitive declaration. To write a concise and carefully worded definition of so abstract a concept requires just as much inspiration as did those who authored the Bible. God's hand is so clearly evident in this amazing statement of faith. It certainly doesn't contradict Scripture but it adds new revelation to our understanding of God.

More than spitting and scourging

Another example of revelation that adds extra information to the Bible is the following: During the passion of Jesus, when Jesus was taken away to be scourged, a lot more happened to him than a few insults, scourging and crowing with thorns. The Roman soldiers had free rein with him. Jesus was comprehensively homosexually raped and abused, including oral sexual abuse. This may come as a shock to some readers but it is quite consistent with treatment given to condemned prisoners by the Romans at that time. Jesus revealed that to me. Sometime later, I had a client who was dealing with a recovered memory involving sexual abuse and wondering how Jesus could possibly empathize. I invited him to bring his truth to her in the midst of the trauma. As part of the comfort Jesus gave her, he told her that he too had been abused in like manner. Since then I have met other people who have said that God told them that he was sexually abused during the scourging and crowning. There is a Christian missions and healing organisation in Australia that incorporates this as part of their teaching[1].

After having received such a revelation, the question to ask is, 'Does this contradict Scripture?' The answer is no. Just because some of what happened to Jesus was recorded in the gospels, doesn't mean all that happened to him was recorded. It is almost certain that the Gospel writers were reporting this part of the passion through second hand information. Jesus was tortured in the Praetorium, a part of Pilate's palace (Mk 15:16), and Scripture tells us that none of the Jews were present for fear of being ritually unclean and therefore excluded from participation in the Passover (Jn 18:28). That means the authors of the gospels received their information second hand. If the gospel writers obtained this information from a Roman soldier or a servant, it could be that this piece of information was omitted by the observer who was relating what had happened. Alternatively, the writers may have known about it but chosen to exclude it from their narrative given the social taboos of the day. Whatever the case, the scenario of sexual abuse is highly plausible and doesn't contradict the Scripture record. Can it be proved? No. It is revelation and the nature of revelation is that it cannot be known by any other means. Why would Jesus reveal that to me and others? Because it provides considerable comfort to those who have been abused to know that Jesus, at a deep personal level, knows what they have been going through.

> *For consider Him who has endured such hostility by sinners against Himself, so that you will not grow weary and lose heart.* (Heb 12:3)

The dilemma with personal revelation is how much, if indeed any, is from God. The first test is whether any of this revelation contradicts the Bible. If it does, it is rejected. If it doesn't, then we next need to ask whether this revelation has a ring of truth about it, whether it 'sits well' with the tenor, the tone, the message of the Bible. Does this revelation bring a deep peace within my spirit? Not just my spirit, for I can be deceived. Do others also sense that this is from God? Does it have that intangible something about it that makes your heart leap? Even if that is the case, there is still a need to exercise caution. Does it stand the test of reason and logic? As a popular saying goes, 'It is possible to deceive some of the people all of the time and all of the people some of the time but not possible to deceive all of the people all of the time'. Could it be that this revelation is in the second category? A new teaching, understanding or interpretation can be widely adopted and not necessarily be true or helpful. Caution and wisdom need to be exercised but be careful not to move into a dogmatic scepticism that refuses to accept the possibility of any new revelation.

3. Experience

As we apply the observational skills God has given us, we acquire greater understanding regarding the meaning of a particular passage of Scripture. We extend its meaning or fill in gaps where Scripture is silent.

Masturbation examined

For example, Scripture appears ambivalent on the issue of masturbation. Nothing is written in the Bible that clearly states whether masturbation is allowable or not. Christendom holds a wide range of opinions on this matter because of the Bible's apparent silence. Some believe there is nothing sinful in masturbating. It is just a normal part of growing up. Others believe it is sinful only if you commit adultery in your heart. Still others believe it is not sinful if you are separated from your wife or husband and you are thinking about your spouse when you masturbate.

Hours of ministering to people has led me to the conclusion that masturbation is sin. It is sin every time. This viewpoint is commonly shared by ministries that utilize the gifts of the Holy Spirit mentioned in 1 Corinthians 12. Why? Because demons are always associated with masturbation. Time after time, when people have a masturbation problem and related demons make their presence felt (manifest), one comes to the very obvious conclusion that masturbation is sin.

Having established that masturbation is sin, we now work backwards to see whether adopting such belief about masturbation is contrary to scriptural principles. Masturbation can be classed as a false comfort. Similar to the abuse of drugs and alcohol, all false comforts take our focus away from God, 'the Father of compassion and the God of all comfort' (1 Cor 1:3). Any action or need for comfort that seeks a resolution outside the comfort offered by God is sin. Of course, I am not talking about a child needing a hug from a parent; I am talking about solace an adult seeks in things or actions that become a distraction from his focus on God. Asking common sense questions helps to further clarify the issue. Does this action result in greater intimacy with Jesus or greater separation from him? I have yet to counsel a man or woman who believes masturbation brings him or her closer to God. All the men and women I have counselled indicate that it does the opposite. Another common sense question to ask is, 'What would Jesus do? Can you imagine Jesus masturbating? Most Christians would answer, 'Definitely not!' Some would find this suggestion abhorrent. There was no need for Jesus to masturbate. All his need for comfort and solace would have found its completion in his relationship with his Father.

Territorial Spirits

Another example of experience increasing our understanding beyond the revelation of Scripture is our growing knowledge of demons and how they function. The idea of demonic princes over territories or countries such as Persia or Greece is outlined in the book of Daniel. The Bible is silent as to whether these heavenly principalities can be further broken down into smaller subgroups. Modern evangelistic and missionary experience indicates that within any country or region there are spiritual microclimates controlled by lesser demons. Why do people come to salvation so easily on one side of the railway tracks, literally, compared to another? Identifying the territorial spirit and the reasons it has to be there and removing those reasons has resulted in greater freedom and acceptance of the gospel. Revelation chapters 2 and 3 show us that angels are over each of the seven churches. We now know, from experience, that Satan assigns his fallen angels over churches as well. These are of similar stature to the angels God uses. The extent of the influence each angel is able to exert over a church is proportional to the choices for good or evil that takes place by the people in that church. Where there is a church that is flourishing for God, you can bet your bottom dollar that the satanic kingdom will have an equal investment in seeing that work of God fall to pieces. None of this experience contradicts the Scriptures.

4. Reason

It is beyond the scope of this book to explore, in any depth, the apologetic for Christianity. In other words, the reasons and logic behind why we believe what we believe. There are many good books that focus on developing logical and well reasoned arguments for the truths of Christianity[2], books that satisfy the requirements of 1 Peter 3:15.

> *But sanctify Christ as Lord in your hearts, always being ready to make a defense to everyone who asks you to give an account for the hope that is in you, yet with gentleness and reverence.* (1 Peter 3:15)

God doesn't just know all truth, God *is* truth. That means all truth has its source and origin in God. Every truth points to some aspect of God; his character and nature. No truth exists outside of God. Philosophy, mathematics and science are all disciplines whose foundation is logical, ordered thinking with more complex truths progressively built on the simpler truths that precede them. Any revelation, whether it is a personal revelation or the Judaeo-Christian Scriptures themselves, must be subject to the scrutiny of logic and reason. Such revelations can be accepted only to the extent that they are consistent with the accepted principles of reason and argument. In my opinion, Christianity is the most logically consistent, viable world view. Other world views require too much faith! They don't stand up to the rigour of consistent logical reasoning.

The uniqueness of Christianity

Here is an example of simple reasoning. Christians believe that Christianity is the truth: that Jesus of Nazareth, who lived 2000 years ago, was God incarnate and that only through him is salvation possible. Logically, this means that all other philosophical systems that contradict Christianity are in error. In the post-modern world in which we live, to hold such a belief is not politically correct. A post-modern viewpoint teaches that truth is relative, not absolute; what is true for you is your truth, what is true for me is my truth and it doesn't matter if they are contradictory. What is important is that we tolerate one another's viewpoint and don't impose our viewpoint on others. If we based mathematics on post modern principles then I could say, 1+1=2 and you could say 1+1=3. We would then agree that both are right; 1+1=2 is true for me and 1+1=3 is true for you.

If Christians are correct that their world view is the truth, then logically, there must be unique aspects to this world view that sets it apart from all other world views. If the Christian religion is fundamentally the same as every other religion, then it has no more of a claim to be the truth than any of the others that also claim to have the truth. So what sets Christianity apart from every other religion, at a fundamental level?

The principle defining difference between Christianity and other religions is that all other religions are based on self effort. You have to earn your salvation. You have to make regular offerings to the gods, pray and visit the temple or mosque, bow towards Mecca, fast, turn the prayer wheel or make sure your good karma outweighs your bad karma so that in the next incarnation you'll be better off! It is all about making sure that you *please* the god that you worship. Only in Christianity is there no requirement to please God. In fact, it is impossible for us to please God. We can't do it through our own self effort. That is why God sent his Son, to reconcile us to himself and provide for us a salvation that is independent of self effort. Salvation cannot be earned in Christianity. It is a gift. It has nothing to do with regular church attendance, baptism, praying, or fasting. This is a concept unique to Christianity.

Other Religions	Christianity
Man has to reach out to god.	God reaches down to man.
Sacrifices of some kind, either physical or behavioural, are offered to the god being worshipped.	No sacrifices required. Instead God offered a sacrifice for us. The sacrifice he offered was his Son.
The god worshipped is distant, too holy to be known, feared, often disinterested and needs to be appeased.	God is personal, wants intimacy with us and uniquely we can call him 'Father'.
Salvation/Nirvana must be earned.	Salvation cannot be earned. It is a gift.
Our own self effort and righteousness pleases the god worshipped.	Our own self effort and righteousness never pleases God. That is why he had to provide another way; his Son..
The god worshipped is always external to the believer.	God takes up residence *within* the believer.
There is a passivity and fatalism about the way their god interacts with them. Whatever happens is 'the will of god'.	God is always on the side of believer and helping her in whatever way he can. Evil is not part of God's will for us.
External observances are more important than heart attitude.	Heart attitude is more important than external observances.
The god worshipped is made in man's image. It is a projection or transference of what man thinks the god should be. The god is constrained to our three dimensional understanding, explained in our terms.	God is presented as multidimensional; a complex interaction of three beings, dimensionally unlimited, who are distinct and one at the same time! Not a tri-theism but a tri-unity or trinity. A contradiction to our 3D understanding.
The gods worshipped have the capability of doing evil.	God is incapable of doing evil.
The body is considered inferior to the soul and spirit.	The body is considered equal to the soul and spirit; a trinitarian unity that is temporarily separated by death.
Worshipping the god is about the completion of a set of rules.	Worshipping God is about relationship.
The gods are capable of love, of providing a 'way', of speaking truth.	God *is* love. God *is* the way. God *is* the truth.

Christianity is fundamentally different from every other religion. With the exception of Judaism, the God Christians believe in is not the god that all other religions believe in and even Judaism has only a partial understanding of God. Christianity is not just another choice among equal choices. It is not even the first among equals. It is in a class of its own. It is not an arrogant or presumptuous claim, it is simply a logical deduction based on presented facts. Christianity is the only consistently logical and liveable world view.

The uniqueness of Jesus

If Christianity is unique and it hinges on the person of Jesus Christ, then, logically, there must be unique features about Jesus that separate him from all other prophets and others who have founded religions. Here are six features about Jesus that set him apart from every other person who has ever existed.

(1) He is the only historical person that has ever claimed to be God. Siddhartha Gautama, the Buddha, didn't. Muhammad didn't. Jesus didn't claim to represent God, he claimed to be God! We are, of course, excluding people who have mental problems and various Indian deities whose existence is mythical rather than historical.

(2) His entrance into the world was unique. Born of a virgin. A supernatural conception. If someone claims to be God, then we would expect his entrance into the world to be unique. If it wasn't, then it would be easy to argue that he was simply another man. No other religious leader has claimed a virgin birth.

(3) His exit from the world was unique. He rose from the dead. No other religious leader or prophet has claimed to rise from the dead. Once again, this is logically consistent with what we would expect God to do if he were to exit this world. He simply couldn't remain dead; otherwise it would be more logical to assume that he was just another man.

(4) He was the only person whose life was completely mapped out before he arrived. The Bible not only predicted his appearing but gave details concerning where he would be born and when. These details (Daniel 9) were comprehensive enough for wise men from the East to arrive at the exact time of his birth. His death was described in so much detail in the Old Testament, in particular Isaiah 53, that it would have been impossible for anyone but Jesus to fulfill it. It is a mark of authenticity that no other religious leader can claim. Muhammad's claim to be a prophet of God is no more valid than if I declare that I, Peter Toth, am a prophet of God sent to bring the truth to the world. There is no independent external verification of Muhammad's claim or my claim. I may even, over time, convince many people to follow me. The number of people who follow me doesn't in any way validate my claim. Whether I knowingly or unknowingly deceive hundreds of millions into following my teaching is immaterial, my claim must have an independent stamp of truth over which I have no direct control.

(5) Jesus' purpose in coming was to die. The high point of his life was his

death. For every other prophet or religious founder, the high point of their lives was their teachings, their death being a relative non-event. Although Jesus is arguably the greatest teacher that has ever lived, his teachings would have meant nothing if it was not for his death and resurrection. Christianity is not about obedience to a set of teachings but about a person. It is about Jesus and his death and resurrection. Christianity is about a *relationship*, not a set of rules that other religions have.

(6) Jesus is the only person who has ever lived who was sinless. No other prophet claimed to be sinless. Muhammad never claimed to be sinless. The Buddha never claimed perfection. Jesus was perfect. Once again, this is logically consistent with his claim to be God. We would expect God to be perfect. God doesn't make mistakes.

God *is* love

Christians make the point that God *is* love. It is not just that God is capable of love. God actually is love. Love is a fundamental aspect of the makeup of God. How does this tie in with the Trinity? Love must have a focus. I must love *something*; my wife, children, pet. Let's assume I have existed in a pitch black vacuum all my life. I exist by myself with no other created being or thing around me. Nothing but black emptiness. It would be impossible for me to experience love because there would be no focus for my love. Now as soon as another being enters my world, it doesn't matter whether it is a person, an animal or an inanimate object, then I am able to experience love for the first time. Let's say a small dog is introduced into my empty black world. I can see, feel and touch the dog. He responds appreciatively to my touch, he licks my fingers affectionately. My love for the dog grows over time. I had the capability to love before the dog came on the scene but I didn't know what love was until there existed a focus for my love. There is a big difference between having a capacity for love, which all humans have, and actually *being* love. For God to be love, for love to be a fundamental aspect of God's nature, there can never have been a time when he didn't love. Since God existed before he created anything, it logically must imply that God had to have a focus for his love within himself! The Trinitarian nature of God is the perfect answer to the problem. There has never been a time when the Father hasn't loved the Son or the Holy Spirit and vice versa. Conversely, it is impossible for the Islamic god to *be love*. The god that Islam understands to be god only has the capacity to love. In that regard, he is no different from us.

Evolution

Sadly, many bible colleges teach the theory of evolution as compatible with Christianity. The teaching often goes along these lines: God created the world and watched it all evolve, monitoring the process and when apes had fully developed, he called it Man. Others are more specific and say he called one particular ape-man Adam and gave him a spirit, distinct from all other creatures. Such beliefs cannot be reconciled with Scripture. They are mutually exclusive. If the Bible is true, then the world was created perfectly and death entered the world as the result of a cognitive choice of a human being to sin; to disobey God. If evolution is true, then death was there long before Adam arrived because he is the final product of a pathway where billions of preceding organisms lived and died. In evolution, death comes before sin. In the Bible, sin comes before death. In fact, evolution renders irrelevant the need for the Garden of Eden and thus the need for Jesus to come and be the second Adam. It strikes at the very foundation of our understanding of sin, death, the Cross and the perfection we long for in the life hereafter. It makes this book not worth the paper it is written on.

5. Knowledge

By knowledge, we mean that as man better understands the world around him, he is able to understand the Bible better. Man's collective and constantly expanding understanding of himself, his world and the universe enables him to reinterpret Scripture with greater depth and insight.

Dinosaurs

'Dad, if God created Adam and the dinosaurs at the same time, how come my teacher says that dinosaurs existed and died out before man was on earth?' This is a common and perplexing question that thousands of Christian children struggle with as the evolutionary paradigm is taught in schools as fact. The reality is that the facts point to the co-existence of man with dinosaurs.

(1) Dinosaur and man footprints have been found together[3].

(2) Dinosaur bones have been found that have blood cells with hemoglobin[4]. Blood cells wouldn't remain intact for millions of years. Such fragile organic material may survive for hundreds of years, possibly thousands at the most.

(3) The fossilized remains of a small dinosaur (psittacosaur) have been found in the belly of a mammal *Repenomamus robustus.* According to evolutionary theory, dinosaurs existed long before large mammals evolved. This indicates dinosaurs existed far later than previously thought.

(4) Frequent references to dragons in many cultures, such as China and Europe, indicate that mankind was acquainted with dinosaurs. Dinosaurs are the only creatures that fit the description of dragons common in literature. The sculptures and pictures of 'George and the Dragon' show a dragon that is surprisingly dinosaur-like. Dinosaurs could have existed as late as 1500 AD. Brass engravings in Carlisle Cathedral in England, from the 1400s show an accurate brachiosaurus that the engraver could not have possibly known how to draw since dinosaur fossils weren't excavated until four hundred years later. Other accounts indicated such creatures existed at the time.

(5) On April 25, 1977, the Japanese fishing ship *Zuiyo Maru*, trawling for mackerel off the coast of New Zealand, snagged a rotting corpse at a depth of 900 feet and hauled in the remains of a beast that no one anywhere seemed to be able to identify 'It's not a fish, whale, or any other mammal,' said Professor Yoshinori Imaizumi of Japan's National Science Museum, in the Asahi Shimbun newspaper story that broke the news to the world. 'It's a reptile, and the sketch looks very like a plesiosaur. This was a precious and important discovery for human beings. It seems to show that these animals are not extinct after all.' Japan even released a stamp with the plesiosaur on it to commemorate the find. According to evolutionary theory, such a sea dwelling dinosaur should have been extinct 60 million years ago.

(6) A plesiosaur is also the most likely explanation for the Loch Ness monster. The long neck and small head fits the picture and descriptions of the animal. Loch Ness is the largest body of contained water in the United Kingdom. Since it is very deep, it is likely that, in the absence of predators, the plesiosaur thrived for many years. Whether the lake still contains an aquatic dinosaur is not known. Where there is smoke, there is often fire so the persistence of rumours and sightings over the centuries shouldn't be dismissed lightly.

(7) God didn't give man permission to eat meat until after the flood (Genesis 9:2,3) and animals didn't have the fear of man until after this time. Like man, most, if not all animals, were vegetarian until after the flood. Yes, that means Tyrannosaurus Rex too! Lions in London Zoo survived well on a vegetarian diet during the Second World War when meat was scarce. Because each wasn't a threat to the other, dinosaurs and man could safely co-exist.

(8) Scripture tells us that God separated the 'waters above' from the 'waters below'.

Then God said, "Let there be an expanse in the midst of the waters, and let it separate the waters from the waters." God made the expanse, and separated the waters which were below the expanse from the waters which were above the expanse; and it was so. God called the expanse heaven. And there was evening and there was morning, a second day. (Gen 1:6-8)

It is likely that this meant that there was a moist thick cloud cover that enveloped the earth. This would have enabled Adam and Eve to live in a uniformly warm climate and not need clothes. Additionally, it would provide the necessary lush foliage to sustain a large dinosaurs.

(9) Consider this amazing passage from Job.

> *Behold now, Behemoth, which I made as well as you; he eats grass like an ox. Behold now, his strength in his loins and his power in the muscles of his belly. He bends his tail like a cedar; the sinews of his thighs are knit together. His bones are tubes of bronze; his limbs are like bars of iron. He is the first of the ways of God; let his maker bring near his sword. Surely the mountains bring him food, and all the beasts of the field play there. Under the lotus plants he lies down, in the covert of the reeds and the marsh. The lotus plants cover him with shade; the willows of the brook surround him. If a river rages, he is not alarmed; he is confident, though the Jordan rushes to his mouth. Can anyone capture him when he is on watch, with barbs can anyone pierce his nose?* (Job 40:15-24)

This is a perfect description of a dinosaur. Yes it is! If I asked you, 'What large animal has a long trunk that sways back and forward?' You would answer an elephant. If I asked you, 'What cat-like animal has its neck covered with a large expanse of long hair?' You would answer a lion. Both these descriptions are unique to these animals. Similarly, if I asked you, 'What large creature has a tail the thickness of a tree trunk?' You would have to answer a dinosaur. The telling feature that distinguishes dinosaurs from all other creatures is the incredibly large, strong tails they possessed. The description of the tail of Behemoth is that it was like a cedar (v17). The NIV says *'His tail sways like a cedar'*. No other creature matches the majestic language used. Elephants have a short stringy tail and hippos have a tiny stubby tail. So the description can't apply to these animals, despite what the reference notes say in most study Bibles. Although nowhere near the thickness of a cedar or a dinosaur's tail, a crocodile could also fit the description with regard to its tail being relatively thick but it doesn't meet the criteria for the rest of the description of Behemoth. The dinosaur that fits the description most completely is a brontosaurus or brachiosaurus. In fact, a common depiction of a brachiosaurus in books about dinosaurs is usually standing in a river or marshes with its long neck reaching out to eat leaves, while the water flows around it.

6. Nature

The most obvious revelation of God is in his creation. His jaw dropping creativity, his quirky sense of humour, his attention to detail, his extraordinary understanding of the delicate interactions required to maintain equilibrium in microclimates and larger ecosystems. God's nature is in nature! At a gross level, it blares to the unbeliever, a megaphone that demands a response and yet so many refuse to hear.

> *For since the creation of the world God's invisible qualities—his eternal*

power and divine nature—have been clearly seen, being understood from what has been made, so that men are without excuse. (Rom 1:20)

At a personal level, God speaks to us through so many metaphors in the relationships within the animal kingdom; the industriousness of the ant and bee; the fearless, sacrificial protectiveness of a mother defending her cubs; the almost machine like dependability and faithfulness of the seeing eye dog[5]. At an intimate level, God may speak to you through a perfect flower in full bloom when you are feeling far from perfect; a tenacious ant struggling with an oversized breadcrumb when you are about to give up; a cheeky clownfish darting around your mask that brings a smile to your face, making you realize how serious you have been lately and that a little bit of cheekiness wouldn't go astray. Elijah, recognizing the gentle way God speaks through the various strengths of the wind, is perhaps the most classic example (see 1 Kings 19:11-12).

In addition to animals, we have the wonder of the electromagnetic spectrum; the way light shafts through a cloud or plays on water, the subtlety of colour both in a Frangipani and on an artist's canvas. The beauty of sound such as melodous birdsong or the majestic combination of sound that stirs the emotions when an orchestra plays the classics.

DIAGRAM OF THE SIX STRANDS OF GOD'S REVELATION TO MAN

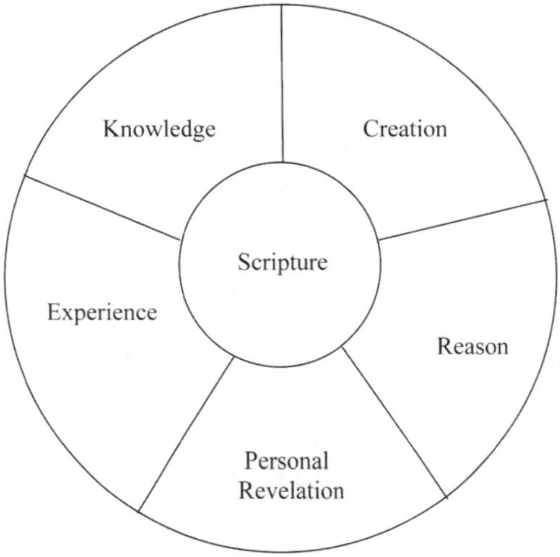

The outer circle represents all spiritual truth capable of being discerned and understood here on earth. Scripture is the core and all additional spiritual understanding that the other sectors bring must be built upon and not contradict the truths of Scripture. The size of each sector has been made uniform but it doesn't mean that all contribute equally.

The conclusions and conjectures presented in this book are a combination of five of the six strands. These, in order of frequency of usage are; Scripture, experience, reason, personal revelation, knowledge.

My position

In my opinion, the Bible needs to be treated like an exciting blueprint; basic structural features upon which we continue to build and add internal partitions, furnishings, embellishments of increasing understanding and utility. The Bible is like a detective story. It has layers and levels of meaning and when God gives us another experience, revelation or increased understanding, we go back to the Bible and add our new puzzle piece to the emerging three dimensional jigsaw picture. The Bible is like a skeleton that is fleshed out with our experience, reason, knowledge, personal revelation and the creation around us.

Some sections of the Christian church believe that revelation comes through Scripture and Scripture only. They allow no place for personal revelation, experience, reason, expanding knowledge or nature as additional sources of extra revelation. They see the Bible as the complete and total revelation of God. I don't adopt that viewpoint.

My attitude is that God's complete revelation of himself to us involves all six aspects discussed. I see personal revelation, nature, experience, reason and increasing knowledge all as ways of adding to, amplifying, and extending or extrapolating God's word. Scripture is clearly not complete. John makes that point at the end of his gospel.

> *Jesus did many other things as well. If every one of them were written down, I suppose that even the whole world would not have room for the books that would be written.* (Jn 21:25)

There are many, many things Jesus talked about that are not included in the Bible. There are letters we know Paul has written which were lost and therefore not included in the Bible. The Bible has everything that is necessary for salvation but it is not the sum total of all spiritual revelation. John does however state that nothing further can be added to the book of Revelation (Rev 22:18,19). In other words, the book of Revelation is complete, a stand alone book in its own right. However, nowhere in the Bible does it say that the Bible is the ***complete*** revelation of God. 2 Timothy 3:16 simply says that all Scripture is inspired by God, which is quite different from being complete. Yet there are many well-meaning believers who hold dogmatically to the belief that the Bible is the complete revelation of God and to challenge such a belief is considered a heresy. There are others who believe that any new understanding of God, any fresh revelation of truth must have some reference somewhere in the Bible. 'Keep searching, brother, you will find it somewhere' has been an exhortation that arises from this irrational thinking pattern.

Dissociation example

My first book, *'The Forgotten Factor in Healing',* which is about dissociation, illustrates this principle well. It wasn't until the last thirty years that the psychiatric profession detailed the condition known as Multiple Personality Disorder and began making progress in bringing some resolution to the disorder. Secular and Christian exploration of this area led to increasing understanding of the formation of alters (alternate personalities, often called 'parts'), their interactions and how they present in the client. Thousands of hours of personal experience with many clients led me to the conclusions detailed in the book. The fact that hallucinations are either entirely demonic, entirely part driven, or a combination of the two, is not included anywhere in Scripture but it is an important spiritual truth.

Finally, when I was examining all the notes and experiences and trying to get to a concise definition of what a part was, the evidence pointed to parts being formed as an addition to the soul, made up of *mind* but I wasn't sure exactly how much *emotions* and *will*, if any, a part possessed. I asked the Holy Spirit for supernatural revelation as to which portion of the soul a part was. He said very clearly it was a replicated portion of the mind, not the emotions or will. I then went back to my observations and reinterpreted these in light of this revelation and all the evidence fitted like a glove. The book was now ready to be written. Throughout this process of truth being revealed through knowledge, experience and personal revelation, Jesus was bringing *long term* healing to clients. This was often accompanied by strong spiritual endorsement. By this I mean that Jesus was graphically appearing to the client, which confirmed I was on the right track.

Then I went back to Scripture to see if any of my observations or conclusions were contrary to the Bible. The answer was no. Do I need to find evidence of dissociation in the Bible for dissociation to be true? No. The truth of dissociation is clearly documented as a reality. Does the Bible have anything to say directly about dissociation? Not that I have yet found. There are many references in Job and Psalms to a man's 'innermost parts' that other writers have quoted as referring to dissociative parts but I think this is stretching the application. Where dissociation *may* play a factor is in sudden behavioural changes and 'supernatural strength'. For example: Samson's rages and his incredible strength and Saul's jealous outbursts against David. Perhaps there were dissociative parts assisting David in his convincing display of mental illness when he was caught by the Philistines. Equally, it could be argued that Samson's incredible strength was solely the Holy Spirit coming upon him, that David was simply a good actor and probably deserved the first Oscar and Saul was driven largely by his own freewill choices and the demon sent by God. Nevertheless, because dissociation is so common and given the fact that many of the biblical characters lived in violent times, it is likely to have played a greater role in their behaviour than we realize.

It is not within the scope of this book to examine the direct control of Christians that Satan has through the use of programmed dissociation. Nowhere is this alluded to in Scripture and yet the stark reality of Satan's agenda is, without question, an established fact. This is confirmed daily around the world by therapists and the satanic ritualistic abuse survivors they minister to. This is the subject of the third book in this series.

Salvation but not Sanctification

The Bible is complete with regard to all that is necessary for salvation, but it is not complete with regard to all that is necessary for sanctification. Sanctification is the process of allowing the Holy Spirit into every area of my soul and body; to expose sin, to illuminate dysfunctions, to heal and renew. Salvation happens in an instant and is a transaction that takes place in my spirit. Sanctification takes a lifetime and is the freewill choice I make to allow the Holy Spirit to enter every area of my life; family and social relationships, finances, leisure time, work, church, prayer, sexuality, physical appearance, exercise, personality, thoughts, my past and in particular the trauma from the past that still bleeds through into my current behavior.

Sadly, there are sincere believers who are struggling with highly developed dissociative parts and who will never experience freedom if they try to find the answers in the Bible. These 'parts of their mind' make the person lose time, do things that she is unaware of and activate a range of dysfunctional behaviours and inappropriate emotional responses that simply perplex her. She has no idea about the origin of these behaviours or even how to get to the source. For almost 2000 years since the Cross, millions and millions of such people have died without receiving the sanctification that God wanted for them. Why? Because no one had the understanding and skill to be able to access these parts and bring resolution to them. These 'parts' can affect fears, phobias, depression, compulsions, hallucinations, delusions and a whole range of mental disorders. They can affect a wide variety of bodily functions included food intolerance, nausea, organ malfunction and weight gain or loss. In such cases, 'Casting your anxieties on Jesus' (1 Peter 5:7), or telling someone that 'Perfect love casts out all fear' (1John 4:18), simply doesn't make any difference. Telling people to trust Jesus and have more faith doesn't even scratch the surface of the problem. Getting them to declare and claim their healing is useless. Reciting aloud appropriate healing Scriptures won't affect the problem. Neither will dealing with demons. In fact, frequently the demons are hiding behind parts and can't be accessed unless the parts are addressed first.

I am not saying that when we try our hardest to find a solution to our problem with the limited revelation we have, that God is passively watching us wallow. He is far too compassionate and loving for that. In many of these cases, he will step in and give grace, as he is able, to alleviate or help us manage our symptoms. Sometimes, dependant on the legal rights balance, he will supernaturally heal or remove the problem. But the point remains that God's grace is not a fresh revelation of truth. God's grace is not deeper spiritual understanding of the core problem. God's grace is sanctification in an instant for one person. What we need is knowledge of *how to be sanctified* so it can be applied methodically to everyone.

Our counselling practice, and others around the world, are bringing deep healing to people who are desperately struggling with behaviours that they cannot understand. No traditional church or prayer ministry seems to help and no amount of spiritual discipline or self effort makes any difference.

Dissociation is just one aspect of sanctification that is available today. Throughout the last 2000 years there have been many books, containing wonderful insights, written by men and women who loved God that have increased our collective spiritual understanding. We understand ourselves much better today than people did in Jesus' time, hence sanctification can go to deeper levels than ever before.

Are you starting to get the picture? Do you really believe that God gave continuous revelation of himself and his purposes to mankind for over 4000 years and then stopped completely after 100 AD? Perhaps you can consider the possibility that God's revelation of spiritual knowledge, truth and his character has been continuous throughout history, continues today and will continue well after the earth has passed away. In fact, can you believe that it will never end?!

Be cautious

The difficult path for every Christian to walk is to read the Bible as the divinely inspired Word of God, keeping to the spirit of God's Word without allowing the letter to kill the intent. It is walking in the freedom that the *spirit* of the word brings without being jailed by bars of legalism. It is knowing when to take the word literally, when to allow the word to speak as a metaphor, and when to accept both. It is being absolutely dogmatic sometimes and, at other times, being prepared to suspend the urge to jump to a conclusion, leaving a difficult passage on the shelf to be re-examined later. It is being able to say, 'I don't know what that means' and being OK with that. It is recognizing that Scripture is, at one and the same time, safe enough for babes to paddle in and deep enough for theologians to drown in!

No one gets the balance right. No one perfectly understands. No commentary is correct in its interpretation all of the time. No version of the Bible is error free in its translation. Unfortunately, one of the biggest blockages to the Church progressing at a faster rate is the legalistic idolizing of the Bible that moves into a rigid dogmatism. This lack of flexibility and unteachability merely plateaus the believer's progress, hamstringing God's ability to use the person in his bigger purposes. God loves you, but can he trust you?

We all put God in box. How cramped is he in yours? Is he so theologically constrained that he can't trust you with fresh revelation about himself because if he did you wouldn't believe it? Is your assurance about your correctness beyond question or, with an attitude of openness and teachability, are you regularly asking God to expand your understanding and enlarge your perspective?

SUMMARY

- God's revelation of truth occurs in six ways: Scripture, personal revelation, experience, reason, knowledge and nature.

- Scripture is pre-eminent and the framework into which the other five must be fitted.

- Personal revelation is revelation from God, given to an individual, that is not included in Scripture but helps us to better understand Scripture. It is extra content, content not found in Scripture. Example: The Nicene creed; sexual abuse of Jesus.

- Experience refers to the application of biblical principles in everyday living and counselling situations. Experience means working backwards from the outcomes to determine a more accurate interpretation of a passage of Scripture or to add to our knowledge of God's total revelation of truth. Examples: Masturbation,; territorial spirits.

- Reason refers to the use of logical, deductive processes to determine whether a belief or interpretation is true. It is applying an impartial consistent rigour to any so called 'revelation' and discarding it, or at least being very cautious, if it cannot pass the test, if it appears illogical. Examples: The uniqueness of Christianity; the uniqueness of Jesus as the founder of Christianity; the notion of God *being* love as opposed to God being capable of love.

- Knowledge refers to our accumulative understanding of the world we live in and how this increases our understanding of Scripture and adds further detail to it. Example: Dinosaurs and man co-existing.

- Nature refers to God's revelations of himself in creation. The majestic vastness of space which contrasts so strongly with my puniness. The incredible detail and complexity of a single cell, and its intricacy, of the most unimaginable fineness, challenges us never to prejudge the ordinary and commonplace as insignificant. The created order speaks both generally and personally of God's nature and character.

- Scripture is incomplete. It is a skeleton to be padded out; a detective story that contains valuable clues that will lead to further truths; an incomplete jigsaw puzzle into which missing pieces still need to be found and added.

- The conclusions and conjectures presented in this book are combination of five of the six strands. These, in order of frequency of usage are; Scripture, experience, reason, personal revelation, knowledge.

- The Bible contains all that is necessary for salvation but not all that is necessary for sanctification. As time progresses, God continues to reveal more tools to set the captive free at deeper levels. Our self-knowledge regarding appropriate boundary setting, rescuing, triangling, codependance and overfunctioning in relationships are example of aspects of sanctification in which our understanding is continually growing.

- In my opinion, the most graphic sanctification issue that God has highlighted in recent times has been dissociation.

- Because of his compassion, God has given grace since the Cross for our lack of knowledge regarding our sanctification. Nevertheless, that is never an excuse for slackness. God wants us to ask for more!

- Holding to a viewpoint that all revelation is through Scripture, and *only* through Scripture, leads to legalism and idolizing of the Bible. It denies God's continuing revelation of himself over the past 2000 years as valid, and it straitjackets our thinking. My God is too excited about revealing more of himself to remain silent for 2000 years!

Anazao

"To come to life again"

Counselling Publishing Training

Anazao is an interdenominational organization, established by Peter and Heather Toth in 2003. Between them they have over seventeen thousand hours of clinical counselling experience in bringing physical, emotional and spiritual healing to others. The long term vision is to establish healing centres around the world. Anazao has a Board of Trustees and a Board of Reference. There are psychologists, counselling professionals, pastors and lay ministers now using the Anazao model around Australia.

Anazao has had considerable success in bringing healing to people who prove particularly difficult for churches and the psychiatric profession. Expertise in ministering to highly traumatized people has given hope to many.

It is our desire to see Christians mature in their approach to their own healing by helping them to understand and remove the blockages that prevent the Holy Spirit from healing. This is achieved by teaching people about these blockages and demonstrating how to remove them. Often overlooked components include the extent of personal sin in our own lives, dissociative factors linked to trauma and the impact of generational iniquity. It is crucial to gain an understanding of the overarching issue of 'legal rights' that intertwines all of these factors and how these legal rights are used by both the Kingdom of Light and the kingdom of darkness to gain control in our lives.

Jesus Christ is the one who has paid the full price for us to walk in wholeness. While the church acknowledges this, most Christians are far too passive in their approach to healing and hence miss out on the physical and emotional health that Jesus wants them to be experiencing. Teaching and demonstrating to people how to appropriate this

Heather and Peter

wholeness is what Anazao is all about. Our focus is always to bring those we counsel into a closer and more intimate relationship with Jesus.

Anazao has run three day healing conferences in most of the State capitals of Australia, and is available to run healing conferences and seminars both nationally and internationally. The seminar section on our webpage will give information on current and up coming seminars available. Training programmes can be run in your area and can cover a variety of topics, including those selected from our four week school.

The four week counselling training school, called the 'Cutting Edge School', is currently run annually and often several times a year depending on demand. This is a modularized course, each week having its own set of learning outcomes with evaluations. This ministry school is limited to a small group of students, making it a hands-on training course designed to equip people to move into truly Christ-centered counselling and healing. Each day consists of teaching in the morning followed by a practical demonstration and then students practice in pairs. This book, *'Darkness in the Light: Underestimating Satan'* and the second book, *'Darkness in the Light: Satan's Legal Rights'* are the basis of the first week in the school which concentrates on deliverance and a correct understanding of the satanic kingdom. The second week of the school is focused on understanding dissociation as an important component in achieving deeper healing and is based on Peter's first book, *'The Forgotten Factor in Healing'*. The third week focuses on ministry to people who have been victims of satanic ritual abuse (SRA). These people are more prevalent than most Christians realize and understanding programmed dissociation is the key to bringing fast resolution to this condition. The third book in the series, *'Darkness in the Light: Satan's Trojan Horse'* is the basis of this week's teaching. The fourth week concerns generational iniquity and how to deal with it effectively in ministry situations. A book will eventually be written for this week.

The four week 'Cutting Edge School' is held on the Gold Coast in sunny Queensland, Australia, where you can swim and surf the whole year round. The climate is sub tropical and the Gold Coast is one of the premier holiday destinations in the world. We are not limited to running this school on the coast and will travel anywhere there is a demand for it.

An addition to these four weeks, Anazao is currently developing a comprehensive healing model for all ailments, physical and mental, both trauma-based and chronic non-traumatic disorders and this will eventually be a fifth week in the school and published as a book.

While we are serious about healing, we are just as serious about having fun and relaxing! Getting the balance right is important to us. We don't want to be so spiritual and driven that we don't have time to savour all the good things in life.

ABOUT THE AUTHOR

Peter is a New Zealander and now an Australian permanent resident, currently living and working on the Gold Coast in Australia.

Peter was a math/science teacher for 17 years, teaching primarily years 8 to 12. The latter years were spent heading the math and science departments of a growing Christian college, writing curriculum and running seminars at teacher training colleges and presenting workshops at Maths Conferences. In 1987 he received a national award for his contribution to mathematics. He has an interest in Christian apologetics and debating with evolutionists.

In 1995, he began fulltime retraining and over the next five years completed government accredited courses in family ministry, family therapy and a two year diploma in Counselling and Family Therapy. For the practical component of his training, he began counselling in a Family Therapy Counselling Clinic, and then opened up his own practice in a Christian medical centre. He was trained extensively in the prevailing secular models such as Cognitive Behaviour Therapy, Rogerian Experiential, the Psychodynamic approach and others. Over time, he began incorporating more and more Christian spiritual tools with deeper and longer lasting outcomes. He adopted the Ellel Ministries approach to bringing healing to those suffering physically as a result of accident and trauma, and this further expanded his counselling. He lectured and counselled overseas in South Korea, USA, New Zealand and Europe on counselling related courses, as well as teaching for one year on staff of an Australian accredited counselling course.

Gaining an understanding of inner healing, based on bringing resolution to the emotional and physical impact of trauma memories in the late '90s, his counselling practice increased in its effectiveness as the Holy Spirit was more directly involved in the healing process. In Traumatic Memory Resolution (TMR), Jesus directly and instantaneously brings his truth into the trauma from the past. The healing is effortless and long lasting. Nevertheless, there were still clients for whom there was no significant long term release from the dysfunctions that were clearly evident in their lives.

November 2000 was a defining moment in Peter's counselling practice. Attending a seminar on dissociation (hidden memory), he understood, for the first time, what it really was and, more importantly, that it was much more prevalent than counselling courses and the psychiatric profession believed. It was the key that Peter was looking for and brought immediate and dramatic freedom to a number of clients, both in his practice in Australia and on teaching and counselling trips abroad. He combined this new understanding of dissociative parts formed during trauma with Ellel Ministries' understanding of healing of accident and trauma.

This combination has brought complete physical healing to some cases where people had only received partial healing previously.

As more complicated cases presented themselves, the current research and understanding of dissociation in the both the secular and Christian world didn't provide any of these deeper answers.

In 2002, Heather joined Peter as a co-counsellor. Drawing from her own experience, coupled with her very clear spiritual discernment and considerable organizational and teaching expertise within the broader church, the effectiveness of Anazao's counselling increased. Heather's skills and experience, in conjunction with counselling trial and error, and the leading of the Holy Spirit, meant that answers to some of these deeper questions were emerging. The counselling practice was soon fully booked nine months in advance, with 80% of the clientele coming from interstate or overseas.

Over the last seven years, Peter has spent over 7000 clinical counselling hours with people with varying degrees of DID (Dissociative Identity Disorder). Anazao Counselling is now achieving long-term outcomes with DID and SRA (Satanic Ritualistic Abuse) clients at a speed that was not previously thought possible.

For example, in most cases, whether the person is mildly dissociative or has extensive well-developed dissociative parts of their mind, including complex SRA survivors, complete removal of their alter systems can be achieved in a matter of hours, rather than weeks, months or even years! Under the current models used by many others, hundreds of hours of counselling would be required. Some who come to Anazao have had extensive counselling using currently accepted models, with little or no real progress. They are amazed and heartened by the results in just a few hours of counselling with Anazao.

Reliance on the Holy Spirit, a scientific background and carefully recorded observations have led Peter to re-evaluate the theory if the outcomes don't follow. Often this means working back from new and unexpected outcomes to fine-tune or even discard the old theory if necessary. Peter and Heather are convinced that basic foundational presuppositions that undergird current DID theory need to be seriously challenged.

His first book, *'The Forgotten Factor in Healing',* presents an approach to dealing with dissociation that simplifies and streamlines the counselling process. Clear and concise, it has demystified what had become a cumbersome and complicated topic. With a practical, step-by-step approach to bringing resolution to dissociation, he has given confidence to many counsellors and others involved in pastoral ministry.

Around Australia and New Zealand, people are achieving counselling outcomes that set clients free, at a far deeper level, quickly and with less effort.

However, to counsel effectively in the field of dissociation, using the steps outlined in his first book, requires a mature understanding of the kingdom of darkness and a streamlined approach to deliverance. Hence the need for this book plus the next two in the *'Darkness in the Light'* series.

Peter has a Bachelor of Science degree, Diploma of Teaching and Diploma of Counselling and Family Therapy. Heather has a Diploma of Teaching, Diploma of Church Leadership and Diploma of Counselling.

The name, '*Anazao*', (pronounced, 'Anna Zay O') is New Testament Greek meaning, '*To come to life again'*. The name and logo is a registered trademark. More information and a list of Anazao's books, which are available for purchase, can be found on their website www.anazao.com.au

Postal: P.O. Box 4102, Elanora, QLD 4221 Australia
Phone: + 61 411 306 590 (cell)
Website: www.anazao.com.au   Email: phtoth@anazao.com.au

OTHER BOOKS BY PETER TOTH

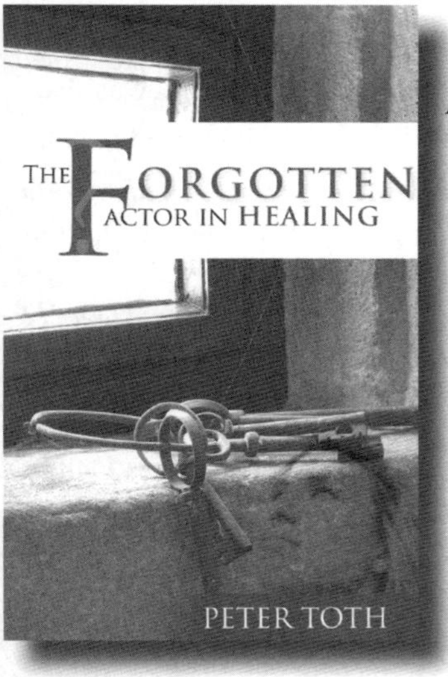

Depression, addictive behaviours, fears and phobias, anger, psychoses, homosexuality.

These are but a few examples of problems that can have the 'forgotten factor' as a major cause. The forgotten factor is Dissociation . Rarely does a book bring a radical change in our perspective, initiate a paradigm shift in our thinking and bring a crucial piece of the jig jaw puzzle that makes sense of the other pieces. This is one of those books.

We have all heard about people recovering memories of events that they didn't know had happened to them. Perhaps you have a healthy skepticism about the validity of these memories. Maybe you don't need convincing. Either way, this book is for you.

Having spent more than 5000 clinical hours bringing resolution to memories held in dissociative state, Peter and Heather not only endorse the validity of these memories but give clear examples of the radical healing that can happen when these memories are exposed and resolved.

That's interesting but it doesn't apply to me. Wrong! 99% of people have had experiences in their lives that they either can't remember or are totally unaware that these events have even happened to them. That means you! Yet these 'forgotten factors' result in numerous dysfunctions of our lives, both mental and physical. In a clear, logical, readable manner, Peter looks at the whole process of 'dissociation', the current secular approaches, how the brain works during dissociation, pitfalls to avoid and how Jesus is the only one who can bring complete healing to these memories. The step-by-step process of how to work through dissociative memories means this is a valuable resource for all counsellors and anyone who likes a self-help approach. Designed to be understood by the non-professional, this 240 page book has many case histories, helpful diagrams and illustrations.

The book is available for purchase from our website www.anazao.com.au or your local Christian bookshop.

ENDNOTES

Chapter 1: Intimacy

1. Jesus was glorified when he ascended into heaven (Acts 1) and was seated at the right hand of the Father. Derek Prince first used this phrasing.

2. *For I will gather all the nations against Jerusalem to battle, and the city will be captured, the houses plundered, the women ravished and half of the city exiled, but the rest of the people will not be cut off from the city. Then the Lord will go forth and fight against those nations, as when He fights on a day of battle. In that day His feet will stand on the Mount of Olives, which is in front of Jerusalem on the east; and the Mount of Olives will be split in its middle from east to west by a very large valley, so that half of the mountain will move toward the north and the other half toward the south. You will flee by the valley of My mountains, for the valley of the mountains will reach to Azel; yes, you will flee just as you fled before the earthquake in the days of Uzziah king of Judah. Then the Lord, my God, will come, and all the holy ones with Him! In that day there will be no light; the luminaries will dwindle. For it will be a unique day which is known to the Lord, neither day nor night, but it will come about that at evening time there will be light. And in that day living waters will flow out of Jerusalem, half of them toward the eastern sea and the other half toward the western sea; it will be in summer as well as in winter and the Lord will be king over all the earth; in that day the Lord will be the only one, and His name the only one. All the land will be changed into a plain from Geba to Rimmon south of Jerusalem; but Jerusalem will rise and remain on its site from Benjamin's Gate as far as the place of the First Gate to the Corner Gate, and from the Tower of Hananel to the king's wine presses. (Zech 14:2-10*

3. When exactly the marriage of the Lamb will happen is open to conjecture. A strong case can be put for it happening before Jesus returns to reign and rule in Jerusalem for 1000 years. The point being made, in the context of this chapter, is not so much when it will occur but that it will be another level of increasing intimacy between God and us.

Chapter 2: No Excuses

1. Jessica Jones, *Ask for the Ancient Paths*. Xulon Press. 2006 ISBN 1-60034-181-0. Details revelations the author believes she has received from God regarding Satan's creation and fall. Being revelation, no one can vouch for its authenticity, but it makes interesting reading. Some aspects of her revelation tie in with our own experience.

Chapter 3: A Promise You Won't Forget

1. Larry Crabb, *The Silence of Adam*. Grand Rapids, MI: Zondervan , March 1, 1998. ISBN-13: 978-0310219392.
2. I first heard the concept of authority lost and regained by Satan at a lecture by Peter Horrobin of Ellel Ministries in Sydney, Australia in 1997.

Chapter 4: Infected

1. Based on the widely accepted chronology developed by Anglican Archbishop Ussher (1582-1656). His chronology is derived largely from age spans given in the Bible.
2. Gen 6:2,4; Job 1:6, 2:1, 38:7; Matt 5:9; Luke 20:36; Rom 8:14,19; Gal 3:26.
   Essentially the phrase 'son of God' or 'sons of God' refers to beings that have their *direct* origin from God. Hence all angels are sons of God, Adam is called a son of God (Lk 3:38), Jesus is the Son of God and we, believers, are sons of God, not in regard to our first birth but with regard to our new birth in Christ, being 'born of God' (Jn 1:12,13). Hosea 1:10 makes a future reference to Israel becoming 'sons of the living God' when they embrace Jesus prior to his return.
3. Number 5303
4. Number 5307
5. Satan is mentioned twice in Enoch as the single chief spirit (1 Enoch 54:3,6).
6. Number 8549
7. The Judaica Press *Complete Tanach with Rashi* is a bilingual Hebrew-English translation of the Bible. The English translations were made by A. J. Rosenberg.
   Joseph Gaer, *The Jewish Bible for Family Reading*. 1957.
8. Keynote 6:4, p10 in the *Hebrew Greek Key Study Bible*, compiled and edited by Spiros Zodhiates, ThD. Published by AMG Publishers, Chattanooga, TN 37422, USA.

Chapter 5: Darkness in the Light

1. See Appendix 1 for further explanation.
2. A common belief among creation scientists is that the conditions on earth after the flood were ideal for the formation of the ice age and that there was only one ice age, not several as evolutionists believe. Currently, the most succinct and 'layman friendly' book that answers difficult questions regarding the Bible and science is, *'The Creation Answers Book'* by Don Batten, David Catchpole, Jonathan Sarfati and Carl Wieland. P.O. Box 4545, Eight Mile Plains, QLD, Australia Creation Ministries

International, Dec 2006, ISBN 978-0-949906-62-5.
3. Job 37:9,10; 38:22,23,29,30

Chapter 6: Reinfected

1. Strong's Hebrew Lexicon. Number 7497
2. Strong's Greek Lexicon. Number 5020
3. *Navs Topical Bible*, Table of Measures.
4. Guinness Book of Records.
5. A Normal Distribution Curve is a mathematical term for the curve that forms when natural parameters, such as height and weight, are graphed. The extent to which any measurement deviates from what is the most common or 'normal' measurement is called the 'standard deviation'. This can be mathematically determined and percentage deviations measured as a result.

Chapter 7: Satan and Israel

1. Matthew Henry's Commentary, Zondervan NIV Commentary, Jerome's Commentary.
2. Isa. 4:2; *The branch of the Lord.* Isa. 11:1; *A branch out of the roots of Jesse*. Jer. 23:5; *A righteous branch*; and Jer. 23:15; *The branch of righteousness*.

Chapter 8: The Greatest Sting of All

1. While Nephilim were fully human in that they could reproduce and produce a generational line, nevertheless there was a taintedness in the human genome produced that God clearly abhorred.
2. I first heard about this paradox stated in a lecture by Floyd McClung, Rotorua, NZ 1995.

Chapter 9: Keys and Captives

1. H. Clay Trumbull, *The Blood Covenant,* p.225. Impact Books ISBN 0-89228-029-8
2. Dt 31:17,18; 32:20; Ez 7:22; 39:29
3. Matthew Henry's Commentary; Zondervan NIV Bible Commentary.
4. Diagram taken from a lecture by Dr Arnold Fruchtenbaum, Tauranga, NZ 1980s
5. I first heard this illustration of the cork in a lecture by Peter Horrobin, Ellel Ministries.

Chapter 10: Re-examining Satan's Defeat at the Cross

1. James Dobson, from 'Focus on the Family', used this illustration in another context.

Chapter 11: Satan's Capabilities after the Cross

1. See Appendix 1

Chapter 13: Satan's Control Over How Long People Live

1. Numerous studies (eg. Article by W.R. Miller, C.E. Thoresen - The American Psychologist, 2003. Also a comprehensive study by John Cacioppo, Professor in Psychology University of Chicago, 2005) indicate positive benefits of religious beliefs. However, there is no apparent additional advantage of being a Christian to being Buddhist, Moslem or Hindu.
2. The seven categories of legal rights that Satan uses will be explored in detail in the next book, *'Darkness in the Light: Satan's Legal Rights'.*
3. God has revealed to us that there are no children under the age of five in hell. It makes sense, in that God would not condemn people to hell who haven't reached the age of reason; who haven't developed the mental capacity to consistently and cognitively reject him.

Chapter 14: Earth, Wind and Fire

1. USGS (United States Geological Survey).
2. As of November 2008, in addition to the 70 000 official deaths, there were 18 000 people still missing.
3. Some Christians don't celebrate Christmas because Christ's birth was not on Dec 25 and it was originally a pagan feast day. Be that as it may, I think God isn't so concerned about when we celebrate Jesus' birthday as long as we *do* celebrate his birthday. If those who don't celebrate it on Dec 25 don't celebrate it at any time in the year, then God is not pleased. Additionally, choosing not to celebrate Christmas on Dec 25 when everyone else is celebrating can lead to exclusivity, a judgmental attitude and young children can feel alienated from their friends. Be careful not to take a narrow dogmatic stance regarding the date and let that override all the other important benefits associated with being part of the season of goodwill.
4. We are including the former USSR in the count of Christian countries since its foundation and ethos for over 1000 years has been Christian and the 70 years of communism are not enough to nullify that. Since the fall of communism, there has been a strong move back to traditional Christian beliefs. Many of the satellite nations have officially renounced communism.

Chapter 15: The Cross and the First and Second Death

1. Use the internet to 'Google' and explore. You will find documented cases of 'healing' under Hinduism/Reike/Buddhism/Acupuncture/Yoga/Homeopathy etc. Clearly not everything written on the internet is true, but many of these therapies have gained Government Medicare support in Australia based on claims of beneficial outcomes.

Chapter 16: Greater Things Than Me You Will Do

1. Charles H. Kraft, ed. *Behind enemy lines: an advanced guide to spiritual warfare*. Ann Arbor, Mich: Vine Books, 1994. Dr Kraft develops this thought to include the position of believers working in enemy territory.

Chapter 17: Can Christians have Demons?

1. First heard this real estate illustration from a lecture by Peter Horrobin from Ellel Ministries.
2. The demons name was 'Legion'. A Roman Legion had 6000 men. Whether the Gerasene demoniac had 6000 demons or simply a very large number is debatable.
3. Quote taken from the documentary, 'Hells Bells'.

Chapter 18: Talking to Demons

1. Bringing resolution to traumatic memories as an important component of healing neuroses, such as phobias, is treated in depth in my book, *'The Forgotten Factor in Healing'*.

Chapter 19: Talking to Demons: They are just like Us!

1. Frank and Ida MaeHammond, *Pigs in the Parlor*. Kirkwood, Mo: Impact Books, 1973 ;
   Noel & Phyllis Gibson, *Evicting Demonic Squatters & Breaking Bondages*. Drummoyne, NSW: Freedom in Christ Ministries Trust, 1987;
   Bill Subritsky, *How to Cast Out Demons and Break Curses*. Auckland: Dove Ministries, 1991;
   Peter Horrobin, *Healing Through Deliverance. Vol. 1: the biblical basis*. Chichester: Sovereign World, 1991; *Healing Through Deliverance. Vol. 2: the practical ministry*. Tonbridge, Kent: Sovereign World, 1995;
   Derek Prince, *They Shall Expel Demons*. Grand Rapids, MI: Chosen Books, 1998;
   Doris Wagner, *How to Cast Out Demons*. Ventura, Ca: Regal Books, 2000;
   H. A. Maxwell Whyte, *Demons and Deliverance*. Whitaker House, 2001.
   John Eckhardt, *Prayers that Rout Demons*. Lake Mary, Fla: Charisma House, 2008;
2. Lawrence O. Richards, Larry Richards, Gleason L. Archer, *New International Encyclopedia of Bible Words*. Zondervan, 1991.

Chapter 20: From Now to the End

1. Elias Joseph Bickman, *Studies in Jewish and Christian History* p125

'Lukan Eschatology and the Missing Fig Tree' 1986 Brill.
Lectures by Lance Lambert, a prominent Jewish intercessor.

2. Based on the last week of Daniel's prophecy in Dan 9:27. Each day represented one year.

Appendix 1: How God Reveals Himself to Mankind

1. 'World to Christ International' Organization, based in Melbourne. Director: June Sutton.
2. Norman L. Geisler, *Baker Encyclopedia of Christian Apologetics.* P.O. Box 6287 Grand Rapids, MI 49516-6287: Baker Books, ISBN 0-8010-2151-0
   Josh McDowell, *Evidence That Demands A Verdict.* Nashville, Tn: Thomas Nelson, 1992. ISBN-13: 978-0840743787
3. Paluxy River Bed, Glen Rose, Texas, USA. A series of 14 human footprints with at least 134 dinosaur tracks in the bed of the Paluxy River, in the Upper Taylor Platform (UTP) near Glen Rose, Texas.
   NOTE: Recently there has been vigorous debate regarding the authencity of these footprints. There are those holding strongly to both sides of the debate. Anazao suspends any judgment on the case. As always, we want the truth and are prepared to discard this evidence should it be inconclusive or erroneous.
4. Carl Wieland, *Dinosaur bones: how old are they really?* in *Creation* 21 (1) 53-55,1999.
5. Founded by Bill Gothard, the Institute in Basic Life Principles produces a range of materials including an excellent series of studies on animals and how they reflect God's virtues. Great reading for children.